# HILLBILLY HIGHWAY

## Politics and Society in Modern America

GARY GERSTLE, ELIZABETH HINTON,
MARGARET O'MARA, AND
JULIAN E. ZELIZER, *SERIES EDITORS*

For a full list of books in this series see: http://press.princeton.edu/ series/ politics-and-society-in-modern-america

# Hillbilly Highway

## THE TRANSAPPALACHIAN MIGRATION AND THE MAKING OF A WHITE WORKING CLASS

*Max Fraser*

PRINCETON UNIVERSITY PRESS

PRINCETON & OXFORD

Published by Princeton University Press
41 William Street, Princeton, New Jersey 08540
99 Banbury Road, Oxford OX2 6JX

press.princeton.edu

ISBN 9780691191119
ISBN (e-book) 9780691250298

British Library Cataloging-in-Publication Data is available

Editorial: Bridget Flannery-McCoy & Alena Chekanov
Production Editorial: Jaden Young
Jacket/Cover Design: Felix Summ
Production: Erin Suydam
Publicity: Kate Hensley & Kathryn Stevens
Copyeditor: Natalie Jones

This book has been composed in Miller

Printed on acid-free paper. ∞

Printed in the United States of America

10 9 8 7 6 5 4 3 2 1

# TABLE OF CONTENTS

# HILLBILLY HIGHWAY

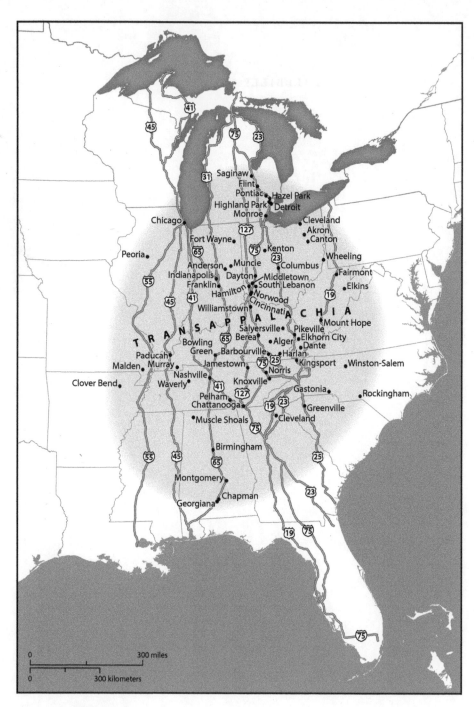

Transappalachia.

# Introduction

A PIONEERING PIECE of cultural anthropology by the husband-and-wife team of Robert and Helen Lynd may have made Muncie, Indiana, the most famous "Middletown" in all of America, but a half century earlier it was a local driller named A. H. Cranell who first put the small midwestern city on the map. In October 1886 Cranell sunk a bore into the belt of limestone that runs across much of the central and eastern portions of Indiana and struck gas 922 feet below the town of Eaton. When he lit a flame to the well, it rose ten feet in the air and could be seen all the way to Muncie, a dozen miles to the south. The fiery beacon drew admiring crowds for weeks afterward—and then, for years, industry, jobs, and people.[1]

The Eaton well was the first commercially viable natural gas well drilled in the state, and it announced the coming of a gas boom to east-central Indiana that lasted more than a decade and transformed the region for much longer than that. The Trenton Gas Field stretched from western Ohio to around Kokomo, Indiana, forty-five miles northwest of Muncie. At roughly five thousand square miles, it was the largest known gas field in the world at the time, and with the bonanza came all the familiar signs of a gold rush. New drilling companies and boosterish boards of trade were hastily organized across the eleven-county region, which historically had been home to sedate county seats and some of the richest farmland in the state. A real estate frenzy saw land prices increase as much as threefold in Muncie and surrounding cities like Anderson, Marion, and Kokomo. Muncie's population more than doubled between 1886 and 1890, and then nearly doubled again by 1900—making it the largest city in the Indiana gas belt at the turn of the century.[2]

Ultimately more significant to the future of the region than the gas itself were the new businesses the boom attracted. Producers in heat-intensive industries like iron and glassmaking in particular were drawn to the region for its cheap and readily available fuel. In 1880, there were just four glass factories in all of Indiana; by 1900, there were six in Muncie alone and 110 across the state. New outfits like the Muncie Natural Gas Land Company, organized in 1889 by a group of eastern investors and led by a former governor of New Jersey, wooed manufacturing outfits from the coal-burning areas of Pennsylvania and Ohio by providing free land and deeply discounted gas prices. Local businessman James Boyce netted Muncie its most famous catch of the gas boom era when he successfully lured the Buffalo, New York–based fruit jar company Ball Brothers to the city, with an offer of eight acres of land, five thousand dollars, and the company's own gas well. After the glassmakers and foundries came wire fabricators and bridge builders and stove part makers and refrigeration companies and, especially, automobile parts manufacturers. Long after wasteful drilling practices had tapped out the Trenton Field reserves by the second decade of the twentieth century, Ball Brothers and the other industrial enterprises that settled in the area would ensure that Muncie's first nickname—"The City of Eternal Gas"—outlived the boom years that had been its inspiration.[3]

Ball Brothers was the first place that Kenny Lewis got a job when he arrived in Muncie in 1942, at the age of seventeen. Kenny was born in the swampy delta region of Arkansas, where his father raised cotton, rice, and soybeans on a small piece of land that provided "just enough to make a living." A friend had moved up to Muncie a couple years prior and wanted Kenny to join him, and by the time Kenny came of age it did not require much convincing to get him to leave too. Kenny said, "I just got tired of working in hot fields. And mosquitoes—mosquitoes was bad down there, with all the water. I didn't want to be a farmer." Muncie's manufacturing economy grew rapidly during the war years—from sixteen thousand jobs before the defense boom to twenty-five thousand by 1944—and Ball was a prime beneficiary of both wartime rationing (which stimulated demand for the company's ubiquitous flagship product, the Mason canning jar) and new government procurement contracts, after it retooled its Muncie operations to produce shells and machine parts for the military. As demand soared, an acute citywide labor shortage worked in favor of recent migrants like Kenny. "I got up here one day, and I went to work the next day at Ball Brothers."[4]

It was not happenstance that Kenny Lewis ended up working at Ball Brothers. Ball had a reputation for hiring southerners that extended well beyond the Muncie city limits. Many of Kenny's coworkers hailed from

Kentucky and Tennessee. Wesley Reagan, who grew up outside of Jamestown, Tennessee—a rural hamlet about a hundred fifty miles east of Nashville and a dozen or so miles south of the Kentucky border—remembers
being young and hearing older relatives talk about moving north. When
they did, it was "mainly Ball Brothers" that they mentioned. Nor was Ball
Brothers the only Muncie employer that looked south when needing to
fill workforce demands. During the boom years of the 1920s, local manufacturers brought in so many recruits from the southern Appalachian
Mountains that they arranged special trains to deliver them to the city.
Companies like Eber Refrigeration, a Muncie firm owned by Tennessee
transplants, often placed job advertisements in local newspapers like the
*Upper Cumberland Times*, published out of Jamestown. Business was
so flush during World War II, in fact, that even the luncheonettes were
known to take out ads in out-of-state newspapers for waiters, cooks, and
dishwashers.[5]

The influx of southern migrants was so great in these years and during the decades immediately following the war that a reporter exaggerated only slightly when he noted that the staff of one local employer that
hired primarily Kentuckians "changes daily." Newcomers stayed "only
long enough to get a stake," which they could bring back home to their
southern places of origin, perhaps to invest in a piece of land or some
new machinery on the farm—or until they could find better-paying work
locally. Kenny Lewis, for instance, put in two years at Ball Brothers, working in the rubber department; but when a job became available at the
nearby Chevrolet transmission plant with pay that started at nearly ten
cents more an hour, he jumped on it, and ended up staying at Chevrolet for the next three decades. In the meantime, the makeup of Muncie's
population—and especially its working-class population—began to change
in ways that drew growing notice and no small measure of ire from longtime residents. "Have you heard that there are only forty-five states left in
the Union?" went one joke heard around town with increasing frequency
during the years when Kenny first got there, back when Hawaii and Alaska
were still only territories. "Kentucky and Tennessee have gone to Indiana,
and Indiana has gone to hell."[6]

Kenny Lewis and Wesley Reagan were just two participants in one of the
largest population relocations in recent American history. Over the first
three-quarters of the twentieth century, somewhere around eight million
poor white southerners—perhaps even more—left economically marginal
parts of the southern countryside and traveled north in search of work.[7]

Some, like Kenny, came from the swamps of northeastern Arkansas, or from among the same rocky ridgelines of the Cumberland Mountains of East Tennessee that Wesley had called home, and from countless farming communities, mill villages, railroad junctions, and mining camps in between. Most left in the years between World War I and the end of the 1960s, when an array of large-scale economic transformations—from the modernization of agricultural technologies to the intensification of resource-extractive industrialization—combined to make traditional agrarian livelihoods increasingly untenable, and when the resulting disparity in the quality of life in the rural South and the urban-industrial North was at its most pronounced. They followed successive waves of relatives, friends, and neighbors who had charted migratory pathways before them, relying on extensive networks of kin and community to navigate far-flung labor markets and secure places to live in unfamiliar and frequently unwelcoming destinations. Some traveled only temporarily, moving back and forth between city and country according to the logic of the seasons or the fluctuations of the business cycle. Many others left the rural South behind for good, bringing with them a set of regionally distinctive experiences and ways of life that conditioned how they settled into their new homes and left an indelible impression on their new urban surroundings. Whatever the case may have been, they journeyed forth on a proliferating network of interstate roadways that would give this massive interregional migration its most abiding nickname: the "hillbilly highway."

Rural white southerners who left the broad region stretching from the Appalachian mountain ranges to the floodplains of the Mississippi River found their way to every corner of the country over the course of the twentieth century. But the majority, by virtue of a combination of geographic propinquity and generational interconnection, headed for the large cities and burgeoning factory towns of the midwestern manufacturing belt that encircled the Great Lakes. They went to smaller regional centers like Muncie and Dayton, Ohio, where Wesley Reagan ended up and put in thirty-two years at one of the four General Motors plants in town while raising four children with his wife, Lula, who he courted during return trips to Tennessee. Or to larger cities like Cincinnati, where so many impoverished refugees from the declining Appalachian hinterland eventually settled that local officials began speaking of them as the city's "second minority." Or to Chicago, where southern newcomers gravitated to a working-class area north of the Loop that by the 1950s had become so chock-full of barbeque joints and country music bars that the neighborhood's residents rechristened it "Hillbilly Heaven." Or to Detroit, where southern migrants became so thoroughly associated in the public eye with job competition, slum conditions, and urban disorder that at midcentury more than one in five city inhabitants selected "poor southern whites" as the most "undesirable" group in the city, with only "gangsters" and "criminals" receiving lower popularity rankings.[8]

Most rural southerners arrived in the industrial Midwest with nothing more than what could be scraped together after the fall harvest, or from the sale of the last remaining parcel of family land, or from a final shift at the local mine or sawmill. When the renowned documentary photographer Margaret Bourke-White traveled to Muncie on assignment for *Life* magazine in the spring of 1937, the resulting eleven-page photo-essay she produced—commissioned to coincide with the publication of *Middletown in Transition*, the Lynds' follow-up to their bestselling 1929 sensation—included one emblematic photo of a pair of destitute white migrants from Kentucky. Scott and Lizabelle Brandenberg were "at the bottom of Muncie's social strata," noted the accompanying caption. Photographed in their home, a "one-room clapboard shack in 'Shedtown,'" a slum district on Muncie's southwestern fringe, the most notable item of furniture pictured is a homemade brooder next to the bed, in which, as Lizabelle explains, they are raising chickens "fer eatin'" rather than to sell. The Brandenbergs' well-worn work clothes, their weathered hands and faces, the simple metal-frame bed on which they sit, eyes averted from the camera, all mark them, in Bourke-White's composition, as recognizable types. "Mrs. Brandenberg talks with the Kentucky hillbilly drawl heard in many Midwest industrial towns," the caption continued, "from southerners migrated north to work in the great auto plants."[9]

In the decades to come, southern migrants like the Brandenbergs would share in the kind of working-class prosperity that jobs in midwestern factories provided to a generation or two of Americans—and most of all to white industrial workers and their families. Although white southerners remained disproportionately concentrated in blue-collar jobs throughout the postwar period, by the end of the 1960s the average family income of southern-born whites living in the Midwest would be roughly equivalent to that of other white residents of the region—and 25 percent higher, by comparison, than the incomes of southern-born African Americans in the Midwest. Similar convergences (and disparities) marked the progress that southern white migrants would make when it came to occupational mobility, residential patterns, and other measures of social and economic well-being. Years later, Wesley Reagan would speak with enduring pride of the moment when he and Lula were able to purchase their first home, in a working-class subdivision just outside of Dayton built by a local developer who put up thousands of such homes across central and southwestern Ohio during the 1950s and 1960s. "A Huber Home is what I bought. Huber was the biggest builder of single-dwelling brick homes in the United States, and that goes back many, many years ago." And after three decades of paying membership dues to the plant's International Union of Electrical Workers local, Wesley, who had left Tennessee with barely a penny to his name, would even be able to retire at the relatively young age of fifty-two, with a union pension and company-provided health insurance for the remainder of his and Lula's lives.[10]

In other ways, however, southern white migrants and their families would remain something of a class apart in the urban Midwest throughout much of the twentieth century. Powerful stereotypes stemming from popular beliefs about the impoverished rural circumstances they came from and the low standards of living to which such "hillbillies" were accustomed made them widely sought-after recruits by northern employers, and just as widely despised by the urban workers they were hired to work alongside (or in place of). The rural accents, styles of dress, modes of worship, and leisure activities they carried with them—to name just a handful of the southern cultural forms whose proliferation in northern cities during these decades antagonized long-term residents—were commonly perceived as lower-class attributes and behaviors, and made southern white migrants frequent objects of derision as well as targets of state intervention, discipline, and reform. For their own part, rural southerners brought a wariness about urban-industrial life that often made them reluctant converts to the metropolitan social orders they came to move within. In neighborhoods like Chicago's Uptown, Dayton's East End, and Muncie's southside, as well as working-class suburbs like Hazel Park, Michigan, or South Lebanon, Ohio, they lived with and around other people of similar backgrounds; formed their own churches, social clubs, and other communal institutions; and danced and got drunk with other people like them. Most of all, they maintained powerful attachments to the southern countryside itself and to the family members and communities they had left behind there.

Rural white southerners in the Midwest returned to the South at significantly higher rates than both Black southerners and white southerners who migrated to other parts of the country during the mid-twentieth century, and as a result many came to lead lives that were in meaningful ways suspended across both rural and urban and northern and southern settings. They returned on weekends between work shifts; to celebrate holidays, prepare for the birth of a child, or help navigate family emergencies; when layoffs sent them packing or when the hurly-burly of the city had simply become too much for them. Even those who made permanent relocations to the urban Midwest, who managed to secure steady work and who raised families in circumstances that far exceeded what they had known from their rural upbringings, often retained such connections to the places they had come from. "I always planned on coming back" was how Wesley Reagan thought about it. By the early 1960s, just as he and Lula were starting their family in Dayton, Wesley had already managed to set aside enough money out of his wages to buy a small piece of land in Fentress County, Tennessee, outside of Jamestown. He and Lula would visit it regularly, preparing for the time they would move there for good. They left Ohio in 1985, on the very day Wesley retired from GM.[11]

The back-and-forth circuits charted by white southerners like Wesley would be one of the defining characteristics of this decades-long migration. For a population that often set out from their native region in response to some sort of economic compulsion—because the farm went under, or the mine closed down, or simply because, as Wesley put it about growing up in his corner of rural Tennessee, "you just wasn't going to be able to make a living here"—the ability to return, whether periodically or permanently, represented a limited yet nonetheless powerful kind of agency. It meant having a say over the terms on which they accepted new forms of work, adjusted to new living environments, embraced new customs and cultures—or didn't. At the same time, the regularity with which such migrants returned to the southern countryside became one of the most frequently invoked charges against them during these years; a reason, in the eyes of others, to question their reliability as workers, their suitability as neighbors, even their fundamental ability to be integrated into the mainstream of American life. And so as these patterns of movement crisscrossed the rural Upper South and the urban Midwest, they both drew together and set apart the communities of displaced white southerners and their families and descendants that lay along the interregional footprint of the hillbilly highway. No longer fully enmeshed in the distinctive lifeways of the southern countryside, not entirely embedded in the urban-industrial milieu in which they sought out work, the complexly interwoven networks of kith and kin that stretched across this broad portion of the American heartland—a region we might think of conjoinedly as "Transappalachia"—became the terrain of a new and distinctive white working-class experience in twentieth-century American life. The story of that region, and the people who brought it into being, is what follows here.[12]

*Hillbilly Highway* is a book about the Transappalachian migration's imprint on the social, cultural, and political map of recent American history. As such, it addresses itself first and foremost to a rather significant gap in the otherwise impressive body of literature that has been produced on the twentieth-century migrations out of the American South. All told, nearly twenty million white and Black southerners—and another roughly one million southerners of Mexican and Hispanic descent—left the region and headed north and west during these decades. The story of the Black Great Migration is well known—so well known, in fact, that today it stands alongside the nineteenth-century migrations of westering homesteaders as one of the heroic grand narratives of American history, a transformational passage out of the darkness of the South's blighted past of bondage, disenfranchisement, segregation, and racial terrorism. Over the last three or four decades, a small library of exemplary works of scholarly and popular history—not to mention numerous television documentaries, major museum exhibitions, and other high-visibility forms of cultural recognition—have been produced about the Great Migration. This stands to reason: the Great Migration represented the most profound shift in racial demography at any moment in the country's past, one that would turn a population that at the beginning of the twentieth century was still overwhelmingly rural and nearly 85 percent concentrated in the states of the Old South, into the most densely urbanized population group in modern America. The Great Migration forever altered Black work roles and cultural identities, and, by facilitating their entrance into the emergent city-based political alliances of the twentieth century, ensured that Black Americans would become the most enduring members of the Democratic coalitions of the New Deal and post–New Deal eras.[13]

The midcentury exodus of white farmers from the southern Great Plains to the Far West and especially California was not quite so epochal. Yet it has nonetheless occupied a similarly prominent place in the American cultural imaginary, thanks in large part to the Depression-era symbolic significance invested in so-called Okies fleeing the twinned environmental and economic calamity of the Dust Bowl by the likes of Woody Guthrie, Dorothea Lange, John Steinbeck, and John Ford. The Okie migration would outlast its Dust Bowl origins, only growing stronger as California rode the wave of World War II–era military spending to become an economic powerhouse and transplanted white southerners continued to flood into booming defense suburbs throughout the Cold War decades. This westward corollary to the hillbilly highway has also received significant historical attention in recent years, especially as scholars have looked to California and its politically ascendant white lower-middle classes for the origin stories of the postwar New Right.[14]

The same cannot be said about the Transappalachian migration, even though the number of white southerners who migrated to the urbanindustrial Midwest roughly equaled those who ended up on the West Coast, and outnumbered *all* Black migrants out of the South by some two or three million. There are shelves worth of country music songs about the hillbilly highway, at least one woefully underappreciated literary masterpiece about the migration, and, most unfortunately, J. D. Vance's bestselling poverty-shaming memoir *Hillbilly Elegy*, published in 2016 and remade as a risible star vehicle by Netflix in 2020.[15] But there is no *Grapes of Wrath* or *Invisible Man*, no Migrant Mother on a postage stamp. Likewise, the scholarship on this migration has been both more limited than in the other two instances, and generally narrower in scope. In the last twenty-five years, there has been only one historical monograph written about the southern Appalachian migration to the Midwest. Chad Berry's *Southern Migrants, Northern Exiles* (2000) is a deeply sympathetic account of this history—Berry's grandfather was himself a migrant along the hillbilly highway—and it excels in its ability to allow participants in the migration to "speak for themselves" and become "authors of their own identities," thanks especially to the scores of oral histories the author either conducted or consulted in his research. But Berry spends comparatively less time situating the migration experiences he gathers within the context of larger histories of economic growth and decline, class formation and conflict, the changing racial composition of American cities, and the overarching political transformations of the period. As a result, *Southern Migrants, Northern Exiles* has relatively little to say about how the Transappalachian migration impacted the broader terrain of American society during these years.[16]

The only more recent work of historical scholarship to address the migration in an extended fashion, James Gregory's *The Southern Diaspora: How the Great Migrations of Black and White Southerners Transformed America* (2005), does considerably more in this last regard.[17] But Gregory's book is largely synthetic in nature and explicitly comparative by design. Leaning heavily on the preexisting scholarship about the southern Great Migrations—including Gregory's own, pioneering earlier work on the Okie migration to California—*The Southern Diaspora* necessarily reproduces that literature's strengths and weaknesses. Detailed and eloquent on how the arrival of Black southerners reconfigured the racial, cultural, and political landscapes of northern and western cities, equally persuasive on how white southerners helped turn California into an unlikely bellwether of the new conservatism, it relegates Transappalachian migrants to an only tertiary role in the grand dramas of recent American history.[18]

These are oversights that *Hillbilly Highway* sets out to correct. A core contention in what follows is that Transappalachian migrants were at the center of many of the defining events of the period—from the country's explosive industrial development around the turn of the twentieth century to the rise of the modern industrial labor movement during the 1930s and 1940s; from the unfolding of the postwar urban crisis to the decisive political realignments that transpired over the course of the 1960s and 1970s. Furthermore, looking at these events through the lens of the Transappalachian migration often forces us to reconsider some of our core preconceptions about them. Most accounts of the early years of the Congress of Industrial Organizations, for instance, locate the midwestern labor movement's roots in the radical political traditions cultivated by the region's polyglot immigrant working classes.[19] Southern white migrants are generally absent from such narratives, and when and where they do appear they are often dismissed out of hand for their "conservative tendencies," for their "staunchly anti-union" cultural dispositions, for "lack[ing] class consciousness."[20] But upon closer examination, Transappalachian migrants were early and eager supporters of midwestern industrial unions, in both radical hotbeds like Detroit and more provincial outposts like Muncie. Similarly, most histories of the postwar urban crisis hardly mention the so-called hillbilly ghettos that began cropping up in midwestern cities like Chicago and Cincinnati during the decades after World War II. Yet these suddenly ubiquitous enclaves of poor white southerners shaped contemporary thinking about the causes and consequences of urban poverty no less profoundly than did the zones of concentrated Black and brown poverty they appeared alongside, and even came to play a pivotal role in the design and implementation of the War on Poverty, postwar liberalism's most ambitious, if flawed, social policy initiative.[21]

The point here is not simply to find traces of the hillbilly highway where others have not bothered to look. Historians have largely accepted at face value contemporary presumptions that transplanted white southerners were constitutionally disinclined to challenge their employers' authority and join in solidaristic activity with other kinds of workers; as a result, we have failed to consider not only the many instances in which their actual behavior departed from such expectations, but also why it so frequently did. How did the material conditions that confronted natives of the rural Upper South during these years also influence the complex movement culture of the country's powerful industrial unions? Why did the persistence of southern, rural, and working-class identities and cultural habits in the communities these migrants formed in the urban Midwest appear for a time to pose such an irreconcilable challenge to the expectations of midcentury consumer society? How did they figure in the intellectual debate about the relationship between racial identity, cultural inheritance, and social class that preoccupied social scientists and policy-makers in the postwar decades, and what did that reveal about growing tensions between more elite interests in the liberal New Deal coalition and the poor and working-class whites who made up its social base? More often than not, the key to these and other questions lay in the circuit-ries of migration that distinguished life along the hillbilly highway—the back-and-forth dynamics of displacement and attachment that shaped the social and cultural geography of Transappalachia as a distinctive terrain of experience whose complex history still awaits its full telling.

If scholars have failed to grasp the significance of this history, the same cannot be said about the working-class white southerners whose personal, familial, and cultural lives have been embedded in the Transappalachian migration and its legacy for the better part of a century. While conducting the dozens of oral histories and other research that went into the produc-tion of this book, I met many natives of the Upper South and the Midwest who knew the "hillbilly highway" intimately, who were long accustomed to using or hearing that phrase to refer to the migration experiences that they or their relatives, friends, and neighbors had known throughout their lives. But the first time I encountered the phrase was actually in a country music song—specifically, on the lead single off Steve Earle's debut album *Guitar Town*, called, aptly enough, "Hillbilly Highway." Earle did not grow up along the hillbilly highway himself. But as a child, he did manage to acquire his own firsthand experience with the frequent relocations that would have been all too familiar to those who did. Born in 1955 on the Army base at Fort Monroe, Virginia, Earle spent much of his youth shut-tling around the South while his family followed Jack Earle's postings as an air traffic controller: from Virginia to El Paso, Texas; the next year to Lake Charles, Louisiana; then back to a little town in the Guadalupe Valley outside of San Antonio called Schertz, where, as Steve would later put it, "I used to get the shit kicked out me by great big square-headed cowboys named Otto on a regular basis." By the time a nineteen-year-old Earle set out hitchhiking to Nashville, where he would begin a long and successful career as a session musician, songwriter, and eventually as a recording artist in his own right, moving had become something of a way of life for him. He would draw on that experience to powerful effect when he entered the studio to record his first full album a dozen years later.[22]

"Hillbilly Highway" is less a work of personal autobiography than it is a kind of collective history, generic enough in the details yet specific enough in what they are intended to evoke that the song manages to capture something fundamental to the experience of millions of Transappalachian migrants. Spanning three generations in the life of the singer's family, the song moves from an unnamed Appalachian coal camp, to Detroit, to Houston, before ending up back on the road—"that old hillbilly highway," as the song's refrain repeatedly intones—destination unknown. The men in the song keep trading dying towns and dead-end jobs for "a dream of a better life" for themselves and their family; the women are always crying and waving goodbye, as the search for work pulls yet another family member away from home. The singer, who quits school to become a musician, thinks he has broken free from these demoralizing routines of working-class life; but the irony is inescapable when he finds himself back in the same old place as those who came before him. "Now I'm standing on this highway and if you're going my way / You know where I'm bound," Earle muses as the song motors toward its interminable conclusion: "Down that hillbilly highway / On that hillbilly highway / That old hillbilly highway / goes on and on." A traveling song that subverts the genre, "Hillbilly Highway" replaces the wanderlust for the open road long celebrated by middle-class artists and intellectuals with the unshakable sense of precarity that more often typified the transient unsettledness of a very particular kind of working-class existence. As much as any other cultural document produced about the Transappalachian migration, it manages to capture exceedingly well the unresolved tension between mobility and marginalization that was at the crux of the migrant experience.[23]

There was something additionally poignant about the timing of the release of Steve Earle's "Hillbilly Highway." *Guitar Town* came out in the spring of 1986—about a decade after the onset of regional deindustrialization had begun to make the country's emerging "Rust Belt" a far less likely destination for job-seeking migrants, and a little over midway through Ronald Reagan's eight-year tenure in the White House. The first development effectively ended the decades-long story of the hillbilly highway; subsequently, it would be the rural South itself, as well as other low-wage, low-union density regions of the country, that absorbed a growing portion of the industrial jobs that flowed away from the old factory towns of the Midwest.[24] The second, meanwhile, marked a no less consequential realignment of twentieth-century American politics. Earle had very personal reasons for abhorring Reagan: Earle's father had been among the more than eleven thousand air traffic controllers Reagan fired during the 1981 Professional Air Traffic Controllers Organization strike (in return, Earle would release a song about Reagan before his second term was out that likened the president to a war-mongering snake oil salesman). And so it only flummoxed Earle that much more that Reagan's ascendancy pivoted to a considerable extent around the changing political allegiances of working-class voters like the hillbilly migrants he identified with and sang about.[25]

The rightward drift of white blue-collar workers and union members over the second half of the twentieth century is one of the more critical events in recent American history, and one that has drawn a significant amount of attention from professional historians as well as scholars working in other disciplines.[26] In many of these accounts, and in much popular commentary on the topic, the conservative political inclinations of the white working classes of the Upper South and the industrial Midwest are largely taken for granted, treated as an almost automatic projection of their diminished economic standing in postindustrial society; their resentment of the social reforms brought about by the civil rights and feminist movements of the 1960s and 1970s; even, according to some, their culturally embedded authoritarian tendencies. One final contention of *Hillbilly Highway* is that this history is more complicated than it might initially appear. Southern Appalachian migrants were no less likely than any other group of white Americans to express such political attitudes during these years. But neither were they any more so, despite deeply engrained assumptions about poor southern whites being a uniquely reactionary force in modern American life. Furthermore, although we have grown accustomed to talking about *the* white working class as if it were a single, monolithic entity, the communities of rural white southerners that formed across the landscape of Transappalachia had their own, historically specific reasons for growing disillusioned with the politics of postwar liberalism. Scorned for their rural attachments and southern cultural identifications, stigmatized by the urban middle classes who increasingly came to dominate the worldview and policy agenda of the Democratic Party, these "hillbillies" had always represented something of a working-class "other" at the heart of the New Deal order.[27] As that order began to decompose in the decades after the 1960s, long-standing divisions of class and culture etched into the terrain of the Transappalachian migration would prepare the ground for one of the most profound and far-reaching realignments of class politics in modern American history.

*Hillbilly Highway* tells the story of the rise and fall of the Transappalachian working class across six chapters. Chapter 1 examines the forces of economic development that precipitated a massive exodus from the southern countryside beginning around the turn of the twentieth century. New patterns of land use, new modes of industrial activity, and new forms of state policy combined to transform the rural South during these decades, nowhere more decisively than in the southern Appalachian region that would send so many migrants out along the hillbilly highway in the ensuing decades. As millions of rural southerners watched viable livelihoods tied to the land disappear, many turned first to the burgeoning mine and mill economy of the Upper South, where first encounters with industrial society would leave lasting impressions—especially as growing numbers began migrating out of the region entirely. Chapter 2 zeros in on the concrete details of the migration process itself: how migrants decided where to go, how they got there, what they brought with them, and when and why they decided to go home again. As more and more natives of the Upper South became adjusted to lives oriented around the proliferating highways connecting the southern countryside with the midwestern factory economy, what had once been a rural surplus population became something else altogether: an increasingly transregional working class.

Chapter 3 moves to the midwestern factories where rural white southerners started arriving in significant numbers in the decades before World War II, much to the satisfaction of northern employers who had already begun sending their emissaries into the southern hinterland in the hopes of recruiting a desperate and docile surplus labor force. The disconnect between that particular image of southern working-class conservatism—the hillbilly scab—and the actual record of workplace ferment among rural white southerners, which marked the critical interwar period in a variety of settings across the urban Midwest, is the subject of this chapter. Chapter 4 focuses on the growing—and increasingly visible—communities of rural southerners that began to materialize in the urban Midwest during and immediately after World War II, when the southern out-migration was at its peak and hundreds of thousands of rural whites were moving in and out of the region every year. As the country at large entered a period of extended affluence, so-called hillbilly ghettos challenged normative ideas about working-class whiteness in ways that seemed to set rural southerners apart from their northern neighbors once again.

For midcentury liberals concerned about the fate of American cities broadly and the intractable problem of urban poverty in particular, the emergence of these hillbilly ghettos ensured that southern white migrants in the Midwest increasingly came to appear as a problem-population. Beginning in the 1950s and 1960s, they also became an object of concern for reform-minded policymakers and intellectuals. Chapter 5 addresses the largely unacknowledged role of the Transappalachian working class in the development of liberal urban and antipoverty policy after World War II, and what ultimately became a missed opportunity for midcentury liberalism to develop a lasting connection with communities of poor and working-class whites. Chapter 6 assesses the consequences of that failure through the increasingly conservative undertones of American country music. By the end of the 1960s, the widening popularity of country music had emerged as one of the more unequivocal demonstrations of the broader cultural consequences of the southern Appalachian migration to the Midwest. Contemporaries often associated the strident patriotism, muscular anti-urbanism, and latent racism of the genre in the era of George Wallace and the Vietnam War with a reactionary political tradition embedded in its rural southern past. But, as I argue there, the music had by that point long since been severed from its hillbilly roots, instead becoming ever more conservative in its tone and message the more it became palatable to middle-class audiences in northern cities. Indeed, it is one of the overarching claims of this book that the particular conjunction of region and class at which poor southern whites found themselves in the urban Midwest blinded not only contemporaries but later scholars as well to the more critical, even radical, potential in hillbilly culture—a radical potential that, for a time, had made even American country music a music of liberation.

One final note, on the use of the word "hillbilly." A contested term, like other examples of sociological shorthand that originated as racial or class slurs its meaning tends to vary depending on who is in the position of the speaker. When Steve Earle uses the term in "Hillbilly Highway," he does so to invoke the perennial rootlessness that had become a defining condition of a certain kind of regionally defined, class-inflected social experience. "If you're going my way," he nods to his audience, "you know where I'm bound." On the other hand, when the *New York* magazine writer Frank Rich greeted the election of Donald Trump in 2016 by declaring "No sympathy for the hillbilly," he did so, at least in part, to put as much distance as possible between conscientious metropolitan elites such as himself, and "the hard-core, often self-sabotaging Trump voters who helped drive the country into a ditch on Election Day."[28]

I do not use the terms "hillbilly" and "hillbilly highway" throughout the following chapters to engage in a similar act of condescension. I use these terms, on the one hand, to call attention to the way contemporaries used them—both the Muncie town trustee who complained to the Lynds of "the cumulating cost of human debris thrown on the city by the heavy importation of 'hillbilly' labor," as well as the millions of migrants and their families who wrestled with the various and at times conflicting implications that were tied up with this kind of language. To be a hillbilly in the urban Midwest during the mid-twentieth century could mean, at different times and in different contexts, to be a farmer or a southerner; to be someone who worked with their hands, or someone who could not find work at all; to be white, or to be not quite white; to be a fellow migrant, or yet another interloper; to be a coworker, or a job stealer; to be a rustic, or a racist, or a hail-fellow-well-met; to be an existential danger to the American way of life, or the most reliable, "old-stock" American WASP you could find. The very mutability of this term is an important throughline in the history of the hillbilly highway, and rather than eliding that part of the story— and not wanting to burden the reader with an excessive number of scare quotes—I have elected to use the term where appropriate, while doing my best to be self-conscious and self-critical throughout.[29]

On the other hand, I also use the term "hillbilly" here in an effort to reverse some of the historical work that has been done—along the hillbilly highway and across the landscape of Transappalachia, no less—to cast uniformly negative aspersions on that term. Rather than an explanation for the conservative turn in postwar American politics, I see the marginalization of hillbilly politics and hillbilly culture as another of its symptoms, and one for which Frank Rich and his predecessors own a share of the responsibility. While deploring efforts to "find common ground with the Trumpentariat"—an election-year neologism that quite intentionally echoed Marx and Engels's term *lumpenproletariat*, or "the passively-rotting mass thrown off by the oldest layers of the old society"—Rich wonders aloud whether we should "waste time and energy" attempting to understand the sources of political disaffection and alienation that drove such voters into Trump's embrace.[30] As I see it, the answer clearly is yes—and to redeem the hillbilly highway from the dustbin of history is, I hope, to take a step in that direction. So if you're going my way, you know where I'm bound.

# CHAPTER ONE

# Changes on the Land

AGRARIANISM, INDUSTRIALIZATION, AND
DISPLACEMENT IN THE APPALACHIAN SOUTH

*"The basic problems of the region, however, grow out of . . . the relation
of population to land."*

—US DEPARTMENT OF AGRICULTURE (1935)[1]

IF CIRCUMSTANCES HAD ALLOWED, Anderson Castle and Lina Sayler
might never have left Scott County, Virginia. Situated in the far southwesterly part of the state, nestled between the peaks of the Blue Ridge
and Cumberland Mountains, the crenelated ridges and valleys of this part
of southern Appalachia had always made for decent farming, especially
along the flatter, lower-lying river and creek beds where most of the county's population had chosen to settle. The Castle and Sayler families had
been farming Scott County for generations, and when Anderson and Lina
married, in 1914, they set about making plans to start their own family,
surrounded by familiar hillsides and within the shadow of their forebears.
First came baby Ruby, in 1916, and then Willard, in 1919, and there would
be more to come—Ruth, and then Charlie, and then Roy, and then Henry,
and, last, Dewey, who would only live to the age of five or six before falling
victim to a fatal bout of appendicitis.

But life on the farm, which had never been easy, was becoming more
difficult in places like Scott County during these years. The first three
decades of the twentieth century saw a 15 percent increase in the number of farms in southwestern Virginia, alongside an even more precipitous
decrease in the total acreage put to agricultural use—in other words, more
farmers were trying to scratch a living from less land. It was a surefire

recipe for declining farm livelihoods; and indeed in most of Scott County, gross farm incomes soon stood below even the relatively low average that prevailed across the broader southern Appalachian region. "You couldn't make enough money on the farm," Anderson and Lina's son Roy would later recall. "You could just survive. You could raise what you eat, but you didn't have anything to buy clothes with." As a result, by the time Roy was born it was not uncommon for Scott County farmers to spend seventy-five or even a hundred days out of every year working off the farm for pay. Others, meanwhile, were beginning to pick up stakes altogether. Among them were Anderson and Lina, who finally packed up the children and moved to the nearby boomtown of Dante at the beginning of the 1920s. A wholly owned outpost of the Clinchfield Coal Corporation—which by then had already bought out upward of three hundred thousand acres of prime coal lands in that corner of the state—Dante was just forty or so miles north of where the Castles and the Saylers had long plowed the earth. Yet in many ways it was already a world away.[2]

The forces then converging on southwestern Virginia came unevenly yet inexorably to the southern Appalachian hinterland over the first half of the twentieth century. In some places, such as the coal-rich Cumberland and Allegheny Plateaus of eastern Kentucky and West Virginia, or the mountainous and well-timbered terrain of western North Carolina and northern Georgia, small holdings and self-sufficing farmland were already disappearing at a growing rate by the turn of the century. Elsewhere, as in the loamy expanses of western Kentucky and Tennessee, agrarian livelihoods remained more viable even into the years during and after World War II. But a pattern was clearly at work throughout the period: already poor living conditions and a deteriorating farm economy across much of the Upper South, along with new pressures on land use engendered by industrial development in the region, combined to set loose a steadily increasing portion of the rural population of southern Appalachia. As they did, they paved the way for what would become one of the most consequential movements of people in recent American history.

The hillbilly highway emerged out of the decomposition of the traditional rural social arrangements of the Upper South, a multifaceted, region-wide, and decades-long process. As was the case in Scott County, in every state across the broader expanse of southern Appalachia, the amount of total land in farms reached its peak around the beginning of the twentieth century and remained flat or declined from there: by 10 percent between 1900 and 1945 in Kentucky and Georgia, 13 percent in Tennessee, and as much as 18 percent in North Carolina and West Virginia. The number of farms in many places, however, continued to increase throughout these years—there were sixty-four thousand more farms in North Carolina in 1950 than there had been in 1900—and as they did, so too did debt loads, farm foreclosures, and tenancy rates.[3] For southern Appalachian agrarians, increasingly tenuous claims to land often translated into stagnant or deteriorating living conditions for those who remained on the farm. Declining farm values, widening income gaps relative to the rest of the country, and consistent shortfalls in other quality-of-life measurements—from basic housing and healthcare amenities to the more disposable items in the emergent mass-consumer inventory—were pronounced across the region, and most acute in the most rural, agriculturally oriented counties.[4]

Ironically, it was not only material deprivation but also its opposite—economic development—that exacerbated the precarious circumstances confronting rural southerners during these years. Resource-extractive industrialization, advancements in agricultural productivity, and state-initiated modernization programs all exerted a steadily downward pressure on the number of people who could support themselves through livelihoods tied to the land. Coal and timber companies purchased vast swaths of land and turned them over to industrial use: already by 1930, 62 percent of all privately owned saw timber in the region was in industrial holdings, and newly opened coalfields not only in Kentucky and West Virginia but also in southwestern Virginia, eastern Tennessee, and northern Alabama had vastly increased the region's share of the nation's fuel supply. New machine and chemical technologies, meanwhile, made even the notoriously laggard southern agriculture increasingly capital-intensive, and as a result the demand for agricultural laborers diminished rapidly. Not least of all, a developmentalist agenda pursued by the federal government, especially during and after the Great Depression, actively sought ways to accelerate the movement of the region's economy away from its historic dependency on small-scale agriculture, and to more fully incorporate the rural Appalachian hinterland into national markets. The combined effect of all this was dramatic. In 1900 more than 90 percent of the population in southern Appalachia had been classified as rural, and the vast majority of that number lived and worked on farms. By 1950 only 30 percent of the region's residents would continue to do so.[5]

Caught in the vice grip of poverty and progress, the forces of displacement stalked rural southerners like the Castles and the Saylers in any number of guises during these decades. For the Minors of Hancock County, Tennessee, each new generation introduced new and ultimately untenable demands on the family homestead, which had once stretched as large as thirty-five hundred acres. "My great-grandfather, he divided up all this land with his children—he had seven," L. F. Minor would later recall. "Well, they growed up and then they had children, and then, they inherited so much and when we left down there it'd got down to where we had 100 acres . . . so we decided that . . . [we would] try something else . . ." For Henry and Catherine Phillips of Dickenson County, Virginia, it was the deep pockets of the Virginia and Tennessee Coal and Iron Company that proved irresistible: tired of eking out a meager existence from the rocky soil, the Phillipses finally deeded over to the company the mineral rights on 503 acres of land for the sum total of $251.50, or just fifty cents an acre. For a group of farmers in Union County, Tennessee, whose marginal lands were to be reclaimed to make way for the construction of a new hydroelectric power facility, it was the power of the state that could not be rebuffed—despite the fact, as their petition to the Tennessee Valley Authority put it, that "those employed by the said authority do not possess an adequate knowledge of land values in this locality; and that their untactful utterances, in public and private, derogatory to our farms, our communities, and to our modes of living have rendered them incompetent to deal with us in the capacity of land appraisers." For George Poteet, who took over the family farm around Bowling Green, Kentucky, and ran it as long as he could, it was simply a matter of the economic math no longer adding up. "Well, at that time I had 10 milk cows and I give $250 for them," Poteet remembered years later, when asked what had prompted him to relocate to Indiana to seek out factory work. "So when I sold them I got $150 a piece for them. That's why I had to quit. Because I was going in debt all the time."[6]

Diminishing landholdings, the insatiable appetite of industrial development, the unforgiving cyclicality of the market: whatever the specific catalysts may have been, the cumulative transformation they wrought was categorical. Over the course of the first half of the twentieth century, the rural population of the Upper South was rendered into a rural surplus population. As millions and millions of southern Appalachian farmers began exiting the countryside—some temporarily, others permanently— they increasingly found themselves absorbed into a ballooning industrial economy that spanned nearby lumber camps, mining towns, and mill villages, as well as faraway cities and factory agglomerations. With each passing year, more and more of them would find themselves drawn into an emergent interregional migration stream, which transported this newly minted rural surplus across the landscape of Transappalachia to meet the growing demand for labor across the urban Midwest. The decisions each of them made to leave the hills, hollows, fields, and forests of their raising would shape their lives—and, indeed, American history—for decades to come. But for many, deep-seated attachments to the land, to rural lifestyles, and to the broader region they had known would remain with them long after their initial experiences of displacement—an imprint of southern Appalachian agrarianism that would leave a lasting mark on what would come to be known as the hillbilly highway.

## The Balancing Act of the Countryside

Margie Hayes was born at home, in a log cabin nestled into a densely forested mountain range known as the Sandy Ridge, which rises as high as thirty-two hundred feet in elevation and winds along the northern border of Russell County, Virginia, a few miles outside the mining hub of Dante. Margie was born in September 1916, just a little over a year after the Clinchfield Railroad had completed work on the Sandy Ridge Tunnel, an undertaking so arduous that Dante residents would talk for years about how the hastily buried remains of dead tunnel diggers could be found under local grazing land, in the deep recesses of nearby hollows, and even beneath one of the town's ball fields. Given the ruggedness of the terrain, the tunnel represented at the time both an engineering marvel and a commercial breakthrough: a mile-and-a-half-long puncture that connected the coal deposits of southwestern Virginia to the rail junction in Elkhorn City, Kentucky, and from there to the industrial centers of the Ohio River Valley and the Great Lakes region along tracks belonging to the Chesapeake and Ohio. And it had been one more example of the way the Clinchfield industrial empire—which by then had also carved six drift mines into the hillsides around Dante, the largest of which contained more than two miles of underground passageways—was already in the process of transforming the natural landscape in this historically remote part of the state. Yet for Margie Hayes and her family, life on Sandy Ridge still bore a strong resemblance to what it had been like before the Clinchfield Coal Corporation arrived on the scene.[7]

Margie's mother, Mary, had also been born on Sandy Ridge; Margie's father, James, was from just across the county line. With the help of James's brothers and a few neighbors, they built the cabin in which Margie would be born in 1906, on land belonging to Mary's father. With four children already in tow and five more to come, James and Mary planted crops and kept some livestock—horses and mules, chickens, a couple of cows. James cleared timber for sale, too, but it was a modest life. "They built their house close to water which was always low [down] on these mountains[,] you know, so that made them have to get down in there, in the lowest place to build the house," Margie recalled. "It was a hard time getting out. There was no road . . . [so] they walked." "We'd go to town maybe once a month to get flour and the stuff that we had to have"—but otherwise, the tasks associated with sustaining the farm and the household were shared broadly among the Hayes parents and children. "All the family, when Dad said 'let's go,' we all went to the corn field. Big ole corn fields, and one of them would plow with a bull tongue plow and all the rest of us would hoe." Tilling the fields was just the start of it. "Everybody had chores to do and mine was to tend the chickens. I tended to the chickens and then I had to carry the wood in for the cook stove and the fireplace. I'd help to do that. But everybody had a job now."[8]

It was a set of circumstances that Myers Hill would likely have recognized. Born a year after Margie Hayes, Myers grew up on a farm in Union County, Tennessee, a hilly stretch between two tributaries of the Tennessee River where in the mid-1930s the newly formed Tennessee Valley Authority would embark upon its first major infrastructure project in the region.[9] When Myers was young, his father, Newton, had raised hay, corn, and tobacco on the cultivated portions of the family plot, which was composed of some more fertile land at the bottom of a valley; the remaining two-thirds of the Hills' acreage were kept in timber. "Nearly all farmers raised and thatched tobacco to give some extra money," Myers recalled. "Outside of that it was just corn and other things we raised for our own consumption." What the Hills could not raise or forage themselves they often traded for with other Union County farmers, through the intermediary of a general store owned by Sherman Hill, one of Myers's uncles. "People would raise chickens, eggs, and . . . butter, and anything they had excess of, they could take it to the general store and trade it for sugar and other staples that you wasn't able to raise or didn't have." A relative lack of social differentiation in the local community—"there wasn't any what you say well-to-do people in the community where I lived" is how Myers would put it—helped imprint patterns of reciprocal obligation and communalism that he would recall fondly as an older man, even though "we didn't have any convenience of electricity or anything like that." Myers recalled, "Anytime there was a tragedy in any family, the whole community would come in. Say the head of the house, the farmer, got sick—they would come in and work his crops and take care of him. If he had a house burn down— all the neighbors would get together and help them rebuild a home and supply them with the furnishings and things like that."[10]

The situation was not much different in Clover Bend, Arkansas, in the years after World War II. The oldest settlement in Lawrence County, which sits astride the Black River in what had long been prime cotton-growing country, Clover Bend in its more modern form was the creation of the New Deal–era Resettlement Administration, which had divided the fifty-six hundred acres of the old Clover Bend plantation into small parcels that the state then resold to local tenant farmers on low-cost, forty-year mortgages. It was an ambitious experiment in land reform—but for families like Jim Hensley's, who had been sharecropping around Clover Bend for decades, "it was still kind of like the Depression [in that] area" by the late 1940s. The Hensleys raised mainly cotton, but also soybeans, corn, and some other garden crops that were just enough to keep Jim and his four brothers fed. "From the time we could walk we worked on the farm," Jim remembered. "We started picking cotton when we—before we started kindergarten really. [We had] small, what we call gunney sacks, they were really potato sacks is what they were, you know, with a string around your shoulder[,] and then it just continued more and more duties from there up." The more complicated farm tasks tended to fall to Jim and his brother Dale, as the two oldest: "We basically did the majority of the chores at that time because we were about the only two that was big enough for the milking, and taking care of the—feeding the hogs, and the chickens, and this type of thing—besides working in the fields also." Jim recalled years later, "It was pretty rough—real bad really." And it would only get rougher, as the intensifying mechanization of cotton production, along with growing price competition from factory-style farms in Arizona and Southern California, steadily undermined what remained of the cotton economy of Clover Bend. By the time his parents finally decided to follow relatives who had relocated to the industrial city of Anderson, Indiana, Jim would be all too glad to leave northeastern Arkansas behind.[11]

The similarities between these snapshots of farm life in Sandy Ridge, Virginia, in the 1910s; Union County, Tennessee, in the 1930s; and Clover Bend, Arkansas, at the end of the 1940s should not obscure their differences: differences in land tenure and ownership, in local farming conditions and the value of farm products, and in the legal and economic standing of farm communities relative to other public and private actors in the local area, just to name a few. But the similarities that do exist are revealing. Across the Upper South, an agrarian society sustained itself throughout the first half of the twentieth century much as it had during centuries prior—by relying on a variety of strategies for making ends meet, which depended first and foremost upon the productive utilization of the resource bounty of the countryside. Like the Hayeses, the Hills, and the Hensleys, most farm families in the region—especially those who lived on more marginal terrain—survived through some combination of subsistence farming, cash cropping, herding animals, raising stock, hunting and foraging, and logging for household use as well as for sale. Arrangements such as these were predicated on practiced methods of land management—which land to put into cultivation and which to use for pasture; how much woodlands to keep in forest as opposed to cutting for timber; what land could be parceled off to adult children and what could not—because land use was at the crux of almost every significant decision rural families had to make. But it was the multiple and complementary productive uses to which that land could be put, rather than its notional value as transferable property, that made it the most critical resource of all for inhabitants of the southern countryside.[12]

Of course, there was very little that was romantic about life in these settings. The balancing act of the countryside was delicately maintained even in the best of times, and crises large and small could easily push sustainable agrarian existences over into scenes of rural desperation. Distant commodity markets might decimate local economies, as they did in Clover Bend, turning cash crops into money-losers. A young Myers Hill may have appreciated the many "conveniences" that the TVA's rural electrification projects brought to the region, but others in his family were less sanguine about the sacrifices they entailed. As the TVA began swallowing up farm properties in Union County for what would become the Norris Dam and Reservoir, Sherman Hill—the uncle who owned the local general store—responded by committing suicide. And when Margie Hayes's father left her mother when Margie was around eleven, alongside the more intimate consequences of family abandonment came the irreparable disruption of the internal division of labor that had long sustained the Hayeses on Sandy Ridge. "It was so hard," Margie recalled of their lives after her father left. "We'd get out in the summertime and pick blackberries. A hundred gallon of blackberries we'd pick every year and take them to Dante and sell them for ten cents a gallon." Their quality of life and their social standing in that community of self-sufficing farmers would never be the same. "Later on, people called us peddlers, you know. They got to making fun of us, you know. Peddlers."[13]

Margie's experience offered a particularly poignant lesson in a second unifying feature of agrarian life across the southern countryside. If access to productive land provided the foundation for agrarian society, on top of that land was often erected complex organizations of labor and exchange that necessarily entailed the coordinated exertions of the entire household—and, in certain situations, extended families and nonrelatives in the immediate community as well. This often remained as true at mid-century as it had at its beginning (and long before that, besides). "The economic activities of [Clay County, Kentucky,] households in 1942," noted one contemporary observer, "were so intricately intertwined with all other activities of the family that it would be exceedingly difficult to discuss them separately except perhaps in an analytical, abstract sense. The farm work was done by family members who were united into a cohesive group by bonds of kinship; familial obligations and work duties were inseparable."[14] Needless to say, such collective endeavors did not always proceed harmoniously, and they were never without their built-in hierarchies. Men, in Clay County as on Sandy Ridge, were "regarded as the director of all activities of the farm family"; they managed the household's land resources, labor power, and cash reserves, and made decisions about how each were to be expended. Women oversaw the duties associated with the reproduction of the household; children, invariably, "were subordinate to their parents' direction" and provided a plentiful source of supplementary labor for nothing more than the cost of room and board. Even when families did not break down under the strain of such arrangements, wives endured the patriarchal authority of husbands; and, as Jim Hensley's memories of his upbringing in Clover Bend made clear, children grated against the physical demands of hard labor and the psychic toll of having parents who doubled as field bosses. Margie Hayes may have rued the day her father's departure sent the family plummeting down the social ladder of Sandy Ridge, but in other ways she was glad he was gone. "I didn't like my dad. . . . I loved my mother so much and Dad was never kind and good to any of us for that matter and he just . . . it was just, say, jerking up by the hair of the head. [It is] said kids [are] jerked up by the hair of the head, well we was jerked up by the hair of the head."[15]

Nevertheless, despite the perennial resentments and occasional rebellions it inspired, the household mode of production was a conditioning force in southern Appalachian agrarian life. Throughout the region, and throughout the first half of the twentieth century, the rural farm population married more frequently and at a younger age than was typical for the country at large. In 1930 the national average was 9.2 marriages per 1,000 people: in Clay County, at the same time, the marriage rate was roughly one and a half times greater; and in Scott County, Virginia, where Anderson Castle and Lina Sayler had grown up, it was as much as double the national figure. Similarly, divorces occurred 20 percent less frequently across the southern Appalachian countryside than they did in the country overall—a result, to be sure, of the censorious attitude toward divorce taken by the more fundamentalist Protestant denominations that thrived in the region, but also of the inescapable importance of the intact family unit to the economic well-being of the farm household. Farm families in the Upper South also tended to be larger than their counterparts elsewhere, and tended to put a significantly higher priority on having children than other American families did. In fact, the segment of the rural population in southern Appalachia that was under twenty-one years of age, which was 19 percent above the national average at the start of the twentieth century, became proportionately larger over subsequent decades—exceeding the national rate by as much as 30 percent by 1930. As American families were electing to have fewer children across the board, agrarian communities in the rural South continued to depend on the labor of minors and to make decisions about family planning accordingly.[16]

During a period when the modern American family was assuming the more specialized functions necessitated by an increasingly bureaucratic and impersonal society, the so-called familism of the southern countryside often stood out, in the eyes of contemporaries, as a sign of the backwardness of such communities—an indication that they were, as the title of one typical piece of pop-sociology from the period put it, "yesterday's people." Yet as a third and final common feature of agrarian life in the region made clear, it was more appropriate to think of the householding arrangements that persisted across the Upper South well into the middle of the twentieth century as existing alongside the transformative influences of industrial modernity, rather than at some prelapsarian remove. Commercial society, in other words, was not so totally foreign to the farm families of Sandy Ridge, Union County, or Clover Bend. In fact, in many such locations, agrarian lifestyles only remained sustainable by way of a growing reliance on the kinds of income-generating opportunities that nonagricultural economic activity in the area made possible; a reality that belied the myth that the Appalachian countryside was, as another expert witness once put it, a "retarded frontier" populated by a bunch of frozen-in-time peasants. By the time the TVA arrived on the scene, for example, nearly one in four farm owners in and around Union County were already reporting earnings from paid labor off the farm. Among the more economically marginal households, who did not own but rented their land instead, the rate was nearly one in two. "He worked around" was how Robert Messer described his father, a Clay County farmer who, like many others across the region, began during these years to add various kinds of nonfarm jobs—for the railroad, or at nearby lumberyards, sawmills, or mining outfits—to the already complex arrangements on which the household depended. "My daddy he made cross ties, he peddled, he peeled tan bark," while young Robert himself picked up small jobs off the farm wherever he could to help his parents make ends meet.[17]

In other instances, "working around" could be a kind of euphemism for the more informal opportunities presented by the rising tide of commercial activity in the region. Before Margie Hayes's father skipped out on the family, he supplemented the family purse with proceeds from an illegal moonshine operation he set up back in the woods on Sandy Ridge. "My dad furnished the big shots in Dante," Margie recalled later, "the doctors and the lawyers" and even some of the company men who began showing up to manage the mines for Clinchfield. "Those people drank all the time," Margie remembered, and they always had the cash on hand to buy the glass jugs James Hayes would distribute out of the family barn. The first time Margie ever saw an automobile out on Sandy Ridge, in fact, was when the town doctor drove out there in a "little one seated job, [a] coupe" to buy five gallons of whiskey from her father. "They all found their way to Dad's door."[18]

Whatever specific form it took—an increase in wage work, the cultivation of new entrepreneurial outlets, the appearance of unfamiliar consumer goods—the pattern was largely the same across the region. The intensification of market-oriented economic activity during the first decades of the twentieth century neither sidestepped the southern hinterland nor obliterated it on contact. Rather, for a time, agrarian society was able to maintain something of an ongoing accommodation with the forces of development, often by incorporating the new opportunities and conveniences created into the traditional balancing act of the countryside. To be sure, this accommodation would prove to be an only temporary one. But for the generations of rural southerners who came of age in places like Sandy Ridge, Union County, or Clover Bend during these transitional decades, it would have a lasting impact. As the ratcheting up of nonagricultural economic activity in the region began to upend the balancing act of the countryside once and for all, a growing number of displaced farmers and their families would continue to try to hold onto agrarian ways of life even amid the onrushing changes brought about by industrialization.

## Resource-Extractive Industrialization and the Demise of the Countryside

By the time Margie Hayes met Joe Lawson, the man who would become her husband, in 1934, the economic landscape around Sandy Ridge had been transformed no less completely than the physical. Production on the southwest Virginia coalfield, which spanned more than fifteen hundred square miles in that corner of the state, had increased roughly threefold since the years when Margie's parents first built their log cabin, and it would double again over the next decade. At the beginning of the 1930s, well over ten thousand men were employed in the area mining coal, while thousands more worked in ancillary roles on which the local coal industry depended—sawing lumber, digging hillsides, hammering pillars, laying track, hauling tonnage, repairing machines, and so on. Dante, meanwhile, had become something of a small city in the wilderness. By 1930 it was home to four thousand people, as well as a power plant, a railroad depot, a post office, a modern hospital and high school, various stores, a movie theater and a fancy hotel, a beer garden, a car dealership, and a gas station. And almost all of it belonged to the Clinchfield Coal Corporation. According to a 1937 assessment of local property records, Clinchfield owned 516 residential dwellings and 59 other buildings in Dante—an economic stranglehold over the town that extended into every conceivable corner of the community. "They controlled your county politics, the sheriffs, the treasurer, the commissioner, every aspect of county office," remarked another longtime resident of Dante, whose ancestors had been among the first to settle in the area. "See, they dominated your whole life from start to go."[19]

The changes that came to the Sandy Ridge area mirrored the transformations that industrialization was bringing to the broader region. In Dickenson County, Virginia, where Margie's family lived, more than seventeen thousand acres of farmland were converted to other uses in the years between 1920 and 1930 alone; the size of the average farm, likewise, contracted by more than 25 percent in that time. All across southern Appalachia, total farmland decreased by 18 percent over the first three decades of the century, and the size of the typical farm shrank from 109 acres in 1900, to just 86 acres by 1930. The driving force everywhere was a rapid uptick in land acquisitions by companies like Clinchfield: deep-pocketed industrial firms, often headquartered in urban markets along the eastern seaboard or overseas, whose demand for the natural resources native to the Appalachian South—coal and timber especially—was nearly inexhaustible. In the parts of far-western North Carolina that would later be incorporated into Great Smoky Mountains National Park, for example, just thirteen timber companies came to own more than 75 percent of the land. In certain counties in West Virginia, coal operators had gobbled up surface lands covering as much as 90 percent of extant mineral reserves as early as 1900. By the 1920s the United States Coal and Coke Company (a subsidiary of the United States Steel Corporation), as well as other companies affiliated with the vast industrial empire constructed by New York–based financier J. P. Morgan, had come to control more than seven hundred fifty thousand acres of Appalachian coal lands—an expanse roughly the size of the state of Rhode Island.[20]

The conversion of a significant portion of the Appalachian countryside into a site of intensive resource extraction was an event of massive consequence for the national industrial economy. Coal output in southern Appalachia expanded almost six times over during the first three decades of the twentieth century. In the most mineral-rich areas, such as the Kentucky Cumberlands, the rate of increase was even greater—from four million tons annually in 1907 to nearly forty-seven million tons by 1929. In the justly famous Harlan County mines, production increased from just fourteen hundred tons in 1910 to fourteen million tons in 1929—by which point Harlan County alone, of fewer than five hundred square miles, was responsible for close to 3 percent of the country's total bituminous coal output. Similarly, beginning in the 1910s, the six states that contained the majority of the hardwood forest of the Upper South—West Virginia, Kentucky, Virginia, North Carolina, Tennessee, and Georgia—would become responsible for more than one-third of the country's annual lumber output. The impact that industrial-scale timbering had on the southern landscape was staggering; in the four years of World War I alone, more Appalachian timber was cut than during the entire period prior to 1900. Overproduction would come at an economic as well as an ecological cost, and by the end of the 1920s the Appalachian timber industry was already beginning to give way to the rising Pacific Northwest—but the southern forests would still be producing roughly three-fifths of the country's pulpwood well into the post–World War II period. One survey conducted in the late 1950s reported at least some logging or basic timber fashioning establishments in 188 of 190 southern Appalachian counties, making it by far the most widely distributed industrial activity in the region at midcentury. Even oil and gas production, though never operating locally at the same scale as the coal or timber industries, nevertheless went through a similar expansion during these years. In West Virginia and Kentucky, where most of the natural gas and crude oil reserves in the region were located, there were some forty thousand wells in production at the end of 1954—more than three times the number active at the beginning of the century.[21]

All this new activity did not enrich the region and its rural inhabitants nearly so much as it did industrialists in other parts of the country. On the eve of the Great Depression, southern Appalachian coal reserves were producing fully 80 percent of the country's bituminous coal supply, and profits on investment for coal operators averaged between 15 and 25 percent, with as many as one in four coal companies averaging rates of return above 25 percent. Yet at the same time, the southern Appalachian manufacturing economy was consuming only a little more than 10 percent of the bituminous coal burned for industrial fuel every year. In every state across the region, the number of manufacturing establishments trailed the national per capita average, by anywhere between 15 and 50 percent. What manufacturing did exist, meanwhile, was overwhelmingly concentrated in less capital-intensive, low-wage sectors, like clothing and textiles, food processing, and lumber—industries that paid, on average, between one-half and three-quarters of the typical manufacturing wage at the time. In 1929 only North Carolina contributed as much 2 percent toward the national sum for value-added through manufacturing; for every other state across the Upper South, the amount ranged from 1.2 to as low as just 0.3 percent. And even this measurement was misleading, as nearly one-quarter of the total for the entire region was generated in just five cities that fell within its most generously defined borders: Winston-Salem, Richmond, Birmingham, Atlanta, and Memphis. If those five cities were removed, the remainder of the area bounded by the Mississippi River to the west, the Ohio River to the north, and the Atlantic Ocean to the east generated less than 6 percent of manufacturing value-added in 1929.[22]

Industrialization, then, arrived both forcefully and fitfully to the rural South. By the end of the 1920s, the southern mountains had become the coal box to the nation's industrial heartland; the Southeast had surpassed New England as the regional locus of cotton textile production; and the southern states were home to nearly half the country's production workforce in lumber and timber goods, generated half of the country's manufactured tobacco products, and processed roughly one-tenth of the country's food supply by value. At the same time, southerners remained three times as likely to be employed in agricultural pursuits as non-southerners; and the South, while home to nearly 30 percent of the country's population, accounted for less than 10 percent of the country's manufacturing income. Parts of the region had become dense with industrial activity: textile manufacturers had installed upward of two hundred thousand spindles in each of more than a dozen counties along the Carolina Piedmont (in four counties—Cabarrus and Gaston in North Carolina, and Greenville and Spartanburg in South Carolina—the numbers reached above five hundred thousand); and so many company towns had sprung up in the coalfields that ran from West Virginia to Alabama that they outnumbered independent incorporated towns there by a ratio of five to one. Still, many stretches of the region saw almost no industrial development at all during the early decades of the twentieth century. In Tennessee, for instance, just six counties contained an aggregate power generation capacity—one way of measuring the presence of industrial machinery and other energy-consuming infrastructure—equivalent to more than four hundred twenty-five thousand horsepower in 1929. Meanwhile, across the state's remaining eighty-nine counties, the aggregate capacity registered just a hundred eighty thousand horsepower.[23]

Even in these relatively undeveloped areas, though, the first half of the century brought economic changes that had disruptive effects on agrarian livelihoods and lifestyles. The mechanization of farms in the South had always lagged behind the rest of the United States, but the general increase in the availability of new agricultural technologies after 1910—from trucks and tractors to mechanical harvesters and chemical fertilizers—eventually rippled through even the most remote parts of the region. In that decade alone, the total value of machinery and tools on Kentucky farms increased by 132 percent; in Tennessee, Virginia, and West Virginia, the increase was over 150 percent; and in North Carolina, South Carolina, and Georgia, it was at or above 200 percent—well ahead of the 184 percent increase for the country overall. Agricultural productivity began to improve even on the historically undercapitalized farms of the southern highlands, and as it did the demand for farm labor began to drop off accordingly. Between 1930 and 1950 the value of farm products sold across 205 southern Appalachian counties increased by 70 percent, even as 1.5 million acres of farmland fell out of production and the total farm population decreased by 10 percent. Machines not only reduced the need for farm laborers; they also made significant inroads into the supplementary work that residents of the rural countryside depended on to make ends meet. In addition to raising corn, wheat, and tobacco in the mountains of western North Carolina, Ernest Hickum's father had supported his family by hauling lumber to a nearby sawmill with a mule-drawn wagon—a side job that did not survive the arrival, in the early 1920s, of a new fleet of chain-driven trucks hired by the logging company. The trucks "could make two trips a day and my daddy couldn't make but one," Ernest recalled. "Now it wasn't but a year or two that they get to bringing them other kinds of trucks in there and just cut the poor farmers plumb out the sawmill, hauling lumber." A year or two after that, the Hickums packed their bags and moved to Greenville, South Carolina, where the Woodside Mill—at one point said to be the largest cotton mill in the world—was then introducing legions of similarly displaced farm families to the new routines of factory labor.[24]

Such was the lay of the land when the US Department of Agriculture concluded, after an exhaustive study of the "economic and social problems and conditions of the southern Appalachians" released at the beginning of 1935, that the principal cause of the region's woes was "an excess of population in relation to the economic opportunities to be found there under prevailing conditions." There was another way of looking at things, of course, which might have noted that it was a very particular set of prevailing conditions, created by the specific form that industrial development was taking locally, that was responsible for producing the region's steadily growing excess population. Intensifying demand for land and locally abundant natural resources; the relative lack of capital investment in higher-wage manufacturing industries within the region; the outsize economic influence exerted by industrial and financial entities based in other parts of the country—the symptoms of uneven development that later critics would associate with a kind of "internal colonialism" were already clearly manifest in southern Appalachia, even before the Great Depression plunged the region to new depths of deprivation. By almost any conceivable metric, the rural population of the Upper South found itself in a more precarious economic position at the end of the "booming" 1920s than it had been in at the turn of the century. In a region historically dependent on small-scale farming, less land was available for agricultural uses, farm earnings supported a smaller number of farm laborers, and fewer farmers owned the land they worked on (in the 1920s alone, a decade of prolonged agricultural depression throughout the country, the ranks of the non-owning farm tenant class in the South swelled by more than two hundred thousand). Growing numbers depended on nonagricultural work to subsidize diminished landholdings; yet the nature of the southern industrial economy was such that the differential between southern and northern manufacturing wages was larger in 1931 than it had been twenty-five years earlier. As a result of all this, per capita incomes across the southern states came out to barely half the national average—worse, by some measures, than it had been in the decades immediately following the Civil War. Even the Department of Agriculture allowed that the recent expansion of the region's most important industry, coal, had failed to produce "permanence of employment and security of livelihood for the laboring population," and that living conditions in the proliferating mining towns it did produce were "squalid."[25]

Nevertheless, the overarching diagnosis in the 1935 report aptly conveyed the bottom-line thinking of Franklin Roosevelt's New Deal government when it came to the problems plaguing the economy of the rural

South. More often than not, the programmatic solutions offered by the New Deal's rural-facing agencies and initiatives focused on how to accelerate the rate of economic development in the region and amplify its effects (or, if necessary, cut its losses), rather than prioritizing the preservation of what remained of Appalachia's traditional, mixed rural economy. Taking for granted decades' worth of conventional wisdom about the Appalachian South as a "retarded frontier," and coupling it with a new faith in state-directed economic "modernization," an increasingly active and interventionist public policy benefited millions—but also reinforced many of the same factors that had been separating southern Appalachians from the land for much of the last half century. Across the Upper South (if to a relatively lesser degree than in the Lower South cotton belt and other staple-crop-producing areas), agricultural price controls aided larger landowners at the expense of smaller ones, while subsidizing increased farm mechanization. The federally sponsored conversion of a neglected nitrate production facility at Muscle Shoals, Alabama, to the production of phosphate fertilizer accelerated a shift in southern Appalachian agriculture in kind as well as degree: over the next two decades, dairy and other kinds of livestock farming increased roughly threefold across the region, replacing smaller and less-efficient row-cropped farms with more extensive operations supporting many fewer farm families per acre. Roadbuilding undertaken by the Civilian Conservation Corps and the Public Works Administration succeeded in opening the more isolated pockets of the rural South to increased traffic, and as a result total highway mileage across the southern states more than doubled during the Depression decade. This was critical for attracting new industrial activity, while also facilitating the development of nonindustrial land in the region for tourism and other recreational purposes, most notably with the construction of the 469-mile Blue Ridge Parkway connecting the Shenandoah and Great Smoky Mountains National Parks. And in just the first year and a half of its existence, the Resettlement Administration purchased more than eight hundred thousand acres of submarginal land in the states of southern Appalachia—nearly 10 percent of the national total—removing them from production and thus further increasing the pressure on available farmland.[26]

Over the longer term, no federal program would have a greater impact on the rural Upper South and its inhabitants than the Tennessee Valley Authority. Much of that was positive, as the TVA improved navigation and flood control, enhanced the productivity and efficiency of local agriculture, and greatly increased the production and accessibility of hydroelectric power for residential, agricultural, and industrial use throughout the Tennessee River Valley. But once again it was those southern Appalachians still attached to the land who felt the trade-offs of regional development most acutely. The construction of the Norris Dam, for instance—the first of seven major dam projects the TVA completed between 1933 and 1941— would ultimately entail the purchase of more than a hundred fifty thousand acres of land, the creation of a nearly seventy-mile-long lake where previously none had existed, and the displacement of more than three thousand local families (including Myers Hill's). All told, over the next four decades the TVA would buy or condemn two million acres and occasion the dislocation of more than a hundred twenty-five thousand people for the purposes of dam construction. In that time, agricultural employment declined from 62 percent to just 6 percent across the forty thousand square miles covered by the TVA's mandate. And as the TVA came to depend heavily on strip-mined coal to fire its proliferating power plants beginning in the 1950s, the public utility once meant to symbolize "democracy on the march" became an unlikely buttress to regional imbalances put into place by the extractive economy. Not only would strip-mining come to make large stretches of southern Appalachia functionally uninhabitable because of its various ecological and toxicological effects on local water supplies and soils; its low-cost, high-productivity, largely mechanized approach to mineral extraction also had devastating and irreversible effects on coal industry employment. To be sure, many other factors helped account for the drop-off in coal employment in the region after its peak in the 1920s. But from 1932 (the year before the TVA's birth) to 1968 (at which point the TVA had become the largest single user of strip-mined coal in the country), jobs in southern Appalachian coal mines declined from 705,000 to just 132,000. Where once the coal industry had absorbed an excess population produced by industrial development, by the postwar decades, thanks in part to the TVA, it was generating its own surplus.[27]

So rather than offering a counterbalance to the trends in land use established by resource-extractive industrialization in the Appalachian South, the developmentalist approach to regional economic policy enshrined during the New Deal period only fueled the forces that had been undermining the balancing act of the countryside since the turn of the twentieth century. Indeed, population relocation was not so much an unfortunate side effect of the central state's vision for the economic salvation of the region, but a core component of it. "Any fundamental alleviation of the conditions of life" in rural southern Appalachia, the Department of Agriculture report argued, "can be achieved only by removing some of the population

from localities in which economic opportunities are too limited to provide a good family living." In the eyes of planners in Washington, poor
farmers like the Hickums and the Lawsons would be better off in places
like Greenville and Dante—growing centers of industrial activity that were
ever more fully enmeshed in national markets, and ever more detached
from the agrarian arrangements that had traditionally prevailed across the
region. For the millions of rural southerners who began embarking upon
similar types of moves during these years, deciding to leave the countryside behind was rarely so straightforward. But as they did, new jobs, living
circumstances, and experiences would shape their identities and outlooks
in ways that would eventually come to have a lasting impact on the emerging social geography of Transappalachia.[28]

## Displacement and the Passing of Provincialism

In many cases, of course, southern Appalachian agrarians did not want
to leave at all, and so did whatever they could to remain in the countryside. When field workers with the TVA surveyed close to two thousand
of Myers Hill's neighbors in and around Union County and asked them
about their relocation plans after construction began on the Norris Dam,
more than 80 percent of farm owners and tenants alike responded that
they hoped to continue to live on a farm. (Two years later, nearly two-
thirds of the families who had been dispossessed of their land by the TVA
had managed to remain within the five-county area that composed the
Norris Basin.) Joe Lawson, too, was "a born farmer," as Margie put it,
and between intermittent and largely reluctant forays into the mines in
Dante—and despite Margie's periodic suggestions that they move to Kingsport, Tennessee, where jobs with the Tennessee Eastman Chemical Company were rumored to be plentiful—he spent as many of his working years
as he could farming a small plot in Dickenson County that the family had
managed to hold onto. For Ernest Hickum's father, the transition to life in
Greenville—the loud machinery of the mills, the new hardships of shop-
ping at the company store and "living out of a tin can"—ended up being
simply unendurable. "He couldn't work in no cotton mill, so he went back
to the mountains," while Ernest and the rest of the family stayed behind
to earn what they could.[29]

Nevertheless, the centripetal force exerted by industry proved too
powerful for much of the region's land-poor and increasingly precarious rural population to resist. Even before the New Deal arrived on the
scene to hasten the process, the Department of Agriculture had noted that

"the chief change in many of the more isolated areas in which limited resources and other factors have hindered or precluded nonagricultural development, has been a more or less continual outward movement of people (mostly young folks) to cities and to other rural areas offering greater opportunities for employment." Already by the time of the 1910 census, the most remote and least developed core of the southern Appalachian region, a 164-county area that stretched from northern Georgia to West Virginia, was exhibiting a net population loss due to migration. All told, the number of farmers across the states of southern Appalachia would fall by 25 percent over the first half of the century (a rate of decline that paralleled the national figure but was felt more acutely in the region, where agriculture continued to account for roughly twice the share of total income payments as it did elsewhere). Another sizable portion of the region's rural population became, in essence, part-time agrarians during these years. By the 1950s the number of farm operators working off the farm more than a hundred days out of every year had increased by at least 80 percent, and the portion that worked off the farm at least two hundred days every year had increased by nearly 175 percent. By 1954, white operators of noncommercial farms in the South—the profile of the vast majority of southern Appalachian agrarians—were more than twice as likely to be working at least a hundred days off the farm as compared to the average American farmer.[30] More than half of these farmers now maintained households in which the largest portion of the family's income came from nonagricultural sources.[31]

With time a growing number of the fully or partially displaced would follow highways north, to the factory cities of the industrial Midwest. But at least initially, the largest beneficiaries of the demise of the southern countryside were the more economically diverse areas within the region rather than outside of it. Cities like Kingsport (and its larger regional cousins like Birmingham, Charleston, Chattanooga, or Knoxville) grew by an average of 32 percent between 1900 and 1930. Over the same period, those areas within southern Appalachia where some combination of mining and manufacturing was the primary form of economic activity saw their populations increase at a rate three to six times faster than predominantly agricultural areas, even accounting for the persistently high birth rates that continued to be found in the southern countryside. The underlying population transfer between agricultural counties and industrial counties that was beginning to remake the internal demography of the region in these years was particularly evident in a place like coal-rich eastern Kentucky. Across the five eastern Kentucky counties that experienced the steepest

population declines due to migration during the 1920s, mining employment made up no more than 16 percent of the local workforce. In the four
counties that saw the most significant population increases as a result of
migration in that time, meanwhile, miners made up anywhere from 40
to 60 percent of the workforce. Harlan County, again, was the pacesetter.
Over the course of the decade, while nearly two million acres of farmland
disappeared statewide and the broader eastern Kentucky region experienced a net population loss due to the migration of 19,730 people, Harlan
itself gained 20,718 more migrants than it lost. By 1927 the county's mining workforce alone (10,980) was larger than its entire resident population
had been as recently as 1910 (10,566).[32]

In practice, these shorter movements within the region represented as
much a geographic extenuation of the old balancing act of the countryside
as they did a definitive rupture with the agrarian past. Limited though
it may have been in comparison to other parts of the country, the availability of local industrial employment meant that even as wage labor was
becoming an increasingly ubiquitous feature of southern Appalachian life,
the first generations of the displaced often retained a welcome ability to
stay relatively close to familiar plots of land and extended kin networks.
It was not uncommon, for example, for those who managed to hold on
to some property in the area to return home at night rather than sleeping in work camps or company towns. An official with the Stonega Coal
and Coke Company, which at one point operated nine such towns in Wise
County, Virginia, acknowledged that many "were reluctant to make this
their new home"; some, as the general manager of a West Virginia mining
outfit attested, might even stay a while and then "go, in the spring of the
year, after the winter's work, back to their farms and return again in the
fall." And what was a comfort in good times quickly became a necessity
in lean ones. After its explosive growth over the previous twenty years,
Harlan County experienced a net population loss due to the migration
of 126 people during the Depression decade of the 1930s, as thousands
of out-of-work miners joined a regionwide "back-to-the-farm movement"
that temporarily reversed the outward flow of people from the countryside. Most of that movement, the Department of Agriculture noted at the
time, "does not appear to have been so much one of reclaiming abandoned
farms as it was a return of persons to the farms of relatives." Somewhat
more churlishly, the patrician reformer Mary Breckinridge referred to the
practice by which recently displaced poor folk fell back on the support of
those who had remained behind as a rural "corn-bread line." But for residents of the southern countryside, habituated as they were to the complex

land- and family-based householding arrangements upon which rural life had always rested, this method of coping with the economic calamity of the Depression was best understood not merely as a country-cousin to the proliferating urban breadlines of the era, but as a modern adaptation with deep historical roots in the region.[33]

In other ways, too, these first movements throughout the region introduced growing numbers of displaced rural southerners to a newly hybrid existence: one that was not nearly so rooted in the agrarian social arrangements that had endured as a result of the region's relatively slow economic development, but not fully severed from them either. Life in the proliferating coal towns and mill villages captured this new reality perfectly. For many of the recently displaced—accustomed as they were to the material deprivation of the countryside—the wages paid in the southern industrial sector seemed considerably higher than their discount on the national average might otherwise have suggested. As a result, not only in their earnings but also, as one of the keenest observers of rural Appalachian life once noted, in their consumption patterns, family structure, levels of educational attainment, and even religious habits and voting behavior, residents of the more industrialized sections of the rural South soon "moved closer to the greater society than [those who remained in] the subsistence agricultural counties." Even on the most quotidian level, the shift involved could seem almost epochal. Gladys Carter, who had grown up on a small farm north of Dante in Dickenson County, would always remember her "first permanent" in the beauty parlor at the Clinchfield Inn: "They hooked you up to all them wires and everything. . . . If it'd come a storm or lightenin' or anything, buddy I'd a tore them off'n my head and come out of there." Raiford Blackstone, who relocated to Dante from northern Georgia with his family in the late 1910s, recalled with a similarly enduring sense of appreciation the newfound thrill of being able to listen to radio broadcasts of the World Series. "We would run downtown to the town news stand, where they sold newspapers and magazines and they would have a radio, and they'd turn the radio loud enough and the men and boys would gather around til' the last man was out." In fact, by the mid-1930s, rates of radio ownership in southern mill villages so closely approximated that of the "greater society" that it hardly seemed out of step when a group of workers at a Gastonia, North Carolina, mill petitioned their employer to begin the day shift fifteen minutes earlier, so they could get off in time to make it home for *Amos 'n' Andy*.[34]

And yet, as Clinchfield did in Dante, employers often ran their local operations like private fiefdoms, retaining ownership over all land and real property, keeping workers and their families dependent on company scrip, and threatening any who brooked their authority with immediate dismissal and ejection. With companies exerting such total control over life and labor, conditions in these southern industrial towns could often sink to deplorable lows. "In the worst of the company-controlled communities," commented the United States Coal Commission, convened by Congress in the early 1920s to investigate conditions in the industry, "the state of disrepair at times runs beyond the power of verbal description or even photographic illustration, since neither words nor pictures can portray the atmosphere of abandoned dejection or reproduce the smells." Dante hardly ranked among the worst; and yet still, as one veteran of the mines there recalled, "there was two classes of people in Dante: there was poor and poorer. It was just slave labor, and people were just surviving."[35]

Surviving, in turn, frequently entailed the preservation of adaptive strategies that the newly displaced had first perfected in the countryside. Since the regularity of wage work fluctuated with the business cycle, and often quite dramatically—in Harlan County, for instance, the mining workforce averaged 217 days of work in 1921 and just 105 in 1922, as a recession and then a nationwide coal strike generated severe disruptions to production— workers and their families remained reliant on a variety of supplementary labors to keep themselves afloat. When possible, they raised vegetables or kept chickens, hogs, and cows, on garden plots attached to their company-owned living quarters. It was not uncommon, especially during periods of extended layoff, for men to head back into the hills to hunt, fish, and trap, as often for much-needed food as for amusement; women, similarly, might bring in some additional cash by performing household labor—cleaning, cooking, caretaking—for the better-off families in town. Other tasks that had traditionally fallen to women in the rural South, like the production of home remedies from herbs, roots, and other foraged materials, persisted in these new settings in no small measure because they remained more affordable options than company-provided doctors and other commercially available amenities. Most significantly in these decades before widespread unionization stabilized earnings in the coal industry (and only in the coal industry, as southern textiles, food processing, and other key industries would remain largely nonunion for much of the twentieth century), old balancing acts continued to provide at least partial subsidy to recently industrialized lifestyles.[36]

But again, old and new ways of life overlapped here as well. Provisioning habits developed across the generations may have sustained displaced agrarians through their initial ventures into industrial society—but these rural holdovers did not prevent many of the same communities from also becoming battlefields in the titanic labor struggles of the period. In all of "Bloody" Harlan County, for example, there were just three incorporated towns not owned by a coal company when the National Guard was first called in to subdue striking miners in May 1931; and it would similarly require squadrons of guardsmen armed with machine guns to reopen the Greenville mills during the Great Textile Strike of 1934. Often enough, these confrontations ended with harsh lessons in the autocratic and at times insuperable power wielded by industrial employers. When organizers from the United Mine Workers first arrived in Dante in the early 1930s, Clinchfield's immediate response was to evict any of its workers who were caught talking to union representatives. "They hauled them out of here and [took] them down there and set their furniture outside on the side of the road," one longtime resident recalled. "If they signed these union cards," another remembered, "they didn't have a job the next day. Even though you paid rent on that house[,] they set you out." But for those who managed to persevere, the transformative effects that collective bargaining could bring to southern industrial life offered enduring lessons of a different sort. "They had a future then, they did," explained Clarence Phillips, who had grown up watching his father, Rufus, dig coal in Dante for what often amounted to less than a dollar an hour. Clinchfield would resist unionization harder and longer than any other mining company in southwestern Virginia, not signing a contract with the United Mine Workers until 1945. But when it did, Phillips noted, the result was more than just "making a little better wages." For the first time in a long time, families like his felt like they "kind of controlled part of their life."[37]

Finally, southern industrial towns not only introduced recently displaced agrarians to new modes of working-class organization and conflict. They also exposed them to a new kind of working class. Compared to life in the countryside, where the nearest neighbor could be miles away and was likely to be a relative anyway, Appalachian mill villages and especially mining towns often teemed with a diverse and unfamiliar humanity. Although the foreign-born populations of many states in the region remained vanishingly small throughout the early twentieth century—ranging from just under 5 percent in West Virginia to less than 0.5 percent in North Carolina—industrial nodes like Dante were already attracting disproportionately large numbers of immigrant workers, as well as Black migrants native to other parts of the South. In West Virginia, according to a large sampling conducted by that state's Department of Mines, fully 40 percent of the mining workforce in 1909 had been born outside of the United States, and another one in four miners were

Black. As a consequence, these growing pockets of rural industry in certain respects came to bear a closer resemblance to the multiethnic landscapes of the urban north than they did to the historically monoracial countryside of the Upper South. By the early 1920s, for instance, Dante was home to enough Hungarian immigrants—many of whom, like Elizabeth Gyetvay's family, had first passed through coalfields in Pennsylvania and elsewhere before turning south—that the town supported a three-story, twenty-eight-room boardinghouse that catered specifically to Hungarians, where old-country traditions like the annual festival to celebrate the grape harvest were restaged every October between shifts at the mines. Greeks, Poles, and Italians were similarly plentiful enough among the local workforce to sustain their own boardinghouses or churches in town. And while Clinchfield, like most employers in the region, generally did its best to keep Black miners in segregated job categories and their families in segregated company housing units, in some parts of Dante, like along the creek bed that wound its way through Cigarette Hollow just east of town, Blacks and whites were known to live side by side even as Jim Crow continued to stalk the land.[38]

In all these ways, then, the cumulative experience of initial forays into industrial labor markets was nothing short of transformational for the people involved. If denizens of the southern countryside had once been a "yesterday's people"—premodern peasants singularly attached to traditional modes of production and communal arrangements—few plausibly could be described that way after decades' worth of dispossession and development had largely done away with agrarian patterns of land use and social organization. Suspended between agricultural and industrial occupations, between self-provision and waged employment, between fewer and more dense residential arrangements, and between parochial and at least quasi-cosmopolitan lifestyles and social milieus, the hybridized existences that many inhabitants of southern Appalachia found themselves leading by the first decades of the twentieth century may not have fully replicated the classical models of rural proletarianization.[39] But neither were they frozen in time and place. "The question of whether the people of the Region have clung to their earlier heritage, steadfastly resisting the secular philosophy of an industrial society, can be answered simply and categorically," concluded another preeminent scholar of southern Appalachia, as he reflected back on the events of the first half of the twentieth century. "The answer is no."[40]

So there was no small irony to the fact that when millions of the displaced eventually began to make their way north, they would often be received—at new workplaces, in new communities, in media accounts, and in political debates—as precisely what they were not: a population of pro-vincial rustics, who fell directly off some remote, ancient hillside into the hurly-burly of the modern city. In reality, as a result of work experiences in coal, logging, textiles, and other southern industries that emerged in these decades, these "hillbillies" were hardly strangers to industrial life when they began arriving in growing numbers in the urban Midwest. Rather, for many of the southern Appalachian poor, movements back and forth between industrial workspaces and rural homeplaces had already become the defining characteristic of a particular kind of class experience, even before they embarked on the longer, interregional migrations to come—a way of negotiating the economic insecurity that had become an unavoid-able condition of their lives as members of a newly landless, increasingly mobile rural proletariat.

This fundamental category mistake would have profound and lasting consequences across the political and cultural landscape of Transappala-chia. And the mischaracterization at its core only became more erroneous with time. Poor southern whites would continue to be regarded as little more than backward hillbillies upon arrival in northern cities well into the 1950s and 1960s—even though, by the postwar decades especially, their ranks had become swollen as much or more by the region's indus-trially displaced as by the agriculturally dispossessed who had been leaving the countryside since the turn of the century. The driving force here was a combination of regional overproduction, the ascendance of oil and other cleaner-burning industrial fuels, and, most significantly, new developments in the intensive mechanization of labor. Each of these factors came to a head in the years immediately following World War II, and together contributed to a dramatic collapse in employment in a num-ber of the key industries that had previously absorbed much of the Upper South's rural surplus.

The effects would be felt in logging and timbering, commercial agri-culture, textiles, and elsewhere; but coal, again, was the prime example. "Continuous mining" machines, first put into regular use in 1948, allowed companies to reduce the size of the average mine work crew from thirteen or fourteen miners to just six or seven, while producing more coal. Strip-mining, which accounted for just 1.5 percent of all US coal in 1920, had come to account for 25 percent of total output by the end of the 1950s and would only increase from there. By 1957 strip- and other surface-mining techniques were able to produce more than twice as much coal per miner-day than traditional deep-shaft mining; auger-mining, another postwar development, produced three times as much. As a result of these and

other changes to the labor process, the output of bituminous coal in southern Appalachia increased by seven million tons, or 17 percent, between
1950 and 1957, even as the average number of miners working daily in the
region decreased by 40 percent over the same period of time.[41]

The demographic impact of all this—particularly in states like Kentucky and West Virginia, which between them accounted for more than
80 percent of southern Appalachian coal output by the 1950s—was catastrophic and fairly immediate. In just ten years, Kentucky's mining workforce dropped from nearly eighty thousand to just a little over twenty thousand; regionwide, there were nearly three hundred thousand fewer mining
jobs in Appalachia in 1960 than there had been in 1950. Unsurprisingly,
instead of gaining migrants as they had for much of the first half of the
century, the Upper South's most mining-dependent counties now began
shedding people by the tens of thousands, experiencing an overall population decline of nearly 20 percent over the course of the 1950s. While the
largest numbers of migrants along the hillbilly highway in the years prior
to World War II had originated in southern Appalachia's more agriculturally oriented sections, in the decades that followed the war—the peak
period of southern Appalachian migration to the Midwest—the balance
would largely reverse itself. In Detroit, for instance, migrants from Kentucky and West Virginia, who had represented well under half of all southern Appalachian migrants to the city during the 1940s, composed nearly
two-thirds of the migrant population by the 1960s. West Virginia alone,
which had produced just 20 percent of migrants who left the Upper South
before World War II, accounted for as much as 45 percent of the total in
the decades that followed.[42]

In the end, the demise of the rural economy of the Upper South, and
the creation of a regional surplus population that could be absorbed into
the industrial labor markets of the urban Midwest, unfolded as a two-
stage process. Resource-extractive industrialization undermined traditional patterns of land use that had long sustained southern Appalachian
agrarians but engendered only a partial and ultimately unsustainable
model of economic development for the region. State-sponsored efforts
to "modernize" the countryside made important inroads in addressing the
material deprivation that decades of this kind of industrial activity exacerbated, but operated from the starting premise that population relocation
was a necessary precondition for correcting the social and economic problems confronting the region. Together, these forces helped accelerate an
exodus from the countryside that by the 1930s had already substantially
remade the internal demography of the region. For a time, these displaced

southerners were able to adapt older lifestyles to new conditions, living and working and above all moving between agrarian and industrial settings within the region—until the region's industrial economy could no longer keep pace with the rising numbers of the displaced, and, in fact, began aggressively displacing its own. And so, at a rate that would increase steadily over the years—from the tens of thousands per decade at the turn of the century, to the millions per decade by its midpoint—poor and working-class residents of the rural Upper South would begin making longer journeys in search of employment outside the region, charting new life courses along the hillbilly highway that would, in turn, change the course of twentieth-century American history.

Still, some chose never to leave. Despite Margie Hayes's best efforts, she was never able to convince Joe Lawson to abandon the corner of southwestern Virginia where they had both grown up. So instead she went to school and became a teacher, while Joe split his time farming and, when the needs of their growing family demanded, picking up work at the mines in Dante. "Clinchfield got some of the first machines, the first miner, they called it a continuous miner, that was ever put in the mines that we know of," Margie would later explain. "And that's when Joe went into the mines. Now he went in to timber after that thing. The machine was up there digging coal like this and raking it back, and he was following way back here, doing the timber work." Joe liked the social aspects of the work—the time spent underground with the other men, the excitement of the union hall—but on the whole it must have been a miserable arrangement for a man who had been born a farmer. "You know, I've never seen one of those things except on television, but Joe said, you know, that was the dustiest thing in the world," Margie recalled. "He said the man that ran that machine back where he was, he said he couldn't even see him. All he could know was there was a light up there. He couldn't see that machine for the dust."

Joe would do that dark and dusty work for about a decade, until Clinchfield had pretty much exhausted the local coal reserves by the end of the 1950s and began pulling up stakes from Dante and the surrounding area. It was not as long a career in the mines as some in Dante had known; but it was still long enough for Joe to contract a case of black lung, which would eventually leave him gasping for air when climbing the steps to his front porch. He would die of a heart attack at the age of just fifty-six.

Margie would live for nearly another half century, most of it in the house she and Joe had lived in up on Sandy Ridge. She would pass away at the home of her niece in the town of Castlewood, just a few miles down the road.[43]

# CHAPTER TWO

# On the Road

## MIGRATION AND THE MAKING OF A
## TRANSREGIONAL WORKING CLASS

*"The folks who ride my line aren't like the passengers most lines have.*
*They all come from Western Kentucky and Southern Illinois and go to the*
*Detroit section to find jobs in the motor plants."*[1]

—J. POLK BROOKS, BUS LINE OPERATOR, PADUCAH, KENTUCKY

*"Loyd Crouch went back to Tenn. Sed the climent diden suit his close."*[2]

—CHARLIE WOOD, FARMER, PALL MALL, TENNESSEE

CHARLIE WOOD WAS BORN in southern Kentucky around the turn of the
twentieth century, but he lived most of his life just across the state line in
Tennessee's Fentress County, which sits astride the Cumberland Plateau a
bit more than an hour's drive northwest of Knoxville. By the early 1920s
Charlie had married a local woman, Delta Hatfield, and together they raised
five children on a piece of land in the hilly northern reaches of the county,
close to the small unincorporated community of Pall Mall. It was not much
land, but they owned it outright, and so Charlie and Delta managed to get
by. They raised some crops—mainly tobacco, corn, wheat, and barley—and
kept hogs and some milk cows. They grew potatoes, Irish and sweet, which
they sold to the local school district. Charlie was handy, and so he would
also bring in extra money for the family by fashioning everything from bas-
kets and wagons for their neighbors, to tool handles for the Works Progress
Administration (WPA) men when they came to build roads in the area during the 1930s. He worked for the WPA himself for a time, and periodically
would pick up paid work cutting timber in the nearby log woods.

And when all that was still not enough, Charlie would pack a bag and head to Muncie, Indiana, a little more than three hundred miles due north of Pall Mall, where he could be sure to get a job at one of that city's many factories. "He didn't like the North," Charlie's granddaughter Kay recalled—but the wages kept bringing him back over the years. "Good money for a kid in my way," the then forty-five-year-old father of five would note in his diary, after one overtime shift at the Chevrolet transmission plant on Muncie's southside.[3]

If Charlie did not know Helen Sells's family from Fentress County, he might have met them in Indiana. The Sellses lived in a community called Double Top—a cluster of farmhouses too small to qualify for a census designation that sat about ten miles south and west of where the Woods lived. More than anything else, Double Top was a small peak, and from the coal seams and shale rock that ran through its middle, as well as the stands of oak, pine, and maple that grew along its ridge line, families like Helen's eked out a living. There were several mines still operating around Double Top when Helen was young, as well as a quarry and a sawmill, but work in the area had always been scarce—it was mainly "a lot of hills and hollers, and a lot of poor people," as she would put it later. And so, almost unavoidably, Helen's family was also drawn north—and specifically to Muncie. Like Charlie Wood, Helen's father would go back and forth to Muncie with some regularity, whenever work was hard to come by in Fentress County, usually spending a few months there at a stretch. He would get jobs doing construction, or at one of the local factories that was known to hire southerners. And not only her father: at various points in her childhood, Helen's maternal grandparents, three aunts, an uncle, and some older siblings all went to Indiana—mostly in or around Muncie, and in some cases to stay. In fact, for people like Helen or Charlie, Muncie could often feel as close by as the most recent letter from a loved one—or at least the next issue of the *Fentress County News*, which for the better part of three decades carried a regular column written by a Fentress County woman who had migrated to Muncie, in which she recounted the local goings-on for friends and family back home. "Everybody had heard of Muncie," Helen would recall when looking back on what it was like to be young in Fentress County. "Everybody, everybody here has somebody that's lived in Indiana."[4]

The economic developments of the first half of the twentieth century impacted life along this stretch of the Upper Cumberland Plateau much as they did life in the rest of the Appalachian South. Fentress County lost nearly half its total farmland during these years, and farms in the county were on average 25 percent smaller at midcentury than they had been at

its beginning. For a time, the familiar forms taken by rural industry created some local opportunities for nonagricultural work, especially in the
complex of mines located around the community of Wilder in the southwestern part of the county. But those industries peaked locally around the
onset of the Great Depression, and by the beginning of the 1950s the last
remaining mines in the area were steadily closing down. Otherwise, Fentress County offered little beyond the kinds of low-wage jobs that tended to
cluster in the rural South, in industries like poultry processing and apparel
manufacturing. As a result, Fentress County and the rest of the Upper
Cumberland region were consistently home to some of the very lowest
incomes in the state. Helen herself went to work at one of the local factories when she graduated from high school, but she did not stay long. "I
worked six months in the shirt factory here, and I thought, 'Can't do this,
there's better.'" And so, as so many others around this time were doing—in
the 1950s alone, Fentress County lost 11 percent of its population—Helen
quit the shirt factory and moved in with her older sister in Muncie, where
she quickly got a job at a wire factory that made replacement parts for
refrigerators. She would stay for nearly four decades.[5]

As experiences like Charlie Wood's and Helen Sells's became increasingly common, they indicated the extent to which the collapse of the rural
economy of the Upper South altered something basic in the orientation
and expectations of the region's inhabitants. Mobility between and among
farm tenancy arrangements, temporary work camps, and seasonal forms
of industrial labor—what one historian has called the "perpetual transience" that landless southerners, both Black and white, came to know
in the decades after the Civil War—had long been a defining feature of
working-class life in the region. But movement took on an added significance for a growing number of southern Appalachian natives during these
years, as the distance, frequency, and duration of their travels increased.
Put simply, once regional out-migration got underway in earnest, rural
people and rural places in the Upper South no longer were as they had
always been. "It was just part of growing up," explained Libby Anderson,
who was born in the early 1950s in the town of Allardt, about five miles
east of Jamestown, the Fentress County seat. "Going to Muncie was just
like going to the bathroom, it was so common." The same could not have
been said just a half century earlier.[6]

The hillbilly highway, in other words, was both an inevitable outgrowth
of forces that had been at work in the region for some time and, for the
people whose livelihoods, families, and sense of community were most
directly affected, something altogether new. As the proliferating interstate

highway system created connections between points on the map previously remote from one another, they brought thousands and eventually millions of natives of the Appalachian countryside into contact with the types of economic opportunities to which the systematic underdevelopment of the region had long denied them access. Suddenly, an essentially limitless supply of good-paying factory jobs—not to mention the various extracurricular amusements that only city living could offer—were no more than an overnight car or bus ride away. Or not: for those who found the northern job market too inhospitable, the rigors of factory life too demanding, or the pace and scale of urban society too unfamiliar, the highways ran in the other direction, too, bringing millions back home again— sometimes for a while, sometimes for good.

Migration studies sometimes have a tendency to focus on starting and ending points while glossing over what transpires in the spaces between them; they operate in these moments in a teleological fashion, concerned more with outcomes than processes.[7] But for many travelers along the hillbilly highway, whose patterns of movement belied any straightforward or permanent division of the migration experience along simple lines of before and after, the process was critical, and the space between as revealing as the locations at either end of the journey. No longer merely transient, natives of the rural Upper South now found themselves navigating existences increasingly suspended between agrarian points of origin and ways of life, and the industrial workplaces and urban cultures that were coming to predominate in the states north of the Ohio River. In such a context, the highways did much more than merely transport migrants between here and there. They became, in essence, the initial staging ground for a new kind of class experience, one that would eventually come to set the economically marginal population of Transappalachia apart as a distinctive group in midcentury American society.

## Hillbilly Highways

In linking together places like Fentress County, Tennessee, and Muncie, Indiana, Helen Sells, Charlie Wood, and migrants like them would forever alter the landscape of Transappalachia. But first they had to get there. And getting there, after all, was no small feat. Years later, Joyce Crouch would still remember the long treks she and her brother made into Jamestown from where they grew up in the most densely wooded portion of western Fentress County. "I rode a mule and my brother just walked. It was a road, but it was just a wagon road, very narrow and when the rains came it was

Jobs with industrial manufacturers like Delco-Remy, a General Motors division headquartered in Anderson, Indiana, were among the most sought-after by Transappalachian migrants. Here, a group of workers in Department 312 of the Anderson Delco-Remy plant pose for a photograph in February 1953. Photograph used with permission of Kay Wood Conatser.

muddy." The roads out in her part of the county "weren't paved until the '40s or '50s—after the war," and so even as late as when she was attending high school in Jamestown, in the early 1940s, Joyce would have to walk two miles just to catch the school bus. Interstate travel, needless to say, was even more prohibitively demanding. As it happened, the first time Joyce ever rode in a car was also the first time she left the county—on a trip she took at the age of seven to visit her mother, who was then working at an automobile plant in Detroit. "We went through Cincinnati about dark," she recalled years later, "and I had never seen so many neon lights in my life. I was in awe of that."[8]

Transportation—or, more precisely, its difficulties—had always been a conditioning feature of life in the Upper South. Particularly in the more mountainous parts of the region, poverty and topography had long combined to limit the construction of paved roads, to an extent that not only constrained the mobility of the region's inhabitants but also seemed, in the eyes of many contemporary observers, to be one of the key factors quite literally cutting the region off from the forward progress of industrial modernity. In one of the earliest comprehensive surveys of southern Appalachia, John C. Campbell's *The Southern Highlander and His Homeland*, published in 1921, the author highlighted "exceedingly poor roads" as an underlying source of the material deprivation confronting the region, and predicted that it would still be many years before that "great civilizer"—the pathbreaking Ford automobile—fully penetrated the most "shut off" pockets of the southern countryside. By the Depression era, when concern for rural poverty generally, and southern poverty most of all, reached one of its periodic zeniths, not much had changed. In its signature 1935 report, the US Department of Agriculture used similar language when discussing southern Appalachia's persistent transportation deficits, which it described as one of the "chief causes" of both the "isolation of much of the region" as well as its "backward economic development." In almost every county situated along the Upper Cumberland Plateau, the report found, fewer than half of all farms were located on improved roads by this time. In Fentress County, the rate was less than one in five.[9]

By the same token, when and where improved roads did begin to penetrate the region, they often acted as release valves. When the Social Science Research Council (SSRC) commissioned a massive national study of population redistribution in the mid-1930s, its authors observed that, following "a century and a quarter of isolation, when communication with the outside world was poor and physical movement exceedingly slow and difficult," out-migration from southern Appalachia quickly "assumed substantial proportions" once the physical landscape had been sufficiently altered so as to allow it. Surfaced highways had started to appear more regularly in the region by the mid-1920s; the first interstate bus lines began running not long thereafter; and local roads were beginning to improve, too, especially following the official launch of the New Deal's public works programs in 1933.[10] As a result, in southern Appalachia as elsewhere, "a new type of mobility and a new form of migration" were already showing signs of taking root. "The evidence of mobility is the more striking when it is remembered that the people of the mountains have been exposed to conditions facilitating migration for a very short time," the study's authors noted, correctly recognizing the Depression's dampening effect on migration as an only temporary reversal of the overall pattern. "The outward movement of the twenties, considerable as it was, is therefore no adequate test of the response which might now be expected were the mountain people exposed to a sustained revival of outside opportunity."[11]

Road improvements not only added to the "ease and freedom" with which residents of the Upper South were able to leave the region, as the SSRC study phrased it. They also determined where people went. The migratory circuits that came to shape life along the hillbilly highway were often initially creations of the specific routes that were carved (or not carved) by the network of paved highways that began to pinstripe the region over the first decades of the twentieth century. Among the more notable were US Route 45, from Mississippi through the fertile farmland of western Tennessee and Kentucky, then up into southern Illinois and on north to Chicago and Milwaukee; US 31, running like a prime meridian from southern Alabama to northern Michigan, passing through Nashville, Louisville, and Indianapolis along the way; and US 41 and 25, two legs of the ambitious "Dixie Highway" that aimed to connect the southeastern states with the metropolitan centers of the Midwest. All would become important traffic corridors—the footprints, more or less, for the arterial interstates (I-55 in the west, I-65 in the middle, and I-75 in the east) that would quadrisect the landscape of Transappalachia after the 1950s. And like the dozens of smaller but no less significant roadways that began to appear in growing profusion throughout the area, these and other routes would leave a lasting imprint on the emergent social geography of the two larger regions they connected.[12]

The impact of these new highways was already evident by the time the SSRC study was being conducted. Pockets of manufacturing activity had begun to develop around larger urban areas within southern Appalachia by the end of the 1920s. But because of the distribution, direction, and variable quality of improved roads throughout the region, the authors observed, "movement entirely out of the mountains may often involve less difficulty than would a transfer from one part of the Southern Appalachians to another." All roads were not created equally, in other words. As a result, it often ended up being "easier for a boy in the West Virginia hills to get down to the manufacturing towns along the Ohio River than to those along the Tennessee; easier for a boy in Breathitt County, Kentucky, to get to Cincinnati or Middletown"—a steel town about thirty miles north of Cincinnati—"than to Charleston, Knoxville, or Roanoke."[13]

Over time, the expanding system of interstate highways would operate like an increasingly complex hydraulic system, guiding southern Appalachian natives not only out of the region but also toward particular midwestern destinations instead of others. By the middle of the 1950s, these roadway-determined migration patterns had become so deeply embedded that it was possible to measure them with a remarkable degree of precision. One sampling of census responses from 1960 given by some hundred thousand southern Appalachian migrants to key midwestern cities found that, of the portion who ended up in the Ohio destinations of Cincinnati, Dayton, and Hamilton, at least 70 percent had originated in the counties in Kentucky and Tennessee that hugged US 23, US 25, and US 127. Cities farther west, like Indianapolis or Chicago, which lay along US 45 or US 41, were the most common destinations for migrants from Tennessee. Farther east—Columbus, Akron, Canton, and Cleveland—and the balance tipped strongly toward West Virginia, the state of origin for at least 60 percent of the migrants to each of those cities. And directional preference of this sort could be even more finely grained. Migrants from West Virginia's most southwesterly counties tended to follow US 35 to Columbus, where they outnumbered West Virginians from the northeastern portions of the state by a rate of thirteen to one. West Virginian migrants to Akron, meanwhile, were more than four times as likely to hail from the state's northern counties, connected to Akron by US 19, US 21, and US 30, rather than from the counties in the southwest that did not sit so conveniently on a direct route to Rubber City.[14]

There was much more that went into the decisions of when and where to migrate, of course, than simply the mute logic of the pavement. But it is also hard to overstate the importance these roadways took on for the generations of people who came of age in the southern countryside during the middle decades of the twentieth century—with one eye already trained toward the North, and a sense that their lives, too, would inevitably play out along this proliferating circuitry of migration. This was precisely what the Pikeville, Kentucky–born (but Columbus, Ohio–raised) country musician Dwight Yoakam had in mind when he wrote a wistful song for his second album, *Hillbilly Deluxe*, about the "three R's" that formed the bedrock of a southern Appalachian child's education: "They learned readin', writin', Route 23 / To the jobs that lay waiting in those cities' factories." And it was what Fentress County residents like Charlie Wood or Helen Sells took away from the hand-painted roadmap of US 127 that adorned the front porch of the Forbus General Store in Pall Mall, Tennessee. A simple yet practical rendering of local points of interest—Jamestown and the Sergeant Alvin C. York property to the south; Dale Hollow Lake to the west along State Route 42—the map itself followed US 127 no farther north than Lake Cumberland in southern Kentucky. But unmistakable were the mileage markers that appeared to the left of the map, in bold black letters painted larger than any of the more nearby place names: Indianapolis, 275; Dayton, 300; Muncie, 325.1.[15]

With all this increased interregional traffic came new opportunities as well. On US 25, for example, just south of Williamstown, Kentucky, an enterprising local opened a filling station, restaurant, and lodging house in the late 1920s, with the hopes of taking advantage of the growing tide of long-distance car and bus traffic frequenting that stretch of highway. In a savvy piece of roadside marketing, he called his business The Halfway House, and for legions of migrants over subsequent decades it became precisely that: a much-frequented midway stop-off on drives to or from the Ohio River bridge crossing between Covington, Kentucky, and Cincinnati.[16]

Another roadway innovation, born to meet a new demand that emerged with the migration, was innumerable informal "taxi" services that popped up throughout the region, to shuttle travelers between the southern Appalachian countryside and various popular destinations in the Midwest. Typically operated by an experienced migrant and often amounting to little more than a large station wagon that a driver would fill however they could, taxi outfits of this sort were as common as the distinctive circuits that came to connect local communities on either end of the Transappalachian migration. Willard Voiles was one of at least three drivers who regularly carried passengers back and forth along the US 127 corridor between Muncie and Jamestown during the peak years of the migration. He was a typical case: a Fentress County native who spent twenty-three years working at Muncie's Frank Foundry, Voiles would carry passengers with him on weekly trips home to visit his wife and five children, who stayed behind on the family's small plot of land just north of Jamestown. For ten dollars a trip (up to fifteen dollars by later years), Voiles's passengers got a no-frills, ten-hour ride that could only be described as moderately comfortable. As Libby Anderson, who rode with Voiles when she went to stay with her older sister's family in Muncie in the late 1950s, put it later, "he would pack you in like sardines."[17]

Most of the drivers who serviced the migration were like Willard Voiles: men with other, primary occupations, usually in the factories, who carried passengers when they could as a way of picking up some extra money. But along the most heavily trafficked routes, there were even occasional opportunities to turn taxi work into something more substantial. J. Polk Brooks hailed from Kentucky's far-western Jackson Purchase region, a low-lying, agriculturally oriented area whose largest city, Paducah, sits at the confluence of the Tennessee and Ohio Rivers. Not quite as poor as the more mountainous terrain in the eastern part of the state, the rural portions of western Kentucky nonetheless experienced a similar population loss in the early decades of the twentieth century—especially after the news of the Ford Motor Company's unprecedented five-dollar day in 1914 initiated what a pair of local historians would describe as "one long Detroit caravan" out of the region. Brooks, who had made his own earlier forays to Detroit, sensed the building demand and began shuttling the northbound traffic between Paducah and Detroit in the mid-1920s.[18]

Encouraged by the response, Brooks decided to expand his operation in 1929 and formally incorporated, first as a permitted taxi service and then as a bus company that he christened Brooks Bus Line. At the outset, "bus" was a relatively optimistic euphemism for the seven-passenger, 1924-model Buick in which Brooks made what was then a twenty-four-hour drive twice weekly, leaving Paducah on Mondays (north on US 45, then east through Indiana and up into Michigan) and returning from Detroit on Saturdays, charging eight dollars per trip. And Brooks's timing was not terribly propitious, as the impending stock market crash soon sent migrants fleeing Motor City's rapidly shuttering auto plants. But Brooks Bus Line would thrive, weathering the downturn and surging over subsequent decades, until it was serving an average of seventeen thousand riders a year by the early 1950s, on what it billed as "The Direct Route Between Kentucky, Illinois, and Michigan"—or, more punchily, "The Paducah Express." At its peak, Brooks maintained a payroll of thirty-five and a fleet of more than two dozen proper buses, allowing the company to promise its riders not only the "shortest route" but also the "fastest time" to Detroit, which Brooks's drivers got down to as little as eleven hours and forty-five minutes with stops. Brooks Bus Line would eventually become collateral damage in the decline of the midwestern industrial economy, but the company did a healthy business well into the 1970s, when the Paducah Express continued to offer daily service to Detroit for less than half the price of a plane ticket, on buses as "neat as a Kentucky grandmother's living room."[19]

Of course, all northbound migrants from Paducah and the surrounding countryside did not travel to Detroit on Brooks's buses. But in an era when so many western Kentuckians were setting out on transformative journeys to the automobile manufacturing capital—by one estimate, as much as one-fifth of the population of Calloway County, Paducah's neighbor to the south, was resident in Detroit during the middle decades of the century—the bus company did assume a kind of icon status across the region. Repeat customers were commonplace; in fact, riders' loyalty to the Brooks brand was so strong that when Brooks had to appeal to the Interstate Commerce Commission to extend the company's interstate service license, court filings recorded "witness after witness [who] testified that they had ridden with him, that his services represented a convenience to them and that they would be inconvenienced if he was denied a certificate of convenience and necessity."[20]

Polk Brooks himself, meanwhile, became a notable local success story, earning renown in the regional busing industry, sitting on the boards of a number of Paducah's leading firms, and even serving as the inaugural president of the Paducah Baseball Association, a briefly lived low-minor league affiliate created in the years after World War II. As a measure of their appreciation—and in what was surely the highest honor ever paid to a man who had started off as one of the migration's myriad taxi drivers—the residents of Paducah even voted to name the city's minor league ballpark J. Polk Brooks Stadium. The stadium, in turn, would outlast the bus line: a monument, long after the heyday of the hillbilly highway had passed, to the central role that the roads themselves had played in stitching together the new landscape of Transappalachia.[21]

### "The Folks Who Ride My Line"

Like many self-made men, Polk Brooks preferred to think that his good fortune amounted to something more than just good luck. "Find a need and fill it" was an entrepreneurial adage he was known to recite from time to time—and to Brooks's credit, he had been right to bet that enduring demand for interregional transportation would outlast the short-term interruption caused by the Great Depression. In another breath, though, Brooks might attribute his success to what he saw as a special kind of familiarity that he enjoyed with his riders; an intimacy that made him uniquely well positioned to attract their business. "The folks who ride my line aren't like the passengers most bus lines have," he once explained to an inquiring reporter, years after that first bet had long since paid off. Overwhelmingly composed of working people—they were all going "to the Detroit section to find jobs in the motor plants"—the profile of the typical passenger meant that Brooks would occasionally find himself out of luck on a fare. "I didn't have the heart to turn them down because they were broke. Sometimes I didn't get paid at all; other times it took years, and then part of the payment was in barter." But as Brooks saw it, the reciprocal sense of obligation instilled in his grateful riders was well worth the small sacrifice on his part. "As a result of all that, there was a more personal relationship between me and my passengers than exists between other bus lines and the people they serve."[22]

A hand-drawn map on the front of the Forbus General Store in Pall Mall, Tennessee, a dozen miles north of Jamestown on US Highway 127, offers Fentress County natives an everyday reminder of precisely how long the trip is to Muncie, Indiana, as well as other familiar destinations on the other end of the hillbilly highway.

Photograph courtesy of the author.

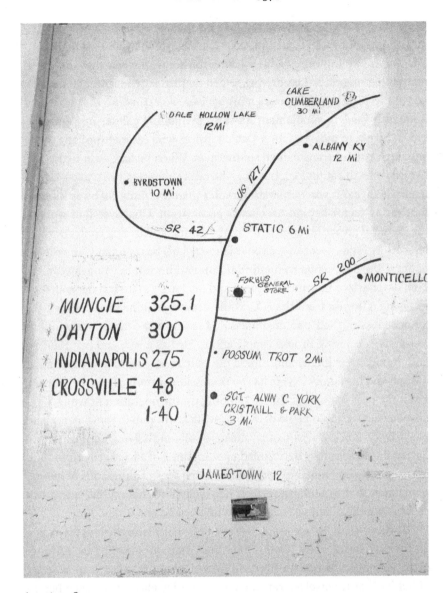

(*continued*)

There was a healthy dose of paternalistic self-regard in this way of seeing things, to be sure. But it was also true that Brooks knew more than
most about the "folks" who were his passengers. Brooks had his own firsthand experience with the economic insecurity that characterized life for
the rural poor of western Kentucky, having grown up on a farm in the
community of Reidland, about five miles southeast of Paducah. He moved
to Detroit before finishing high school and tried his own hand at factory

work—first at Briggs, which made chassis for many of the major car companies, then at Chevrolet Gear and Axle—but recurrent layoffs eventually sent
him and his young wife, Sadie, packing for home, the way they did for so
many other migrants. Taxi-driving helped them make ends meet for a while;
but in the early years, Brooks's margins were so razor-thin that he would
frequently have to supplement his fares by hauling gallons of Kentucky-
grown sorghum molasses for a Detroit grocer who catered specially to the
culinary tastes of transplanted southerners. When he first went to the ICC
to receive certification for a bus line, the brief submitted by Brooks's lawyer
made clear that it was desperation rather than ingenuity that was the true
motivating factor behind his client's application. Unable to find work in
the Paducah area after a job at a "local cleaning and dyeing concern which
lasted only for a short time," Brooks launched his bus company "in order to
fight off the depression as it affected him and his family." Repeatedly, the
brief emphasized how much Brooks and his family's survival depended on
receiving a license from the ICC, while drawing distinctions between the
tenuousness of their circumstances and those of the larger national bus
companies opposing Brooks's application. "He has a wife and two children
and the business he has built up is the only means he has of supporting
himself and his family. . . . He has no profession or trade of any sort, having
given the best years of his life to building up the operation in which he is
now engaged. Should he be denied a certificate of public convenience and
necessity he would have no other means of making a living for himself and
his family." Brooks may have ended up something of a local celebrity, but in
his origins he had much in common with the tens of thousands of anony-
mous men and women in western Kentucky for whom a bus ride north
could mean the difference between getting by and not.[23]

Working-class backgrounds were not all that distinguished the riders
on Brooks's buses, meanwhile. Other bus companies catered to working-
class passengers; what set Brooks's passengers apart were a specific set
of habits that themselves reflected a distinctive class experience beginning to take shape along the interregional roadways networking the Upper
South and the Midwest. For instance, Brooks was offering more than just a
casual observation when he noted that, with many of the riders on his line,
"I've hauled them, their children, and by now some of their grandchildren." Multigenerational pathways of this sort were at the crux of virtually
all the chain migrations that guided traffic along the hillbilly highway—
not only between Paducah and Detroit, or Jamestown and Muncie, but
throughout the broader expanse of Transappalachia. Having relatives or
even friends at the other end of the highway inevitably made everything

from finding work to having a place to stay easier to manage upon arrival. And so, as one characteristic study of movement between Magoffin County, in eastern Kentucky, and Cincinnati determined, nearly four out of every five migrants chose where to move because a family member or at least a friend was currently living there or had done so previously. Two out of every three had already had occasion to visit someone in Cincinnati before relocating. And at least one-third of the migrants surveyed lived with a relative or a friend for a period of time when they first arrived in the city. It was to be expected, then, that as successive waves of western Kentucky migrants made the trip north on US 45 to Detroit, many of them rode in the very same bus seats that had once transported older members of their own families.[24]

Family ties—or more to the point, the household economy—shaped the traffic on Brooks's buses and elsewhere along the hillbilly highway in other ways as well. For at least half a century, residents of southern Appalachia had been growing accustomed to moving back and forth between the countryside and various centers of industrial activity within region. For those who managed to retain some access to workable farmland but who struggled nonetheless due to diminishing farm incomes, the improved roadways connecting the Upper South and the urban Midwest made possible similar kinds of movements, only now across an even greater spatial expanse. Charlie Wood was a perfect example of this tendency. Charlie was powerfully attached to his life as a farmer, and so even as conditions confronting farmers in Fentress County began to worsen, his trips to Muncie remained a way to subsidize—rather than to replace—the family's traditional livelihood. Charlie was able to set aside enough money to purchase all the supplies he needed for the 1944 crop year, for example, over the course of a six-week sojourn to Muncie earlier that spring. He left Tennessee with a carful of friends one Friday in April, arrived in Muncie the following afternoon, and by Monday had hired on at Delco-Remy, a General Motors division that specialized in car batteries but was then repurposed for defense production like many of Muncie's factories. Putting in six eight-hour shifts a week—"I like my job very well," he noted in his diary after his first day at work; "Its easie anough"—Charlie made a few hundred dollars before quitting at the end of May. Two days after he got home, he went into Jamestown to buy four hundred pounds of fertilizer, and then the whole family spent the remainder of the week in a whirlwind of digging and hoeing and seeding and planting.[25]

Although it is difficult to calculate with any precision how many "shuttle migrants" of this sort traveled the highways of Transappalachia during the middle decades of the twentieth century, anecdotal indications would suggest that their numbers were substantial. They presented such a persistent issue for one manager at a rubber products company in Indiana that he would always inquire of southern-born job applicants whether they were traveling alone or with their families. "If he comes up here alone it's a good bet he won't stay six months," the manager explained; in his experience, solo travelers like Charlie Wood were planning to leave as soon as "the weather gets nice." An article about Brooks Bus Line noted that, especially in the early days, Brooks's passengers were also "mainly farmers"—cyclical travelers who "would plant crops in the spring, work in the expanding Michigan automobile plants in the summer, return for the fall harvest and back to the Michigan jobs in the winter." Nor was it only single men who shuttled back and forth according to the rhythms of the agricultural calendar. Similar patterns were noted even among migrant families traveling with children. As one Chicago commission convened in the late 1950s observed, enrollment in city schools with significant populations of southern-born white children fluctuated dramatically between November and December, after the fall harvest, when attendance was at its highest, and April and May, when attendance dropped to a low point as migrant families returned to the South to plant the next year's crop. "They'd come in when school started in Kentucky, which wasn't until mid-October," remarked a veteran of the Indianapolis school system, who identified an identical ebb and flow during her many years in the classroom, "and leave early before Memorial Day when school was out in Kentucky."[26]

At least as common as the short-term trips many migrants made were the frequency with which those who succeeded in finding employment in the North sent a portion of their earnings back to family members who had remained behind. According to one more extensive sampling of Transappalachian migrants, as many as two-thirds sent at least some money south during their time away from their families. Charlie Wood was again a case in point: he would try to set aside as much as half of every paycheck he received in Muncie for these purposes. And it was not only husbands and wives who did so. The same survey found that sons and daughters who migrated north were just as likely to send money home to support parents and siblings who chose not to relocate, as were members of conjugal households. The total significance of such influxes to any given household budget could range widely—but invariably, as one southeastern Kentucky farmer who spent time working in Ohio noted, they elevated the basic standard of living for cash-poor rural families. "[They] bought more food, clothing," he remarked when asked how his family fared during his time away. "I think they lived better than if I'd been here." And indeed, the meticulous regularity with which Charlie sent remittances home hints at something of the full scale of their importance to his wife, Delta, and their children. If payday was Friday, by no later than Saturday Charlie had made a trip to the post office in downtown Muncie to mail a letter and an envelope full of cash back to Pall Mall.[27]

Households that relocated more permanently depended on the movement of still other types of traffic along the roadways connecting south and north. For southern Appalachian migrants who suddenly found themselves far from traditional networks of family and communal support, the maintenance of the home itself often demanded the supplementary labors of additional members of the extended family. Libby Anderson, for instance, was still in high school when she first left Jamestown and moved in with an older sister and her husband in Selma, Indiana, just outside of Muncie. At the time, Libby's brother-in-law was working the night shift at a local meat-packer and sleeping during the day; Libby's sister, meanwhile, was trying to complete school herself. And the two had just had a baby. So Libby caught a ride north on US 127 with Willard Voiles and moved to Selma for a year, where she took care of her niece and lent a hand with the cooking and cleaning, while going to class at Muncie's Central High School. Frances Hurd, another Fentress County native, initially relocated to Muncie to help her aunt and uncle open a fourteen-room boardinghouse on the city's heavily industrial southside, which catered largely to the single men, like Charlie Wood, who came in from Tennessee to work in the factories. Frances helped her aunt paint, wallpaper, furnish the efficiency-style apartments, and manage the boardinghouse. She even lived in one of the apartments for a few years with her husband—until the birth of their first child necessitated moving into a larger place.[28]

Given the economic reliance of migrant households on the often-unwaged labor of female family members, it was not surprising that girls like Frances and Libby, or married women traveling with husbands, were the most likely groups of female migrants along the hillbilly highway. In Magoffin County again, just eight of ninety-eight female heads of household identified in one survey left Kentucky in search of work during World War II; nearly two-thirds of the women who did move, on the other hand, did so with families. Among men, by comparison, the number traveling with families amounted to just 30 percent. The most commonly reported occupation among female migrants from Magoffin County in these years was "housewife." This was a pattern that likely held across the region, as southern-born white women generally showed lower rates of formal labor-force participation in the North throughout the peak decades of southern out-migration, especially when compared to southern-born Black women—a reflection of both the even more acute poverty often confronting Black southerners, as well as the persistence of racially discriminatory hiring practices and segregated workplaces in many of the male-dominated northern industries. But informal labor-force participation was another story. As had been the case in the coal camps and company towns of the Upper South, it was relatively common for southern Appalachian women in the Midwest to take in laundry or share childcare arrangements with friends and relatives in the local community. One study of southern Appalachian migrants to Chicago noted that southern white women often functioned as building managers in buildings occupied by other southern migrants—effectively exchanging the performance of house-maintenance duties in the homes of other families, for preferential access or discounted rent for their own.[29] In whatever fashion, whether as temporary caregivers, full-time homemakers, or in any number of more complex arrangements, the interregional transportation of gendered domestic labor was a common form of traffic along the hillbilly highway.[30]

Even in those instances when women and girls did not travel north with husbands and fathers, their labor might be put to use generating additional income for households that now stretched across an expansive new geography. Delta Wood produced a steady supply of quilts, bonnets, and aprons, which her son Howard—who relocated permanently to Muncie as soon as he came of age—would load up in his trunk after visits to Tennessee and drive back north, where he would sell them to other displaced southerners he knew through work at Chevrolet-Muncie. Other handmade reminders of home, from southern foodstuffs—like the local black walnuts that Delta would collect, crack, and send north to "sell in the factories"—to traditional home-remedies, were also regularly transported to reliable markets on the other end of the hillbilly highway. Polk Brooks even found ways to capitalize on this kind of activity: by the end of the 1940s, he was charging rates to carry not only family members but also what one might call the material culture of family—express mail, newspapers from home, even flowers—across state lines.[31]

Perhaps none of the familiar artifacts that traveled along the hillbilly highway during these decades was more significant—at least by volume—than illicitly distilled moonshine. Typically the province of men rather than women, unauthorized backyard stills were commonplace throughout the Upper South in the middle decades of the twentieth century—and likewise could be put to new use feeding a demand that grew alongside the emerging contours of Transappalachia. In the woodlands along Fentress County's eastern border with neighboring Scott County, one later investigation found evidence of more than a hundred seventy-five distillery sites across an expanse of a hundred twenty-five thousand acres. Peak years of activity, it was noted, were from 1930 to 1960, during which time local moonshiners "sold their products far and wide," often transporting them to larger cities in "gallon jars, false gasoline tanks and any number of available yet inconspicuous and ingenious large volume containers." When the money he put together from his regular shifts at the foundry and the weekly taxi rides was not enough, Willard Voiles would make a little extra by hauling some of those large containers on his rides north to Muncie, where moonshine whiskey was easy to find at the gates of many of the factories in town that employed significant numbers of Tennessee transplants. Whether or not Polk Brooks made similar accommodations on his early runs between Paducah and Detroit is unclear—but it is certain that carloads of homemade liquor fermented from the sassafras bushes that grew in the wet, loamy western Kentucky soil regularly made the trip north alongside Brooks buses on US 45. In fact, interstate bootlegging became such a scourge along the most regularly frequented roadways of the Transappalachian migration that some drivers came to believe northern police officers and state troopers had developed a habit of singling out cars with southern license plates to stop for "random" searches.[32]

As the decades of the migration wore on, even dead bodies became an important form of traffic along the highways traversing the region. Inevitably, some of the Paducah-area natives who made the trip north on Brooks buses made their final return in the back of a hearse, where local mortuaries did a steady business interring the remains of southern migrants who elected to be buried closer to their place of birth. When Virginia Rust, for instance, passed away in Pontiac, Michigan, in 1976, Roth Funeral Home coordinated the transportation of her body back to the area so that Virginia could be buried in the family plot at Paducah's Maplelawn Cemetery. Likewise, when Robert Hampton passed away in Illinois, where he worked for Del Monte Canning, Roth billed his family for the expenses associated with having a local funeral director prepare Robert's body ($70), plus transportation back to Kentucky ($115), where he was buried in the cemetery of the Spring Bayou Baptist Church in nearby Kevil. Similar arrangements were made over the years for Otis Burroughs of Cincinnati; James Bridges of Cleveland; Mildred Smith of Greenwood, Indiana, just south of Indianapolis; and many others besides.[33] Nor was Roth Funeral Home unique in this regard. Over the course of a fifteen-year period beginning in the late 1960s, roughly one out of every twelve burials arranged by Jennings Funeral Home in Jamestown, Tennessee, was for someone who was living in the Midwest at the time of their death. Predictably, given the direction of the migratory circuits that networked that part of the region, more than half had been in Indiana. The vast majority of them had lived in or around Muncie.[34]

Displaced natives of the Upper Cumberland Plateau or far-western Kentucky or any other corner of the Upper South had their bodies shipped "home" for any number of reasons. Burial costs tended to be lower south of the Ohio River—by as much as 60 percent, according to some measures—enough, certainly, to factor into the considerations of more than a few working-class households. Just as important, though, was the symbolic significance accorded to burial practices in many southern religious traditions and folk cultures. This was notably true in rural southern Appalachia, where yearly "Decoration Days" devoted to cemetery maintenance and beautification had long functioned as "a major season of the year," in the words of one expert in the field: a time for family gatherings, communal celebrations, and the collective memorialization of intertwined local histories. For some migrants, then, the decision to be buried in family plots was more than simply a sentimental one, especially in the face of the various and throughgoing upheavals that had accompanied the emergence of the hillbilly highway and swept aside generations-long connections to particular parcels of land. It reflected a desire to remain attached to these older, place-based customs—and through them, to a time when the places themselves, and the families and communities that lived there, were still comparatively intact.[35]

## A Transregional Working Class

More than anything else, it was these kinds of attachments that Polk Brooks had in mind when he spoke of the passengers on his buses as a particular kind of "folks." Brooks knew the importance of Decoration Day celebrations well: around Memorial Day (a loose relative of the southern tradition, and the closest analog on the vacation calendars of many northern factories), he would often double- or even triple-up the end-of-week southbound runs to accommodate the rush of visitors, and then do the same after the weekend for the return legs to Detroit.[36] He did something similar around the other major holidays of the year, when family gatherings were sure to draw comparable swells of transplanted southerners back to the region. "I took them to Michigan originally to

Brooks now operates modern buses. This one is stopping at Mayfield. Brooks operates feeder lines out of Paducah to round up his passengers to make the long trip to Detroit.

♦ THE COURIER-JOURNAL MAGAZINE

J. Polk Brooks began his career as one of the innumerable "taxi-drivers" who serviced the Transappalachian migration by shuttling southerners to and from midwestern destinations. At its peak, Brooks Bus Lines was providing daily round-trip service between western Kentucky and southeastern Michigan to an average of seventeen thousand riders a year. Here, passengers board a Detroit-bound bus in Mayfield, Kentucky.
© Thomas V. Miller Jr.—USA TODAY NETWORK

find jobs," Brooks attested about his most reliable customers, "and I've hauled them back to make visits to Kentucky two or three times a year ever since."[37]

Regular return trips of this sort were not only limited to the holidays. In fact, they were one of the defining features of the Transappalachian migration. Like the phenomenon of southern burials, they represented a kind of reverse-traffic that revealed as much about the people whose lives were transformed along the hillbilly highway as the journeys that brought them north in the first place. Joyce Crouch's mother, Cassie Greer, would come back to Jamestown as often as she could during the years she was living and working in Detroit and then Cincinnati, while Joyce and her brother and sister were "farmed out to different relatives" in the area. Cassie would try to come for a week at a time on those visits, as Joyce recalls, because the twelve or fifteen hours the trip typically took by bus or train during the 1930s made shorter visits impractical. Ray Owens, who also grew up in Jamestown before moving to Dayton after World War II, would return frequently to Fentress County in the early years. "When my mother and dad was living I would come home quite often and see them, see their needs and all. Every three or four months I'd come home." For James Shelby, who hailed from across the state in Hardin County, Tennessee, the regular trips back south from Mishawaka, Indiana, were less about upholding family responsibilities and more about blowing off steam. "I went home pretty often from there," he explained to the historian Chad Berry. "You know, we was single, maybe four or five of us guys would get in a car and drive there over a weekend, because back then we'd swap up driving. We didn't get much sleep, but we was young."[38]

Visits were significant occasions for the southern migrants who moved away, as well as for the rural communities they left behind. Nowhere was this made clearer than in the "society" pages of local newspapers, which gave regular notices of the comings and goings of Transappalachian migrants and their families. A typical issue of the *Upper Cumberland Times*, published out of Jamestown, was full of items like the following, all of which appeared on just a single page of one July 1955 edition of the paper: "Here from Detroit for the weekend were Milton Frogge, George Ellis Delk, and the Hull Brothers." "Miss Joyce Hinds of Muncie, Ind., girlfriend of Richard Conatser, who is now stationed in Korea, visited with his parents, Mr. and Mrs. Roy Conatser." "Mrs. Ray Williams and children of Middletown, Ohio are spending their vacation here with relatives." And these did not even begin to cover all of that week's announcements about out-of-town visitors. Sometimes, these write-ups revealed the more somber occasions that might bring a migrant home for a visit, as when the *Campbell County Times*'s weekly "Jellico Social Scene" column reported that "Mr. and Mrs. Ray Hicks of Dayton, Ohio, and Mrs. Earl Baker were in Middlesboro on Monday due to the illness of Mr. Hicks' mother, Mrs. Mary Solomon, who is a patient in the Appalachian Regional Hospital." In other moments, they offered glimpses into the distended familial arrangements that came to proliferate across the region, as when the *Morgan County News* reported that "Mr. Leon McPeters, Sr., and son Leon, of Cincinnati, Ohio spent the past week with their families in Wartburg." One type of event that was sure to attract visitors—and to receive write-ups in local papers—were annual family reunions. At the 1975 Huddleston family reunion, held near Static, Tennessee, attendees "came from Ohio, Michigan, Indiana, Kentucky, and Tennessee," according to the *Pickett County*

*Press*. Not surprisingly, the *Press*, whose readership was also concentrated along the footprint of US 127, reported more family members present from Indiana—thirty-one—than from any state other than Tennessee.[39]

In some cases, return trips were dictated by forces outside of the migrants' control, such as changing labor market conditions in the North. This was true from the very earliest period of the migration, in the years during and immediately after World War I, when job seekers from the rural South and especially southern Appalachia first earned special reputations as "floaters" or "drifters" in a number of midwestern cities. Depictions of southern Appalachian migrants as improvident treasure seekers—transient types "imbued with the idea of getting rich quick and getting easy money" before moving on, as one Akron industrialist put it in the early 1920s—certainly fit the needs of employers, who enjoyed being able to hire migrants during periods of peak demand and then let them go just as quickly when business slowed down again. But the reality was that many recent arrivals to northern cities did beat a hasty retreat back south when economic conditions soured. This was particularly the case during the worst years of the Great Depression, when migrant flows reversed themselves dramatically across the region. As the economic collapse precipitated a nationwide "back-to-the-farm" movement, a place like Flint, Michigan—where at least one in ten white residents hailed from the South at the onset of the 1930s—saw its population of southern-born whites decline by roughly 35 percent in a matter of just a few years. And the same was true during less catastrophic downturns as well. At the height of the 1958 "Eisenhower Recession," for instance, the Kentucky Department of Economic Security found that more than twenty thousand Kentucky residents had recently returned to the state to file unemployment claims against out-of-state employers. Not uncommon among Brooks Bus Line passengers were people like Wayne Shelton, who, at twenty-six, was already wrapping up his sixth stint in Michigan when a reporter from *Newsweek* caught up with him on a Paducah-bound bus during the doldrums of the mid-1970s—"each time going home when the work ran out."[40]

In moments like these, cycling back and forth between city and country was in essence an extension of one of the key adaptive strategies that rural Appalachian households had developed during their earliest forays into industrial employment. But at other times, Transappalachian migrants opted to reverse course for reasons that were not first and foremost economically determined. For a significant number of travelers along the hillbilly highway, migration was always only a temporary arrangement: an opportunity to sock away some years of high wages before returning to the communities in which they had been raised. "I always wanted to come back south" was how Forrest David "Hamp" Nunley thought about it. Hamp grew up on a small farm in Pelham, Tennessee, near the base of the Cumberland Plateau and not far from the Alabama border. At the age of eighteen, he moved to Cleveland, where he spent the better part of a decade moving through a series of factory jobs—first making stove parts, then artillery shells, then car bumpers, and finally at a paper mill. But as soon as he had finished paying off the mortgage on a piece of land he had bought in Pelham, he moved back home: "I didn't want to owe nothing when I came back to the country." For Franklin Hargis and his wife, Opal, both of whom had grown up around the coal mines of Davidson and Wilder in southwestern Fentress County, the decision had more to do with how they wanted to raise their children. "Me and my wife, we discussed about when they get school-age, we decided we wanted our children to go to school down in Tennessee," Franklin explained. So after a six-year stretch in the Chicago area during the 1950s, as their oldest was getting ready for elementary school, they returned to Fentress County. Others turned around simply because they never managed to feel at home in their new surroundings. For Cassie Greer, "the tie was always to the farm," as her daughter Joyce put it—and so after a few years navigating between her children in Jamestown and her life in the North, she finally threw in the towel and moved back home for good. Lloyd Crouch, one of Charlie Wood's closest friends and a traveling partner on one of his trips up to Muncie in 1943, did not even make it that long. "Loyd went back to Tenn.," Charlie noted in his diary, just two weeks after they had arrived. "Sed the climent diden suit his close."[41]

Whatever circumstances guided these and other individual decisions to reverse course, the overall frequency of return migration proved to be one of the more persistent features of life along the hillbilly highway—if also one of the most difficult to measure accurately. According to the best estimates that scholars have been able to generate, every five years somewhere between 6 and 12 percent of all white Americans who had previously migrated out of the South elected to return. Very roughly speaking, this would have amounted to anywhere between four and eight million people over the entire period of the Transappalachian migration. In some decades, rates of return may have been as high as 20 or even 25 percent; at times, for every four white migrants leaving the South, there were three who were simultaneously returning to the region. Furthermore, by the same scholars' admissions, these figures represent only "crude" and "very conservative" measures, "severe undercounts" resulting from the "incomplete or even biased" data produced by census questions that demographers and historians have had to rely upon when trying to quantify the larger tendency.[42] In all likelihood, a full accounting that managed to more accurately capture shorter-interval migrations would produce still larger numbers than those indicated by the higher-end estimates.

Even the very concept of return migration—implying as it does a single round-trip journey, whether made over the course of a discrete period of years or a lifetime—fails to convey the dizzying complexity of the circuits that migrants navigated across the landscape of Transappalachia. Charlie Wood's seasonal shuttles up US 127; Wayne Shelton's back-and-forth bus rides set to the rhythms of the business cycle; Libby Anderson's trips to Indiana in the back of Willard Voiles's station wagon to look after her niece; Cassie Greer's years spent suspended between Michigan, Ohio, and Tennessee: none of them, quite possibly, would have ended up in the census tabulations of the overall migration. And yet for millions of southern Appalachian households, these innumerable temporary sojourns were as much a reflection of the epoch-making transformations of the first half of the twentieth century as the more easily counted permanent relocations. While a final measurement of the Transappalachian migration that manages to take all of these back-and-forth trips into account as well may never be possible, the near-constant circular traffic they represented was, as the historian James Gregory has written, in many ways the "key dynamic of the [southern] white diaspora."[43]

It was also, as Gregory and others have noted, a dynamic that largely distinguished the migratory experiences of white and Black southerners during this period. Of course, Black migrants also found opportunities to return to southern places of origin throughout the decades of the Great Migration, most commonly on holidays, for social visits, or during family emergencies. For those who were able, a visit to former homes was a "moment of glory" that some "prepared all year for," as the daughter of one Mississippi-born transplant put it; and numerous scholars have highlighted the essential roles that such return visits played in maintaining familial bonds, relaying information about employment opportunities, and preserving traditions within Black households and communities.[44] But far less common were the kinds of reversals that so regularly appeared along the hillbilly highway, whether of the cyclical or permanent variety. Shuttle migrations of the sort practiced by farmers like Charlie Wood were a negligible occurrence among Black migrants—in no small measure because rates of land ownership remained so much lower for Black southerners as compared to those in even the poorest pockets of

rural southern Appalachia.[45] In moments of acute economic stress, like
the Great Depression, Black southerners also retreated from centers of
northern industry—but, taking Flint, Michigan, as an example again, at
something like half the rate of white southerners.[46] Nor did Black southerners as often make the shorter-duration relocations that white migrants
like Hamp Nunley or Franklin Hargis did, taking advantage of boom years
in northern labor markets to build up cash reserves that could be brought
back south and invested in a piece of land or to secure a more comfortable living.[47] Black southerners who left the region were far likelier not to
return, at least not before the so-called Great Return Migration got underway in the 1970s and 1980s. According to one estimate, for every Black
migrant who had returned to the South by 1970, there were thirty-three
who continued to live in the North. For white southerners, the comparable
number was seven.[48]

A combination of factors endemic to southern society during these
years accounted for the discrepancy between rates of return exhibited by
Black and white migrants. By the 1930s if not sooner, the reorganization
of southern agriculture generally, the intensive mechanization of cotton
farming in particular, and the compounding effects of "a half-century of
southern industrialization on a segregated basis" all ensured that the economic disadvantage confronting large swaths of the southern Black Belt
had no true equivalent in southern Appalachia or anywhere else across the
broader South. As late as 1965, the poverty rate among African Americans
in the rural South would remain an astounding 78 percent—as compared
to 55 percent for rural farm dwellers in Appalachia, and 39 percent among
rural whites in the region overall.[49] Needless to say, the indignities of life
under Jim Crow acted as an equally strong disincentive to returning, even
as Black migrants encountered new forms of racial discrimination, segregation, and injustice in northern and western cities. Still, most determinative of all may have been the pervasiveness of white mob violence
and other forms of racial terrorism, an inescapable reality confronted
only by Black southerners and one that remained an omnipresent threat
throughout the decades of the Great Migration. "Every time a lynching
takes place in a community down south," Thomas Arnold Hill of the Chicago Urban League observed as early as 1919, "you can depend on it that
colored people will arrive in Chicago within two weeks." Such experiences,
in turn, fueled a kind of collective common sense in the new communities that formed at the other end of the southern diaspora, one that even
children who had never known the South could hardly forget. Carl Stokes,
who grew up in Cleveland in the 1940s before becoming the city's first

Black mayor in 1968, later recalled his Georgia-born mother making sure he understood from an early age that "in the South the white man could kill any black person he wanted to."[50] And whether they were of Stokes's generation or his mother's, few Black Americans mistook the very specific circumstances surrounding the single most notorious act of racial violence in the twentieth century: the 1955 killing of Emmett Till, the fourteen-year old Chicago native who was brutally lynched while visiting relatives in Mississippi and who quickly became "perhaps the most memorialized black northerner ever to go south." Given everything, it was little wonder that relatively few Black migrants "even contemplated a return to the South," as the African American poet-intellectual Arna Bontemps, himself the Louisiana-born son of southern migrants, once put it.[51]

Even in their shared experiences of dispossession and displacement, then, poor southern whites enjoyed tangible advantages that Black southerners did not. If Appalachian migrants came to navigate the vicissitudes of life in the urban-industrial Midwest in part by retaining relatively unimpeded access to southern "havens of refuge," as the rural sociologist James S. Brown once put it—homeplaces where they could "stay for a while, lick their wounds, and then perhaps return to the urban fray"—doing so also signified a kind of informal economic security that Black southerners could not so easily avail themselves of during difficult times. And if a result of this arrangement was that white natives of the Upper South were more able to accommodate what Chad Berry has described as their "emotional ambivalence about leaving"—not only by way of the traditions they held on to, or the reconstructed communities that former southerners sought out in northern cities, but also through ongoing and regularly revitalized attachments to southern places of origin—their "divided hearts" were also a luxury that fewer African American migrants could as readily afford. To be sure, not every southern Appalachian migrant felt so ambivalent about their new surroundings; most, after all, stayed where they ended up. But the unusually high rates of return that characterized the Transappalachian migration—not to mention all the other circular traffic that tied together communities on either end of the hillbilly highway—was a reminder that even the ability to go home again could hinge on its own form of racial privilege.[52]

At the same time, there was a critical irony here. As migrants from the Upper South moved in growing numbers into midwestern jobs and communities, the very same interregional attachments that marked their preferential racial standing in the South would become cause for suspicion, resentment, and even contempt in the North. What developed first as a strategy of survival, deployed by a displaced regional working class to maintain a modicum of continuity in the face of economic forces beyond their control, became in the eyes of their northern coworkers and neighbors a mark of the same population's rural backwardness, hidebound traditionalism, and almost pathological failure to adapt to "modern" ways of life—ultimately, even, to its unreliable or inadequate *whiteness*. As a result, southern Appalachian migrants and their families often found themselves suspended not only between old and new homes but also between degrees of belonging and not-belonging—privilege and its opposite—in ways that persistently cut across the more conventional lines of race and class that shaped the contours of midcentury American society. As members of a distinctively transregional working class, travelers along the hillbilly highway were both like and unlike the wider working-class communities in which they came to move within the industrial Midwest. And the tensions that this discordance would arouse would shape the emerging social and political landscape of Transappalachia for decades to come.

# CHAPTER THREE

# Green Peas and Hotheads

## THE PARADOX OF THE HILLBILLY HIGHWAY

*"In 1922 we were so rushed with orders we couldn't possibly fill them or get enough men here in town to carry on, so we had to import some men from Kentucky and West Virginia. . . . We brought two train loads of them down. Some of them learned quickly, and some of them didn't. Most of them have drifted back by now."*[1]

—AN UNNAMED MANUFACTURER IN MUNCIE, INDIANA

*"You and I know who these strike agitators are. They are these uneducated tobacco chewing geetar playing hillbilly illiterates from West Virginia, Kentucky, and Tennessee."*[2]

—"UNION HATER," LETTER TO THE *AKRON BEACON JOURNAL* (1938)

IN JUNE 1937 A WRITER named Claude Trimble Martin, who went by Deac and who was soon to become known—to the extent that such a thing is known—as the "first international historian" of the Society for the International Preservation and Encouragement of Barber Shop Quartet Singing in America, arrived in Akron, Ohio. He had come to Akron on assignment not for the SPEBSQSA, but for the *Nation's Business,* the official publication of the United States Chamber of Commerce and at the time one of the most widely circulated business periodicals in the country. And he was there because by the summer of 1937, Akron—itself better known in these years as the Rubber Capital of the World—had been in a state of almost uninterrupted industrial warfare for nearly eighteen months, ever since a sit-down strike that began in February 1936 had shuttered Goodyear Tire and Rubber's massive flagship plant before spreading throughout the rest of the city.

As he laid it out for his readers, there were a number of things that struck Martin about the labor unrest in Akron that summer. "In Akron," he observed, "we find the highest wage levels of any city in 1936 rubbing elbows with the greatest number of strikes in the same period." Likewise flying in the face of conventional wisdom, which generally attributed blame for workplace conflict of this sort to immigrant radicals and various foreign ideologies, Martin noted that "almost every informant capable of analytical comment brings out the fact Akron men are largely native born." Most incomprehensible of all was the substantial representation of migrants from the farms and mining towns of southern Appalachia among the city's rubber workers. "It is said that personnel records would reveal a majority of workmen as of Anglo-Saxon descent, hailing from southern hill and mountain districts," Martin wrote. "We might assume that this racial stock, weaned on Bible teachings, would have an unusually high regard for property rights. The sit-down record reads differently."[3]

Martin and his editors at *Nation's Business* referred to this unexpected turn of events as "the paradox of Akron," but it might better have been thought of as the paradox of the hillbilly highway. First confronted by a set of emergent challenges in the years during and after World War I, it was during these interwar decades that industrial employers across the Midwest began to pursue a workforce recruitment strategy that self-consciously targeted rural white southerners.[4] They did so for reasons that were at once pragmatic and ideological: out of a need, on the one hand, for increased flexibility in tightening labor markets; and, on the other hand, out of a belief that the recently displaced rural population of the Upper South represented a particularly docile—and therefore exploitable—labor pool. Poor, provincial, and not incidentally "of Anglo-Saxon descent," as Martin had put it, southern Appalachian migrants seemed to combine an ideal set of attributes in the eyes of many employers when they first began arriving in midwestern cities. "These people," as one executive in Flint, Michigan, explained, "could do the unskilled jobs all right and were glad to get whatever wages were given them." "Those people aren't like us," echoed an employer in Muncie when queried about that city's growing population of working-class migrants; "they *love* that kind of job!" In Detroit, reports confirmed that hiring managers deemed such newcomers "much safer" than other elements in that city's substantially foreign-born workforce, in large part because they had not yet been "poisoned by ideas of unionism." In fact, demand for southern "hillbillies" was so high among

Detroit's automakers by the mid-1930s, one journalist claimed, that he had even met a local man who had "practiced up on the Southern drawl and dialect, then presented himself at the factory gates, and was hired as soon as he opened his mouth."[5]

Significantly, it was not only interwar capitalists who were responsible for producing this image of the conveniently exploitable southern hillbilly, which Deac Martin and others accepted almost as a matter of faith. Union leaders, left-wing radicals, and liberal activists of various stripes were equally likely to express skepticism of and even outright hostility toward poor white southerners as they began showing up in northern factories in significant numbers. Often, they did so in terms that echoed, rather ironically, the tendentious ideas about race, region, and rurality that had led employers to seek out those workers in the first place. In the eyes of these critics, economically marginal southern whites composed a classic *lumpenproletariat*: a particularly demoralized and deferential class in American society, whose complicity with employers was predestined by their supposedly all-consuming race hatreds, their faith-riddled backwardness, their transient nonattachment to the midwestern communities in which they sought work—or some combination of all three. "They are the type newly come from the country," went one such missive from the period; "Southern hillbillies who have no experience in industry nor in labor organization, who are not class conscious and who have themselves traditions that fit in with the [Black] Legion"—the last a reference to the quasi-fascist white supremacist group that terrorized midwestern cities during the 1930s. Their recruitment by northern industrialists was "definitely a policy to split the ranks of labor."[6]

The great industrial upheaval of the latter half of the 1930s, in which southern white migrants often ended up playing critical roles, would reveal a fundamental flaw in this kind of thinking. In Flint, Detroit, and Muncie, as in dozens of other midwestern locations, southern Appalachian migrants time and again confounded the expectations of their employers. They walked away from poorly paid jobs, confronted abusive bosses, and went out on strike with their coworkers. Rather than split the ranks of labor, many of them joined the founding cadre of the newly formed Congress of Industrial Organizations, which emerged from the same midwestern landscape during these years and left an enduring imprint on American society and politics for decades to come. In Akron, they even became the driving force behind a nearly two-year-long shop-floor insurrection against the largest rubber company in the world—one that would get their actions likened to "labor terrorism" in the local press, send their own union leadership scrambling to restore order at the workplace, and, finally, leave one barbershop quartet enthusiast scratching his head in confusion.[7]

If the interwar decades began with rural white southerners being seen as capital's solution to the labor problems of the period, by their end these same workers had become a labor problem in their own right. And yet, there would be one final irony to the paradox of the hillbilly highway. Despite their very real track record of workplace militancy during this period, the stereotypes that first attached themselves to southern Appalachian migrants as they began entering northern labor markets en masse in the years around World War I would prove remarkably persistent. Powerful social and cultural forces came together in rendering poor southern whites as a uniquely exploitable "racial stock"—or, more darkly, as a desperate and menacing hillbilly *lumpenproletariat*—and those twinned images would cast a long shadow over the remainder of the twentieth century. Indeed, as misleading as they may have been, these ideological creations of the early days of the hillbilly highway would shape the course of American history—and even how American history is written—in ways that continue to reverberate into the present.

## An Industrialist's Happy Hunting Ground

From the vantage point of the midwestern manufacturing sector, the collapse of the agrarian economy of the Upper South could not have occurred at a better time. World War I had disrupted global migration flows, driven up demand in defense-related industries, and compelled the federal government to take on a more direct role in organizing production and mediating labor disputes—all of which led to a marked increase in wages over the second half of the 1910s. Weekly earnings in manufacturing jobs doubled between 1914 and 1919, even as factory workers managed to extract a reduction of three hours in the length of the average workweek. At the same time, however, comparable increases in the prices of consumer goods were eroding much of the real value of wartime wage gains. Food prices rose by more than 80 percent during the war years, while the cost of clothing soared by more than 140 percent. As a result, when firms sought to recoup the lost ground after the armistice, they provoked one of the largest waves of labor unrest in American history. More than four million workers went on strike in 1919, bringing critical national industries like steel and coal to a grinding halt and even shuttering a major city in Seattle, where a five-day general strike that February stoked business leaders' fears about a home-front restaging of the Bolshevik Revolution.[8]

Though the uprising would be quelled—often quite brutally—a lasting legacy of the 1919 strike wave was a sweeping revival of xenophobic sentiment across the country. This new nativism crystalized in the systematic harassment and persecution of political dissidents and the foreign-born during the First Red Scare, and, even more enduringly, in the passage of the landmark Johnson-Reed Act of 1924, which imposed severe restrictions on immigration that would remain in place for the better part of half a century. The effects of the law were dramatic and immediate: from an average of more than one million immigrants annually between 1910 and 1914, the number of foreign-born arrivals to the United States plummeted to just over three hundred thousand per year between 1925 and 1929. Of greatest significance for many midwestern employers were the especially strict limitations put on immigration from the poorest countries of southern and eastern Europe, curtailing their access to what had been a steady supply of readily exploitable industrial labor throughout the first decades of the century.[9]

So the earliest waves of the Transappalachian migration presented employers with a particularly well-timed alternative. Needing a reliable source of low-cost factory labor—and persuaded that American-born workers would be more immune to the "foreign" contaminants of socialism and anarchism—employers across the Midwest turned with new emphasis to the rapidly growing surplus populations of the rural South. Nowhere was this more evident than in a city like Akron, which was undergoing a period of phenomenal growth in the 1910s and 1920s. Home not only to Goodyear but also to fellow tiremakers B. F. Goodrich and Firestone Tire and Rubber, Akron boomed with the domestic automobile industry: in the decades between the wars, two-thirds of all rubber goods made in the United States would come out of Akron. And as Akron's rubber companies flourished, they came to depend heavily on a steady influx of southern migrants, who poured into the city looking for work in the tire plants. Almost overnight, Akron grew from a moderately sized city of less than fifty thousand in 1900 to an industrial powerhouse of more than two hundred fifty thousand in 1930—and one in which roughly 85 percent of the city's workforce was employed in its singularly dominant industry. By that point, migrants from Appalachia and the broader South accounted for nearly 60 percent of Akron's overall population, and more than 70 percent of all American-born white residents of the city. Fully one-third of the city, by one estimate, hailed from West Virginia alone—enough, even if exaggerated, to earn Akron its other unofficial nickname as "the Capital of West Virginia."[10]

John House did not come to Akron from West Virginia, but he did come from southern Appalachia—specifically, from Cleveland, Georgia, a town of some four hundred inhabitants nestled in the rugged hills of the northeast corner of that state. Life in Cleveland when John was growing up in the 1910s was like that in much of the rest of the region: there were some small mines and a lumber mill in nearby Helen, but the closest centers of industrial activity, in Atlanta or Chattanooga or Greenville, South Carolina, were one hundred miles or more away. Otherwise, there was little to do in the area, aside from farming and orchard work. John tried doing a little of the latter as he got older, but the wages were terrible. "The highest rate of pay I received was 20 cents an hour for picking peaches in the rain," he recalled later. "When the weather was dry the rate was 15 cents an hour." And so in 1922, just after he had graduated from high school, John boarded a northbound train and soon debarked at a crowded and soot-blackened Union Station, where a prominently displayed billboard welcomed the tens of thousands of newcomers like him to Akron, "City of Opportunity."[11]

House was following a familiar path when he set off for Akron: his older brother had spent some time there previously, working for Goodrich during the war, and the elder House brother promised their father that he would keep an eye on seventeen-year-old John when they traveled back north together in 1922. And while Goodrich and other midwestern firms would eventually be able to rely on these characteristic kin-and-community-driven migratory circuits to bring a steady supply of new workers to them, few were prepared to leave things entirely to chance—especially as business soared during the heady years of the 1920s. In fact, it had been large-scale agricultural enterprises, uniquely dependent on flexible and mobile workforces due to the inherent seasonality of their labor needs, which were among the first midwestern employers to tap more directly into the stranded labor reserves of the rural South. By the beginning of the 1910s, onion growers along the Scioto River in central Ohio were already relying on an annual springtime influx of workers from eastern Kentucky, whom they recruited via local intermediaries (such as one particularly ambitious Magoffin County native, who had spent a season "on the marsh" before becoming an informal hiring agent for the growers) and the promise of expenses-paid travel to the onion fields. During the 1920s, tomato growers in central Indiana, berry growers in central Illinois and southwestern Michigan, and sugar-beet growers in Michigan's Saginaw Valley—just to name a few of the more significant midwestern agribusinesses of the period—all recruited heavily from migratory labor streams that came down from the highlands of the Appalachian Mountains and up from the floodplains of the Mississippi River. Some, like the tomato growers of Johnson County, Indiana—the hub of Indiana's tomato crop—would take out advertisements in Kentucky newspapers at the start of each harvest season, announcing the date and time when company-owned trucks would be leaving local towns, headed north for the tomato fields. By the end of the decade, at least one thousand Kentucky migrants were traveling to Johnson County this way every August.[12]

Manufacturers would not be far behind. As early as 1915, Champion Paper of Hamilton, Ohio, the country's larger producer of commercial packaging, magazines, and other coated paper products, began sending company representatives into the eastern Kentucky backcountry to augment its workforce. The first recruiters even traveled with hammers and nails, so they could hang job advertisements to tree trunks as they went. The paper mills that ringed the Michigan coastline along Lake Erie began recruiting workers in east Tennessee and other parts of southern Appalachia around the same time, as did the steel plants of Ohio's Mahoning and Miami River Valleys. Armco Steel in Middletown, Ohio, for instance, dispatched its recruiters primarily to Wolfe, Morgan, Menifee, Breathitt, and Bath Counties, in eastern Kentucky—and brought back so many local workers that they would soon hang signs between departments in the Middletown factory that jokingly read: "Leave Morgan County and enter Wolfe County." For their part, Muncie's glassmakers made their first significant forays into rural Appalachia in 1922, when, as one local executive explained, "we were so rushed with orders we couldn't possibly fill them or get enough men here in town to carry on, so we had to import some men from Kentucky and West Virginia." In the end, Muncie employers "brought two train loads of them down," kept them on until business slowed, and then, "when the slump came, we fired them and kept our old men."[13]

Even the Detroit automakers, whose reputations for offering high-paying jobs had no equal in the region, sent recruiters throughout the Upper South—and even, on occasion, company-chartered buses to bring out-of-work farmers and miners directly to the factory gates. General Motors first began recruiting southern workers to fill its plants in Flint during World War I, mostly from in and around the cotton lands of the Missouri bootheel, northern Arkansas, and West Tennessee. The poverty that marked these areas created a situation that was ripe for abuse: in one locally notorious case, an employment manager at Chevrolet orchestrated an elaborate scheme to extort bribes from desperate sharecroppers and tenant farmers. Recruits paid a fee to associates based in Malden, Missouri, which in effect bought them a job in Flint; they then boarded buses owned and operated by the same men, and in doing so paid an additional fee that ended up in the pockets of the employment manager and his co-conspirators. The buses, in turn, delivered them to a local poolroom, operated by a Missouri-born man named Oscar Martin, that was popular with southern whites in Flint and was conveniently located just down the street from the Chevrolet employment office. "They had rooms all ready for them and everything," one autoworker later recalled. "[Martin] fed them, packed their lunch for them to go to work and had their beds up there for them"—and received a kickback from the scheme operators for his troubles. Since the southeastern Missouri cotton fields produced an almost inexhaustible supply of potential recruits, ready and willing to pay for the same jobs, bus tickets, and beds, many were fired soon after arriving in Flint so the cycle could repeat itself. It is impossible to know how many southern recruits fell victim to this scam over the years, but their numbers must have been legion: by the time the scheme was uncovered in the late 1930s, Chevrolet's Flint workforce seemed to have become "85 percent hillbilly," in the estimation of one industry veteran, and there were so many natives of the Malden area living and working in town that it was as if "they moved the whole city up," as another Flint native would put it.[14]

The three Akron tiremakers recruited in the South as well—Goodyear perhaps most aggressively. World War I was a critical turning point for the firm: its annual sales figures increased by a factor of nearly five between the beginning of the European conflict and the armistice, surpassing $100 million for the first time in 1917. And as Goodyear's business took off, it reached deep into the Appalachian hinterland to staff its factory complex on Akron's east side, which included eighty buildings and spanned more than one hundred acres of floor space. During these years, the company routinely took out advertisements in larger circulation regional newspapers like the *Wheeling Register*, where one ad that appeared for four weeks in March and April 1918 touted the "enormous business" the company was doing, while promising "steady employment" and wages that ran between three and five dollars per day, for men between the ages of eighteen and forty-five as well as "a large number of girls, ages 21 to 35." Goodyear also stationed recruiters throughout the Upper South, where they posted notices in local papers, met with potential recruits in hotels or at lunch counters, and handed out slips that promised the holder a job when they arrived at the hiring office in Akron. According to Fred Yoak, himself a West Virginian who rose through the ranks to eventually become head of the company's employment division, Goodyear deployed as many as thirty-six such labor agents during these decades. The combined effect of all this was impressive: by its own accounting, Goodyear's Akron workforce in 1929, which averaged just under fourteen thousand, was composed of nearly three thousand West Virginians, thirteen hundred Tennesseans, nine hundred Kentuckians, and at least another thousand workers who hailed from various southern states.[15]

Like other midwestern firms, Goodyear and the other tiremakers had compelling reasons to look South around this time. Rubber workers were among the better-paid manufacturing workers in the country, and rubber workers in Akron most of all. Already in 1909, before the industry entered its years of most robust growth, Akron rubber workers averaged $562 in annual earnings, just slightly below Detroit autoworkers; by 1936, when the Goodyear sit-down strike began, workers in tire and pneumatic tube-making jobs were averaging thirty-one cents an hour above the typical manufacturing wage. Even within the rubber firms, there was a clear "Akron advantage": wages at Goodyear's flagship plant, for instance, regularly exceeded those at the company's Los Angeles plant by more than 30 percent, and at its Gadsden, Alabama, factory by as much as 80 percent. At the same time, the implementation of new factory technologies and labor arrangements that characterized tiremaking's development into a mature, mass production industry—and which often boiled down, at least from the workers' perspective, to the ubiquitous and broadly despised "speed-up"—had also produced repeated waves of worker unrest over the first couple decades of the century, climaxing in a citywide strike in 1913 that dragged on for six weeks. In light of both challenges, the economic precariousness that was becoming endemic to the southern countryside presented the tiremakers with an attractive way to remake their Akron workforces, while driving down labor costs and undermining shop-floor cohesion.[16]

Most brazen in this regard, especially in the eyes of many current and prospective rubber workers, was the way Goodyear and the other rubber companies persisted with their recruiting efforts regardless of local business conditions. When John House first arrived in Akron, he was greeted by what became a grimly familiar sight for many of the city's working men and women. Each morning, he would "join the long line of men stretching for at least a city block before the employment office would be opened for interviews—men who, like me, had been lured to Akron by the widely advertised promise of good jobs at high wages." House managed to make it to the front of the line after several days, but many others in his position were not so lucky. "I was attracted to this fair city by an ad in the paper by one of the rubber companies," another migrant complained in the form of a letter to the *Akron Beacon Journal*; "but when I visited the company that had advertised, I was informed they were laying off men instead of hiring them." Longer-tenured workers in the city, meanwhile, routinely remarked upon seeing "men from other states . . . being hired" while "we Akron men are left stranded"; of seeing "experienced men turned down by the scores without even the opportunity of an examination, men who are permanent residents of this city," at the same time that "men who claim they have never had any experience are hired." Even the *Beacon Journal* itself, only rarely known to take sides against the tiremakers, balked in the late spring of 1922—not long before John House got off a train in Union Station—when the companies issued a call for one thousand new workers while thirteen hundred recently laid-off rubber workers remained on the backlogs at the state employment agency. "It does seem strange," the *Beacon Journal* pointed out, "when but a few weeks ago the papers were being importuned to aid in finding work for thousands that could not find it for themselves [that] we should now begin to import labor." Was it really a matter, as the companies claimed, of there not being enough available rubber workers to fill a recent spike in orders; or was it, the newspaper's editors wondered, "a method to insure a surplus of Labor"?[17]

In Akron and beyond, the initial results from northern manufacturers' recruiting efforts were encouraging. After more than doubling between 1914 and 1920, average annual earnings at Goodyear hardly budged once the company accelerated its southern hiring, growing roughly one percentage point a year on average for the next ten years. Maybe even more significantly, there was no recurrence of the labor unrest that had rocked the tire plants in 1913. How much of this was attributable to the increased presence of southern newcomers in the city's rubber industry was debatable; these were, after all, generally bleak times—"lean years," in historian Irving Bernstein's memorable formulation—for American workers and the American labor movement.[18] But similar patterns were discernible elsewhere along the expanding footprint of the hillbilly highway. In Detroit—where, by 1935, there was "but one union in the automobile industry of any consequence, and this one of no great consequence," as the labor writer Louis Adamic put it in the pages of *The Nation*—the auto companies' recent decision to import "tens of thousands" of rural white southerners had proven "very, very clever." "Any kind of solidarity between these newcomers and the old-timers of Detroit is out of the question in the immediate future," Adamic concluded somberly.[19]

In city after city, similar situations prevailed. When Robert and Helen Lynd returned to Muncie to follow up on their original *Middletown* study, they found that the city's well-established tradition of craft unionism stretching back to the late nineteenth century had been supplanted by "an industrially open-shop town," which the Lynds attributed at least in part to a "working class in recent years [that] has been heavily recruited from first- and second-generation farm stock." "An industrialist's happy hunting ground" was how they summed up the new employment scene in Muncie. By the time the Depression brought the post–World War I boom to a crashing halt, the same desultory description could have been applied broadly across the landscape of Transappalachia.[20]

## Fresh from the Farm

The first job John House got in Akron was at B.F. Goodrich, and it paid twice what he could make in the peach orchards back home. Nevertheless, like so many southern newcomers to Akron's rubber plants, he found the adjustment to the factory labor regime to be daunting. Layoffs were frequent and unpredictable: six months after he started, he was included in a group of "some fifty-odd men who were laid off as surplus labor"; two months later he was brought back, only to be laid off again two weeks after that.[21] When he could get it consistently, work itself was an unremitting war of position with shop-floor management, which pressed incessantly to increase the rate of production while maintaining a system of near-constant surveillance. Workers were punished or fired for any kind of infraction or mistake—putting a tire in the wrong-size mold; leaving a small gap in the gum strips that were used to cover the tire plies—and "there wasn't a damned thing we could do about it," as House put it. The physical conditions were no better. "There was little or no ventilation other than the windows that were kept open during the hot months[,] and occasionally someone would be overcome by the intense heat and be taken to the plant hospital to recover," he recalled. The tire companies did not exactly deny the problem—"in the summer, men in the pit fall like flies," one Goodrich official acknowledged privately—even as they publicly shifted the blame for such matters onto the newest workers themselves, who "have not the grit or stamina to remain here long enough to learn our processes and earn good wages," as Goodyear management claimed in the pages of the company's in-house newspaper, the *Wingfoot Clan*. True or not, turnover in the plants, especially among more junior workers and the city's most recent arrivals, was astronomically high. In the years between

1921 and 1929, Goodyear's employment rolls averaged a little under 13,000 workers and never went above 18,766—but in order to maintain those numbers, the company had to hire a total of 87,255 workers over the same period. Voluntary quits accounted for as much as two-thirds of tiremakers' workforce turnover every year. House was one of them: after a year and a half of sporadic work at Goodrich—and one too many frustrating run-ins with management—he gave his notice in January 1924.[22]

As initial experiences with midwestern factory employment went, House's was fairly typical. When Lucian Gupton got a job as a tool-and-die worker at Ford's massive River Rouge complex, he began at a dollar and a half an hour, which was "big money" for someone who had grown up on a tobacco farm in western Kentucky, not far from Paducah. But the factory environment was suffocating. "When you went to work there you had a stick over your head" was how he would describe it later. "You worked until you were done, whenever they told you, when they told you. . . . If you had to go to the toilet, you didn't go until they said. And then when you'd go, you'd have four men in there. By gosh, you'd darn near burst your britches." "They fired me sometimes four times a day," Gupton recalled— until eventually he decided he had had enough of the treatment and quit. Lloyd Jones, who hailed from southeastern Kentucky near Barbourville, not far from the borders with Virginia and Tennessee, had a similar experience at Ford's Highland Park plant when he arrived in Detroit in January 1925. He was hired on to work in the powerhouse, where red-hot metal was hammered into axles for the Model T: a steaming, punishingly loud, and overcrowded misery that he would later liken to "a new jungle." Jones did not last three weeks before turning in his identification card at the timekeeper's office. "I said, 'Write out my time, I'm quitting. . . . This is not for human beings. Human beings are not supposed to work on a thing like this. This is for something else.'"[23]

The high quit rates that southern migrants like John House, Lucian Gupton, and Lloyd Jones demonstrated upon first arriving in northern cities was a perennial source of frustration for midwestern manufacturers. But it was also largely a problem of their own creation. Just as General Motors focused its attentions on the impoverished cotton fields of southeastern Missouri, Arkansas, and Tennessee, northern employers often intentionally targeted their recruiting efforts in areas where there was little or no existing factory employment, and where they could be quite certain about the type of workers they would be able to hire. Even though there were thousands of skilled rubber workers and already trained factory operatives who lived in Akron and its nearby environs in Ohio's densely industrialized northeastern corner, Goodyear often wrote into the job postings it circulated throughout the Upper South that it was hoping to fill openings with "inexperienced men," and made sure to appeal directly to the growing population of landless farmers and transient migrant workers who composed the region's most desperate and vulnerable residents. "Are you tired of moving around from one job to another losing time and money?" read one typical ad that Goodyear ran in southern papers in 1920. Meanwhile, on the ground, Goodyear representatives made a special point of paying frequent recruiting visits to the region's overworked coalfields— places like Fairmont and Elkins, West Virginia, where Fred Yoak's labor agents found that the regular boom-and-bust cycle in mining produced a reliable supply of potential hires from among southern Appalachia's rural proletariat. In Muncie, employers even deployed a special lexicon that distinguished the local population from the less experienced outsiders they preferred to bring in during peak periods. "Our men from the local district here, born and bred on the farms near here, knowing the use of machinery of some sort from their boyhood, reliable, steady, we call 'corn-feds,'" one such employer explained. "These men we brought in from the mountains, we called 'green peas.'" As the name implied, it could be safely assumed that a fair number of these rawest of recruits would not work out—but that was a tradeoff the companies were prepared to live with. "Some of them learned quickly, and some of them didn't. Most of them have drifted back by now."[24]

So well known, in fact, was this managerial preference for "inexperienced workers" that at times it could be used by workers to their own advantage. When he quit his job at Goodrich, John House's first stop was across town at rival Firestone, where the employment office was presided over by Lou Hannah, a legendary local figure known to make hiring decisions based on the results of a simple imperative: "Let's see your hands!" Perhaps sensing that House was no longer such a novice, Hannah turned him away without offering him a job. "After leaving his office," House recalled, "I helped my brother overhaul the motor on his auto that he had driven to Georgia and back recently and was covered in Georgia red clay dust and some of this dust and grease still stained my hands." Deciding to go back and try again at Firestone the following day, this time House made a point of not washing up, and "deliberately dressed like someone fresh from the farm, whereas yesterday, I had worn my Sunday best." Not recognizing him, Hannah must have liked what he saw on House's hands the second time around: he hired him on the spot and put House to work the next day.[25]

In addition to being a deft piece of workplace subterfuge, House's experience "dressing up" as a hillbilly to get a job revealed a lot about the deeper context framing the way midwestern employers thought about their rural Appalachian recruits. "Green peas" and other "fresh from the farm" southern migrants appealed to the likes of Firestone not only because the ongoing collapse of the rural economy of the Upper South made them a widely available and relatively cheap source of labor. Prospective employers were also often operating with a common set of assumptions about such workers; assumptions that ascribed to them certain indelible characteristics that differentiated them from the longer-tenured members of the urban workforce they were brought in to work beside. Familiar stereotypes that had been attached to the rural poor from the very earliest period of American history took on a new salience in the modern crucible of the industrial Midwest. In Flint, southern cotton farmers had a reputation for being willing to "work until they couldn't walk"; other workers would later recall the way the "hillbillies" were dispatched in the auto factories to drive up production rates whenever foremen needed to increase output. In Detroit, southern whites were set apart in the eyes of local employers by their lack of "close contact with modern industry," and the "extremely low standard of living" to which they were supposedly accustomed. As one contemporary report noted, it was an open secret that "no one has a better chance of employment in Detroit these days than a Southerner of unsophisticated mien." Like dull animals, the thinking went, such men could be relied upon to work hard without complaint. In Akron, the West Virginians who came to make up such a large portion of the rubber company's semi- and unskilled workforces were widely referred to as "snakes," "snake-eyes," or, more to the point, "snake eaters"—an allusion to the urban myth that these Appalachian migrants were so destitute that they had subsisted on snake meat before leaving their mountain homes. The green pea/corn-fed distinction drawn by Muncie's manufacturers echoed a similar dietary logic of degradation; in their eyes, the super-exploitability of the men "from the mountains" was likewise a quite literally *embodied* character trait. "It seems to me that the working class are different here from any other place" was how one local business leader explained it to the Lynds. "They are more incapable, stupid—just a crummy lot, biologically inferior, with a lot of these dopes from Kentucky and Tennessee."[26]

Almost inevitably, given the circumstances under which southern workers were entering midwestern factories, these kinds of attitudes permeated the thinking of northern workers as well. Hillbilly stereotypes resonated far beyond the personnel offices of industrial firms; as one Akron native later recalled from growing up in the city during these interwar decades, "the association was massive and thorough in Akron between ignorance, shiftlessness, illiteracy, and the West Virginians, Tennesseans, Georgians, etc." During his time reporting from Detroit, Louis Adamic found that poor southern whites were "looked down upon by all but the most intelligent local workers, both native and foreign-born." Job competition, real or perceived, was often at the crux of the resentments that northern workers harbored against southern migrants: as Adamic concluded, southern whites were "despised also—indeed mainly—because they take employment from the old-time automotive workers." But it was easy for such workplace-based resentments to evolve into more categorical denunciations of poor white southerners as something of a race apart. In fact, even though white southerners were being recruited under the assumption that they would prove more reliable than the recalcitrant immigrant workers of the pre–World War I period—that they were, in the language of the day, "100 percent Americans"—it was not unusual to hear longer-tenured members of northern workforces refer to these rural newcomers explicitly as "foreigners," as did one Akronite in a letter to the *Beacon Journal* during the height of the 1922 controversy over labor recruiting. In Flint, "the people with whom they [come] into contact distinguish between themselves and *all* southern white laborers and tend to treat to them as members of a single homogenous group," another contemporary observer noted. The same was true in Muncie, where, as Phyllis Johnson would later recall from her childhood years before World War II, everybody "hated the hillbillies." "They came up here and took the people who lived here's jobs. The hillbillies, when I was growing up, were thought of worse than the Negroes."[27]

Even the era's socialists, labor radicals and liberal activists tended to view the first waves of southern white migrants to the Midwest largely according to the framework established by their employers. Like Deac Martin of the *Nation's Business*, who fixated on the influence of their racial "heritage" and their religious fundamentalism, many took these workers to be an inherently conservative group. Marxists like James Cannon, a leading American Trotskyist of the period, and Albert Weisbord, an important figure in various Communist Party formations during the 1920s and 1930s, were typical in this regard, emphasizing as they did the essentially reactionary tendencies of the "masses of 'hillbillies' from the impoverished districts in the South," who, upon arriving in northern cities "with their ignorance and their prejudices," dumbly joined the ranks of "the tremendous army of the unemployed [employers used] as a whip to beat down wages and conditions."[28] Akron's own B. J. Widick, a Serbian émigré who worked as a beat-writer for the *Beacon Journal* before becoming an activist in the United Rubber Workers and the United Auto Workers (UAW), likewise wondered whether the city's "so-called hillbillies" were capable of "a class solidarity strong enough to overcome their prejudices," especially in the face of their "fanatic allegiance [to] the Ku Klux Klan."[29] This last was a question that particularly preoccupied individuals and organizations on the American left during these years, when the Klan and the Black Legion experienced a notable surge in popularity across the same parts of the Midwest that were seeing a simultaneous influx of job-seeking migrants from the rural South. Many took for granted, as the radical intellectual Dwight Macdonald did, that southern Appalachian migrants "provided the backbone of the powerful Ku Klux Klan organization in Ohio, Michigan, and Indiana," while Walter White, the longtime head of the National Association for the Advancement of Colored People (NAACP), even went so far as to suggest that the Black Legion was "originally conceived to secure and insure jobs for white Southerners."[30]

For the more conventionally minded old guard of the midwestern union movement, which was not especially interested in revolutionary socialism or civil rights, the biggest perceived threat posed by southern Appalachian migrants was often their lingering attachment to their rural places of origin. If Muncie's employers prized the expendability of the green peas in part because they believed "a substantial marginal number of them [are] able to live on the farm during slack periods in the industrial year," an officer of Muncie's Central Labor Union was saying effectively the same thing when he complained to the Lynds that "these hillbillies can be educated into joining the union, but as soon as they do, they lose their jobs and drift off." Clearly, there was some truth behind this, as the notable phenomenon of shuttle migration and the particularly high rates of return that characterized the Transappalachian migration made clear. And yet too often, the transience such migrants demonstrated—whether of their own volition or not—prompted midwestern trade unionists to treat newcomers from the Upper South as if they were all men like Charlie Wood, making seasonal forays into the factories before returning to his Fentress County farm. When, for example, the American Federation of Labor granted its initial charter to a national union of automobile locals, in 1934, one of the very first orders of business taken up by the new leadership of the UAW was to recommend that rural migrants "be placed on the 'preferred list' for being laid off." As the reasoning went, these "agricultural workers" had "outside means of subsistence" on which they could

rely during periods of economic downturn in the industry. It was a dubi-
ous assertion at any time, but an especially unpersuasive one at a moment
when farm foreclosures were at an all-time high, and agricultural wage
rates were at their lowest since 1906.[31]

## Paradoxes

One way or the other, the picture that emerged of rural southern whites
in the Midwest during the interwar period was a damning one. But it was
also one that, from the very start, proved to be a particularly poor predic-
tor of their actual behavior in the workplace. Before Lloyd Jones had his
ill-fated stint in the powerhouse at Highland Park, for example, he was
an itinerant Pentecostal preacher, earning a reputation for his ability to
speak in tongues and heal the sick through the laying on of hands, along
a circuit that took him through the most remote, densely wooded pockets of southeastern Kentucky and western Virginia. And yet less than a
decade later, he was on the strike committee during a walkout at Briggs
Auto Body in Detroit. Just four years removed from the peach orchards of
Cleveland, Georgia, John House found himself part of a failed attempt to
form a union among Akron rubber workers, which ran aground when the
companies banded together to fire and blacklist the campaign's most visible leaders. Nine years after that, he would be elected president of Goodyear Local 2 of the United Rubber Workers. Despite their shared lack of
experience with "modern industry," despite the traditionalism—even, in
Jones's case, the charismatic supernaturalism—that characterized their
spartan rural upbringings, neither had any trouble embracing "the idea of
industrial unionism," as Widick had feared.[32]

And these were not just anomalous, individual cases. While the prepon-
derance of contemporary opinion presumed southern whites to be incor-
rigibly individualistic and either too simple or too desperate to buck the
status quo, already by the 1920s a growing number of reports were singling
out the rural migrants then pouring into northern factories for, among
other things, their lack of "loyalty to the establishment," the particularly
low esteem in which they held "corporate property rights," and their generally "hostile attitude toward all supervision." For every account of "hillbilly"
scabs and rate-busters, there were others that attested to how quickly these
new recruits learned the techniques of machine-breaking, "systematic sol-
diering," and other "time-honored practices of self-protection" that more
seasoned manufacturing workers deployed to resist managerial control
over the pace of work. This was especially true about Transappalachian

migrants who had had some prior experience in the mines in the region, and for whom, in the words of one management expert, the "method of handling disagreements in the mines"—in other words, through direct action at the workplace—was already a well-established tradition. "Transplant such a man into a factory where production is speeded and no imagination is required to picture what will happen," the expert warned. As the wider region was convulsed by labor unrest throughout the 1930s, the wisdom of such warnings would prove itself time and again.

The events that transpired in Anderson, Indiana, one county over and twenty miles west of Muncie, were a perfect case in point. Anderson was another beneficiary of the Indiana gas boom of the 1880s; and like Muncie it had grown into an important node in the midwestern automobile supply chain by the end of the 1920s, when two General Motors subsidiaries, Delco-Remy (which made batteries) and Guide Lamp (which made headlights), between themselves employed more than eleven thousand workers in a city of less than forty thousand people. Also like Muncie, Anderson entered the Depression decade as a viciously open-shop town. When a veteran organizer from the 1934 Toledo Auto-Lite strike arrived in Anderson to assist workers at Delco-Remy and Guide Lamp in their efforts to form a union, city officials and the local police promptly ran the organizer out of town and warned him not to return. Such actions created a palpable climate of fear among Anderson's auto workers: after Joseph Wilson, who had grown up on a small tobacco farm outside of Bowling Green, Kentucky, joined the union at Guide Lamp, he was "afraid to tell anybody"—including his own father, who also worked at Guide Lamp. Organizing had to be extremely "secretive," Wilson recalled later, "because everything was against us, the politicians was all against us." Nonetheless, the Guide Lamp workers persisted in their efforts inside the plant, and on the morning of December 31, 1936, the day after the famous General Motors sit-down strike began in Flint, Michigan, Wilson and his coworkers shut down their machines, called on the company to recognize their union, and began a sit-down strike of their own.[33]

The Anderson Guide Lamp strike was the most explosive episode of industrial unrest to hit the cities of the Indiana gas belt during this formative decade, and Transappalachian migrants were critical in launching the strike and maintaining it in the face of overwhelming local opposition. Support for the UAW was strongest among Guide Lamp's youngest workers, who, like younger workers throughout the region, were more likely to be newcomers to the cities of the industrial Midwest. "What we had mainly in there was a lot of people out of the mines," Wilson recalled.

"The mines was down, the coal mines was dead, [but] them old mines was union—that was beat in their heads two hours after they was born." As Wilson remembered things, it was "some of them boys from the mines" who were first to stop work and call for a strike; and it was their reputations for toughness—their "habit of going home to get their guns when a strike broke out and there was a possibility of terrorism," as Victor Reuther, who came to Anderson to help lead the strike, later put it—that buoyed the other Guide Lamp workers at crucial moments over the next month and a half. One such moment came on the evening of January 25, when a mob of local vigilantes invaded and destroyed the local union headquarters, burned down picket shacks in front of the Guide Lamp plant, and beat whatever union workers they could get their hands on. Even after General Motors settled with the sit-downers in Flint in early February, its Guide Lamp division refused to budge and Anderson's self-appointed civil constabulary continued to terrorize the workers. On February 11, in what was perhaps as clear an indication as any of which side southern migrants found themselves on as Anderson descended into a virtual civil war over the question of the union, workers held a rally at an old downtown theater while a crowd of a few hundred vigilantes gathered outside and began firing shots through the theater's windows. Outside, the chief of police stood idly by, watching as the crowd brandished rifles and pitchforks; inside, an "improvised hillbilly band," as one witness put it, played feverishly through the night to keep up the spirits of the workers. Finally, the vigilantes dispersed. In another few days, law and order was restored as Governor Maurice Townsend begrudgingly declared martial law and negotiations began with Guide Lamp. "It was the turning point," Reuther would later write; "after that, UAW membership in Anderson moved up and up."[34]

Even in Muncie, the green peas would end up playing an essential role in the resurgence of the local labor movement. The turning point there was also the Guide Lamp strike in Anderson, as it turned out. Factory workers in Muncie watched the strike unfold closely—especially at Warner Gear, at the time a key supplier of transmissions for at least a dozen midwestern automakers and one of the city's largest employers. Independent parts makers like Warner Gear were particularly sensitive to interruptions in production during these years, which jeopardized their ability to deliver on their all-important contracts with the industry's largest assemblers. As a result, workers at the factory had received a series of unexpected raises during the fall and winter of 1936 and 1937, all "for no explainable reason by management," as one Warner Gear worker rather ingenuously noted (the explanation, he suspected, could be found "in Detroit and the UAW").

But Warner Gear's attempts to bribe its workforce into docility were no match for the inspiring drama on display in Anderson. In mid-February, just as the Guide Lamp strike was reaching its triumphant conclusion, a contingent of Warner Gear workers traveled to Anderson to meet with the strikers and organizers from the UAW, from whom they "obtained union cards and headed back to Muncie ready to organize." A little over a week later, the inaugural meeting of what would become UAW Local 287 was convened, with forty-two new members in attendance. By the late spring of 1937, enough workers had signed membership cards for the local to approach Warner Gear to request that it recognize the union and begin negotiations on a contract. Company executives dragged their feet—but the wintertime raises had already revealed their desperation to avoid a confrontation like the one at Guide Lamp. Once the Supreme Court delivered its April ruling upholding the constitutionality of the National Labor Relations Act—and thus entrenching the new federally sanctioned regime of contractually enforced collective bargaining—Warner Gear was left with few options. A representation election was scheduled for the end of June, which the union won by a four-to-one margin. By the first week of July, a little over half a year after Guide Lamp workers in Anderson first sat down at their machines, Local 287 in Muncie signed a contract with Warner Gear—the first union contract representing nonskilled trades workers at any of the major Muncie manufacturers.[35]

It is a challenge to determine with complete precision the part that southern migrants played in this formative period for Local 287, which would remain one of the galvanizing forces in the Muncie labor movement for decades to come. But it is possible to draw certain conclusions from the available evidence. Nearly twenty-four hundred employees were eligible to vote in the June 1937 union election; a partial survey of Warner Gear workers from around that time suggests that roughly 20 percent of the workforce—or just under five hundred workers—would have been born in the states of southern Appalachia.[36] Given the margin of victory for Local 287, it seems likely that a sizable majority of them voted with the union. One of the workers who had gone to Anderson in February was Vades Norman, a thirty-one-year-old father of four who had moved to Muncie from Kentucky, and who went on to be one of five men chosen to serve on Local 287's first executive board. Another Kentuckian, Ray Babbitt, moved to Muncie when he was seventeen, just after the outbreak of war in Europe; he would sit on the seven-person bargaining committee that negotiated the local's first contract with Warner Gear, and went on to a long career as a leader in Local 287 and within the broader labor movement in the region.[37]

Babbitt and Norman may have been relatively unusual—most of Local 287's elected leadership during these early years were native to Muncie or elsewhere in Indiana—but on the level of the shop floor, it was more common to find southern-born workers playing active roles in building a union culture at the workplace. Of the ninety-nine Warner Gear workers who functioned as union stewards and committee members during Local 287's first two years of existence, at least thirteen were born in southern states. That ratio was below the 20 percent of Warner Gear's overall work-force that hailed from the South—but it was still more than double the rate at which southern-born white men appeared in the general population of Indiana at the time.[38] To be sure, some of this early cadre lost interest after the excitement of the first union campaigns had passed; by 1941 Vades Norman had drifted on to a job first as an officer with the Muncie Police Department, and then with plant security for Warner Gear of all places.[39] But for other southern-born workers at Warner Gear, even the grinding and often thankless work that stewards and committee members do representing coworkers, processing grievances, and enforcing contracts—the day-to-day manifestations of the promise of industrial democracy that was so central to the institutional culture of the early CIO—was a responsibility they took up eagerly and actively during these critical years. Indeed, Local 287 may never have become the force that it became in the local economy without them.[40]

Nowhere did the workplace record of rural white southerners diverge as dramatically from expectations during these decades than in Akron. The strike at Goodyear in February 1936 inaugurated the climactic struggles that would, in the ensuing years, finally lead to the organization of the Akron rubber industry. And not only that: preceding as it did the sit-down strike at GM in Flint by more than ten months, the Goodyear strike also launched the very "sit-down era" in American labor history, from which would emerge the fully formed CIO and the modern American labor movement.[41] It started with a wildcat stoppage in the company's tire-building department, where the workforce by that point was disproportionately composed of southern-born recruits and other rural migrants. And when the strike ended some five weeks later, following a tenuous settlement between the company and URW Local 2, which reopened the plant but left most of the core issues at stake essentially unresolved, it was those workers, primarily, who carried on the conflict in an unremitting series of sit-downs, slowdowns, and other kinds of stoppages, most of which were conducted without the formal authorization of the Local 2 leadership.[42]

Goodyear Tire and Rubber workers in Akron celebrate the March 1936 agreement that brought an end to the first major sit-down strike in the region. Although the agreement secured some of the union's demands, the issues it left unresolved would provoke a wave of smaller sit-downs and wildcat shop-floor actions led largely by Transappalachian migrants that lasted through 1937. © *Akron Beacon Journal*—USA TODAY NETWORK.

Between the date of the settlement and the end of the year, in fact, Goodyear recorded at least ninety-four such workplace incidents, or roughly one every three days. Some were as short as a single shift or part of a shift; others were extensive enough to idle the entire factory for a full day or more. Already by the end of May, the *Beacon Journal*—which along with the other local papers had come around to a begrudging kind of neutrality during the larger strike of February and March—was likening the wave of "disruptive, outlaw sitdowns" sweeping through the city's rubber plants to an "epidemic" in one breath, and "guerilla warfare" in the next. Into 1937 and even 1938 the strike wave continued, until one labor beat-writer could not help but conclude that "the rubber workers of Akron have engaged in more sitdowns than any other group of workers in this country, and probably in the world." And as the chaotic situation dragged on, there became little doubt among an increasingly hostile general public about who was responsible for the ongoing turmoil in the city's key industry. "You and I know who these strike agitators are," complained one Akron resident, in a letter to the *Beacon Journal* signed "Union Hater." "They are these uneducated tobacco chewing geetar playing hillbilly illiterates from West Virginia, Kentucky, and Tennessee."[43]

That the tiremakers' migrant workforce, not long ago attacked for undermining wages and stealing jobs from Akron's homegrown population, should now be demonized as "strike agitators" was in some sense predictable. Stereotypes can be elastic, even as the underlying antipathy they articulate is unchanged—and as a contemporary observer of Akron's social landscape would note, the most intractable dividing line in the city during the Depression years remained that "between the oldtimers and the Snakes."[44] At the same time, Goodyear's "hillbilly illiterates" were more than just convenient scapegoats. There was quite a bit of truth, if not much sympathy, to the contemptuous assessment offered up in "Union Hater's" letter. According to most reports from inside the factory, southern-born workers, and especially those with fewer years of accumulated service, were among the more common agitators during the long, post-settlement period of shop-floor upheaval. And it was certainly true that many if not most of the stoppages in these months originated in the factory's tirebuilding rooms and curing pits, where so many of the company's Appalachian recruits were concentrated. In Department 251, for instance—the same department where the February strike had begun—Goodyear recorded at least twenty-seven sit-downs in the period between March and July 1936 alone. Likewise, most of the disruptions were initiated by workers on the fourth shift: a twelve-to-six-in-the-morning graveyard shift to which the younger and most junior employees tended to be assigned. Other departments and shifts participated in the post-strike sit-down wave as well, of course. But as time wore on, it became increasingly common to hear complaints about "red-hot tire builders" being drawn to trouble like "molasses draws flies," as Goodyear's general counsel phrased it in one court filing; about "fourth shift radicals" who were prone to bullying and harassing their nonunion coworkers if they refused to join Local 2, as one such worker groused; or about the "hotheads" in the Plant 2 tire room, whose incessant striking was making impossible the union's efforts to present itself as a responsible bargaining agent in the factory.[45]

Among the more notorious of the hotheads to emerge during this period was James "Jimmy" Jones, a "dapper Georgian" who worked on the fourth shift in Department 251.[46] A union steward and committee member, Jones had been one of the organizers of the wildcat sit-down that launched the February strike. Along with his fellow fourth-shift tire builder Charles Lesley—who had grown up in similar circumstances on a farm in southern Ohio—Jones remained a constant thorn in the side of Goodyear plant management throughout the strike's tumultuous aftermath. "During the several months which elapsed [after] the time of the settlement of the strike in 1936," a Department 251 supervisor would later testify, "I do not believe that [Jones] worked ten complete six-hour shifts without interruption by sit-downs or by him running about the Department or the Plant on union agitation." In one particularly incendiary instance, after Goodyear promoted a nonunion worker to a senior position in the Plant 2 tire room, Jones and Lesley responded by announcing that "the factory would be shut down for a while." They then led a group of Local 2 members around the plant, gathered up some twenty foremen, shift supervisors, and nonunion workers, and corralled them into a makeshift "bullpen" built out of stacks of tires, where they effectively held them—and the larger factory—hostage for the better part of a day and a half, until Goodyear agreed to replace the nonunion worker with a Local 2 member. It was, according to the company, "one of the worst [disruptions] experienced during the entire period of labor trouble and represented a complete seizure of the factory and absolute workers' control or domination of all operations in Plant 2."[47]

Episodes like this one, which resulted in criminal charges against Jones and thirty other workers, may have been extreme. (Jones, as it happens, was the only one whose case made it to trial, although he would be acquitted on all counts.)[48] But they were not altogether unusual during these months of chaos. "There have been many times when I have come to work on my regular shift only to find the plant shut down and completely out of the hands of the supervisors and foreman who were supposed to be in charge," another Goodyear manager would later attest. "During these times, the plant was in the hands of a mob of riotous union men usually headed by J. Jones and C. Leslie [sic]." And it was not only Jones. There was also Gibb Giles from Tennessee and Hokey Twyman from West Virginia: union stewards in Plant 1 who were fired after leading fifty coworkers in a department-wide sit-down that eventually shuttered the whole building and ended only after the police had been called in. Local 2 representatives managed to get Giles and Twyman their jobs back with a formal apology—although the most Twyman was able to muster was "According to the executive committee [of the union], I guess I was wrong." Or Earl Graham (Kentucky) and Frank "Red" McClain (West Virginia), union committeemen who fought a pitched and ongoing battle with plant supervision over piece rates in the Plant 2 inspection room, which not infrequently ended with "the floor literally covered with tires" that Local 2 members in the department refused to handle. Or Clarence Mathews, another West Virginian, who "held no official union position" and yet was "one of the hottest union men" on his shift, according to his foreman—an assessment that was borne out when Mathews, angered by a pair of nonunion workers who were violating the informal limit on production established by Local 2 members in the department, called a sit-down that quickly engulfed the whole Plant 2 tire room.[49]

Mathews and the others also drew a revealing contrast with the Goodyear employees who lined up against Local 2 and behind the company during this period. As opposed to the hotheads, Goodyear's most reliable employees were significantly more likely to be veteran workers and members of the factory elite. As the sit-down wave continued, a group of these employees formed the Akron Goodyear Employee's Association, a rival union that emerged to challenge Local 2 and enjoyed the tacit backing of the company. The differences between the AGEA leaders and the Local 2 militants were striking. Of the eleven rubber workers present at the founding meeting of the AGEA, there was only one who had been born in southern Appalachia, and he had been employed at Goodyear for twenty years. The others in attendance were overwhelmingly Ohio natives, other northern WASPs, or "older" immigrants from the British Isles. Unlike the rank-and-file militants, they were more likely to hold salaried jobs at Goodyear as engineers or office clerks; a significant number had previously served in the Industrial Assembly, an earlier company-sponsored employee association; and at least two were members of the Stahl-Mate Club, an anti-union group that had emerged during the strike wave to spy on and intimidate union activists.[50] On one notable occasion, members of the Stahl-Mate Club set fire to a pair of giant crosses outside the gates of Plant 2, just before the fourth shift reported for work—as clear an indication as any that despite the "fanatic allegiance" to the Klan that southern Appalachian migrants purportedly brought with them to Akron, local vigilantism "seems always to have been under the control of respectable Protestant social and political leaders."[51] Two of the founding AGEA members had even traveled to Washington at Goodyear's expense in 1935, to testify against the passage of the National Labor Relations Act. As Arthur Boggess, the one West Virginian in the group, later acknowledged, "From my personal experience in my department, it seems as though the old employees were more against Local 2 than the younger ones."[52]

By the time Deac Martin arrived in Akron in the summer of 1937, the conflict at Goodyear was proceeding along two distinct tracks.[53] For the elected leaders of Local 2 and the international union, the top priority had become getting the largest rubber manufacturer in the country to engage in good-faith negotiations toward a first written contract. "Union heads themselves are now discouraging the sit-downs," Martin noted in his reporting; "It is general opinion that Akron labor leaders now want to stabilize their members, make them responsible to sounder organization." On at least fifteen separate occasions that spring and summer, URW leaders met with Goodyear representatives, and attempted to persuade them, as House would later put it, "that genuine collective bargaining leading to the execution of a labor contract would be the best possible solution to our mutual problems." But they got nowhere. "It was probably [one of] the most frustrating periods in my life," he recalled.[54]

In the meantime, so long as Goodyear continued to drag its feet, sound organization came to seem like an increasingly worthless objective to Local 2's rank-and-file militants. Besides, on the issues that those workers tended to care most about—production quotas, staffing, and piece rates— all the wildcatting proved quite effective. Even stoppages of a limited duration translated into costly shortfalls in Goodyear's output—production losses during the "bullpen" incident, for instance, ran to thirty-two thousand tires—at a time when the company, still just barely recovered from the worst years of the Depression, could ill afford them. As a result, while Local 2 leaders continued to have little to show for their efforts at the bargaining table, the hotheads won their conflicts with plant management more often than they lost them, if for no other reason than because shop-floor supervisors found themselves "virtually compelled to [acquiesce to workers' demands] in order to prevent serious injury to the nonunion men as well as keep up my production schedule," as one department foreman explained. Factory-wide, it amounted to a de facto labor policy of "peace at any price," Goodyear's personnel manager, Cliff Slusser, acknowledged. "We've given concessions, put extra men on pools, have increased rates, have accepted production limits—because we had to."[55]

It was a remarkable admission. Without having secured a contract— without yet even having secured exclusive bargaining rights, which would only come after the National Labor Relations Board certified a consent election that finally took place that August, won by Local 2 at a margin of roughly three to one—Goodyear's Akron-based workforce had managed to secure for itself an extraordinary amount of direct control at the workplace. That the driving force behind this wave of militant self-assertion came in many cases from the ranks of the very same workers that Goodyear and the other rubber producers had spent much of the last two decades recruiting could hardly have been anticipated. But maybe it should have been. After all, few sizable cities of the period were as exclusively focused on a single industry as was Akron. Fewer still also shared the peculiar demographic profile that years of intensive migration from the states of southern Appalachia had given to Akron and particularly to its rubber factories. In a sense, the tiremakers' plans had precisely backfired: instead of a super-exploitable labor force whose loyalty to the companies was predetermined by their extreme desperation, their presumed cultural deficiencies, and their permanent status as outsiders in the local community, Goodyear and the others had ended up with an unassimilable core of economically precarious and socially marginalized malcontents, who were primed for a fight when the time came. This, then, was the final paradox of Akron: appearances aside, there was perhaps no other city in the region where the conditions were quite so conducive to an uprising of the green peas.[56]

But an uprising was one thing; maintaining a protracted struggle against a powerful antagonist like Goodyear, especially as economic conditions began to worsen in the second half of 1937, was a challenge of an altogether different order. The recession that began that fall brought successive rounds of mass layoffs at Goodyear and surging unemployment in Akron—which may well have been enough to diminish the appetite for confrontation inside the factories on their own. Just as important, though, was the ongoing campaign by the Local 2 leadership to contain the militancy of the hotheads. Already by the middle of 1936, Local 2 had begun holding special memberships to publicly remonstrate against "'wild cat' sitdowns," while warning any "ring leaders" that they would face discipline if they "did not carry on through orderly procedure." And such efforts only intensified in 1937. In February the union and the company agreed to the creation of a so-called supreme court within the factory: a labor-management committee designed to resolve shop-floor disputes before they got out of hand, which became, in effect, an in-house mechanism for reining in the rank and file. In one indicative instance, a group of fourth-shift union members approached a nonunion worker in Department 232-B and tried to compel him to join; in response, "the union members of the committee . . . agreed to talk to these men this afternoon. . . . [They were] of the opinion that they would be able to handle the situation and went on the record as disapproving of this method of getting men into the union." For good measure, Local 2 leaders also arranged with the international leadership of the URW to have some of the most visible figures in the union's "radical element" sent away to assist with other organizing campaigns outside of Akron. Among those so redeployed was Charles Lesley, Jimmy Jones's close associate in the Plant 2 tire room.[57]

The combined effects of all this proved decisive. By the spring of 1938, as the recession stretched into a second year and discouragement and desperation set in among the workforce, the sit-down wave had almost completely subsided. As tempers cooled in the tire rooms and curing pits, URW leaders finally managed to obtain the sound organization they had been seeking since the end of the 1936 sit-down strike. But other goals remained more elusive. With shop-floor peace no longer coming at such a high price for Goodyear, it would be another three and a half long years before the company would sign a first union contract with Local 2 to represent its Akron workforce.[58]

## Quiescence and Rebellion in Transappalachia

While by no means a forgotten story, the events that took place in the Rubber Capital of the World between 1936 and 1938 have remained mostly peripheral to the dominant narratives of the formative years of the CIO. More focused on developments in other heavy industries like automobiles and steel; on the polyglot working classes of major cities like Chicago, Detroit, or New York; or on the cultural influences of immigrant ethnic identities and various European socialist traditions, such historical accounts have largely neglected to consider the broader significance of the paradox that unfolded within Akron's tire plants.[59] And compared to this collective picture of the cosmopolitan origins of the labor movement of the 1930s, Akron and its rubber workers surely were exceptional. Unlike the working-class Jews and Catholic immigrants who flocked to new unions in the garment trades, mining, steel, and other key sectors, the rubber workers tended to hail from Protestant backgrounds that were broadly similar to those of their employers. As noted by Daniel Nelson, the rubber workers union's exemplary chronicler, the southern Appalachian roots, rural upbringings, and limited industrial experience that characterized the founding cadre of the URW meant that they often had "little . . . in common" with the prototypical CIO leaders of the period.[60] Furthermore, especially compared to the role they played within a number of other industrial unions in these years, among them the International Ladies' Garment Workers' Union, the United Electrical Workers, and the UAW, neither the Communist Party nor the various socialist formations held much appeal for the membership of the URW. By John House's best estimate, card-carrying Communists among the tens of thousands of workers who passed through the gates at Goodyear "numbered less than five hundred," while the vast majority of the rubber workers, according to Nelson, found Akron's "avowed radicals" to be "redundant and their ideas unappealing."[61]

The focus on these other settings and types of workers has coalesced into a certain kind of conventional wisdom about the social milieus that were at the forefront of the heroic factory struggles of the 1930s. At the same time, it has also resulted in a one-dimensional and ultimately tendentious depiction of the role that rural southern whites played in this decisive period in American labor history—one that, rather ironically, ends up reiterating many of the same erroneous ideas about southern white migrants that employers first articulated when they began recruiting them into midwestern factories back in the 1910s and 1920s. When Appalachian migrants appear at all in historical accounts of the period, they have done so almost exclusively as company loyalists and anti-union reactionaries; or as conservative followers of the likes of Homer Martin, the leader of the right-wing faction within the early UAW, or J. Frank Norris, the Southern Baptist preacher and demagogue who established a beachhead in Depression-era Detroit.[62] Of course, there was some truth to this. Some southern whites in midwestern cities undoubtedly did join vigilante groups like the Black Legion, which were frequently deployed to intimidate union organizers and striking workers (although so too, and by all accounts in far greater numbers, did working- and middle-class natives of the Midwest).[63] Likewise, Homer Martin's oratorical repertoire "full of biblical imagery, moral exhortation, and instructive humor" clearly did speak to southern Appalachian migrants in UAW locals in places like Flint, Anderson, and Muncie, where the former preacher enjoyed considerable popularity for a time (although even those locals were quick to support efforts to depose Martin from the UAW presidency in 1938, as his increasingly vindictive red-baiting, thuggish behavior, and backroom dealings with management became more widely known among the membership).[64] But while the singular attention that has been paid to these instances of conservatism may reveal something about why some rural Appalachian migrants did not rally to the cause of the early industrial union movement, or only to its more parochial expressions, it fails altogether to explain why many more of them found themselves at the center of the same transformative workplace battles that engaged their more urban and cosmopolitan peers.

A fuller appreciation of the particular class experience that took shape along the hillbilly highway begins to clarify the picture. Rather than mutely acquiescing to the treatment foisted upon them by their employers, in Anderson and Muncie, Detroit and Flint, and above all in Akron,

Appalachian newcomers developed a distinctive labor politics all their own during the interwar decades. When the first waves of dispossessed tenant farmers and out-of-work miners began arriving in the industrial Midwest, many did so with lingering attachments to the homes, communities, and lifestyles they had left behind—in some cases, quite adamantly and intentionally so. Recruited explicitly as disposable workhorses, many found that they were disinclined to create permanent attachments to new and frequently hostile communities, or unfamiliar and frequently alienating types of work. Exacerbating matters was the fact that rural Appalachian migrants generally arrived in the North without an industrial trade, at a time when the mass production industries were adopting technological advancements that vastly increased the demand for unskilled and semi-skilled labor. The jobs they ended up taking, in the tire pits at Goodyear or the powerhouse at Ford, did pay far better than the work such migrants could get in the rural South. But within the factory ecosystem itself, these were also likely to be the lowest-paid and most laborious jobs to begin with, as well as those in which the effects of the ever-present speedup inevitably felt the most inhumane. Whether in the impersonal quasi-police states created at the massive auto assembly plants, or the more intimate managerial bureaucracies of places like Guide Lamp or Warner Gear, such jobs also fell under the most intensive supervision of factory foremen, whose authority—especially when exercised capriciously, unreasonably, or simply arrogantly, as it so often was—represented another unfamiliar imposition of industrial life. Not surprisingly, then, when they did not simply quit and go home, or try their luck somewhere else, the formal and informal tactics of resistance deployed by rural southern migrants most commonly indicated a desire to regain a greater measure of autonomy over the rate, method, and general conditions of their labor.

To what extent these attitudes translated into an embrace of the various anti-capitalist projects that took root in American workplaces during these decades—or, no more straightforwardly, into an appreciation for the "sound organization" that an emergent trade union bureaucracy was simultaneously coming to raise to the level of a singular imperative—was another question. In Detroit, Lloyd Jones's path from the cabin churches of southern Pentecostalism to, eventually, the presidency of UAW Local 2 and a seat on the union's international executive board, took him first through the Industrial Workers of the World, which he joined soon after hiring on at Briggs in the early 1930s. Compared to the more ideologically dogmatic party factions on the contemporary left, it is not hard to see why that organization's particular blend of non-doctrinal antiauthoritarianism and democratic control at the workplace might have been an appealing fit for the industrial novices of the hillbilly highway—although considering the IWW's already much-reduced state by the early days of the Transappalachian migration, it is also not surprising that Jones's experience seems to have been relatively rare. And yet, as the events in Akron made so abundantly clear, southern Appalachian newcomers could just as often *behave* like Wobblies: remaining unpersuaded about the value of (or even potential for) non-conflictual relations with their employers; having greater faith in the efficacy of direct action on the shop floor rather than negotiations at the bargaining table; and rebelling against any form of hierarchical command at the workplace, even when the orders were being issued by a worker-led organization like the union.[65]

That they acted like this, again, was more a mark of their particular circumstances within the broader constellation of the interwar industrial working class, rather than an indication of some cultural predisposition that left southern Appalachian migrants constitutionally ill-suited for union discipline, or—worse yet—"lack[ing in] class consciousness," as some of the more dismissive historical accounts have concluded.[66] In fact, the "peace at any price" policy, to quote Goodyear's Cliff Slusser, which the tire builders and pit workers managed to secure from the company at the peak of their sit-down activity, required a great deal of self-conscious coordination. But the object of the Goodyear wildcatters' collective action, while certainly parallel and in many cases overlapping with the efforts of the Local 2 leadership, was not always identical. Pay rates, seniority rights, layoff protections: for southern migrants who did not always think of themselves as permanent members of the midwestern industrial workforce anyway, and for whom regional wage disparities were already so steep to begin with, these union priorities could feel unrelated to their needs and irrelevant to their increasingly transregional identities. Shop-floor issues, and above all the control of production and the exercise of authority in the plants, were far greater preoccupations of the Appalachian rank and file. After all, what did a "fair day's pay [for] a fair day's work" even mean, noted Leslie Johnson, an Alabama-born Goodyear worker, union committeeman, and sit-downer, "when you had a supervisor driving us along like slaves used to be driven"? Given how successful they could be at securing such things for themselves, directly at the point of production, it was no wonder that some balked at the tradeoff that John House and the early URW leaders were prepared to make, of a return to the managerial status quo in exchange for the still-uncertain promise of a union and a contract.[67]

Seen in this light, the hotheads of the Akron tire rooms and curing pits were perhaps not so exceptional to the broader culture of the early CIO as they might have appeared. Take, for instance, the career of Chester Mullin, another Appalachian-born migrant who become a rank-and-file leader at the Kelsey-Hayes Wheel Company in Detroit and in Local 174 of the UAW during the 1930s and 1940s.[68] Particularly popular among the other rural white southerners at Kelsey-Hayes, Mullin was a natural choice to represent his coworkers as a shop steward, as well as on the plant-wide union committee that met regularly with Kelsey-Hayes management to negotiate everything from pay and benefit provisions to a range of shop-floor policies.[69] On the committee, Mullin quickly established himself as a militant, a perennial thorn in the side of both management and Local 174 officialdom alike. In one indicative instance, he was charged with leading an "undisciplined mob of Union workers who left their jobs and by force and violence displaced Company management representatives," leaving one foreman "bruised and injured." The disagreement was over whether the foreman had been improperly promoted over one of the hourly workers in Local 174; as Mullin offered by way of explaining his actions, "we weren't going to wait for the grievance procedure to be followed." In another such episode, which occurred while Local 174 was operating under the World War II–era no-strike pledge, Mullin led a walkout that spread through the entire plant, after a union steward had been discharged for forcibly objecting to the installation of a company "scorekeeper" to monitor workers' productivity. According to the committee chairman, "it took two mass meetings before we finally sold our people on the idea that it was in their best interests to go back, regardless of grievances, and give the committee a chance to iron out the dispute."[70] A "hillbilly anarchist" was how Local 174 vice president Victor Reuther would describe Mullin—and he did not mean it in a nice way.[71]

Like the hotheads in Akron, Mullin increasingly found himself at cross-purposes with the emerging union bureaucracy, and especially so during the war, when the no-strike pledge seemed to deprive him and other Kelsey-Hayes rank and filers of their most effective mechanism for enforcing terms at the workplace. By the summer of 1941, Mullin had risen to the position of union committee chairman at the McGraw Avenue plant; but he was also publicly castigating the Local 174 executive board for "impinging upon our plant autonomy" and spearheading an effort to have the Kelsey-Hayes shop split off from the rest of Local 174 so as to retain more direct control over their bargaining with the company. Among his supporters in the divisive campaign, which consumed the attention of the Detroit-area UAW for a time, was Lloyd Jones, who in his capacity as president of Local 2 wrote to Kelsey-Hayes workers expressing his belief that "with a local charter of [their] own," they would be better able to ensure that "the representatives of the shop are directly responsible to the workers for their actions."[72] As the war continued, and Mullin and his followers continued to stage periodic walkouts over shop-floor issues, it eventually proved too much for both Kelsey-Hayes executives and the union leadership. When Mullin and two other committeemen were finally discharged after an April 1945 walkout, forty-five hundred Kelsey-Hayes workers waited only until V-J Day to launch what became an eight-week wildcat strike to demand their reinstatement. Despite the popularity of the rank-and-file leaders involved, the UAW executive board refused to authorize the strike, and, when the striking workers still balked at going back to work, put the Kelsey-Hayes unit of Local 174 under administratorship and replaced its elected leaders. More than a year later, resentment over the ousting of Mullin and the two other committeemen would continue to simmer inside the factory. In December 1946 the Kelsey-Hayes bargaining committee voted unanimously to request that the international union "reopen negotiations on the reinstatement of the three members who were discharged." "It is our opinion that a grave injustice was done in this case," wrote the committee chairman. "It remains a blot on the history of the UAW-CIO to permit some of its oldest and most militant members to be made martyrs to the cause of unionism."[73]

The language here was a bit melodramatic, to be sure. But it was an excusable offense on the part of Mullin's supporters at Kelsey-Hayes, who must have felt compelled to correct for the dismissive way detractors in Local 174 wrote Mullin off as "the poet of the West Side beer halls," as an "irresponsible" hick from "way down yonder in the paw paw patch"— in other words, as an irredeemable hillbilly.[74] And in a sense, Mullin *was* a martyr to a certain kind of unionism—the kind of unionism that had convulsed industrial workplaces across the Midwest during the 1930s and especially in the latter half of the decade. From the first sit-down strikes in Akron in 1936 until the Supreme Court's 1939 *Fansteel* decision, which effectively outlawed the tactic, there were nearly six hundred sit-down strikes of at least one day's duration in the United States. In the moment, they represented an extraordinary breach of prevailing practice, a complete abnegation of the unquestioned rights of property and a remarkable assertion of workers' moral and legal claim to "legislate and enforce unilateral rules directly regulating relations of production." Not all Transappalachian newcomers to the Midwest became union militants during these years, of course. But that so many of them did, despite the near-universal presumptions about their innate quiescence, suggested something quite profound about why and how much this more direct form of industrial democracy resonated with their particularly vulnerable class position and their increasingly delocalized and migratory working lives.[75]

By the beginning of the 1940s, however, the more radically participatory visions of shop-floor governance that burst forth during the sit-down era would increasingly give way to a state-endorsed system of collective bargaining that, as one labor historian memorably put it, "ate at the vitals of the shop-floor impulse." For Transappalachian migrants like Chester Mullin and the hotheads in the Akron tire rooms—and many other kinds of rank-and-file militants besides—the trade-offs embedded in this new contractualist regime, of fatter paychecks and more comprehensive benefits packages in exchange for a tightly administered system of rules delineated by collective bargaining agreements, grievance procedures, and no-strike pledges, could appear to give up too much of what mattered most of all. And for the more experienced industrial workers and seasoned political activists who filled the ranks of the trade union bureaucracy that came to jointly administer this new industrial order—the same working-class milieus that had harbored such antagonism for the poor white southerners who began arriving in their midst after World War I—the "hillbilly anarchist" emerged as a new version of an old problem. Stubbornly recalcitrant, too quick to act, prone to disruptive, violent, or otherwise anti-collectivist behavior,[76] unschooled in the disciplined procedures of "modern" industrial unionism—much had changed since the first trainloads of green peas and "snake eaters" had shown up in the urban-industrial Midwest, but one thing that had not was the collective sense that the Transappalachian working-class represented a fundamentally problematic segment of the twentieth-century industrial workforce, a working-class "other" at the heat of the American labor movement and the broader liberal Democratic political order that came to orbit around it. Condemned equally for the quiescence and their rebelliousness, this was the ultimate paradox of the hillbilly highway, and one whose legacy would shape regional and national politics for decades to come.[77]

As for Mullin himself, after his 1945 discharge he would never work at Kelsey-Hayes again. Efforts to win his reinstatement went nowhere, and he ceased to play an active role in union politics in Detroit. By 1948 he had drifted on, to a job at Kaiser Frazer, a newly formed car company that briefly completed with the larger automakers, and started paying dues to UAW Local 142. After that, he is too difficult to trace.[78]

CHAPTER FOUR

# An Other America

HILLBILLY GHETTOS AFTER WORLD WAR II

*"These migrants are United States citizens, free to roam anywhere they wish. But they have turned the streets of Chicago into a lawless free-for-all with their primitive jungle tactics."*[1]

—WALTER DEVEREUX, CHIEF INVESTIGATOR,
CHICAGO CRIME COMMISSION (1957)

*"And there will be more of these music-filled, miserable country neighborhoods springing up in the cities of the other America."*[2]

—MICHAEL HARRINGTON, *THE OTHER AMERICA* (1962)

IF THE HILLBILLY HIGHWAY produced a singular work of art, it is Harriette Arnow's social realist novel *The Dollmaker*, published in 1954. A moving depiction of the struggles endured by an eastern Kentucky family that relocates to Detroit during World War II, and the extraordinary physical and emotional labors that the young mother, Gertie Nevels, puts toward keeping the family together, *The Dollmaker* is also a work of semi-autobiography. Arnow, who grew up in a small mill-town on the Cumberland River before attending Berea College, hailed from a rather more urban and middle-class background than does Gertie. But in other ways their stories closely overlap. Like Gertie, Arnow left Kentucky for Detroit during the war, following a husband who moved there to find work. And like Gertie, Arnow made her first home in Detroit in a public housing development that had been hastily erected to accommodate the recent flood of migrants, drawn to the city by the wartime economic boom. In the novel, the Nevels family finds itself living in a temporary housing project not-so-comfortably nestled between an airport and a steel mill, which upon first encounter Gertie describes as "rows of little shed-like buildings, their low roofs covered with snow, the walls of some strange gray-green stuff that seemed neither brick, wood, nor stone." Its real-life counterpart, a similarly unnatural-looking development that sat along a busy set of railroad tracks in northeastern Detroit, was called the Emerson Homes.[3]

Places like the Emerson Homes were fraught terrain during these years. More than four million southerners left the South during the 1940s—roughly twice as many as in any previous decade of the twentieth century, and more than three times the number that had migrated out of the region in the Depression-hobbled 1930s. Most headed to industrial cities along the Atlantic seaboard, in the industrial Midwest, and in the Far West, where opportunities for work in defense-related production jobs, or in ancillary sectors battened on the recent resurgence of economic activity, were essentially inexhaustible. Living space was not so limitless, however, and acute housing shortages were the inevitable result across much of urban America. In the most densely industrialized Detroit neighborhoods, where Arnow and her fictional alter ego settled, populations increased during the 1940s at a rate that surpassed the commensurate increase in available housing by as much as 60 percent.[4] Emergency construction of public housing developments like the Emerson Homes, meanwhile, barely addressed the shortage problem—while introducing new issues. In February 1942, less than a mile from Emerson, white Detroiters from surrounding neighborhoods rioted at the opening of the Sojourner Truth Homes, a wartime housing project that had been designed specifically to house Black defense workers. At least forty were injured in the incident, and more than two hundred were arrested.[5]

Within the contested racial ecology of wartime Detroit, southern whites like Harriette Arnow occupied an ambiguous middle ground. They did not encounter anything like the organized resistance that greeted the Sojourner Truth residents and other Black migrants from the South. But the reception that Detroit's longer-tenured inhabitants granted the city's southern white newcomers could hardly have been described as welcoming. Mean-spirited jokes about "ignorant hillbillies," Arnow later recalled, would make regular appearances in Detroit newspapers in the years when she arrived in the city. It was not uncommon to encounter landlords who posted "No Southerners" signs in the windows of rental properties, and city officials were known to engage in all sorts of public hand-wringing about the deleterious effects that "Dixie Whites" were having on the communities in which they were arriving in growing numbers. "Detroit was a good town till da hillbillies come," one of Gertie Nevels's neighbors—a self-described "dacent, respectable, religious good American"—spits at her at one point in the novel. "An den Detroit went tu hell."[6]

At times, the suspicion and resentment that white migrants from Appalachia and other parts of the rural South aroused among their new neighbors could take on an even darker cast. When, in June 1943, the city exploded in one of the worst race riots in the country's history—which left thirty-four people dead and hundreds wounded, most of them Black— local leaders and opinion-makers tripped over themselves to lay blame for the orgy of violence on "ignorant Negroes and southern whites," as mayor Edward Jeffries put it in the riot's aftermath. Despite southern-born whites accounting for only about 6 percent of Detroit's population at the time, Jefferies and others were quick to attribute what happened to "Kentucky 'hillbilly' and Georgia 'red neck' notions of white domination," which had imposed a "predominantly Southern white psychology" on the otherwise blameless city. In a strange twist, Detroiters' popular scapegoating of the city's marginal population of southern outsiders echoed the nativist hostility that had targeted immigrants and ethnic Americans in the wake of World War I and the 1919 strike wave—and which, in turn, had played such a critical role in spurring on the first great waves of the Transappalachian migration. Even after a report by the Michigan State Department of Social Welfare concluded that roughly 75 percent of those arrested in the riot had been in Detroit since well before the war, some city officials still bandied about the idea of imposing an immediate ban on all further southern migration into the city, "white and black."[7]

The exaggerated if not altogether false accounts of the "southern roots" of the 1943 Detroit race riot recalled the stereotypes of an inveterately reactionary hillbilly *lumpen* that had first taken root in midwestern workplaces during the decades between the world wars. They also prefigured a new anxiety, in Detroit and elsewhere throughout the region, which stemmed less from uncharitable ideas about the type of workers southern whites might be, and more from equally uncharitable ones about the kinds of neighbors they would make and communities they would form. By 1951, in fact, a citywide survey of Motor City residents found that more than one in five respondents named "poor southern whites" or "hillbillies" as the most "undesirable" group in the city—almost four times the number of Detroiters who answered "foreigners," nearly twice the number who chose Black Americans, and second only to "gangsters" and "criminals" among survey responses. Speaking more anecdotally, a reporter for the *Chicago Tribune* soon thereafter observed that the influx of southern white migrants who had "descended on Chicago like a plague of locusts in the last few years" were "currently the number one concern of police and crime experts, school and church authorities, organizations such as the Mayor's Committee on New Residents, the Chicago Commission on Human Relations, the Uptown Chicago commission, Northtown Ministerial association, and others." If anybody was left, presumably they just had not been paying attention to what one quoted source referred to as the worst thing to "hit our town since the Chicago fire."[8]

As the wartime housing shortages evolved into a full-bore, region-wide urban crisis, and as many of the same inner-city neighborhoods into which so many southern whites had crowded during the war years became increasingly visible problem-areas over the decades that followed, resentful urbanites increasingly came to fixate on the question of how growing pockets of poor and working-class southern Appalachian migrants would alter the social landscape of midwestern cities. It was in this context that a new and distinctly Transappalachian creation emerged: the so-called hillbilly ghetto. In the two decades between 1945 and 1965, in both large and small midwestern cities, zones of concentrated poverty where white southerners made up sizable portions of the population became suddenly ubiquitous features of the Transappalachian migration. For many recent arrivals from the rural South, such neighborhoods—places like Chicago's Uptown, Cincinnati's Over-the-Rhine, Indianapolis's Stringtown, or a part of Muncie that locals commonly referred to as Shedtown—were often inevitable landing points: urban thresholds where cheap rent and familiar faces helped smooth the transition to city living. In the eyes of longer-tenured residents, however, those same neighborhoods appeared as growing sinkholes of rural backwardness and urban dysfunction, incontrovertible signs of the economic, social, and cultural deterioration that heralded the onrushing decline of the American inner city. And even though all, or even most, southern-born whites in the Midwest did not ultimately settle in culturally and economically homogenous urban ghettos composed primarily of other white southerners, the proliferation of such neighborhoods during the peak decades of the Transappalachian migration attracted an inordinate amount of contemporary attention and concern.[9] "These neighborhoods of Southern mountaineers," one reporter noted in the mid-1950s, in one of dozens of such articles that appeared in midwestern newspapers and national periodicals around this time, had become "as easily recognizable" as any of the more familiar quarters of minority group impoverishment clustered in the region's rotting urban cores. "Down from the hills and into the slums" was how the reporter summed up the phenomenon.[10]

Given its prominence in the moment, it is something of an irony that the hillbilly ghetto has disappeared so thoroughly from standard accounts of the postwar urban crisis. It is not that these accounts, which almost invariably take the Black ghetto as their spatial and thematic focus, misrepresent the "color" of the urban crisis. Rather, by reducing the role of white urban dwellers in this period to a singular one of resistance and then flight, they misrepresent something about the nature of working-class whiteness in postwar America—a lesson Gertie Nevels, for example, learned all too clearly from her ill-tempered neighbor. Far from a monolithic category of identity, the experience of the hillbilly ghetto made clear that for some urban residents, whiteness was a much more contingent and ambiguous social position during these years. Arriving in midwestern cities at the same moment that longer-established and more affluent white residents were abandoning them in accelerating numbers; living in neighborhoods that more closely resembled—and oftentimes overlapped with—nearby inner-city communities of color, rather than more distant, lily-white suburbs, Transappalachian migrants embodied tendencies that were irreconcilable with the dominant modes of midcentury whiteness. To contemporaries, the hillbilly ghetto posed many of the same social problems that other ghettos did—in fact, it was with the hillbilly ghetto in mind, as much as with more familiar Black and brown ones, that policymakers, city officials, and liberal elites would begin to formulate new ways of talking about and addressing the confounding persistence of urban poverty amid the generalized prosperity of postwar America. The hillbilly ghetto, it turns out, is as much a part of the narrative of the postwar urban crisis as the Black ghetto. And in the racially uncertain position in which the hillbilly ghetto found itself during these years, an ambiguous political future for the Transappalachian white working class would begin to emerge.

## The Hillbilly Ghetto Takes Shape

Even if Highway 41—one branch of the famous "Dixie Highway" that runs between Chicago and Miami, designed by the early twentieth-century real estate developer Carl G. Fisher and later inspiration to legions of blues singers and country musicians—did not cut right through the heart of Monteagle, Tennessee, it was probably inevitable that a generation of Grundy County natives coming of age during and after World War II would find themselves drawn to the road north. Farming had always been a relatively small-scale affair in that hilly stretch along the Lower Cumberland Plateau, just a dozen miles or so from the Alabama border; and automation was rapidly transforming what remained of the mining and logging activity that traditionally had been the most reliable supply of industrial wage-work in the area. The Tennessee Consolidated Coal Company, the largest outfit operating mines locally, began introducing auger and other machine-assisted drilling techniques in the Grundy County mines in the years immediately after the war, with dramatic effects for the local workforce. By 1950 TCC had opted to close its largest mines around the old company town of Palmer, and replaced them with a new, fully mechanized mine in nearby Whitwell. More than seven hundred men had worked in the Palmer mines at their peak, but by 1954 TCC employed fewer than a hundred fifty in the area—a rate of decline that the local United Mine Workers union would resist forcefully, if ultimately in vain, in a series of violent skirmishes over the subsequent decade. For all but the most committed, the writing was already on the wall. "There was nothing to do here," recalled Gene Myers, whose family was put out of work as the mines around Tracy City began closing down. "Killing squirrels, that's about it."[11]

For Grundy County natives—especially those who, like Gene, grew up "down the mountain" in Pelham and the other unincorporated valley communities nestled into the base of the plateau—the journey north most often pointed them toward Cleveland, Ohio. When Gene left Pelham at sixteen, he went to Cleveland because his father, some uncles, and an older brother had already established roots in the city—a pattern that was common within Grundy County at the time. "Lots of people from around here went to Cleveland," said Janelle Taylor, another Pelham native who, at the very end of the 1940s, moved there as a young girl with her family. "They were always either going or coming or visiting. It was *the place* to go from this area." And Grundy County was not the only southern locale that was sending people to Cleveland during these years: by one estimate, a greater proportion of migrants from southern Appalachian states settled in Cleveland than in any major midwestern city during the 1950s, with at least forty thousand arriving over the course of a decade in which the city's overall population declined by more than 4 percent.[12]

"These newcomers," noted a contemporary account in the *Cleveland Press*, "have come from the mountains and the meadows of Dixie in such numbers that their impact is felt in every section of the city." But it was more than just their sheer numbers that made the new arrivals stand out, the *Press* reporter explained. "Unlike the relatively few white-collar Southerners here who live generally in the suburbs, these former coal miners, farmers and mountaineers work almost exclusively in factories and live overwhelmingly in the city proper," typically in Cleveland's

"shabbier residential areas." Like Gene and Janelle, when Hamp Nunley
left Grundy County, he gravitated to one "shabby" neighborhood in particular, an industrial area south of Lake Erie and the Collinwood Railroad Yards known as Five Points, which was the primary settlement zone
for Grundy County natives in Cleveland. "I had some folks around in east
Cleveland there," Hamp explained. "I had a brother and a sister there; and
then I had cousins and an uncle. They was all right near where Lake Erie
is at." So many southerners lived in Five Points, in fact, that, as Janelle
recalled, "there weren't really any northerners that we were acquainted
with—with the exception of the people that worked in the grocery store."
By the 1950s as many as one-third of the white students enrolled in the
local public school, East Clark Elementary, had been born in the South;
and local music halls like the Eclair Theatre, on St. Clair Avenue, or bars
like the Buckeye, on East 152nd Street, were well known as spots where
southerners gathered to hang out, enjoy a beer, and listen to music from
back home.[13]

Prior to World War II, hillbilly ghettos like Cleveland's Five Points did
not really exist in the urban-industrial Midwest. Especially in the wake
of the "back-to-the-farm" movement of the first half of the Depression
decade, this was most often simply a function of numbers: in very few
locations were sufficient concentrations of permanently relocated southerners in place to produce such dense migrant enclaves. A city like Akron,
with its distinctively Transappalachian rubber workforce, was again
much more the exception than the rule in this regard during the interwar
decades. Still, even there, southern-born heads of households accounted
for no more than 30 percent of residents in any single ward of the city, even
in the most densely working-class districts. In rural areas that depended
on migratory labor networks, such as the tomato fields of central Indiana
or the onion marshes of northwest Ohio, it was not unheard of for locals
to complain of the sudden appearance of "bad little towns" composed of
migrants from Kentucky or Tennessee during the 1920s and 1930s. But
population influxes of this sort were typically quite seasonal and would
vanish as quickly as they had appeared when the crop was picked. Far
more typical of these years was a city like Flint. As one local report from
the 1930s noted, southern white migrants in Flint confronted various economic and social restrictions on their "choice of residence"—among them
the cost of housing, the proximity of industrial activity, and the "frequent
objections to them as renters." Yet they demonstrated no observable tendency toward "residential segregation similar to the foreign language colo-
nies," and could be found living "in all areas of workingmen's homes."[14]

The unprecedented migratory event that was World War II altered the calculus of southern Appalachian settlement in the Midwest.[15] The exigencies of war mobilization and the new geographies of production created by the defense boom uprooted and transplanted Americans of all races, classes, and regional backgrounds during these years. But few were as likely to depart their place of birth as natives of the Upper South. In just the first three years of the war, the most rural districts of southern Appalachia saw their population shrink by roughly 10 percent. Migration rates were most negative in the most economically marginal parts of the region, especially along the Cumberland and Allegheny Plateaus and in and around the Blue Ridge Mountains. But even in more fertile agricultural zones, like those throughout the Tennessee River Valley, wartime population losses could be staggering. In Humphreys County, Tennessee, some seventy-five miles west of Nashville, the population declined by nearly 20 percent between April 1940 and November 1943, and by 1945 had shrunk to the size it had been in the 1870s. Only in the states of the old Southwest and the Great Plains, still reeling from the back-to-back calamities of the agricultural depression of the 1920s and the Dust Bowl of the 1930s, were there similar rates of exodus in this period. And yet what further distinguished the regional outflow from the Upper South, even from some of those other areas, was that it not only continued into the immediate postwar period but even accelerated. Seven of the ten states with the largest net losses in interstate migration during the 1950s lay within the footprint of the Transappalachian migration. Not only for the region's rural-agricultural population but also, increasingly, its rural-industrial workforce, the watershed of World War II extended well into subsequent decades, as the extractive industries that had transformed the southern countryside during the first half of the twentieth century moved rapidly to mechanize production, or else began to decamp altogether.[16]

By every measure, the decades between the 1940s and the 1960s represented both a numerically larger phase in the half-century-long Transappalachian migration, and a generally poorer one. Annual migration outflows were as much as two and a half times greater in the later period than they had been in the interwar decades, and in the 1950s every state in the region except Georgia and Mississippi experienced its highest single-decade loss in net migration of the twentieth century. While farmers still registered the highest rates of out-migration during the 1940s, in the following decade they were overtaken by the region's rural nonfarm population, who accounted for more than half of net migration losses during the 1950s.[17] Although exclusively agricultural counties in the Upper South still tended to exhibit the highest levels of absolute poverty in the region, the forces of displacement were often further advanced where farming had already given way to rural industry, leaving residents of those areas little to fall back on when work at the local mine or sawmill began to dry up. In either case, rural-agricultural and rural-industrial counties were on average considerably poorer than those counties with more significant employment in manufacturing or high-wage services (which, not incidentally, had the lowest rates of out-migration during the postwar decades), and coal-dependent counties began to undergo a population exodus that would prove to be quite nearly catastrophic. As the southern Appalachian mining workforce collapsed over the course of the 1950s, net migration losses for these areas soared as high as 37 percent. After being one of the fastest growing parts of the region during the first decades of the twentieth century, the coalfields of eastern Kentucky and West Virginia—where per capita incomes stood at only half the national average—saw their overall populations drop by as much as 10 or 15 percent between 1945 and 1960.[18]

Of course, all of these southern Appalachian evacuees did not relocate to the factory-dense region north of the Ohio River. But millions of them did, and it was in this context that places like Five Points emerged suddenly and noticeably across the landscape of the postwar Midwest. In the Uptown neighborhood of Chicago, once a fashionable area along Lake Michigan north of the Loop before it became perhaps the most notorious hillbilly ghetto of the postwar period, white southerners eventually came to make up as much as 60 percent of the local population in certain census tracts. In Indianapolis, where the southern-born population exploded from under 15 to nearly 25 percent of the city's total in the years between 1940 and 1960, neighborhoods like Stringtown, a traditional port of entry for successive waves of urban in-migrants since the nineteenth century, became almost exclusively associated with southern white newcomers.[19] As one longtime resident of the neighborhood noted, beginning during the war years, "about the only people that ever'd come to Stringtown were from Kentucky"—or, more generally, "Appalachia people," in the inelegant phrasing of another local observer. Similar influxes transformed dense inner-city communities like Over-the-Rhine and Lower Price Hill in Cincinnati; the Jefferson Corridor area, Midtown, and the Briggs neighborhood in southwest Detroit; and places like Franklinton on Columbus, Ohio's west side and the East End neighborhood in Dayton. And it was not only the larger cities in the region where such visible migrant clusters began appearing after the war. Southern Appalachian enclaves sprouted up in Middletown, Ohio, birthplace of Armco Steel, and Peoria, Illinois, home to the Caterpillar Tractor Company; in working-class suburbs like Hazel Park, Warren, and Madison Heights, outside of Detroit; and even in bedroom communities like South Lebanon, Ohio, where one reliable source estimated the population to be "composed of well over 90 percent Kentuckians" during the immediate postwar decades.[20]

Despite the notable variation in the types of communities toward which southern Appalachian newcomers gravitated, the economic composition of these increasingly ubiquitous migrant enclaves proved more similar than not. As the *Cleveland Press* had noted, there were relatively few white-collar professionals among the southern whites arriving in that city in surging numbers, an observation borne out by occupational and earnings profiles within different types of residential communities.[21] Southern whites living in Cleveland's suburbs, according to one local study, were more likely to be employed in skilled trades than those living in the city proper during these years—but both groups were overwhelmingly employed in blue-collar work, and average wages for southern whites living within the Cleveland city limits were actually slightly higher than they were for those in the suburbs.[22] According to another postwar survey, nearly 80 percent of all southern white migrants to the Cincinnati metropolitan area, whether they resided in the suburbs or the city, found themselves living in communities where the average income was below the national median—a ratio closer to the concentration of metropolitan Cincinnati's Black population in below-average income neighborhoods (86 percent), than to either Cincinnati-born whites (66 percent) or white migrants from places other than the South (55 percent).[23] In Hazel Park—which earned the nickname "Hazel-tucky" around this time because of the large numbers of Transappalachian migrants who settled there—white-collar professionals made up only 9 percent of the workforce even as late as 1980, while the median family income hovered at just over half the average for the Detroit metropolitan area throughout the postwar period.[24]

Most typically, especially initially, rural southern whites established beachheads where newcomers to industrial communities had always been most likely to concentrate—in poor or declining neighborhoods, where rents were relatively cheap, single-family dwellings had already been broken up into multifamily units or boardinghouses catering to solo migrants, and the proximity to industrial sites rendered neighborhoods less physically attractive and desirable to begin with. As one contemporary study of Chicago noted, "ecological factors"—key among them "the availability of cheap, furnished flats and easy access to industrial plants"—played as large a role as "in-group ties" in determining where southern whites were settling in that city. Property values remained low in Cleveland's Five Points, according to an assessment of that neighborhood, "because of its advantageous location to nearby industries and transportation and occupancy desirability for the low income group." But as the newly relocated quickly realized, the advantages of proximity and affordability came with their attendant trade-offs. For Hamp Nunley, fresh from the Tennessee countryside, acclimating to life in a heavily industrial neighborhood like Five Points was among the hardest adjustments he had to make after leaving Grundy County. "See, that coal smoke—I couldn't hardly stand that smell at all, because I wasn't used to it." Like Gertie Nevels in *The Dollmaker*, similarly crammed between rail yards and factories in northeastern Detroit, Hamp's initial revulsion was downright visceral. "I couldn't stand the smell of Cleveland," he would recall years later.[25]

Comparable forces tended to concentrate migrants in neighborhoods south of the White River in Muncie, where the vast majority of the city's industrial activity and working-class housing had been located since the turn of the twentieth century. By the 1950s fully 75 percent of Muncie's southern migrant population lived south of the river—most in a factory-dense zone just beyond the downtown business district; or else in and immediately around Shedtown. Located along Muncie's southwestern margin, Shedtown had long been one of the poorest parts of town—at least since its earliest denizens, many of whom arrived with the Indiana gas boom and the sudden expansion of the local glass industry, had been forced to live in crate-and-cardboard shacks they hastily assembled for themselves. As one Muncie native later recalled, after the neighborhood had become almost exclusively associated with recent migrants from Kentucky and Tennessee, in the "pecking order of residential areas . . . the absolute bottom in Muncie was the region called Shedtown."[26]

Aside from their location within the larger geography of the city, hillbilly ghettos were often marked by a set of other common features. Substandard or deteriorating housing stock was one of them. In Shedtown, a real estate appraisal produced on the eve of the war found nothing but "one- and two-room houses built by the occupant," all in "poor condition" and "practically no homes equipped with a flush toilet." That was before the wartime population boom left many of the newest arrivals to the city, in the words of one local columnist, "tearing their hair" to find decent housing—so much so that one family had moved into the back half of an unused barn while another had been reduced to taking up living quarters in a 288-square-foot chicken coop.[27] By the end of the 1940s, the downtown

Kentucky-born migrants Lizabelle and Scott Brandenberg in their home in the Shedtown neighborhood of Muncie, in 1937. This photograph originally appeared in *Life* magazine, where the accompanying caption identified Transappalachian migrants like the Brandenbergs as being "at the bottom of Muncie's social strata."

Margaret Bourke-White/The LIFE Picture Collection/Shutterstock

core ringed by Detroit's circumferential Grand Boulevard had become home to the city's "worst slum and blighted areas," according to the Detroit Housing Commission—and had also been given over almost entirely to the city's newest arrivals. Migrants to the city outnumbered native Detroiters nearly five to one in neighborhoods within the central city, and fully 50 percent of the population there hailed originally from southern states. "Most recent arrivals tend to be highly concentrated in the area within four miles of City Hall," noted the managing director of Detroit's United Community Services, "[an] area [that] includes thousands of dwellings in various stages of decay and deterioration, the majority of which are utterly unfit for human habitation." Similar patterns obtained in city after city across the region. In Indianapolis, southern white migrants were disproportionately represented in "the least desirable housing in the poverty areas"; in Cincinnati, the neighborhoods where "inferior housing conditions" were more the norm than the exception. In Uptown, more than one-quarter of the residential buildings were in a state of serious decay by the end of the war—among the highest incidence of blight anywhere in Chicago.[28]

Overcrowded living quarters was another common attribute of the urban neighborhoods where southern white migrants were most likely to concentrate. In some instances, this was a function of the characteristically larger family units that migrants brought with them from rural Appalachia—the rising numbers of "families of six or more persons," which the Lynds attributed to Muncie's "considerable minority group of indigent Southern mountain families." In Cincinnati, such families were half as likely as native Cincinnatians to live in single-family homes, and twice as likely to live in homes with fewer than three rooms. But residential overcrowding in hillbilly ghettos was just as often an indication of the way profit-minded landlords had transformed the physical environment of declining urban neighborhoods as it was a reflection of the types of families that ended up living there. Uptown, which had once been a "lovely district; all residences, lovely homes," as one longtime resident would recall, was a case in point. Uptown went through a steady residential downgrading over the first half of the twentieth century, as "many desirable people moved farther north" and property owners began relentlessly subdividing the neighborhood's historic buildings into a bevy of one- and two-room apartments tailored for working-class renters. At the onset of the postwar period, only 5 percent of Uptown's residential properties remained owner-occupied, and the neighborhood was home to a larger concentration of rooming houses than any other community in Chicago. By the beginning of the 1960s, Uptown had the highest population density of any neighborhood in the city outside of the poor Black ghetto of Lawndale.[29]

Like overcrowded apartments and decrepit buildings, high rates of residential turnover tended to distinguish hillbilly ghettos from their urban surroundings as well. Southern migrants moved frequently, so much so that it was one of the most regularly remarked upon characteristics of these newly formed communities. A reporter for the *Cincinnati Enquirer* noted one short block in a local pocket of southern whites that functioned as "staging area" for new arrivals, where "in the last six months at least half a dozen families have moved on and off" the street—in some cases on their way to more permanent residences in the city, in other cases to return "back home disappointed." Another study of households in a Detroit neighborhood that was fast giving way to newcomers "from [the] hills of neighboring states [in the] Deep South" found that nearly half had lived at no single location for longer than five years, while 10 percent had moved more than ten times over the same period. "There's just continual moving in, moving out, moving in, moving out," remarked one older Stringtown resident, voicing a familiar complaint about the neighborhood's southern Appalachian newcomers. "Used to be all homeowners when I moved up here," another echoed; "[now] its more of a transient lot." The pattern was so notable among southern migrants living on Chicago's Near West Side that one contemporary observer described a pervasive "transient psychology" that made poor southern whites the bane of employers and landlords alike. Another noted that in Dayton's East End, landlords would only rent to southerners by the week, so that if they "slip off quietly for Eastern Kentucky, at least the landlord will only lose a week's rent, not a month's rent."[30]

Residential mobility of this sort was typical of low-income neighborhoods generally, of course, and reflected the acute housing insecurity that many rural migrants experienced upon their initial arrival in northern cities. So it was for James and Donna Fair, two migrants from the Carolina Piedmont who settled in Uptown with their seven children in the mid-1950s. The first two apartments they found to live in were in "only marginal" condition, and the third was so infested with rats that one of their children began showing up to school with bite marks. The city eventually ordered their landlord to address the problem, but he refused. When the Fairs finally found a new place to live and moved—for the fourth time in four years—their landlord sued them for $176 in back rent.[31]

At the same time, the high rates of return migration that always distinguished life along the hillbilly highway also tended to accentuate the dilapidated conditions of these emerging migrant enclaves. Just as it was the economically better-off migrants, especially those who worked in the professions, who could most easily make the return trip South, so too was it the poorest migrants, like the Fairs, with less to return to or with, who most often found themselves "stuck" in these postwar ghettos, shuttling between derelict apartments and vermin-infested buildings.[32] For longer-term residents, it was a common mistake during these years to assign responsibility for decaying buildings, crumbling sidewalks, and trash-strewn front lawns or back alleys to the pick-up-and-go mentality of a migrant population with no investment in the larger community. "We just can't seem to get them interested in anything to make this a nicer place to live," one Uptown native complained about his new, southern-born neighbors. "I don't know what it is," echoed a Stringtown resident, "but it's like they don't care if their yard looks like the city dump." In fact, it was often the opposite problem. As neighborhoods like Stringtown and Uptown became magnets for a transregional working class increasingly bereft of resources, the residential neglect that old-timers tended to associate with hillbilly disinterest or "transiency" emerged as one more sign of the intensifying poverty of these declining urban zones.[33]

By the beginning of the 1960s, conditions within such communities were, if not equivalent, then certainly comparable to that encountered in the other growing urban ghettos of the period, whether populated by similarly transplanted Black southerners; migrants from Puerto Rico and the wider Caribbean on the East Coast and Mexico on the West Coast; or American Indians throughout the country's interior. In Muncie, in the three census tracts that were home to the largest concentrations of southern migrants, between 20 and 35 percent of all families lived below the federal poverty threshold—as compared to just 5 or 10 percent of families in parts of the city where southern whites were least represented.[34] In Columbus, Ohio, indices of poverty, residential overcrowding, educational attainment, and single-parent households were all likewise significantly worse in neighborhoods inhabited by white southerners than in the city overall.[35] In Uptown—"seedy, dreary, congested, despairing," as the *Chicago Daily News* described it around this time; "Appalachia in Chicago"—more than one in four apartments lacked adequate plumbing. Poverty-related health hazards, like lead poisoning, were rampant, and the neighborhood recorded the second-highest tuberculosis rates anywhere in the city.[36] When Cincinnati's Community Health and Welfare Council compiled a "Problem Index" to rank the city's neighborhoods according to a range of quality-of-life criteria, Over-the-Rhine finished in thirtieth place overall, out of a possible thirty-three. According to the director of health education for the city's Health Department, southern Appalachian migrants living there, in Lower Price Hill, and in other such corners of the city, exhibited higher infant and maternal mortality rates than the rest of Cincinnati, were more likely to experience persistent malnutrition, and were significantly less likely to have received vaccinations against common viruses. "Severe dental disease," meanwhile, was "almost universal." Southern-born white children in Cincinnati's schools also showed significantly higher rates of "retardation," dropped out of high school at faster rates than any other group in the city, and ultimately averaged nearly two full years less education than did white residents native to the city.[37]

It bears repeating that most southern Appalachian migrants in the Midwest did not end up living in such neighborhoods. Some left the South with more to begin with and settled more naturally into middle-class communities in the North. Many others did well enough upon arrival that they were able to pass through hillbilly ghettos fairly quickly or not at all, opting instead for more stable areas within the urban core; or, more likely, for outlying suburbs where it was possible for blue-collar workers to qualify for a mortgage and purchase property—granted, of course, that their skin was white. By the 1970s, in fact, as the historian James Gregory has found, southern-born whites living in the Great Lakes states were roughly two and a half times more likely to reside in suburban areas or smaller townships than they were in the region's larger cities—a ratio that not only more than reversed itself in the experience of southern-born African Americans, but which outstripped that of locally born whites as well. Nevertheless, fact and perception do not always align. The reality was, despite their only partial representativeness, hillbilly ghettos attracted an extraordinary amount of popular attention in the decades between the end of World War II and the beginning of the War on Poverty. And as these suddenly visible enclaves of poor and working-class white migrants began to leave a noticeable imprint on the postwar urban landscape, so too did they begin to attract an increasingly hostile kind of attention from their new northern neighbors.[38]

## Heavens and Jungles

The dense pockets of Transappalachian poverty that emerged across the region during the postwar period stood out for reasons that went beyond broken-down buildings and overcrowded apartments. Hillbilly ghettos were also marked by distinctive ways of life and patterns of social activity that troubled longtime residents, city leaders, journalists, and other outsiders. The way these southern newcomers talked and dressed, their leisure habits, the music they liked, how they worshipped God, even what they ate and how they drank—all these and more stood at odds with norms and conventions embraced by middle-class midwesterners. Such aberrant behavior would have made hillbilly ghettos problematic zones of communal activity in any moment. But in the context of the manifold challenges confronting American cities during the postwar period, when the economic and racial composition of urban areas was so in flux, they appeared particularly menacing. Ultimately, although they did not always speak of it in precisely these terms, it was the class-inflected nature of these different cultural practices that made northern city-dwellers so uncomfortable. Nowhere was this clearer than in the outright hostility midwestern natives often directed against the most visible communal institutions of the hillbilly ghetto, whose appearance marked the emergence of a palpably rural and explicitly southern working-class subculture in the heart of the region's rapidly transitioning urban centers.

Few institutions generated as much controversy in this way as the so-called hillbilly tavern. Drinking culture, of course, is an important component of the social life of many working-class communities.[39] But in the eyes of both Transappalachian newcomers and their often-unwelcoming neighbors, identifiably southern drinking establishments, which proliferated in large and small midwestern cities during the post-war influx, assumed an added significance. Northern urbanites, for their part, frequently fixated on southern bars when marking the progress of neighborhood change, seeing in the sudden multiplication of such culturally alien landmarks—"the one institution they have originated up North," as a writer for *Harper's* sneeringly put it—one of the clearer indications of the shifting demographics of the larger city. Southern migrants did not disagree; marked as outsiders by not only their class status but also their rural and regional backgrounds, they embraced these informal spaces of collective leisure as rare locations in the urban Midwest which they could call their own. "The bars are one of the social gathering places in the city," one Uptown resident explained. "When you get off work you go right to one of the hillbilly bars, where you're among your own people and you feel free and don't have to worry about how your voice sounds, how you're dressing." For many resident Chicagoans, the bars that came to line Uptown's commercial thoroughfares and seemed to spill forth with "drunks of both sexes, loud screeching jukeboxes of idiotic music, arguments, knifings, crime, empty whiskey and beer containers in doorways," may have appeared as breeding grounds for a particularly threatening and vice-ridden southern "low culture." But for thousands of displaced southerners, it was precisely because of the familiar faces and well-lubricated excitement that could be found in the growing number of beer joints and honky-tonks that dotted the area that Uptown earned its more affectionate nickname: "Hillbilly Heaven."[40]

In addition to sharing common places of origin, patrons of these establishments often shared the same place or at least type of work, and they imbibed a spirited, working-class camaraderie along with their pints of beer. Contemporary descriptions emphasized how the prevalence of blue-collar attire made it "easy enough to tell a hillbilly dive from the ordinary saloon," as a reporter for the *Chicago Tribune* put it. "Men are in work pants, coveralls, leather motorcycle jackets, and Presley sideburns. (In some 30 joints, we only saw one 'square' in a suit.)" A Detroit bar that attracted southern migrants was invoked in similar terms: "Clientele has been in the habit of coming in 'as is,' some in usual street clothes, some in working clothes and a few in modified but obviously hillbilly style, with oversized hats."[41] In the early years after Amanda Hicks and her husband, Omer, relocated from Fentress County to Dayton, Ohio, where Omer got a job at the Frigidaire plant, Amanda would go whole days without seeing him. "Now, on the weekends, all of the guys would get together on the weekends; and, like, go to work on Friday, and then I would see him again on Sunday, because they were at pool halls, beer joints, or wherever."[42] When he was not working one of his two jobs in Dayton—the first as a mechanic in a General Motors factory; the second as a short-order cook in a nearby restaurant—Wesley Reagan, another Fentress County native, also "drank a lot of beer." "I never drank a beer at home in my life. I never took a drink of anything by myself. I was always with friends," usually his coworkers or people he knew from back home, and typically at one of the many Dayton bars that had country records on the jukebox. "A lot of [the bars] had music in them—all of them had some," Wesley recalled.[43]

As much as the southern accents and the working-class clothing, the ubiquity of country music marked these establishments as distinctive from the "ordinary saloon." In 1943 the recording industry magazine *Billboard* recounted the story of William Levin's Jefferson Inn, an "East Side working class spot" that, thanks to the wartime population boom, had suddenly found itself surrounded by a "whole colony of recent Southern migrants . . . centered around the Continental, Chrysler and other factories where they are employed." Sensing an opportunity, Levin had decided to "revamp his operating policy to cater to these new customers," and began booking "as many hillbilly acts as available"—including local notables George and Leslie York, a Kentucky-born country duo who performed as the York Brothers and whose 1940 single "Hamtramck Mama" had sold three hundred thousand copies in the Detroit market alone. Levin's gamble worked, and soon "scores of bars and nightclubs featuring country-western music across Southeast Michigan" had followed the Jefferson Inn's lead.[44] The same was true in hillbilly ghettos throughout the region. "Wherever you find furnished rooms and low-priced hotels, you find country-and-western music," remarked George Topper, who owned a record store on Wilson and Kenmore Avenues in the center of the Uptown entertainment district during the mid-1950s. According to one estimate, the neighborhood would eventually become "home to more than 150 bars, dozens of which booked nightly live country music to attract southern migrants."[45] Hamp Nunley,

# Hillbilly Disc Arouses Ire Of Hamtramck

## BY LOU SCHURRER

Hamtramck, Mich.—A hot hillbilly recording, *Hamtramck Mama*, is getting a cool reception by city fathers in this Detroit suburb. Their request to pull it from the thousands of juke-boxes in the largest Polish city in the country is ironical in the fact that the town is one of the most prominent in the operation of pigs and brothels.

Recorded by the York Bros. Hillbillies, the platter was "just plain nasty and our people are angry," stated City Attorney William Cohen after Hamtramck civic organizations had protested to the police.

When the Kentucky-born duo of George and Leslie York, who performed as the York Brothers, released their 1940 single "Hamtramck Mama," they could hardly have expected the response it would generate. The disc went on to sell three hundred thousand copies in the Detroit market alone—but, as this article from trade magazine *DownBeat* made clear, also aroused the ire of Hamtramck city leaders who did not appreciate being immortalized in the honky-tonk sensation.

Excerpt from *DownBeat*, Lou Schurrer, "Hillbilly Disc Arouses Ire of Hamtramck," p. 4, used with permission of *DownBeat* (May 15, 1940).

who played the electric bass in a country band alongside his brother and a couple other Grundy County natives, performed in bars and music venues all over Cleveland and as far away as Akron—but especially at local Five Points establishments like the Buckeye. "That's where all the hillbillies went," he explained. "And we played out of that Eclair Theatre. We used to have that rented, we played there often." Hamp only started playing the bass after he came to Cleveland—"I was eighteen years old. None of us could read music; we just played by ear"—but he found a receptive audience nonetheless. "There was a lot of people listening to country music there."[46]

By all accounts—including those of many southern migrants themselves—hillbilly bars were also defined by a characteristic rowdiness. "Sometimes they'd have a brawl in there, you know, get in fights," Hamp recalled about his nights playing the Buckeye; "that was just part of it." Janelle Taylor, whose parents rented an apartment above the Buckeye when they first arrived in Cleveland, remembered the raucous scene with a bit less sanguinity; as a young girl from Grundy County, the regular fistfights and occasional knifings that went on downstairs were distressing introductions to city living. Another Tennessee native, William Breeding, who grew up in Pontiac, Michigan, and performed and recorded under the stage name Arizona Weston in the decades after the war, would later describe one favorite Detroit hangout—Ted's 10-Hi, just down Jefferson Avenue from the Jefferson Inn—as "one of the roughest damn bars in history." In Uptown, the bars that lined Madison Street between Kedzie and Homan Avenues were said to be "solidly hillbilly and wilder than any television western." So too the stretch of bars catering to the city's working-class migrants that ran along South Walnut Street in Muncie, where fights broke out on such a regular basis that one local columnist waggishly suggested that what the city really needed to do was build "one of those outdoor beer gardens." "People seem to behave better in one of those dark outdoor spots because its calm and quiet," the *Star Press*'s Bob Barnet went on, "and when there are no bright lights there isn't any reason for the boys to get up and show off in front of the girls by staging a Jamestown, Tenn., knife burying contest."[47]

The "knife burying contests" and other such incidents that made hillbilly taverns favored police-blotter fodder during these years were typically little more than internecine squabbles, familiar by-products of the regionally specific masculine subculture that so many migrants had known growing up in the southern countryside, which prized assertiveness, a defensive regard for masculine honor, and an easier recourse to certain kinds of violence. James Gregory noted a similar dynamic in the Okie bars that proliferated in the Central Valley boom towns in which white natives of the western south came to predominate in the years during and after the 1930s, where "fist fights occurred frequently" and "the migrants' cult of toughness represented an adjustment of old values to a new setting." But as was the case in California, where a not insignificant number of the bar brawls pit "resilient Okies [against] insolent Californians," the physical violence that occurred in and around hillbilly bars in the Midwest could also reflect the contested terrain such clearly defined migrant spaces occupied in the urban landscapes that surrounded them. So it was when the Mace brothers, Arnold and Ernest, used "two rocks" and an "impressive looking butcher knife" to beat up a local Muncie tough who had bragged of being the best fighter in town at a bar on Howard Street, one block east of Walnut. According to a story that ran in the next day's newspaper, when the police came to take them away, the Mace brothers were heard "announc[ing] proudly they were from Jamestown, Tennessee."[48]

Altercations such as these, and the rough-and-tumble behavior that generally obtained behind saloon doors, invariably marked hillbilly taverns as uniquely threatening disruptions to the urban social order. As the commander of the Nineteenth District of the Chicago Police Department, which included most of Uptown, explained, "A hillbilly tavern starts up in the neighborhood and they want to know what you're going to do about it. We have other kinds of taverns too, where pervers [sic] hang around—but that doesn't seem to attract attention like the hillbilly tavern." As a result, bars and centers of after-hours activity that catered to southern migrants often became the target of municipal anti-vice campaigns and crackdowns on street crime during the postwar decades. "These migrants are United States citizens, free to roam anywhere they wish," warned the chief investigator of the Chicago Crime Commission, a business-led anti-crime organization that dated to the Prohibition Era, when it had set its sights on such mortal threats to law and order as Al Capone and John Dillinger. "But they have turned the streets of Chicago into a lawless free-for-all with their primitive jungle tactics." In response to such forms of public pressure, the Chicago Police Department flooded the streets of Uptown with extra officers and by the beginning of the 1960s was arresting southern-born whites for crimes like public intoxication, disorderly conduct, and assault at roughly twice the rate at which such migrants appeared in the neighborhood's general population.[49] Similar disparities were evident in other highly visible migrant enclaves throughout the region. In Cincinnati, natives of Kentucky, Tennessee, and West Virginia accounted for nearly 50 percent of all white arrestees in the city by the mid-1950s. On eleven types of charges—typically those, one local reporter remarked, "where impulse, not intellect, is the trip-hammer"—they easily outnumbered natives of Ohio.[50] Numbers like these, in turn, only confirmed the most outlandish stereotypes of hillbilly depravity, and reinforced the official consensus about the relationship between growing migrant populations and rising crime rates. Southern whites "cannot drink liquor like a sensible person," one senior Cincinnati police officer concluded; "excessive drinking and family fights" were simply in their nature. "The average Chicagoan doesn't realize it, but it isn't our own people committing the crimes," a Chicago lieutenant reported to the *Tribune*. "It's the migrants taking over."[51]

The reality, many migrants claimed, was that police bias, rather than uncontrolled drinking and lawlessness on the part of transplanted southerners, was at work behind the inordinately high arrest rates noted in hillbilly ghettos. "[The police] didn't like anyone that they thought was a hillbilly," one Tennessee-born migrant felt. "Oh gosh, as soon as you opened your mouth" to reveal a southern accent, concurred another, "you got a billy club upside the head."[52] Profiling of this sort occurred throughout the region, especially in big cities like Cincinnati, Chicago, and Detroit—but also in smaller ones, like Muncie, where many migrants "had the impression that the Police Department treated Appalachians unfairly."[53] An analysis of Uptown arrest records revealed that a particularly large proportion had been made "in the vicinity of Wilson Avenue where a number of cheap bars have existed for years." Similar concentrations were identified around other pockets of southern bars, restaurants, and dance halls throughout the neighborhood, all of which were unusually "heavily policed." According to one Kentucky-born migrant who hung out at the Dixie Hut on Leland Avenue with a group that was "all from the South," the police "were always comin around, searchin us, bustin up eight or ten guys."[54] And as tensions in the neighborhood between the community and the police escalated through the mid to late 1960s, it was not uncommon for southern whites in Uptown to describe instances in which police officers enforced curfew and loitering laws against them with a particular strictness; assaulted them in the course of making arrests; or in some cases even planted drugs or other evidence so as to manufacture criminal charges against migrants they deemed to be especially troublesome.[55] Michael Maloney, director of the Urban Appalachian Council in Cincinnati, likewise described "officers who persist in harassing and abusing citizens living in these neighborhoods[,] . . . who are either unqualified by reason of training or attitude and who commit acts of brutality." As a result of the "invidious discrimination" to which poor white southerners in the city were frequently treated, concluded a report of the Ohio Advisory Committee to the United States Commission on Civil Rights, "virulent anti-police feelings in the predominantly Appalachian community" had become the norm in centers of migrant settlement like Over-the-Rhine.[56]

Southern drinking establishments were not the only institutional embodiments of an emergent migrant subculture to draw the attention and opprobrium of urban midwesterners during these years. Another significant landmark of the social and cultural life that developed in hillbilly ghettos was the southern or "storefront" church—the latter being used so regularly at the time to imply the former that they effectively became

synonymous with each other. In fact, in the eyes of many midwesterners, the sudden appearance of dozens of new Protestant churches—many
quite small and belonging to denominational traditions with no prior
roots in the region—made an unlikely twin with the hillbilly bar; a further
indication of the way the arrival of southern migrants was contributing
to a wholesale refashioning of urban neighborhoods. Frequent were the
accounts that made mention of both, in some cases in the same breath:
"In these neighborhoods," observed one report on southern migrant life in
Cincinnati and Indianapolis, "bars and store-front churches exist in about
equal profusion, and, on summer nights, the impassioned exhortations
of the preachers and the blaring 'country' music from juke boxes merge
in furious cacophony." "The activities that gave the white southerners
their highest visibility as a group took place in the hillbilly taverns and,
paradoxically, in the churches," went another. "In the case of the latter, a
minority of the migrants attended storefront churches of various 'holiness'
sects. The shouting, the spirited singing, and the twanging of guitars and
banjoes impinged harshly on the ear of even the casual passerby."[57]

It was no coincidence that established urbanities tended to bundle
together these two most common creations of newly formed communities of transplanted white southerners. Indeed, the storefront churches
erected in migrant neighborhoods often stood out for precisely the same
reasons that southern bars did. Both were clearly working-class and "low-
culture" institutions. In physical appearance, the hastily constructed
southern churches often bore a greater resemblance to the flourishing
"hillbilly dives" than they did the columned grandeur of the typical downtown cathedral. As one study of southern church life on Muncie's southside noted, "none of the buildings [occupied by migrant churches] are
architecturally imposing symbols of religious worship . . . with a bell tower
or a steeple rising above the surrounding buildings." More commonly, at
least initially, such churches were convened in living rooms, above corner stores, or in small streetside shacks clustered between the factories
and tenements where working-class southerners spent most of their time.
Furthermore, among the clergy at these new churches, seminary training
and formal ordination were notably rare. In the early 1950s, by one estimate, there were as many two thousand lay preachers among the union
autoworkers in Detroit's Ford local alone, most of whom hailed from the
South. Some had preached to home congregations before migrating north;
others were like Wesley Brown, a native of Casey County, Kentucky, who
moved his family to Muncie in 1952, got a job driving a truck, and found
God a few years later. After being saved at the Twentieth Street Church

and baptized in the White River, Wesley began pastoring to three local churches when he was not delivering fruits and vegetables for Ace Produce. "A year or two later he started," his daughter Sharon recalled. "He was called to preach, he wasn't—he did become ordained, but he didn't go to college for it."[58]

Denominational nonconformity made the southern church stand out as well. "Perhaps the growth in Metropolitan Chicago of the Southern Baptist Church, the church that claims the largest membership in southern states, provides the most substantial index to the rapidly increasing number of persons migrating from the south," observed a committee of concerned citizens in Lake View, a neighborhood directly adjacent to Uptown. "In 1950 there were 9 churches in what are now the Great Lakes Baptist and the Chicago Southern Baptist Associations. By 1959, this number had increased to 67!"[59] While attendance declined steadily at "all of the 'old line' Protestant churches," one Detroit pastor remarked at the end of the 1950s, "store-front churches . . . mushroom continually"; within a two-mile radius of the city's downtown core, he counted twenty-two such southern churches that had opened in a matter of just a few years.[60]

In Akron, too, the influx of southern Appalachian migrants transformed the city's denominational landscape in profound and far-reaching ways. Dallas Billington was just twenty-two years old and working in a shoe factory in Paducah, Kentucky, when he and his wife-to-be decided to move to Akron in 1925. Recently born-again, Billington found the booming city of Akron to be "the wickedest place this side of hell" and the churches there to be "cold and dead," and so it was not long before he was ministering to his new coworkers at Goodyear and beginning a self-directed course of Bible study with the intention of becoming a preacher. His first opportunity came in 1930 at the Furnace Street Mission, a "shacklike little mission" in an old, repurposed pool hall, which sported a neon cross on its roof and a sign identifying it as "The Brightest Spot in the Underworld." Billington quickly developed a following at the mission, which he augmented with a weekly fifteen-minute radio broadcast on a local Akron station and a steady preaching circuit across a fifty-mile radius surrounding the city, all while continuing to work at Goodyear. In 1934 he began meeting with a half dozen families at an elementary school not far from the Firestone tire factory in south Akron, with the intention of starting a church with "warm informational services and gospel preaching that Southerners in Akron could attend." The next year, the Akron Baptist Temple was organized, with eighty-one charter members and Billington at the helm. By 1949, according to a photo-essay in *Life* magazine, the Akron Baptist

Temple had grown into the "biggest Baptist church" in the country, with a weekly Sunday crowd of some fifteen thousand attending services and Sunday school in a recently constructed megachurch facility that boasted forty-one thousand square feet of floor space, multiple auditoriums and classrooms, a nursery, and a parking lot with room for fifteen hundred cars (as well as the fleet of forty free buses Billington operated to shuttle "the working class factory worker who could not afford an automobile"). Even in its new grandeur, though, the *Life* editorialists remarked on how much Billington's church remained true to its founding mission as a place of worship for the city's working-class southern migrants. "Many of congregation are factory workers from the South," read the caption to one photo of the jam-packed main auditorium room; while another noted that the newly built, ninety-seven-foot-high brick building that housed the Akron Baptist Temple "looks something like a factory."[61]

Patterns like these prevailed across the region. In the two decades after World War II, the Southern Baptist Convention (SBC) would become the most rapidly growing Protestant denomination of any kind across the state of Ohio, and experienced equivalent surges in membership in the other states in the Great Lakes region over the same period of time. By the end of the 1960s, there were 169 Southern Baptist churches in Michigan, 230 in Indiana, and close to 900 in Illinois, where the SBC had had a downstate presence since the turn of the twentieth century. All told, by the end of the southern migration, the number of state conventions affiliated with the SBC had grown to thirty-four, from sixteen at the beginning of the century, with many of the newest appearing outside of the region. As a result, as Baptist church historian Leon McBeth has noted, while the denomination's name had once "reflected accurate geography," by the end of the 1970s it could "be defended only as a doctrinal description."[62]

Although Southern Baptists made up the majority of southern-born migrants to the North and West during these years, contemporaries paid a disproportionate amount of attention to the Pentecostal churches or "Holiness sects" that some poor southern whites gravitated toward upon arrival in the urban Midwest.[63] More often than not, northern clergy attributed white southerners' refusal to be "readily assimilated in the city's conventional churches" to their adherence to the more charismatic traditions associated with the Pentecost, which had deep roots especially in the mountainous regions of southern Appalachia; and to which, as the wife of an Episcopalian minister in Cincinnati's Lower Price Hill neighborhood put it, southern whites maintained "a faith which is individualistic, strongly held, and seemingly impossible to shake."[64] And there was some

The Akron Baptist Temple was started by a Kentucky native named Dallas Billington, who moved to Akron from Paducah in the mid-1920s to work in the city's tire plants. By the time this photograph was taken, in 1949, the Akron Baptist Temple had become one of the largest Baptist churches in the country. A fleet of free buses operated by the church carried "the working class factory worker who could not afford an automobile" to weekly services.
Courtesy of the Ohio History Connection.

considerable truth to this. By one measure, southern whites in the city were more than twice as likely as white Cincinnati natives to be members of Holiness churches, and overall were "drawn to fundamentalist groups" at a rate that was matched only by Black migrants to the city. Already by the middle of the 1930s, the Lynds had noted a "resurgence of earnest religious fundamentalism" on Muncie's working-class southside, which they concluded was "probably due in part to the number of casual workers that have drifted in from the Southern Mountains." Since 1925, they estimated, nearly two-thirds of new congregations in the city were affiliated with "the marginal groups somewhat deplored by the older denominations," "weaker worker-class sects" that fell "in the general classification of Spiritualist, Holiness, Apostolic Faith Assembly, and so on."[65] Such patterns would continue after the war: of the thirty-seven southside churches founded during the peak years of migration, well more than half had southern denominational origins or represented independent, nondenominational churches that were particularly prevalent within those parts of southern Appalachia that produced most of the city's migrants.[66] Likewise, one in four Kentucky-born migrants living in South Lebanon, Ohio, according to another study, identified with the "Church of God, Holiness, and similar sect groups," while "extremely fundamentalistic position[s]"—including beliefs in biblical inerrancy, dispensationalism, and the sinfulness of all drinking, gambling, and card playing—were held by nearly 40 percent of all southern-born men and almost 65 percent of southern-born women, regardless of church affiliation. In some instances, southern-born preachers even managed to transplant the more arcane worship practices that endured in the rural South to their new homes in the industrial Midwest. Arnold Saylor, who grew up around Berea, Kentucky, and moved to Fort Wayne, Indiana, with his family in the early 1950s, drew congregants of a similar regional background (as well as a great deal of hostile attention from locals) when, in 1968, he opened the Hi-Way Holiness Church of God in nearby Riverhaven, where among other traditions typical of certain mountain churches he began "preach[ing] snake handling in the eastern Kentucky style."[67]

Nevertheless, the disproportionate focus placed on "Holiness and Pentecostal 'lower class' [churches]," as another contemporary account put it, was more often than not a function of precisely that: the heightened attention paid to "lower class" social behaviors generally among southern migrants in the urban Midwest, and the understood class composition of those kinds of churches. Descriptions that northerners offered of migrant churches quite often were redolent with the same kinds of class and cultural biases that likewise informed their criticisms of southern living arrangements and drinking habits. A pastor in one of the city's longer-established churches could hardly conceal his sneer in describing services presided over by "some southern preacher who is now a laborer in Detroit," who tended to preach "in all directions at once" while deploying "a cadence not unlike that of a tobacco salesman." "Good preaching consists in working the people up to a high emotional pitch, so they can speak with 'tongues' and 'git happy' with their religion," went an observation of migrant church life in Cincinnati. "Most of the time the preacher is so worked up that he is unintelligible." And in fact, prejudicial attitudes of this sort among midwestern churchgoers and leaders were just as likely to be responsible for the creation of a separate southern church tradition in the urban North as the migrants' own denominational preferences or doctrinal differences. John Donovan, a Chicago city official who conducted youth services work in the Uptown area, noted that a number of local ministerial associations led by long-established churches "work[ing] off of $250,000-a-year budgets" had drawn their geographic boundaries so as to have effectively "boxed out" Uptown. Donovan attributed this congregational gerrymandering to the influx of southern migrants—"some people don't want to associate with the blue shirt or lay work types"—and their attendant social problems, for which the better-off churches "are not assuming any responsibility."[68]

In certain instances, the social ostracization practiced by northern churches could have the ironic consequence of making migrant churches unlikely sites of social inclusion. It was noticeably more common, one Cincinnati resident pointed out, for the churches attended by southern white migrants "to have both white and Negro members," who likewise received a cold welcome from the northern churches that catered to middle-class Blacks. This was not true always and everywhere—Dallas Billington's Akron megachurch would become a notably segregated institution, and especially so as its phenomenal growth began to attract better-off city residents beyond "the hillbilly transplanted from West Virginia and Kentucky"—but similar patterns were observed in Detroit, and likewise attributed to the common rural origins of Black and white migrants to the city. "In some instances, southern whites and negroes worship together," remarked a local clergyman. "They feel that they have more in common than they do with 'city people' who go to the 'big churches.'"[69] In this again, the southern church shared a kinship with the southern bar, which, as John Hartigan Jr. has noted, in certain circumstances could be a more racially integrated space than its non-southern equivalent. In the Detroit neighborhood of Briggs, for instance, southern Blacks and whites who arrived during and after World War II each found themselves "broadly barred" from neighborhood drinking establishments by reason of racial animus and ethnic parochialism; as a result, the hillbilly bars which emerged throughout the neighborhood developed a laxer commitment to enforcing the color line than was otherwise common in postwar Detroit. Helen Elam, a southerner who arrived in Uptown in the 1960s, noted similar patterns in the bars there: "I remember going out to this place on Lawrence [Avenue] and seeing blacks and whites out together. Everybody dancing, blacks and whites. Everybody getting along good; having a good time. No fights or nothing. I said, man, you wouldn't find that down south." "As a group," Hartigan Jr. found, "'hillbillies' were the whites most frequently and elaborately engaged in interracial social ties in Briggs"—a tendency that some southern churches in migrant neighborhoods only reinforced further.[70]

Like the work clothes of the congregants, the emotionalism of the services, or the ramshackle appearance of the church buildings themselves, the race-blind confraternity that could be observed in certain migrant churches confirmed their status as lower-class institutions in the eyes of urban midwesterners. Yet for the migrants themselves, these same markers of informality were often precisely the point—as important if not more so than some "impossible to shake" doctrinal adherence they carried with them from their places of origin. Many southern migrants felt so uncomfortable among more middle-class congregations, noted a group of Cincinnati social workers, that they "will not attend larger, established, or 'more formal looking' churches." Southern migrants in Detroit likewise frequently invoked differences of class rather than theology to explain their preference for attending churches of their own: "I'm afraid I wouldn't know what to do. I have been used to a small church," remarked one white southerner by way of declining an invitation to attend services in one of Detroit's more established churches. "I don't have clothes good enough to go there," offered another.[71]

In the end, southern churches and bars, like the hillbilly ghettos in which they were located, could be sites both of exclusion and inclusion, sometimes at the same time. "I don't think there was ever any people we knew that was born and raised in Muncie," recalled Mabel Guffy, who moved there as a teenager in the early 1950s. "I don't know why. I guess maybe 'cause we was from the hills of Tennessee and we weren't—we weren't northern people and we was, I guess, backwards, to them, to the northern people, you know." Instead, Mabel spent time with other girls from down south, babysat for another Tennessee family whose parents worked at Ball Brothers, and attended a Baptist church like the one she knew from back home—all because, as she put it, "we wanted to stay with our own type."[72]

Understood in that context, hillbilly bars and storefront churches played a more complex social role than merely as places of escape or collective commiseration—or as "haven[s] for the lonely exile," as one influential interpretation of the northern expansion of the southern church has put it. For his part, Wesley Brown, who had been raised a Methodist in Kentucky, became a Free Will Baptist after moving to Muncie because the local Methodist church was attended mostly by the city's middle-class, native-born residents, while the congregants at Twentieth Street Church "were from the South, from Kentucky and from Jamestown." The same was true of the churches where he would pastor over the coming years. "One was on a side road by Frank Foundry, I do remember that," recalled Wesley's daughter Sharon. "Because some of the men that went to our church worked there, second shift; and on Wednesday nights they'd come to the side door, when we were out in the church yard, and they'd come out the side door and they'd all wave at us." "Us men in overalls" was how the minister at one such southside church was known to address his congregants. To Kirby Garrett, who grew up in Pickett County, Tennessee, and moved to Muncie in 1952, the appeal of Jackson Park Baptist Church had everything to do with the common backgrounds of the congregation. "They were all southern—when they come here, they'd just grab them." Like many of his fellow worshippers, Kirby spent thirty years working in one of the city's auto parts factories, while raising a family in a series of apartments and modest homes on Muncie's southside. "You felt like when you met them, you had something in common—and you did." In the bars and churches that popped up on Muncie's southside, in Cleveland's Five Points or along Wilson Avenue in Chicago, a very specific, regionally and class-inflected process of community formation was taking place.[73]

## Whiteness and the Other America

Once more, most southern white migrants to the urban Midwest did not end up settling in hillbilly ghettos. Even at its peak, only about one-half of the total population of Uptown—the migrant neighborhood that consistently generated the most national attention and public consternation throughout the 1950s and 1960s—was born in the South. In Detroit, smaller clusters of southern whites developed in neighborhoods like Briggs and along the Cass Corridor; but dispersion rather than concentration proved to be the dominant pattern of settlement across the larger metropolitan area over the duration of the postwar period.[74] With time, the enclaves of southern migrants that had initially gravitated toward declining inner-city neighborhoods or working-class urban fringes would begin to radiate outward toward the suburbs—places like Mill Creek, outside of Cincinnati; or Yorktown, just west of Muncie. By 1970, as James Gregory notes, only 10 percent of southern-born whites living in the six largest metropolitan areas in the Midwest (Chicago, Detroit, Cleveland, Milwaukee, Indianapolis, and Cincinnati) resided in neighborhoods where southern whites exceeded 30 percent of the population. And over the course of the coming decades, as regional deindustrialization slowed the rate of new migration to the Midwest to a trickle, those numbers would erode even further.[75]

Nevertheless, it is a fundamental mischaracterization to argue, as Jacqueline Jones and others have, that because poor southern whites "were more dispersed throughout metropolitan areas and so more difficult to count and study," social elites concerned with the fate of declining American cities "ignored them altogether" in discussions of urban ghettos that otherwise focused on the Black and brown poor.[76] Communities of poor and working-class white southerners loomed much larger in the imaginations of urban contemporaries—so large, in fact, that many of them came to see hillbilly ghettos as racially and culturally suspect places despite the apparent consanguinity of their residents. "The first Southern white Anglo-Saxon Protestant to move in on a Chicago block has about the same impact as a Negro," noted one account of the reception to which these migrants were often treated. "Chicagoans panic and move out as fast as possible, though a few remain to fight a rear-guard action." The journalist who wrote those lines exaggerated, grossly: the hostility that greeted southern white migrants during these decades would never approach the level of the often-violent campaigns of organized resistance that greeted the simultaneous arrival of southern Blacks, in Chicago and other cities across the region. But the comparison, imperfect though it may have been, captured something crucial about the way many midwesterners viewed the increase in southern white migration over the two decades following the war, and the critical importance they gave during these years to the problems associated with the hillbilly ghetto.[77]

By some measure, this was simply a matter of timing. It was during these same years, after all, that the racial composition of the urban Midwest was experiencing its greatest flux, making the "Southern white Anglo-Saxon Protestant" something of an anomaly in a rapidly shifting urban landscape. For the first time in the twentieth century, Chicago's white population actually began to decrease during the decade of the 1940s, while its Black population increased by more than 80 percent. By 1960, Black Chicagoans accounted for nearly one-quarter of the city's population, after having made up less than one-tenth on the eve of the war. In Detroit, the Black population increased from 16 percent to 29 percent between 1950 and 1960, and again to 45 percent by the end of the next decade. Cleveland lost a hundred forty-five thousand white residents over the course of the 1950s, and gained Black residents at a rate that exceeded the national average for urban areas by nearly 35 percent. Even Muncie—which like other smaller cities in the region did not attract Black southerners over the course of the twentieth century at anywhere near the same rate as the larger cities of the Midwest—saw the Black portion of its population increase by nearly 60 percent in the years between 1940 and 1970.[78]

Arriving in urban areas at the very moment that other groups of whites were leaving, and as the Black population, confined to metropolitan cores by the "white noose" of the suburbs, was becoming an ever more defining presence in midwestern cities, poor southern whites struck more than just one contemporary observer as being at variance with the dominant trajectory of northern white identity. "The so-called hillbillies," remarked Daniel Seligman of *Fortune*, "who now constitute a major slum problem in several midwestern cities . . . are about the only sizable group of white, Protestant, old-line Americans who are now living in city slums." "Their neighbors often find them more obnoxious than the Negroes," claimed Albert Votaw, executive director of the Uptown Chicago Commission, an association of conservation-minded neighborhood homeowners and business leaders, founded in 1955 amid a citywide anti-blight campaign; "or the earlier foreign immigrants whose obvious differences from the American stereotype made them easy to despise."[79] Even those "earlier immigrants," like Gertie Nevels's neighbor in *The Dollmaker*, were quick to assert their claims to full-blooded Americanism—to middle-class notions of decency, respectability, and, by implication, whiteness—as against the compromised stock represented by poor white newcomers like the Nevels family.[80] If not quite Black by association, in the changing racial landscape of postwar urban life, southern white migrants suggested a similar threat to the established order of things.

The experience of the hillbilly ghetto was also at odds with one of the dominant narratives about postwar American history. An operating premise in much of the scholarship as well as more popular writing has long been that between the 1930s and the 1960s was an era of steadily increasing stability and socioeconomic security for American working people, and especially for white blue-collar workers. Unprecedentedly high rates of union membership and low rates of long-term unemployment, consistent wage and income growth, expanding rates of homeownership and university attendance, a diminishing wealth gap between rich and poor—economic trends such as these were indications that these were historically good times for the country's laboring masses. As a result, this was also a period when American workers were seen to be becoming more culturally "middle class" in a variety of ways: from their consumption habits and family structures to their domestic arrangements and residential patterns, to their ideological orientations and worldviews. Politically, meanwhile, it was during these years that the white working class found itself at the core of an electoral coalition that, from its base in the industrial cities of the North and the coasts, dominated much of national political life for the better part of two generations. For the most part, exceptions to this narrative—of the postwar decades as a kind of workers' paradise, American style—have focused on groups of people whose race, gender, or citizenship status denied them full participation in what Steve Fraser and Gary Gerstle have called the "New Deal Order"; or equal benefit from what Robert Self has described as the political-economic ideology of "breadwinner liberalism," which placed the white male worker and head of household at its center and undergirded the social policy reforms and governing priorities of the period.[81]

Southern Appalachian migrants in the Midwest both were and were not a part of this larger narrative. Despite the very real conditions of poverty many would encounter in the urban neighborhoods they first settled in upon arrival in the North, the truth of the matter was that most southern Appalachian migrants also shared in the steadily improving material conditions of the postwar white industrial working class. In general, southern white migrants to the Midwest experienced wage and income growth during these years that was more or less equivalent to their northern-born neighbors. As beneficiaries of a common racial privilege, southern-born white migrants in the Midwest stood significantly better chances than Black southerners of finding employment in the leading heavy industries of the postwar period— where jobs tended to be better paying, more densely unionized, and more secure—and of moving up the occupational ladder to skilled and supervisory positions within those industries. Likewise, southern-born whites in the Midwest were significantly more likely to become homeowners than southern-born African Americans, and participated in the postwar trend toward rapidly growing working-class suburbs at rates that were basically similar to their northern-born white coworkers.[82]

And yet, the persistent focus on the "problem" of the hillbilly ghetto during these years suggests that all was not right here. It was not for nothing that "urban hillbillies" were the only population of non-elderly, non-disabled, non-rural whites—besides the "the intellectual poor" and skid-row alcoholics—that Michael Harrington included in his pathbreaking 1962 work on the persistence of poverty in postwar life, *The Other America*. "Where the ethnic slum once stood, in the 'old' slum neighborhood," Harrington writes, "there is a new type of slum. Its citizens are the internal migrants, the Negroes, the poor whites from the farms, the Puerto Ricans. They join the failures from the old ethnic culture and form an entirely different kind of neighborhood." Harrington describes one midwestern neighborhood of displaced sharecroppers and cotton pickers from

Arkansas as "one of the worst urban slums for white people that I have ever seen," where the familiar offenses to hygiene and domesticity, the propensity for delinquency and marital breakdown, and "the casualness of a people who expected little," sooner called to mind the conditions of life in a contemporary "Negro ghetto" then in the immigrant neighborhoods of old. "Above all," Harrington explains, "these people do not participate in the culture of aspiration that was the vitality of the ethnic slum." "The backwoods has completely unfitted them for urban life"; as a result, he predicts, "there will be more of these music-filled, miserable country neighborhoods springing up in the cities of the other America."[83]

These notions—that the forms that urban poverty took on amid the relative plenty of American society in the 1950s and 1960s were somehow anomalous with what had come before; that the urban ghettos of the postwar period were creations more characterological than structural in nature; and that a culture of fatalistic dysfunction was shared in common by poor Americans across lines of race and ethnicity—would go a long way to shaping popular attitudes at the time. In ways the following chapter will address, they also would provide an essential theoretical framework that would come increasingly to guide the social policy innovations of postwar liberalism.[84] Southern whites were not only settling in northern cities as the racial complexion of those cities was beginning to darken; in the hillbilly ghettos where they became most visible during the postwar decades, white southerners also seemed to demonstrate many of the same behaviors and encountered many of the same problems that were observed in communities of Black and brown newcomers to the city. In doing so, these Transappalachian migrants presented a very real threat to the normative image of midcentury whiteness.

By some measure, hillbilly ghettos really were part of an "other America," where the types of behaviors that middle-class urban society valorized most readily—acquisitiveness, rationalism, self-discipline; the celebration of the nuclear family over the extended clan, and market society over the traditional community—seemingly were not only absent but abjured. One Cincinnati school principal remarked that the families of her southern students seemed "to move around in a world without the restrictions of time and the clock." A Cleveland minister pointed to the economic underdevelopment of the rural South to explain why the white southerners he encountered in his parish had "never had to develop the characteristics of the aggressive and suave 'organization man'"—a revealing if rather confused invocation of the midcentury conformist archetype described by the popular journalist and urbanologist William H. Whyte, who himself once attributed the struggles that rural southerners encountered in northern cities to "the new arrivals' lack of knowledge of such rules of the game as not throwing garbage out the window." Less sympathetic voices interpreted these kinds of behaviors not as a sign of not knowing the rules, but as a willful refusal to follow them: "Those people are creating a terrible problem in our city," complained one particularly aggrieved Indianapolis resident. "They can't or won't hold a job, they flout the law constantly and neglect their children, they drink too much and their moral standards would shame an alley cat. For some reason or other, they absolutely refuse to accommodate themselves to any kind of decent, civilized life."[85]

For their part, the inhabitants of hillbilly ghettos approached these rules differently. It was less that southern newcomers to northern cities were not "time-conscious," as the Cincinnati principal put it; but that, for at least some of them, nonindustrial time—be it the planting and harvesting schedule, or the rhythms of family life—continued to be an operative frame of reference as well. The "lack of strong success motivations" to which middle-class urbanites often attributed poor southern whites' inability to get ahead in northern cities, meanwhile, was often merely a matter of perspective. For many migrants, after all, success was measured by the ability to earn enough in northern factories to return to the South; and in any event, nothing other than "success motivations" had driven cycles of intra- and interregional migration by a displaced rural southern proletariat since the turn of the twentieth century. Likewise, the fatalistic resignation to their conditions, which Harrington, Seligman, and so many others read into these "environments of misery," was difficult to square with the well-established patterns of individual and collective resistance that poor southern whites frequently demonstrated in northern workplaces; or the traditions of rural working-class life they managed to preserve in the churches, bars, and other spaces of their own that they managed to carve out of their new northern homes.[86]

Instead, as the next chapter will discuss at some length, northern contemporaries looked at these behaviors and saw in them the imprint of the premodern past. Some situated that past in agrarian traditions and cultural forms endemic to the Appalachian countryside and the American South more broadly; others looked even further back to a stubbornly independent Scotch Irish "mountain folk" heritage claimed by some (although by no means all) European-descended whites of the rural Upper South.[87] And surely there was considerable truth to the idea that Transappalachian migrants brought with them cultural habits, practices, and worldviews that diverged from and were even, perhaps, fundamentally incompatible with those embraced by the mainstream culture of urban America. But just as it had been an ideological fiction to believe that rural white southerners were simply babes in the woods when it came to their experiences with industrial labor and class conflict, so too was it a mistake to read the distinguishing features of the hillbilly ghetto merely as the extension and continuation of one or another form of hidebound traditionalism—or even to imagine that such cultural traditions could somehow have survived the epochal disruptions of transoceanic immigration, mass dispossession, intensive industrialization, and regional dispersion entirely and pristinely intact. The rapid spread of southern churches during these years, for instance, was clearly a reflection of both the strong identification many migrants still felt for certain regionally defined worship traditions; and also a response to the particular form of class society that was mapped onto religious practice and institutional life in their new homes. One of these impulses was doctrinal, the other was sociological; one had elements of a backward-looking cultural conservatism to it, the other suggested how even fundamentalist religiosity could be a means not only of resisting capitalist modernity but also of learning how to navigate life within it. Any attempt to fully disentangle the two could not help but engage in an ideological mystification of the distinctive migratory experiences that unfolded across the landscape of Transappalachia.

Ultimately, the hillbilly ghettos of the postwar period were problematic precisely because they were such perversely liminal spaces. Pockets of poverty amid the relative plenty of the midcentury consumer's republic; markers of divergent racial identity at the dawn of white flight; marginal and transient communities in the era of the crabgrass frontier; redoubts of rural and working-class nonconformity in the very heart of an ascendant urban middle-class culture—no matter how broadly representative these highly visible creations of the hillbilly highway truly were, they troubled the waters of midcentury American society in ways that made them impossible to ignore. Like the green peas and hotheads of the sit-down era, the hillbilly ghetto residents of the postwar decades stood for something larger than themselves: an incommensurable working-class subject at the heart of the modern political order, whose very existence seemed to call the racial and economic foundations of that regime into question. And as those foundations began to show serious signs of cracking beginning in the 1960s, the problem of the hillbilly ghetto would by no means disappear. In fact, if anything, the figure of the Transappalachian migrant and the future of postwar liberalism would become even more decisively and fatefully intertwined.

# CHAPTER FIVE

# "An Exaggerated Version of the Same Thing"

## SOUTHERN APPALACHIAN MIGRANTS, CULTURES OF POVERTY, AND POSTWAR LIBERALISM

*"The city proper we progressively leave to those even more rural and backwoods in their culture than we: Negros from the rural South, mountain folk from the Ozarks and Appalachians, Puerto Ricans from the island villages."*[1]

—PAUL YLVISAKER, SPEECH TO THE ANNUAL MEETING OF THE ASSOCIATION OF URBAN UNIVERSITIES (1958)

*"Negro poverty is not white poverty."*[2]

—LYNDON JOHNSON, COMMENCEMENT SPEECH AT HOWARD UNIVERSITY (1965)

IN THE SPRING OF 1953, a group of social workers and teachers in Cincinnati reached out to the Mayor's Friendly Relations Committee (MFRC) for help with a problem. A citizens' advisory commission to municipal government, the MFRC was one of dozens of such city and state committees then active around the country, created in the immediate aftermath of the 1943 Detroit race riot "to ease group tensions and build healthier community relations." Torn between these essentially pluralist beginnings and the prodding of a more reform-oriented bloc of members representing local chapters of the NAACP, the CIO, and the Cincinnati Community Chest's Division of Negro Welfare, the MFRC had become by the early 1950s a reliable if programmatically incrementalist ally of Cincinnati's burgeoning

Black civil rights movement, taking halting but nonetheless important steps to put the city behind notable campaigns to eliminate workplace discrimination and desegregate public facilities.[3] Under the stewardship of Marshall Bragdon, its long-serving executive director, the MFRC had also begun to work to address the challenges confronting other residents of Cincinnati's inner-city neighborhoods, many of whom were relative newcomers to the city. Among them were the rural southern whites who so confounded the social workers and schoolteachers who reached out to the MFRC in 1953.

By that time, at least 10 percent of the city's population hailed from the poorest parts of southern Appalachia. As Cincinnati's middle class continued its exodus to the suburbs, the clusters of rural southern whites that were developing in declining neighborhoods like Over-the-Rhine and Lower Price Hill were becoming sources of mounting concern for long-time residents, local business leaders, and civil servants alike. And for many, the obstacles to addressing the emergent social problems in these types of communities seemed to center as much around matters of cultural understanding and communication as they did around resources. As the MFRC would later recall in an organizational document, a number of the most directly implicated city agencies admitted that they simply "don't know how to help the migrants." Bragdon felt that he did, or could— and so, beginning in 1953, the MFRC "turned part of our attention to the city's 'second minority,' the Appalachian migrants." The ramifications of that decision would eventually come to be felt in communities of transplanted southern whites across the region.[4]

The immediate outcome was a citywide workshop, cosponsored by the MFRC and the Social Service Association of Greater Cincinnati, held in April 1954 and attended by some two hundred social workers, educators, and health and welfare professionals, as well as representatives of law enforcement, the religious community, private charity organizations, and the personnel departments of local employers. The purpose, as Bragdon put it, was to "de-stereotyp[e] the city man's and urban agency's views of and attitudes toward hill folk," and to that end the MFRC also brought in Roscoe Giffin, a sociologist at Berea College in Kentucky who specialized in rural Appalachia, as the workshop's principal speaker. Focusing his attention on "the culturally determined patterns of behavior which the Southern Mountaineers bring with them when they come to live north of the Ohio River," Giffin used his talk to attempt to explain to the uncomprehending city representatives a series of traits and characteristics that had become sources of conflict in the migrants' new urban settings. After hearing from

Giffin, workshop attendees broke into discussion groups in which they shared impressions of the migrants gleaned from their own experiences working with them in a variety of contexts, before Giffin offered some final thoughts on what he, Bragdon, and the assembled urban representatives agreed was the core challenge confronting the city in its dealings with rural southern whites: the "struggle for urban adjustment."[5]

Clearly, as Bragdon had suggested, some "de-stereotyping" was in order. "They work for a day or two and you see them no more. They seem to do everything wrong because of lack of training, poor physical stamina; they are not used to strong competitive rivalry like we are—can't stand the pace," remarked one employer during the discussion period. And the litany of criticisms only descended from there. "Education does not have importance to these people as it does to us," observed a teacher. "Some don't want modern facilities—if they have a bathtub, [they] don't use it," complained another workshop attendee. "[I] recall a family with 13 children of its own," one social worker told the group; "sister has four illegitimate children, each one with a different father who has departed." "They let the children run wild," claimed another. Familial dysfunction and juvenile delinquency, others argued, eventually begat even more scabrous offenses. "They do not understand laws here, such as it being a felony to have sexual relations with a member of their own family or with a girl who consents [i.e., statutory rape]."[6]

Faced with such accusations, Giffin did not try to disabuse the Cincinnatians of their opinions—far from it, in fact. While pointing out that "the experiences which the discussants presented are not the result of the sort of investigative process" that could be accepted "with any degree of statistical accuracy," Giffin nevertheless reaffirmed their more anecdotal observations in his own, rather torturous academic prose: "However, as I have studied them in relation to the information which provided the basis for my earlier address, I am of the opinion that many of the ideas expressed by the discussants represent hypotheses which have a high probability of being verifiable." Instead, Giffin sought to provide his audience with a context in which to understand these and other behaviors, whose "pathological quality," as Giffin put it, seemed undeniable. For instance, what a number of the urban professionals castigated as an impenetrable clannishness among poor southern whites—"They will not go away from their own people," observed one workshop attendee; "They regard those who wish to help them as a threat rather than a help," claimed another—Giffin described as a culturally reinforced "familism," which had held together extended family networks as the basic units of the rural economy but could produce an "emotional deficit" that made urban migrants resentful of outsiders, prone to loneliness and homesickness, and socially detached in their new homes. Likewise, the large number of children that this family orientation and the material demands of the rural household necessitated became a liability in the more crowded living quarters of the urban North. Giffin provided similar explanations for the poor school performance of the children of southern migrants (the inevitable fate for "carriers of a cultural tradition which considers a little readin' and writin' the goal of formal education"); the migrants' reported lack of thrift (resulting from an impoverished mindset in which "immediate consumption rather than future need is dominant"); and their apparent lack of ambition to improve their circumstances once settled in their new homes (born, as it were, of a fatalistic culture in which "the significance of life is in eternal salvation rather than present rewards"). Originating as natural and even rational adaptations to the rural settings from which the migrants hailed, these behaviors could, Giffin emphasized, be unlearned, after sufficient time and exposure to the different way of life they encountered in their new homes. But until then, it was reasonable to expect that poor southern whites would continue to demonstrate a deficiency of, among other things, "the motivations and behaviors which go with formal education, dependable work habits, maintenance and improvement of housing conditions, more realistic usage of cash income, and sharing in the community responsibilities which accompany urban living."[7]

By all accounts, the Cincinnati workshop was a resounding success. For their part, the local representatives were grateful to have a better understanding of what one called "the significance of [the migrants'] cultural heritage," and a number echoed the sentiment expressed by one social worker, who remarked afterward that "[the workshop] gave me the positive side; my previous observations of them had been only on the negative." Others came away feeling like a school counseling director who noted that she was now "better able to help new counselors to understand problems of [this] group with whom we do a great deal of work." And after the *New York Times* covered the publication later that year of a report on the workshop produced by the MFRC, interest quickly spread beyond the two hundred Cincinnati attendees. Requests for information about the workshop and copies of Giffin's talk soon came in from cities across the country. By the end of 1954, the MFRC had issued a second printing of a thousand copies, and by the end of the decade it would go through two more. Giffin himself would be invited to deliver talks on the subject at the 1956 convention of the National Federation of Settlements and Neighborhood Centers, during similar workshops convened in Chicago and Dayton in 1957, and in subsequent years before audiences in a host of other cities that had recently received large influxes of migrants from the Upper South.[8]

At the same time, the conversation that Giffin and the MFRC had initiated began to resonate beyond the boundaries of the hillbilly ghetto. In the immediate aftermath of the 1954 workshop, the MFRC received requests for copies of Giffin's talk, as well as consulting services, from the Puerto Rican Labor Department's Migration Division, located in New York City, where tens of thousands of Puerto Rican migrants were relocating annually during the 1950s. In January 1957 Chicago's Commission on Human Relations—an advisory committee formed along similar lines as the MFRC—inaugurated a Committee on New Residents, the first public body of its kind, "based on a recognition of the adjustment problems presented by the migration to Chicago of Southern Whites, Negros, Puerto Ricans and American Indians seeking increased economic opportunity." Detroit followed shortly thereafter, creating a Committee on Urban Adjustment to tackle the challenges, in the words of its chairman, in "assimilating" the city's influx of rural southern whites, Blacks, and Puerto Ricans, who refused to "shed some of their thornier and no longer functional traits." Like the attendees at the Cincinnati workshop, the members of the Detroit committee—which included representatives of the Detroit Department of Health, Board of Education, and police department, as well as local employment and youth services agencies, and religious and charitable bodies—saw their responsibilities as being "to try to change some of the values, attitudes, and behavior patterns . . . of the existing and continually arriving members of the rural lower class." Not surprisingly, one of the committee's first orders of business was to invite Roscoe Giffin to Detroit as part of a citywide workshop "whose core subject . . . would be the Appalachian highlander."[9]

The Cincinnati workshop would have enduring implications as well. By the middle of the 1950s, a growing consensus among social welfare professionals and policy experts would come to focus on the cultural handicaps of the rural working classes as an explanation for rising rates of poverty in urban America. In this sense, Bragdon and Giffin were neither iconoclasts nor innovators—the MFRC was, in effect, only applying this emerging conventional wisdom to the particularly intractable problems presented by Cincinnati's poor southern whites. But in helping establish a pattern for how to think about those problems, the Cincinnati workshop marked the beginning of a brief but important chapter in postwar liberalism, during which a mounting political concern with the fate of American cities, the disruptive effects of rural migration, and the causes and consequences of urban poverty intersected most directly with the interregional landscape of Transappalachia.

For a time, an unusual combination of elite condescension, political opportunism, and genuine compassion made newly formed communities of southern white migrants in the urban Midwest a unique object of focus for liberal policymakers and intellectuals. In their eyes, the challenge of urban adjustment in the hillbilly ghetto represented, as one prominent foundation leader put it, an "exaggerated version of the same thing" that rural migrants of various races and backgrounds were encountering in the postwar city. In that context, the relative whiteness of hillbilly ghettos provided important ideological cover, at a critical juncture in the development of liberal social policy—a way of talking about urban poverty as a problem of culture without talking explicitly about the politically explosive issue of race. But before long, the rising influence of the civil rights movement and the changing political and racial landscape of the 1960s would make the Black ghetto the near-singular focus of urban antipoverty policy. And in the process, poor and working-class communities of southern white migrants in the industrial Midwest would assume a new invisibility in the political landscape of postwar America.[10]

## Applying Theory to Practice

The "urban adjustment" framework that Roscoe Giffin and the MFRC adopted for the 1954 workshop owed as much to prevailing lay opinion as it did to cutting-edge sociological theory.[11] For a decade or more, longer-tenured residents, landlords, and community leaders, who were experiencing firsthand the neighborhood transformations associated with the postwar urban crisis, had been saying much the same thing: namely, that poor southern whites brought with them a set of behavioral traits that were not only ill-suited but actively detrimental to the urban communities in which they settled. It was only inevitable, then, that the same kinds of criticisms would begin to issue forth from those civil servants and representatives of municipal agencies who had the most direct contact with the migrant influx. School personnel, for instance, often attributed the battery of performance- and attendance-related issues noted among migrant children to what a group of elementary school teachers in Chicago's Lake View neighborhood called "a conflict of cultural values"; or what another group of teachers on Detroit's west side similarly referred to as "community attitudes and mores entirely foreign to [the] area."[12] "The lack of cultural press toward formal education" was one of the greatest obstacles confronting southern white migrants, concurred the assistant director of Intercultural Relations for Detroit's public schools. "Most of these parents do not seem to be against the educational systems but, equally delimiting, they are *indifferent* to it," he concluded.[13]

Law enforcement officials, meanwhile, increasingly explained the "disproportionate amount of lawbreaking in the city" that poor southern whites were supposedly responsible for as resulting from a similar conflict in values and culture. "Our laws and customs are different from anything they've known," explained one Cincinnati police officer. Although there was clearly some truth to the notion that migrants brought with them different cultural ideas about manhood and honor from the rural South, it was not uncommon to hear city police officials speak of an entirely alien "code of the hills," which gave license not only to near-biblical forms of retributive violence but also tolerated a whole host of sins against propriety, such as incest and child marriage. "The attitude of the Southern Appalachian migrant toward the law probably reflects his closeness to the frontier era of our society," concluded one Cleveland-area public official. When "transplanted into the urban setting," he continued, such premodern tendencies could not help but translate into "anti-social behavior."[14]

Public health advocates, likewise, spoke of an almost-superstitious aversion to formal medicine on the part of southern migrants, which they attributed to "traditional behavior patterns and attitudes" carried over from their impoverished rural backgrounds. A representative of Dayton's Division of Health, for instance, felt that families of southern migrants were so ignorant of basic healthcare practices that the city's welfare services should begin providing instructions on "cleanliness, immunizations, sanitation, and nutrition . . . intelligible to a fourth-grade education." Despairing even of the effectiveness of that approach, Chicago's director of Migration Services proposed "forced medical examinations of students in the schools," as the only way to corral the untreated health issues that were particularly acute among migrant children from the upper South. "They have no conception of what we consider adequate medical standards," complained one Cincinnati doctor. Even by the standards of other poor city-dwellers, southern whites seemed uniquely unwilling to avail themselves of the medical resources available to them in their new urban homes. An observer of the cultural practices of "the medically indigent urban white" in Detroit could not help but notice that "every single health service contacted reported that the overwhelming majority of the people who used their facilities was black. Where was the black Detroiter's neighbor, the southern mountain white, when it came to utilizing the medical aid from which he could so clearly benefit?"[15]

Given all this, it hardly came as a surprise that audiences made up largely of middle-class professionals and city officials would respond as enthusiastically as they did to Giffin's presentation. His diagnosis of the underlying causes of the various quality-of-life issues observed in communities of southern white migrants appealed because it placed the blame for those poor social outcomes not on factors endemic to the cities where they moved, or to the often-hostile receptions they received there—but on the newcomers themselves. The complaints that northern city-dwellers so often lodged against southern whites about their substandard housing conditions, dismal school performance, or frequent run-ins with the law, by Giffin's account, were not a function of the unenforced building codes, overcrowded public schools, and biased police practices that plagued lower-income urban neighborhoods generally, but rather were causally attributed to "a society with the foregoing cultural patterns." "It applied theory to practice," one participant in the 1954 workshop explained; or, in other words, Giffin's framing gave a theoretical coherence and the imprimatur of sociological authority to what was already a well-established operating premise in many northern cities.[16] Although they did not share the most obvious ascriptive markers of difference— race and language—that had set apart previous generations of slum-dwelling urban migrants, there was something likewise innately problematic about these poor southern whites, who seemed to have such a difficult time acclimating themselves to the expectations of middle-class society. "The trouble with the latter, as with the rural Negroes, Puerto Ricans, and Mexicans," observed one journalist at the time, echoing and encapsulating this popular consensus, "is that they simply don't know how to live in cities."[17]

Successful adaptation, then, was a matter of learned behavior—of culture—and Giffin's argument about the cultural unlearning that southern migrants first needed to do conformed nicely to the widely shared assumption that it was the migrant community, and not urban society itself, that was in need of adjustment.[18] In this, Giffin's framing of the issue of the cultural conflict that accompanied rural-to-urban migration also reflected the rising influence of the behavioral science "revolution," which was in the process of transforming social science research broadly in the decades after World War II.[19] By treating what was, in essence, a problem of public welfare in the postwar city, as a creation of what he described as the "character structure or basic personality structure" of the transplanted southerner, Giffin reduced complex and power-laden social interactions to more elemental personal attributes of individual and collective psychology. At the same time, Giffin, like the other contemporary social scientists who gravitated to the more practical implications of the behavioral turn, held out hope that if his audience of teachers, law enforcement officials, welfare professionals, and urban leaders came to better understand these defects of personality, they could effectively engineer those attributes out of existence. "The basis of all human relations work with all people," Giffin told his audience, "is that you have first to accept them as they are before they are willing to modify their behavior."[20]

In doing so, Giffin laid out a course of corrective action that prioritized neither structural change nor even extensive self-reflection on the part of the city representatives, but instead placed the emphasis almost entirely on a need "to know and to understand" the cultural habits that obtained in these communities of migrants. One obvious consequence of that approach was that it further normalized those aspects of urban society that might otherwise be held up to scrutiny, while exacerbating the cultural distance between poor southern whites and the urban professionals in the audience by treating the former as if they were something akin to a foreign population. In fact, Giffin began his remarks by bemoaning the fact that "we do not have a body of anthropological studies [on the people of southern Appalachia] rivaling in quality those done on many tribes in the far-away corners of the earth, such as those of the South Pacific." The "struggle for urban adjustment," in this light, was as much one *between* middle-class urbanites and an uncouth population of rural working people, whose behaviors flouted the norms of bourgeois civil society at every turn, as it was a struggle waged by the migrants themselves to find decent housing and employment in their new homes. A purpose of the workshop, as the MFRC's Marshall Bragdon suggested, may have been to disabuse Cincinnati's social service bureaucracy of some of the more persistent and unhelpful stereotypes that attached themselves to the cultural habits of southern hillbillies. But as Giffin's remarks made clear, doing so was intended not as an end in itself; nor in the interest of some benign, pluralist notion of intercultural understanding; but as the first step in a program of behavioral modification aimed at eliminating aspects of that foreign culture which did not immediately conform to the conventions of middle-class urban life.[21]

Giffin's analysis also fit well within a long and robust tradition of social scientific thinking that treated the South generally—and southern Appalachia specifically—as regions that suffered from a particularly acute form of

*When Cultures Meet—*

# MOUNTAIN
## and
# URBAN

**In one day's time, a whole family can move
from mountain hollow to city tenement. By understanding the newcomers' attitudes and needs,
we can help them adapt to their new home**

The "urban adjustment" framework adopted at the 1954 Workshop on the
Southern Mountaineer in Cincinnati would largely define the way city officials,
social scientists, and concerned policymakers thought about the challenges
many Transappalachian migrants confronted in finding decent employment
and housing in their new homes.

Excerpt from *Nursing Outlook*, Vol. 11, E. Russell Porter, "When Cultures Meet—Mountain
and Urban," p. 418, Copyright Elsevier (1963).

arrested cultural development. William Goodell Frost, a prominent southern sociologist who spent nearly three decades as the president of Giffin's
own Berea College, had famously described southern Appalachians as "our
contemporary ancestors" at the turn of the twentieth century; a native
population untouched by the "progress of the metropolis" and the "great
avenues of commerce and thought," who lived on as "an anachronism" in
their own time.[22] In the mid-1940s Howard Odum, the dean of southern
regionalism at the University of North Carolina, whose work and that of
his students had helped shape significant portions of New Deal develop-
mental policy in the South, continued to speak in terms of a "chronological lag" that was as much cultural as it was economic or industrial when
it came to the region's rural inhabitants.[23] By the 1960s this representation of the region and its people would reach its fullest expression in
such widely read texts as Harry Caudill's *Night Comes to the Cumberlands*
(1963) and Jack Weller's *Yesterday's People* (1965)—works of popular sociology that each emphasized "handicaps" associated with southern Appalachia's tradition-bound culture and folkways, and in doing so helped shape
the Kennedy and Johnson administrations' strategic approaches to the
Appalachian theater of the War on Poverty.[24]

Giffin's most significant contribution to this familiar litany was his near-singular responsibility for the invention of the character of the urban Appalachian—or "SAM," a popular shorthand for "Southern Appalachian Migrant" that social scientists, philanthropic organizations, journalists, and midwestern social welfare professionals increasingly began to employ in the years after the 1954 workshop. Before settling on SAM, Giffin had experimented with various proper-noun identifiers for southern migrants— among them "Southern Mountain Newcomers" and "Southern Mountain Whites."[25] But by the end of the 1950s, as the initial work of the Cincinnati conference gave birth to various "urban adjustment" workshops and committees across the region, SAM emerged as the clear consensus choice.

To some extent, the impetus for the new nomenclature was an essentially dignifying one. As E. Russell Porter, Cincinnati's director of health education and an early supporter of the MFRC's work with southern whites, explained, "Most Americans refer to the mountain people as 'hillbillies.' Sociologists identify these people as *Southern Appalachian migrants*, naturally shortened to the initials S.A.M." Nevertheless, the nominally more objective and dispassionate sociological terminology also contained a countervailing subtext. According to Giffin's usage, the most salient characteristics in the group identity of the urban Appalachian were those particularly dysfunctional cultural traits that had long been associated with the southern mountains—the clannish "familism," the fatalistic worldview, the limited value placed on formal education and other commonly accepted markers of social status in urban communities, the tradition-bound approach to everything from medical care to fundamentalist religiosity. There were some positive attributes that came with that identity, Giffin allowed, that might function as "assets" to the migrants in their endeavors to integrate into new urban settings—among them a strongly expressed individualism, "an ethical code which is rooted in the Bible of Christianity," and, above all, "the undeniable fact that the mountaineers are 'Old American' stock." But for the most part, urban Appalachians were defined as a doubly disadvantaged population: one that combined the out-of-timeness of Goodell's contemporary ancestors, with the out-of-placeness of an uprooted peasantry. "Adjustment patterns satisfactory for the rural regions of Eastern Kentucky [were] most inappropriate for Cincinnati," Giffin explained. "When such people came to live around Liberty and Sycamore Streets of Cincinnati, they were in a world for which they had little advance preparation."[26]

There were multiple ironies here. On the one hand, of course, not all southern white migrants to Cincinnati, or to any other midwestern city,

were properly "Appalachian"—in other words, from the most geographically remote, mountainous regions of the Upper South. A statistical breakdown of new migrants to Cincinnati revealed that while 40 percent of new
migrants to the city in 1950 came from the states of the Upper South, only
12 percent hailed from the census-designated portions of those states that
formally composed southern Appalachia. In Indianapolis, the ratio of "flatlanders" to "highlanders" was as high as six to one. A well-informed observer
in Chicago estimated that "only a fraction of these people are from the highlands. Most are from the flat country"—and indeed, southern migrants to
Chicago were nearly five times as likely to originate in places like the tobacco-
rich counties of alluvial western Kentucky as they were in the coalfields of
the eastern mountains.[27] But once the southern Appalachian migrant category had been defined and embraced, urban midwesterners began to see
the corrosive signs of "mountain habits" everywhere—even ascribing supposed southern Appalachian traits to working-class whites who turned out
to have no connections not only to Appalachia but even to the South more
broadly. In one instance, public school personnel in Chicago identified a
group of twenty families whose children demonstrated problems the teachers and administrators attributed to their southern roots—only to discover,
in a subsequent investigation, that seven of the twenty families were not
originally from the South at all, including one "who claimed never to have
lived outside Chicago." Similarly, after an analysis of arrest records in the
city confounded popular perceptions of a hillbilly-driven crime wave, its
author concluded that "perhaps the factor which may account for persons
born in the South being blamed for a much higher proportion of unlawful
conduct than they are responsible for is the similarity between them and
other persons in the area, particularly farm workers from the mid-west."[28]
"I thought I was an authority on knowing who is and who isn't [a southern
Appalachian migrant]," acknowledged one senior Chicago police official.
"Actually, I can't distinguish them. They have the same accents. This man
said he never left the state of Indiana until he came to Illinois."[29]

On the other hand, by attributing the struggles that these poor and
working-class southerners encountered in northern cities to a fundamentally irreducible set of regionally defined character traits, the SAM appel-
lation often ended up accomplishing in practice much the same thing as
the hillbilly stereotype, if with a somewhat gentler touch. It was not beside
the point that Chicago residents seemed to have a tendency to confuse
southern Appalachian migrants with "farm workers from the mid-west,"
or even low-income whites who were born and raised in the city: many of
the so-called adjustment issues that SAMs faced, in the end, were typical

of displaced rural workers or the urban poor generally, rather than specifically symptomatic of those with "Appalachian" cultural habits.[30] SAM might have been conceived as a way of offering a culturally sensitive alternative to the hillbilly label, but it shared with Giffin's broader diagnosis the ultimate effect of pathologizing the very people it aimed to assist. "We are talking about a minority group," explained Cincinnati's Porter. "[They are] native Americans of several generations, who are of the white race and generally are Protestant in religion. But still they are different—different in speech, in dress, in culture, in habits and mores, in education, in social status, in work experience, and in health."[31]

Above all, it was this notion of difference that would prove to be the most enduring legacy of the early framing that Giffin and the MFRC gave to the social problems confronting Cincinnati's population of southern white migrants. Southern whites had been seen as a potentially threatening group of outsiders in the urban Midwest since the beginning of the hillbilly highway, whether as low-wage green peas, apathetic strikebreakers, reckless shop-floor militants, sowers of racial discord, or spreaders of urban blight. But it was only with the invention of a distinctive cultural profile for the southern Appalachian migrant—by a sympathetic group of urban liberals, no less—that popular representations of maladjusted southern whites came to resonate with broader interpretations of postwar poverty that were gaining traction around the same time. In one more irony, it was what set these rural newcomers apart from middle-class midwesterners—with whom, as Porter noted, they shared so much—which also made them more like various other groups of poor and working-class migrants to the postwar city, who enjoyed fewer of the benefits of common nativity or racial and religious identity. And as a growing universe of city officials, liberal intellectuals, and policy professionals turned with renewed interest to poverty as a social and political issue during the late 1950s and early 1960s, it was these perceived shared dysfunctions that would shape some of the more consequential social policy developments of the period.

## Sturdy Oaks and Great Cities

By the latter half of the 1950s, the decision that Marshall Bragdon and the MFRC had made to train their focus on Cincinnati's "second minority" was starting to have its intended effect. In Cincinnati, charitable institutions, beginning with the Methodist Church–affiliated Emanuel Community Center and a local philanthropic organization called the Appalachian Fund, led the way in dedicating resources and personnel to assisting the new migrants to Over-the-Rhine. In keeping with the philosophy behind the 1954 workshop, the idea, as the Appalachian Fund's Stuart Faber put it, was to adopt a "sympathetic approach to lend a hand and steer them in the right direction." To that end, the Fund allocated money to cover the cost of hiring two social workers through the Emanuel Community Center, who would focus their energies on community outreach and "mak[ing] sure the migrants are aware of the agencies and facilities they can turn to for help in Cincinnati."[32] A seven-part series of articles appeared in the *Cincinnati Enquirer* in July 1957, which did not mince words about the various difficulties that recent migrants to the city were encountering but also went out of its way to correct certain common misconceptions. At a time when the city was debating extending its residency requirement for those receiving social welfare assistance, the director of the Hamilton County Welfare Department went on the record to state that "a relatively small percentage of the Kentucky-born are receiving help. Infinitely more of them are not on relief." Another article in the series reported on migrants who had "won out" after arriving in the city, among them a Clay County, Kentucky, native who had started out working a grill at a local White Castle restaurant and had since gone on to open a chain called Johnson's Country Kitchen, which had restaurants across the state and was doing $2 million in business annually.[33] Meanwhile, the MFRC, in its studiously nonpolitical way, continued its efforts to elicit wider understanding for the plight of Cincinnati's poor southern whites from the city establishment. Bragdon himself—whose "personal desire and his commitment outside the committee," in the words of one local activist, was often the driving force—met with a range of civic organizations to present the results of the 1954 workshop and enlist their support in easing the adjustment of rural southern whites. "The men guffawed wryly at the first mention of the migrants, conditioned by standard jokes and jeers at 'hillbillies,'" Bragdon reported from his meeting with the Junior Chamber of Commerce in Norwood, Ohio, home to a General Motors assembly plant that attracted thousands of southern jobseekers. "But [they] quickly caught the more serious aspects, [and] listened accordingly."[34]

Outside of Cincinnati, the MFRC's work resonated as well. In several cities, the MFRC's organizational counterparts began to develop related initiatives designed to educate members of local civic bureaucracies about the specific needs and cultural "handicaps" of rural southern whites. In Chicago, for instance, the Committee on New Residents was able to take advantage of its "direct pipe-line to the mayor" to secure support from

Richard Daley's administration for what were, in effect if not in name, sensitivity training programs in city schools and at the police department. Similar article series appeared in local newspapers throughout the region, echoing the more sympathetic portrayals given in the *Enquirer* series and likewise sharing the paper's (and the MFRC's) cautious optimism that, with proper care and instruction, the migrants would successfully adjust to the complexities of urban life.[35] National media attention followed as well, with even the most salacious reports of hillbilly misbehavior demonstrating the influence of the Cincinnati workshop in reframing the conversation surrounding southern white migrants. One widely discussed and reprinted 1958 article in *Harper's*, which began by likening the migrants' arrival in Chicago to that of an invading army's and went on to accuse them of a litany of abuses that "confound all notions of racial, religious, and cultural purity," nonetheless hailed the MFRC for making the "first major approach" to dealing with the problems posed by the migrants, and concluded on a note of Appalachian fancy worthy of Roscoe Giffin: "For this Southern migrant—the white Protestant artisan or farmer—is the descendant of the yeoman of Jeffersonian democracy. No matter how anti-social he seems, he has every attribute for success according to the American dream—even in its narrowest form."[36]

Most significantly, the MFRC's initiative drew the attention of two larger institutions that would, in the years ahead, play critical roles in linking the fate of white southerners to broader political conversations around rural-to-urban migration, cultural adjustment, and poverty: the Council of the Southern Mountains (CSM) and the Ford Foundation. Initially founded as a project of the Russell Sage Foundation, the CSM had been headquartered in the small town of Berea, Kentucky, since 1925, where it came to share an institutional home and common purpose with Berea College, which had maintained a missionary interest in the poor youth of southern Appalachia since its inception in the middle of the nineteenth century. Like the college, the CSM was a nonsectarian but decidedly Christian institution; for much of the twentieth century, it embraced a role in the region as an ecumenical clearinghouse for spiritually inflected social service work that targeted the more isolated and under-resourced portions of the mountainous hinterland at whose base it sat. Though its focus had traditionally been on the region's rural poor, by the 1950s the CSM was coming to recognize—largely at the behest of its new executive director, Perley Ayer, a "self-made sociologist" who shared research interests and teaching quarters with Berea's Roscoe Giffin—that out-migration was having a transformative impact not only on the region itself but across the contiguous urban landscape north of the Ohio River as well. With Ayer and Giffin at the fore, the CSM began to devote increasing attention to the issues surrounding rural-to-urban migration. In the fall 1956 issue of *Mountain Life and Work*, the CSM's quarterly journal, Giffin published a follow-up to his talk at the 1954 workshop, based on extensive interviews conducted with migrants in Cincinnati; and for the first time at its annual conference in 1958, the CSM organized a panel on the themes of regional out-migration and urban adjustment, which was well attended by representatives from the urban Midwest.[37]

The Ford Foundation also took a natural interest in the work that had begun in Cincinnati and was quickly spreading throughout the region. Along with the other major philanthropic foundations, Ford had helped pioneer the behavioral sciences movement at the beginning of the 1950s—although by the end of the decade its focus would already begin to shift away from "the psychologized 'individual pathology' diagnosis that prevailed at the time," and toward an operating theory that viewed social dysfunction as "a product of community, not individual, 'disorganization.'"[38] The change in focus could be attributed to a significant degree to the rising influence within the foundation of Paul Ylvisaker, a liberal urbanologist who had done graduate training in public administration and government at Harvard before working as an aide to Philadelphia's reform mayor Joe Clark. Ylvisaker took over Ford's Public Affairs division in 1955 with the ambition of reinventing its urban programming in response to the evolving circumstances of the postwar urban crisis. Like Bragdon and the MFRC, Ylvisaker had come to see the influx of rural migrants as one of the preeminent challenges confronting American cities at the time, and one that had created conflicts not only over limited space and resources but also around the ease with which cities were able to integrate communities of newcomers. "I had the sense that we were dealing with people problems, not bricks and mortar and not power structure problems so much," Ylvisaker would later recall, "and that we were witnessing the vast migration into the central city and I shifted at that point, to a concern with the migrant flows and what could be done about that." And like Giffin, Ylvisaker tended to attribute the obstacles to integration largely to the cultural maladjustments of the migrants themselves—a polyglot and multiracial peasantry composed of "Negroes from the rural South, mountain folk from the Ozarks and Appalachians, [and] Puerto Ricans from the island villages," all of whom, as Ylvisaker glibly put it in a 1958 address before an audience of urban university professionals, arrived in the city "even more rural and backwoods in their culture than we."[39]

SELECTED PAPERS

# INSTITUTE on CULTURAL
# PATTERNS of NEWCOMERS

Mexicans

Puerto Ricans

Southern Negroes

Southern Mountain Whites

Sponsored by

**WELFARE COUNCIL of METROPOLITAN CHICAGO**

with the cooperation of

Migration Services Committee of the Chicago Commission on Human Relations

The Mayor's Committee on New Residents

Third Printing, October 1960                    Chicago, Illinois

In Chicago and other cities across the Midwest, poor rural migrants of various racial and ethnic backgrounds seemed to pose a common set of problems in the decades after World War II. In the many local committees and working groups established by social service professionals and municipal leaders to aid these rural "newcomers" during the 1950s and 1960s, "southern mountain whites" were often discussed in terms that directly echoed those used to describe Black southerners, migrants from Puerto Rico and Mexico, and American Indians. Berea College Special Collections and Archives.

Ford's interest in the causes and consequences of "community disorganization" had led to an initial collaboration with Berea College in early 1957, on the first extensive study of the southern Appalachian region produced since the Great Depression. Supported by $250,000 in foundation grants, the resulting product was a 320-page volume called *The Southern Appalachian Region: A Survey*, edited by Thomas R. Ford, a professor of sociology and behavioral science at the University of Kentucky, and introduced with a foreword by a current Berea trustee and future president, Willis D. Weatherford. The book included nineteen essays on topics ranging from the region's economy and social institutions to the traditional folkways and cultural habits of its population, and would effectively launch the academic subfield of Appalachian studies. It also put the work being done with southern Appalachian migrants in Cincinnati and elsewhere on the Ford Foundation's radar. *The Southern Appalachian Region* featured two essays on the topic of regional out-migration—one of which, naturally enough, was by Roscoe Giffin. Bragdon and the MFRC, meanwhile, served as the northern spoke of the team at Berea for the purposes of gathering migration data, as well as a regional hub for conveying the informational needs of various city agencies and institutions, who eagerly anticipated the publication of the study in the hope that it would shed further light on the migrants' "capacity for adjustment to city ways." And although migration was only one piece of the larger regional study, it was understood to be a critical one: an effect, on the one hand, of what the study's authors treated as the near-total social and economic disorganization of southern Appalachia itself; and, on the other, the issue that most clearly linked the region's fortunes as a "problem area" to the broader national concerns that were increasingly coming to preoccupy the Ford Foundation. "The Appalachian [migration] stream was ruining a lot of people coming into the Akrons" and the other industrial centers of the urban Midwest, concluded Ylvisaker. "They were worse problems to those cities in the eyes of those cities than were the blacks."[40]

Race was a critical subtext to Ylvisaker's evolving interest in Appalachian migration. Throughout the 1950s the Ford Foundation was besieged in the public by right-wing Congressional commissions and media figures like Fulton Lewis Jr. who viewed the foundation's initiatives as liberal social engineering at best and radical subversion at worst; and, more privately, by the southern segregationists of the White Citizens Council, who threatened to organize boycotts of Ford automobiles if the foundation's programming interfered too directly with southern race relations. As a result, Ylvisaker was looking for a way to target what were often racially determined patterns of inner-city poverty, without addressing the issue of race directly. In this context, Appalachian migration proved to be a doubly useful stand-in. Most immediately, the rural-to-urban migration framework provided Ylvisaker with an "overarching process" that encompassed many of the various symptoms of the emergent urban crisis—the concentrated pockets of joblessness and underemployment; the neighborhoods marked by extreme residential overcrowding and infrastructural decay; the obvious inadequacies of existing systems of social service provision—yet supplemented the race-neutral concept of "urban adjustment" for the more hot-button topics of employment discrimination, housing segregation, and racial disparities in access to power and resources in the city. As Ylvisaker would later explain his thinking, "If you could conceive of an overarching process within which one could deal with the *verbotens* of race relations and so forth, and where you weren't talking black immediately, which raised all the hackles, then you had a much better chance of getting a program accepted." At the same time, as Giffin and others had been so quick to note earlier in the decade, the southern Appalachian migrant offered a unique kind of racial and cultural surety, which in the case of the Ford Foundation's public relations challenges could disarm even the most inveterate of racists and red-baiters. Compared to the various minority groups who were simultaneously crowding the expanding ghettos of the postwar city, "it was so easy," Ylvisaker recalled, "to deal with the sturdy oaks of our culture . . . these craggy, furrow-lined faces of Appalachian pioneers"—echoing, as he did, Giffin's depiction of the southern Appalachian migrant as "Old American stock." "Nobody could say, 'This is socialism or radicalism' or anything else." And while the initial appeal of addressing the adjustment problems encountered by southern whites may have been how it allowed Ylvisaker and Ford to avoid "talking black," Ylvisaker nonetheless believed that focusing the foundation's energies on an issue like migration "and the problems it involved" could also have broader, if unspoken, ramifications—potentially even "perk[ing] solutions through the whole system" and not only for the southern white newcomer to the postwar city.[41]

And so, building off the relationships that had developed out of the urban adjustment work and the production of the regional study, southern Appalachian migration became, as Ylvisaker would put it, "the first real entry point" for the Ford Foundation's growing engagement with the complex of issues surrounding community disorganization and the unfolding urban crisis. In late 1958 Marshall Bragdon, Ira Gissen of the American Jewish Committee in Cincinnati, and Wendell Pierce, who was soon to become Cincinnati's superintendent of schools, approached Berea's Weatherford with an idea for an expanded version of the 1954 workshop, which would bring city representatives from across the Midwest down to Berea, to, in Gissen's words, "study the mountaineer migrants in their native habitat." Weatherford in turn pitched Ylvisaker on the idea, who quickly agreed to provide $20,000 in foundation funding to cover the costs of the workshop, which was to combine a bus trip through eastern Kentucky and Tennessee with a three-week program of presentations and discussion in Berea. Perley Ayer of the Council of the Southern Mountains, who was in the middle of a sabbatical year in Columbus, Ohio—spent partly in study and partly "soaking up the facts and feel of the migration's urban complex"—agreed to cut his leave short and assume responsibility for running the workshop. Bragdon, in turn, offered to put the Cincinnati contingent's extensive "contacts and resources" at Ayer's disposal, and to assist in "mobilizing 'teams' in other cities," focusing especially on enlisting participation from "top support in other school systems," "social agencies' planning executives," senior police officials, as well as "various other organizations which have inquired about our workshops and publications—and so on, through universities, employers, etc." Weatherford, meanwhile, took responsibility for planning the tour portion of the workshop, which would cover roughly four hundred miles over the course of six days, beginning in Berea and winding its way down to Knoxville, Tennessee. Along the way, Weatherford arranged for "these middle western industrial city representatives" to visit area mining camps, factories, schools, and churches, while hearing from various locals who together "represent a cross section of the entire Appalachian Mountain Region."[42]

Billed as "a unique social exploration," the resulting workshop, which ran from July 8 to July 30, 1959, was a modest yet not insignificant success. All told, fifty-nine delegates from seven cities—Akron, Cincinnati, Chicago, Cleveland, Columbus, Dayton, and Detroit—attended either the sessions at Berea or the bus tour. Among them were relatively highly placed individuals like the heads of the Cook County (Chicago) and Hamilton County (Cincinnati) Welfare Departments, and the director of Detroit's Commission on Community Relations, who worked out of the mayor's office; as well as representatives of a half dozen metropolitan school systems and police departments, reporters from an equal number of local newspapers, and one Ford Foundation officer. The midsummer weather made for rather inhospitable living arrangements in the cramped and un-air-conditioned dormitories at Berea, and the tour group may have logged more miles on bumpy mountain roads than they did contacts with local informants—but the experience was still largely a positive and useful one for the northern visitors. A workshop attendee from Cincinnati remarked that she came away with "many insights into the S.A.M. attitudes and feelings plus cultural background," and noted that "one can not get at the grass roots nearly as effectively unless one is or has been where the grass grows." The Chicago contingent was similarly grateful to observe firsthand the "disastrous, bleak, horrible closed mine counties of Kentucky," where "abandoned cabins, abandoned tipples, hundreds upon hundreds of coal cars standing on rusty tracks, with the grass growing between the cars" revealed a landscape of absolute desolation. For his part, Mathew Cullen, the Ford Foundation representative, saw resonances not only between "the problems with the Southern Whites [and] the Southern Negro," but also "California [with] the influx of Mexicans into the small cities surrounding the metropolitan area" and even "London with the West Indians and the incipient possibility of fascist developments." Ford had been coming to the conclusion that "in-migration is a major problem which the residents of metropolitan areas don't understand," Cullen explained to the other attendees, and the tour and workshop "give us more basis for our judgment." Overall, the feedback was positive enough that the organizers decided, with some ambivalence—"I don't want to saddle myself to another organization," Weatherford grumbled—to repeat the workshop "with modifications" in 1960, and in the meantime to launch an "exploration with other organizations of their possible role in follow-up action."[43]

As it happened, the urban adjustment workshops at Berea would be continued for another nine years, during which time well over two hundred additional individuals from two dozen more cities and as far away as The Hague would attend.[44] By the second year, the Ford Foundation transferred its funding to the CSM, which took over the planning and administration of the workshop and established an Urban Adjustment Workshop Committee, chaired by Perley Ayer. After the third workshop in 1961 brought the number of participants to 141, Ayer moved to create a program for keeping workshop alumni in communication with each other and with the CSM in Berea, called Hands-Across-the-Ohio, which maintained a directory of contacts and local resource-people, arranged periodic workshops throughout the urban Midwest, and published a regular newsletter. By 1963 the Berea workshops had so clearly struck a nerve that the CSM moved to broaden the purview of the Workshop Committee and for the first time in its nearly half-century existence established a permanent Committee on Urban Affairs, to address the needs of southern Appalachia's increasingly visible transplanted urban population. That same year, the CSM even opened a branch office on Kenmore Avenue in the heart of Chicago's Uptown, "to encourage the mountain people to find or develop skills and job opportunities that will enable them to live as contributing citizens in whatever community they choose to live."[45]

But the greatest impact of the Berea workshops would be felt even farther afield than Uptown. For the program officers at the Ford Foundation, the urban adjustment framework first devised in Cincinnati and thereafter applied on a larger, regional scale with the subsequent workshops represented, as Matthew Cullen put it at the time, "a tentative interest which could become a major emphasis." "Our first two [workshops] were . . . small investments in bringing the people from the cities of Akron, Cincinnati and the rest . . . down to Appalachia where they could see the local people and begin understanding," Ylvisaker recalled later. "And then we wanted to seed the passage with helping points," which would get beyond the narrower objective of fostering intercultural understanding between established urbanites and rural newcomers, and begin to make tangible interventions in the way cities dealt with the growing pockets of poverty in their midst.[46]

By this point Ylvisaker was coming to see these urban neighborhoods—in his words, the "deteriorating real estate between central business district and suburbs, which economists are calling the gray area"— as both "magnets" for new groups of rural migrants to the city, and zones of divestment and neglect, where the process of urban adjustment was being allowed to stall out to the detriment of the migrants and the larger metropolis alike.[47] If instead these port-of-entry neighborhoods could function effectively as areas for "citifying our in-migrant population," Ylvisaker argued, the gray areas might yet be reclaimed from the pathological and unassimilable behaviors that poor newcomers brought with them from their rural places of origin. "That also then became the theme for a lot of the other work we did in the other [migration] streams; in the Mexican stream, in the black stream, and so forth," Ylvisaker explained. The southern Appalachian migrant had become more than just a convenient way to avoid "talking black": Marshall Bragdon and the other urban liberals at the MFRC in Cincinnati, along with Roscoe Giffin and his colleagues in Berea, had provided the Ford Foundation not only with a "conceptual framework" for understanding the rural roots of postwar poverty and urban decline, but also the beginnings of a "strategy of development" that Ylvisaker could imagine deploying beyond the boundaries of the hillbilly ghetto as well. "Appalachia gave us a chance to touch off the concern with the whole process."[48]

The first step in that direction was a Ford-funded pilot program called the Great Cities School Improvement Program, launched in March 1960 with a $1.25 million appropriation to seven northern and midwestern cities: Chicago, Cleveland, Detroit, Milwaukee, Philadelphia, Pittsburgh, and St. Louis.[49] Supported as a joint initiative between Ylvisaker's Public Affairs program and Ford's Education Division, the proposal for Great Cities had emerged out of a series of meetings between the superintendents of fourteen big-city school systems that had recently been the recipients of significant numbers of poor rural migrants of various racial and ethnic backgrounds. Key among them was Cincinnati's Wendell Pierce, who had conceived of the idea for the Berea workshops with Marshall Bragdon and Ira Gissen. Overwhelmed by the needs of these "culturally deprived," "disadvantaged," or "handicapped" newcomers—the clinical language applied to the adjustment problems encountered by migrant children varied slightly by grant application—the school officials envisioned the Great Cities programs combining educational reforms like curriculum revision and special-needs training for teachers, with school-based mechanisms for interacting with families, providing resources directly to households, and coordinating action with municipal agencies engaged in social welfare activities.[50] All told, between 1960 and 1961, Great Cities directed nearly $4 million to an array of city-sponsored initiatives, from adult education classes, to preschool programs for the children of poorly educated parents, to after-school facilities for teenagers. At the same time, extensive support was given to cross-site trainings, evaluations, and conferences like the workshops at Berea, which received an additional $70,000 in funding over the course of the first two Great Cities grant cycles. Berea's Willis Weatherford joined future Housing and Urban Development secretary Robert C. Weaver and Clarence Senior, the director of the Puerto Rican government's Migration Division, on a three-member committee to oversee an intensive process of what Ylvisaker called "continual evaluation" of the Great Cities programs. And the ever-useful Perley Ayer took an administrative leave from his duties at the Council of the Southern Mountains to become the initiative's floating "secretariat," charged with maintaining links between the various programs and to the foundation.[51]

From the outset, Ylvisaker saw the schools program more as an opening gambit than a conclusive solution—or, as he put it, "a stepping-stone to larger grants that would stimulate broader and more coherent community approaches to the physical and human problems of the gray areas." Although Ylvisaker felt strongly, as he told a contemporary audience of municipal leaders, that "it is one of the blocks to an effective urban program and policy in this country that the school system and City Hall have kept, and been kept, splendidly aloof from each other," he also readily acknowledged that "the schools can't go it alone." So by March 1961 Ford was ready to embark on "a full fledged program of action and reform," which would adopt the name of Ylvisaker's favorite sites of urban dysfunction and became known as the Gray Areas program. In keeping with Ylvisaker's growing belief that comprehensive urban reform was necessary to address the problems of the inner city, Gray Areas grants would be awarded to "broader-than-school approaches," which encouraged institutional coordination between mayors' offices and various agencies of the city bureaucracy, and supported citizen participation in the reinvigoration of declining urban neighborhoods under the rubric of what would come to be known as "community action." By the end of 1963, Gray Areas had become Ford's largest urban program to date, distributing nearly $23 million to five demonstration cities and the state of North Carolina, for initiatives that "encouraged urban communities to fashion more effective ways to speed the transition of the urban in-migrant and slum resident of low educational achievement and inadequate work skills to full economic, social and cultural participation in the urban community."[52]

The Ford Foundation's Gray Areas program—and Ylvisaker himself—would also become a critical bridge to the incipient War on Poverty, the seeds of which were already beginning to germinate in internal discussions centered around President John F. Kennedy's Council of Economic Advisers (CEA). In the summer of 1963, Ylvisaker took Michael Sviridoff, who ran the Gray Areas–funded antipoverty initiative in New Haven, to meet with key staffers in the Kennedy administration, including William Capron, then assistant to CEA chair Walter Heller. Ylvisaker's experience "designing programs," Capron would later recall, "took us a major step . . . beyond" the study-and-report approach that had defined the Kennedy administration's earlier and more limited forays against urban poverty, which had been carried out under the mantle of the President's Committee on Juvenile Delinquency and Youth Crime. It also brought the concept of community action to the center of emerging discussions of how to craft and implement policy. According to Capron, "A lot of the ideas that ended up actually in the legislation, the ground rules for how you go about organizing CAPS [community action programs], really were developed out of the Ford experience." After Lyndon Johnson took up the mantle of the antipoverty campaign following Kennedy's assassination, and tapped Sargent Shriver in February 1964 to run a Task Force on Poverty to begin drafting a bill, one of Shriver's first orders of business was to call Dick Lee, mayor of New Haven, to talk with him about the Gray Areas program. Ylvisaker, meanwhile, was present at the task force's first meeting and would become part of a "core group," which included Daniel Patrick Moynihan and Eric Tomlach from the Labor Department; James Adler and Andrew Brimmer from Commerce; Harold Horowitz from Health, Education and Welfare; and Shriver's deputy, Adam Yarmolinksy.[53]

Ylvisaker's experience developing the Gray Areas program would prove decisive in the task force meetings, as competing visions and priorities brought members into conflict. At one point "community action was out, the group had rejected it," recalled William Cannon, who represented the Bureau of the Budget. "I kind of encouraged Ylvisaker to bring it up again," and before long it was back in the mix. "He maintained contact with us throughout," recalled James Sundquist, who joined the task force from the Department of Agriculture. "He was always available if somebody needed to consult with him." By the time the Economic Opportunity Act was being debated in Congress, Ylvisaker could fairly claim that "the Community Action section of the poverty program builds heavily on the experience of the Gray Areas project"—an assessment confirmed by Frederick Hayes, who would become the deputy director of the Community Action program in the Office of Economic Opportunity after the EOA was signed into law in August 1964. "If there was a model for community action," Hayes observed, "it came from the Ford Foundation Gray Areas Program."[54]

And when, just two years later, OEO director Sargent Shriver was photographed sharing a pone of cornbread with Ernie Mynatt at the Over-the-Rhine headquarters of The Hub, a newly created neighborhood social service agency, it was a visceral reminder of the role that urban Appalachian poverty had played in setting in motion the events that would lead to the enactment of one of the signal social policy experiments of postwar liberalism. Shriver was visiting to determine whether The Hub should be funded by the OEO's local administrative agency, the Cincinnati Community Action Commission; Mynatt, a native of Kentucky's Harlan County, was by that point a senior figure among the community organizers in Over-the-Rhine, having been one of the first social workers hired by the Emanuel Community Center and the Appalachian Fund in the years after the 1954 MFRC workshop. As the story goes, Mynatt used the southern food staple to turn the tables on Shriver,

Ernie Mynatt, right, presents Office of Economic Opportunity director Sargent Shriver, center, with a pone of cornbread, on the occasion of Shriver's 1966 visit to The Hub, a social service agency working with residents of Cincinnati's Over-the-Rhine neighborhood.
Berea College Special Collections and Archives.

informing the Washington Brahmin and Kennedy in-law, "We can't do any business or transactions or anything unless you break bread with the poor." "Give me that bread and I'll break it," Shriver responded—and soon after he left town, The Hub became an official representative of the War on Poverty in Cincinnati.[55]

## Cultures of Poverty

As it happened, the meeting between Ernie Mynatt and Sargent Shriver turned out to be something of an anticlimax. The Hub got its War on Poverty funding, which allowed it to hire Over-the-Rhine residents to conduct neighborhood canvasses, identify potential clients and assist them in accessing existing social service resources, and begin to organize local block associations and tenant councils. But over time, the Cincinnati Community Action Commission proved to be far more responsive to the demands of the city's larger and better-organized poor Black population than it did to Cincinnati's poor white southerners. Until Stuart Faber of the Appalachian Fund was able to force his way onto the CAC board, the commission's leadership included no representatives of the southern Appalachian migrant community, and that omission led to perennial complaints from Faber, Mynatt, and others that southern white neighborhoods like Over-the-Rhine and Lower Price Hill did not receive their fair share of local antipoverty funds. "The Community Action Commission picked up on a survey done by the United Appeal that identified nine disadvantaged Cincinnati neighborhoods. The one with the worst problems was Over-the-Rhine and that's the one they didn't do anything about," Faber claimed at one point. Feeling neglected, by 1968 many of the activists who had been behind The Hub's creation were already coming to despair of its effectiveness, and began discussing plans for a new organization that would "engage with policy makers and power structures of Cincinnati, to look out for our civil rights."[56]

Michael Maloney, another southern Appalachian migrant who had left seminary training to become an organizer with The Hub, was one of them. He would later attribute these problems to a broader pattern in the War on Poverty's Community Action Program, which by the second half of the 1960s had become the site of a fraught political tug-of-war between Washington liberals, territorial city governments, and an increasingly assertive Black civil rights movement.[57] Even as the federal poverty initiative was devoting considerable resources to assist the Appalachian poor in southern Appalachia itself, Maloney pointed out, it soon became "clear that Model Cities and urban community action programs—not just in Cincinnati but throughout the country—were not going to have the will or ability to include poor whites."[58] Much of this, in Maloney's eyes, boiled down to the significantly more developed "social infrastructure" that was already in place in Black Cincinnati, "even before the War on Poverty," as compared to that which existed in neighborhoods like Over-the-Rhine.

"We had a sort of community structure in white Appalachian areas, too, but it wasn't nearly, nearly as advanced." And as a result, southern whites and the relatively novice community organizations that represented them were far less likely to secure the kind of federal support that the Community Action Program provided. "People were quite willing to have us as the token white or token Appalachian in the meeting," Maloney concluded. But beyond that, "we weren't wanted." So Maloney followed the advice given to him by a Black organizer in the city, quit The Hub, and started doing "some consciousness-raising with our own people."[59]

Maloney knew the Cincinnati experience firsthand, but he was right to note that the marginalization of southern Appalachian migrants within the urban-focused programs of the War on Poverty was a dynamic that was replicated elsewhere. When the Senate Subcommittee on Employment, Manpower and Poverty held hearings on the effectiveness of War on Poverty programming in Chicago in May 1967, one Kentucky-born migrant testified that whenever someone from Uptown's southern Appalachian community tried to secure a seat on the advisory council of the Montrose Urban Progress Center—one of eight OEO-supported community action programming hubs in Chicago, and the only one not located in a predominantly African American neighborhood—the response was always the same: "'We will let you know.' We never did hear." Uptown remained disproportionately Appalachian, and one of the most economically distressed neighborhoods in the city—by 1966 unemployment in the neighborhood stood at 27 percent, and only 39 percent of adults had full-time jobs—and yet, as the same migrant confirmed, "I am the only employment man on this war on poverty program from the Uptown area."[60] A white minister who worked with a large community of southern Appalachian migrants in the Cass Corridor, one of four blight-ridden zones that had been designated a target area by Detroit's Model Cities program, noted similar patterns there. Although the area's population of just under a hundred twenty thousand was split evenly along racial lines, Black residents, led by a well-organized group of women who had been active in local welfare rights organizing, had won fifteen of the sixteen seats on the Citizens Governing Board, which had a hand in determining how Model Cities grant money would be spent in the community. "They're growing Negro leaders while the poor whites go down, down, down," the minister concluded. Even the Black director of the Detroit Model Neighborhood Agency had grumbled, after seeing the results of the Governing Board election, that he wanted an "open affair with true representation, but they want the whole cake."[61]

There was more than a little irony to the fact that southern Appalachian migrants, who had played such an important role in the prehistory of the War on Poverty, now found themselves increasingly overlooked by the federal programs they had helped inspire. But there had been warning signs. Already by the time the Ford Foundation had officially launched its Gray Areas program, which became the most direct conduit between the early urban adjustment framework and the later antipoverty initiatives, there was a notable absence among the cities selected for inclusion of significant populations of southern white migrants. There was nothing obviously intentional in this: demonstration sites were chosen through a rigorous selection process, which required cities to submit exhaustive applications showing commitments of matching local funds, plans for interagency coordination and mayoral support, and programmatic innovations that promised to be not only of local relevance but also "of national significance."[62] Nevertheless, unlike its predecessor Great Cities, which had addressed itself to the challenges encountered by migrant families in primarily midwestern destinations that drew heavily on the Upper South during the postwar decades, the initial Gray Area cities ended up being uniformly coastal cities, in which the postwar urban crisis was playing out along more clearly and simply racial lines. So too did it become clear from an early stage that the "majority drift" of Shriver's Task Force on Poverty, as one task force member would later put it, "was focusing on low-income, black, inner-city [communities]." "There was lip service given to the fact that there was a whole lot more poor white people than there were poor black people in the United States," noted John Baker, who came to the task force from the Department of Agriculture and a career working on rural poverty matters. "But when they started talking plans and policies, their stereotype that they were trying to get operating programs to operate on was the inner-city black poor." Even Ylvisaker himself, who had once depended on southern whites as the "sturdy oaks" upon which he could erect programs that might "perk solutions through the whole system," no longer seemed to have a need for them. "The Ylvisakers and the Yarmolinskys and the Dick Goodwins," Baker recalled, "just kind of snarled when they'd think about rural or white southerners."[63]

To a significant extent, the shift in the color of the urban crisis was a function of the growing national presence and political influence of the civil rights movement, which by the early 1960s had begun to initiate a congruent shift in the way liberal intellectuals and politicians discussed the issue of urban poverty. The decade's highly visible urban uprisings, which began in northern cities in the summer of 1964 and continued in earnest through 1968, would only further solidify, in the popular eye as well as the political mind, this increasingly uniform association between urban poverty and the Black ghetto. And of course, southern white migrants, in Cincinnati and elsewhere, had access to means of escaping the unfolding urban crisis that were effectively denied to the Black poor during these years. As Jacqueline Jones notes, "in Northern cities, plain white folk from the rural South were afforded advantages in jobs and housing not because of some putative superiority (to blacks) in formal education, in 'factory sense', or in personal values, but because of the color of their skin"—and as growing numbers left the poverty of the inner city for working- and middle-class suburbs, or to return to southern points of origin, the complexion of the northern gray areas tended to darken further. Even Over-the-Rhine, which had become among the most densely settled of hillbilly ghettos during the two decades after World War II, would see its demographic profile begin to alter dramatically once again by the latter half of the 1960s. By 1980 roughly three-quarters of the neighborhood's population was Black.[64]

A further effect of all this would be the replacement of rurality with race as the dominant explanatory factor for the behavioral deficiencies of the urban poor. By the end of the 1960s, the comparisons that liberal intellectuals like Roscoe Giffin and Paul Ylvisaker had once drawn between southern whites, Blacks, Puerto Ricans, and other rural newcomers to the urban ghettos of the North and West were becoming far less common. The first step in this direction had come in 1959, when the anthropologist Oscar Lewis introduced the notion of a separate "culture of poverty," which more than mere "economic deprivation" had become a "way of life . . . passed down from generation to generation along family lines." Lewis developed his influential theory in ethnographic studies of poor families from Mexico and Puerto Rico, but the catalog of pathological behaviors and attitudes that he identified among his subjects—"a strong feeling of marginality, of helplessness, of dependence and of inferiority[;] . . . a lack of impulse control, a strong present-time orientation with relatively little ability to defer gratification and plan for the future, a sense of resignation and fatalism, a widespread belief in male superiority, and a high tolerance for psychological pathology of all sorts"—in many cases directly echoed the portrayals of maladjusted southern white migrants that had been painted by Giffin and others.[65]

Yet as his ideas entered the political mainstream, the sensitivity that Lewis had maintained to the particular contexts in which a culture of poverty developed—often as an adaptive strategy to "cope with feelings of hopelessness and despair" that would be familiar to displaced rural people of various backgrounds—increasingly came to be replaced with blanket indictments (and misrepresentations) of the cultural habits of the Black poor.[66] Most notable in this regard would be the 1965 publication of assistant secretary of labor Daniel Patrick Moynihan's influential report "The Negro Family: The Case for National Action." Moynihan borrowed Lewis's concept of the intergenerational transference of poverty and infamously attributed it, in the Black ghetto, to the marital breakdown of the Black family and the "matriarchal" household structure it supposedly produced. Not incidentally, another key idea that appeared in Moynihan's report—the notion that family dysfunction produced a self-reinforcing and perpetual "cycle of poverty and disadvantage"—had seen its first extensive use in the literature of the Gray Areas program, specifically in the grant application submitted by the North Carolina Fund on behalf of the state of North Carolina, which was added as a demonstration site in 1963.[67] Moynihan and others would later insist that the report's emphasis on family structure was taken out of context. But appearing as it did in the immediate aftermath of the first wave of urban uprisings, the report's central claim that there was something uniquely dysfunctional about the form that poverty took in Black communities nonetheless resonated with its intended audience in the White House.[68] Lyndon Johnson drew heavily on Moynihan's report in his pivotal public address at Howard University later that summer, which reflected the administration's growing conviction that urban poverty was a distinctly Black phenomenon. "Negro poverty is not white poverty," Johnson exclaimed. "Many of its causes and many of its cures are the same. But there are differences—deep, corrosive, obstinate differences—radiating painful roots into the community, the family, and the nature of the individual."[69]

In a country that had only one year earlier granted full civil rights to its Black population—and was still some months away from passing a legally enforceable Voting Rights Act—the recognition that race played a determinative role in the experience of poverty was in obvious ways a salutary development. Yet in emphasizing the cultural manifestations of poverty in the Black ghetto, rather than its structural roots, the Johnson administration's War on Poverty would also consistently mistake symptoms for causes, leaving unaddressed both the large-scale changes in the postwar economy and the political factors that reproduced racially disparate outcomes in the first place. "In thus disconnecting the poverty problem from the issues of urban transformation with which the [Ford Foundation's] public affairs program started out," Alice O'Connor writes, "the thinking behind Gray Areas and the War on Poverty perpetuated the notion of poverty as a problem confined to *other* people and diverted attention from its links to economic restructuring, population movements, racial discrimination, and government policies that perpetuated inequality."[70]

And in ways that other scholars have been less likely to note, it also signaled a significant focal shift that had occurred in the years between the MFRC's first workshop in Cincinnati and when Johnson spoke those words. No longer were migration and urban adjustment the "overarching processes" through which postwar liberalism would seek to address the problem of poverty in American cities. If migration had once appealed to liberals like Ylvisaker because of the political cover it offered as a putatively race-neutral concept, the changing political circumstances of the 1960s had produced a framing for the discussion of urban poverty that had become quite clearly coded as Black. In the process, however, the Transappalachian poor had been allowed to fall out of the equation. Only in their rural Appalachian homes did poor southern whites continue to register in the policy discussions of the period; and yet, as the Ford Foundation–funded regional study had only most recently noted, interregional migration between the southern mountains and the urban-industrial Midwest had become a common survival strategy of the region's rural poor for decades by that point.

For Roscoe Giffin, Marshall Bragdon, and the other early proponents of the urban adjustment framework, the rural backgrounds of southern whites in Cincinnati and other midwestern cities were understood as explanations for the individual struggles and collective backwardness that inhibited their full incorporation into modern urban society. The rising contemporary influence of the behavioral sciences, on top of long-standing beliefs about the peculiar culture of the Appalachian South, combined to produce a unique profile of pathology—the southern Appalachian migrant, or SAM—which echoed comparable portrayals of other populations of poor newcomers to the postwar city, all of whom, as Ylvisaker put it, were "more rural and backwoods in their culture than we." To be sure, this had been a fundamentally condescending way of diagnosing the social ills observed in the expanding ghettos of the urban Midwest—one that expressed a rather automatic preference for urban norms and values over rural ones, breathed new life into old hillbilly stereotypes, and at least implicitly accepted the logic of the marketplace as the only appropriate calculus for determining whether rural migrants encountered "success" in their new urban lives.

But it also, for a time, held out the prospect of a broader and more sensitive understanding of the underlying causes and effects of the changing economic landscape of postwar American society than the later and more explicitly racialized culture of poverty framing would allow. By emphasizing the common experiences uniting dislocated rural workers of various races, the urban adjustment framework could have been a means of drawing attention to the emerging weak points in the country's industrial economy, which by the 1950s was starting to show signs of sliding into reverse. With the economy's rate of growth slowing by more than half over the second part of the decade, and unemployment ticking steadily upward even during periods of recovery, the early effects of economic stagnation were already being felt at the bottom end of the labor market, where most rural migrants found themselves. Inner-city whites were dropping out of the workforce over the course of the decade at rates comparable to inner-city Blacks, and already by 1960 only two in three whites living in urban America were employed full-time for any portion of the year.[71] In nearly every major northern city where southern whites settled in great numbers during the two decades after World War II, the gap in income between those confined to urban gray areas and those who were able to escape to surrounding suburbs widened by considerable margins: by more than 4 percent in Chicago, 5 percent in Cleveland, and well over 6 percent in Detroit.[72] As one contemporary analysis pointed out, "Blue collar workers, those in good producing industries, teenagers, those with less than eight years of education, and non-whites suffered more sharply than average."[73] This was not an exact restatement of Ylvisaker's catalog of "Negros from the rural South, mountain folk from the Ozarks and Appalachians, Puerto Ricans from the island villages"—but it was close enough.

But instead of seeing the fate of the rural in-migrant as a bellwether of things to come for the midwestern industrial economy, liberals like Ylvisaker, Giffin, and Bragdon spent the 1950s and 1960s drawing inferences about the characterological defects of those left behind. The consequences of that oversight, ultimately, would prove to be twofold. Where once the visibility of the hillbilly ghetto might have allowed policymakers to address broadly the social and economic challenges associated with rural-to-urban migration, its relative invisibility as the 1960s wore on signified what would ultimately prove to be a conservative triumph: the "blackening" of culturalist theories of poverty and the political isolation of the Black ghetto from communities of poor and working-class whites.[74] And as liberalism became increasingly tied, fairly or otherwise, to the fortunes of the Black ghetto, it would appear to have less and less to offer the southern Appalachian migrants who had once served as its critical bridge to the postwar city. Having first objectified them as the ideal test-subjects for reforming the behavioral maladjustments of the urban poor, after the 1960s the white poor and working classes of the Upper South and the Midwest would increasingly become personae non gratae in the eyes of postwar liberals. In the meantime, a culture of urban resentment and anti-elitism, which had long been nurtured by the experiences of exploitation and marginalization that characterized life on the hillbilly highway, would begin to make an ominous new sound in the shifting political landscape of postwar American society.

# CHAPTER SIX

# Lost Highways

## COUNTRY MUSIC AND THE RISE
## AND FALL OF HILLBILLY CULTURE

*"I was just a lad, nearly twenty-two,*
*Neither good nor bad, just a kid like you.*
*And now I'm lost, too late to pray.*
*Lord, I paid the cost, on the lost highway."*[1]

—HANK WILLIAMS, "LOST HIGHWAY" (1949)

*"I live back in the woods, you see.*
*A woman and the kids and the dogs and me.*
*I got a shotgun, a rifle, and a four-wheel drive,*
*And a country boy can survive."*[2]

—HANK WILLIAMS JR., "A COUNTRY BOY CAN SURVIVE" (1982)

IT WAS NEW YEAR'S EVE 1953, and Hank Williams—the so-called "King of the Hillbillies," as he was soon to be memorialized in newspapers around the country—was driving from Montgomery, Alabama, to Canton, Ohio. Or rather, he was being driven—as was often the case during his last months as a touring musician, when he spent most of his time marinating in a steady bath of booze and painkillers, Williams had hired a chauffeur for the trip, in this instance an eighteen-year-old college student and part-time taxi driver named Charles Carr. Carr was responsible for delivering Williams to a pair of New Year's Day performances at the Canton Memorial Auditorium, alongside fellow country music headliners Hawkshaw Hawkins, Homer and Jethro, and the Webb Sisters. But the two would never make it beyond West Virginia.[3]

Snowy conditions almost convinced Carr and Williams to wait out the weather at a hotel in Knoxville, where they had stopped to rest on the evening of December 31. "It's a tough drive, I promise you that," Carr would later remark, about the two-lane highways that wind through the mountainous counties of East Tennessee and between the Appalachian ridgelines that stretch across West Virginia and southeastern Ohio. "If I had known what was going to happen, I would not have made the trip." But the Canton date, though hardly the most glamorous that Williams had played in his young life, had recently become too important to miss. Though only twenty-nine years old at the beginning of 1953—a mere six years removed from the release of his first chart-topping single—Hank Williams had spent much of 1952 doing everything he could to bring his meteoric recording career to a crashing halt. First, Williams's tumultuous marriage to his first wife, Audrey Mae, had reached its inevitable dissolution amid rumors that Williams had fired a gun at her four times following a drunken spree. Williams had "been engaging in the wildest extravagances, and wasting the funds which [had] come into his hands," Audrey Mae wrote in her divorce complaint; worse still, he became "a man of violent disposition when aroused, and this violence is particularly aggravated when the complainant, herself, is the object thereof." A few months later, Williams's out-of-control drinking got him ousted once and for all from the *Grand Ole Opry*, country music's biggest stage. Desperate to protect their star investment, executives at Nashville's WSM radio station had even taken to sending a private detective on tour with Williams to keep him sober toward the end, but it had proven a fool's errand: when he encountered Williams on the morning the station decided it had finally had enough, WSM manager Harry Stone recalled, "he was the most pitiful-looking thing I'd ever seen." The nadir point came that October, when Williams resorted to marrying his second wife, the nineteen-year-old Billie Jean, in front of a paying audience at the New Orleans Municipal Auditorium. "He didn't have any money, and he needed some stuff to start the marriage with, especially furniture," explained Williams's manager, Oscar Davis. Williams was so hard up by that point, in fact, that he and Billie Jean ran through the performance twice: once for a matinee crowd and then again that evening, charging separate admissions each time. One of Williams's more reverential biographers describes 1952 as a "troubled" year for the singer, but when all is said and done it was probably more appropriate to call it a tailspin.[4]

Canton, then, was supposed to be the beginning of a comeback—and although his records were continuing to sell despite his very public struggles (Williams just then had three singles on *Billboard*'s top-ten country-and-western listings), it was a chance at a comeback he knew he was lucky to get. After being fired from the *Grand Ole Opry*, Williams had been forced to retreat to Shreveport, Louisiana, where he resumed playing for radio station KWKH's regionally popular but lower-profile *Louisiana Hayride*, on which he had begun his career. Though the familiar audience took him back without reservations, Williams quickly returned to form and was soon bombing or altogether missing performances there due to drinking. For its part, Harry Stone later confirmed, WSM "wouldn't have given him a job back for anything in the world"—and the *Opry*, broadcast over WSM's fifty-thousand-watt frequency every Saturday night since the station had received its clear-channel designation in 1932, was still the surest way to reach the steadily growing markets for country music that were emerging outside of the rural South during these years. The Canton concerts were to be Williams's first dates north of the Ohio River since he had been fired from WSM and left Nashville—if not quite in disgrace, then at least surrounded by serious questions about whether his better years were already behind him.[5]

As it happened, Hank Williams would survive his catastrophic 1952—but only barely. During the early morning hours of January 1, 1953, drunk and high in the backseat of his Cadillac, Williams suffered a massive heart attack and died instantly. Somewhere between Mount Hope and Oak Hill, West Virginia, along US Highway 19, an early long-haul route connecting the Gulf of Mexico with Lake Erie, Carr reached back to adjust a blanket that had slipped from the singer's shoulders and found his body cold and stiff. A subsequent autopsy discovered copious amounts of alcohol and morphine in Williams's system, and police officers would also find chloral hydrate on his person—a combination sometimes used to euthanize the critically ill, though rumors of a suicide could never be substantiated. Fittingly enough, given the singer's preoccupation with the subject and his posthumous canonization as country music's preeminent tragic troubadour, the unfinished lyrics to yet another song about faded love were found strewn among the empty beer cans at his feet. In the days to come, few of his many mourners would fail to note the morbid irony of the title of his latest single—"I'll Never Get Out of This World Alive," which was just then beginning its climb up the *Billboard* charts—and twenty thousand of them would attend his funeral in Montgomery, the biggest the city had ever seen. "Bankers, jurists, physicians, writers, governors and philanthropists have been returned unto dust in Montgomery," the *Montgomery Advertiser* genuflected on the morning after, "but the coffin of none was followed as was that of the dead singer."[6]

To say that much has been written about Hank Williams's extraordinary career, his sudden and premature demise, and his influence on postwar country music is to run the risk of understatement.[7] Rarely, though, have these myriad reflections on his life and legacy noted the relationship between Williams and the evolving regional geography of southern working-class culture during the same period. Indeed, it is not beside the point that the most notorious car ride in country music history took place on the hillbilly highway, along the very same roads that so many southern-born men and women like Williams—who was raised in Georgiana, Alabama, a small town once described as "sixty miles south of Montgomery, one hundred and fifteen miles north of Mobile, meaning that it is practically nowhere"—were then taking north in search of work. Not altogether unlike Williams, desperate as he was to get his career back on track, they were heading to places like Canton in search of the kinds of economic opportunities that life in the South failed to provide.

A midsized steel town that had become an increasingly attractive destination for migrants from the Upper South in the years during and after World War II, Canton's population of working-class southern whites increased nearly tenfold over the course of the 1950s. During these years, more southern Appalachians from the Blue Ridge area of western North Carolina and northern Georgia ended up in Canton than in any midwestern city outside of Detroit. All the new arrivals helped ensure that the recently constructed Canton Memorial Auditorium was filled to capacity that New Year's Day. Another regional transplant, the Kentucky-born Cliff Rodgers, who had also found success in the North as one of the top country music disc jockeys in the country at nearby WHKK in Akron, was on hand to introduce Williams and emcee the event. It was no accident, in other words, that the "King of the Hillbillies" was on his way to a place like Canton, Ohio, when he died.[8]

But there was more that connected Hank Williams and the hillbilly highway than just the symbolic location of his final ride. Most significant was his role in bridging the divide between country's largely regional origins and its growing popularity across wide swaths of the country and with an audience that was no longer confined to the rural poor and working classes. That is not to suggest that country music had never before been enjoyed or performed outside the South. As early as 1928, in fact, just a few years after the first commercial recordings of country music were produced, a promoter with the Loew's theater chain named H. M. Barnes arranged a touring show for a group of musicians from Virginia, North Carolina, and Tennessee who he called the Blue Ridge Ramblers. Touting these overalls-wearing, banjo-strumming Ramblers as "real mountain recording and broadcast artists," Barnes booked dates for the band all across the northeast. The audiences they played before were uniformly enthusiastic, with many finding themselves pleasantly transported, in the words of the local newspaper in Lowell, Massachusetts, to "the environment of the Kentucky hills." By the middle of the 1930s, according to the Lynds, Muncie's radio-listening public had become so fond of the danceable string-band music that originated in the southern mountains that "as many as 12,700 'fan letters' have been received in a single week commending these 'hillbilly' [radio] programs"—a rather shocking total that, if accurate, would have amounted to roughly one fan letter from every four or five city residents at the time. Early country music celebrities like Jimmie Rodgers and the Carter Family, meanwhile, had already achieved the kinds of national reputations and followings that Williams would later attract during his brief career (even if Williams was the first to be lauded by the New York City papers as the "Hillbilly Shakespeare"). And the notable popularity throughout the Midwest of "barn dance" radio shows like the *Opry*—one of which, the *National Barn Dance* on Chicago's WLS, even predated the creation of the *Opry*—during the pre–World War II period further testified, in one scholar's assessment, to "the spread of country music and the enlargement of its audience well before the mass migration of southern whites."9

Still, it was no coincidence that the explosion in country music's popularity after World War II overlapped with the most intensive period of outmigration from the rural South. The expansion of southern leisure and recreational culture in destination cities throughout the industrial Midwest had not only stimulated the proliferation of hillbilly taverns throughout the region, but also pointed the way to an expanding geography for country music record sales, radio airplay, and tour revenues that would allow a musical genre long derided in both casual conversation and official industry jargon as "hillbilly music" to begin to transcend its historic regional and class origins. Though the growth of radio and the touring performances of curiosity acts like the Blue Ridge Ramblers had begun to expose other portions of the country to the type of music recorded by white musicians of the rural South, even as late as the second half of the 1940s, country music was still overwhelmingly consumed by rural southern audiences. As noted by the longtime industry executive Henry Glover, who then worked for King Records in Cincinnati ("If It's a King, It's a Hillbilly"), before country's explosion onto the national stage in the 1950s and 1960s, the label saw most of its country sales in "remote" markets, "in the backwoods in the country." "I wouldn't give you two cents for a country record during that time in New York or Chicago," Glover explained. Stephen Cisler, who helped launch WLS's pioneering *National Barn Dance*, offered similar observations about the station's local audience. "We didn't care a hoot for Chicago. We were broadcasting for Bloomington, Illinois, or downstate, or anywhere we could reach a farmer or a small town."[10]

To say that Hank Williams changed all that is a bit of an overstatement—but not much of one. To be sure, it helped that many of his fans were themselves moving out of "the backwoods," and in the process creating parallel new markets for country records throughout the urban-industrial North and West. When Gene Myers relocated from Pelham, Tennessee, to the Five Points neighborhood in Cleveland, for instance, he and his brother Bernice made sure to dig deep into their repertoire of Hank Williams songs when they played shows at local southern bars like the Buckeye. Gene played the guitar, while Bernice sang and alternated between the banjo and the fiddle. "There wasn't a song he didn't know by Hank Williams," Bernice's wife, Barbara Myers, recalled later. "In the bars, he couldn't go in without them women hollerin', 'Hank! Give us a Hank song!'" Still, as the ethnomusicologist D. K. Wilgus noted at the height of the postwar country music boom, "Williams' popularity did not stop with what should have been his 'normal' audience, but . . . spilled over into general American culture." Never before, after all, had popular musicians the likes of Rosemary Clooney or Tony Bennett covered the songs of a "hillbilly musician." But they did Williams's, with Bennett spending twenty-seven weeks atop the pop charts in 1951 with his rendition of "Cold, Cold Heart," and Clooney scoring a number-one hit of her own the following year with "Half as Much."[11]

Explaining the source of Williams's all-encompassing popularity was not immediately straightforward. Williams, Wilgus noted, "was as country-based as they come, or rather he was a typical product of the forces of urbanization on the southeastern poor white. He reeked of the parched fields of Alabama, the dirty streets and dives of Montgomery. He embodied drunken Saturday nights in the tavern and soul-saving Sundays in the country church." And as such, Williams embodied everything about the hillbilly *lumpen* and the maladjusted rural migrant that had made poor and working-class southern whites such as himself objects of continual scorn, derision, and reform-minded condescension across the wider landscape of Transappalachia. There was perhaps no clearer indication of what Wilgus calls "the polarization of the urban hillbilly" than the fact that the year of Williams's death—a star-making tragic end that would mark the beginning of country music's vault into the high terrain of American popular entertainments—coincided so precisely with the Mayor's Friendly Relations Committee's first stirrings of interest in Cincinnati's southern Appalachian community. In the same midwestern markets where Williams's telltale country warble was becoming such a sensation among urban audiences, middle-class residents were simultaneously identifying the influx of rural folkways and "mountain habits" as an existential threat to the rational order of the postwar city.[12]

Resolving this tension, between the negative cultural associations tied up in country music's hillbilly past, and the mass appeal and acceptance that would define its future, is the goal of this final chapter. The story of country music's crossover from a regional idiom and lower-class subculture to something that *Billboard* magazine would soon lionize as "our native art" was, in a sense, the story of the unmaking of the hillbilly ghetto, the final—and perhaps always inevitable—assimilation of the Transappalachian working class into the mainstream of American life. But if so, it was a more complicated and multidirectional process than the classic assimilation experience, previously undergone by successive waves of European immigrants to the United States during the nineteenth and twentieth centuries. While there may have been some truth to the notion, as others have argued, that for travelers along the hillbilly highway—as, with slight variations, for the Irish, Slavs, and Italians before them—"it was possible to leave the 'ridgerunner' and 'briarhopper' taunts behind forever by losing their accents, adopting Northern dress fashions, and switching the radio dial from Hank Williams to Frank Sinatra," the reality was, over the final two decades of the Transappalachian migration, many more midwestern urbanites began turning the dial in the opposite direction. As they did, the cultural divide that had separated rural white southerners from their northern neighbors throughout the half-century-long Transappalachian migration began to grow smaller. And if by the late 1960s and early 1970s it was in country music, as much or more so than in any other terrain of American culture, that the fates of the white South and the larger nation seemed most expressly and evocatively intertwined, it was because country music, too, emerged from this crucible period very different, in form and in meaning, than it had been earlier in the century. More tragic in its bearing, increasingly defined by stylistic conventions determined by the industry in Nashville, different in its class inflections, and, for the first time, markedly rigid in its ideology—the evolution that country music underwent to become widely recognized as "one of the bright ornaments of America's musical heritage" itself reflected larger changes in the direction of American politics over the latter half of the twentieth century. It was here as well that Hank Williams and the hillbilly highway crossed paths, in a confluence of cultural and economic transformations that helped turn hillbilly music into country music—and in the process, helped turn this supposedly native genre into a far more conservative art form than it had been at its birth.[13]

## Hillbillies and Highways in Early Country Music

Singing careers aside, Hank Williams certainly had more in common with a Bernice Myers than he did with a Tony Bennett. After he was rejected from military service in the fall of 1942—the result of a chronic, degenerative back condition he suffered with most of his life, which likely contributed to his dependency on painkillers—Williams took a job at the Alabama Drydock and Shipbuilding Company, in Mobile, where he worked as a welder, on and off, for the next year and nine months. By that point Williams had spent the better part of the last six years trying to get his singing career off the ground, mostly unsuccessfully. Although he continued to perform locally while he worked in the shipyards, Williams was beginning to despair of his ability to make a living as a full-time musician.

For a time, then, it seemed as if Williams might go the same route as so many other young men from the South during the war years, leaving the countryside behind for a life of industrial employment. Years later, after he had returned to music, Williams would explain to an interviewer that it was his familiarity with work, and the arduousness of the working-class life he had known first in Georgiana and later in Mobile, which made his songs resonate so widely. "There are more people who are like us than there are the educated, cultured kind. . . . You got to know a lot about hard work. You got to have smelt a lot of mule manure before you can sing like a hillbilly. The people who has been raised something like the way the hillbilly has knows what he is singing about and appreciates it."[14]

However belabored, the association Williams drew between a particular kind of class experience and singing "like a hillbilly" was an accurate enough description of the socio-historical origins of early country music. Like the hillbilly highway itself, country music emerged out of the multifaceted regional transformations brought about by the rise of market relations and the various processes associated with proletarianization in the rural South. But however self-evident such an assertion may appear in retrospect, to the earliest generations of folklorists and musicologists, southern rural music—and especially music that originated in the Appalachian South—seemed to be about anything but the sweat and stink of work. When the British ethnomusicologist Cecil Sharp and his American collaborator Olive Dame Campbell ventured into the Appalachian hinterland in the 1910s in search of folk songs and ballads, they encountered what they perceived to be a "fascinating and well-nigh magical" mountain culture, which "for a hundred years or more [had] been completely isolated and cut off from all traffic with the rest of the world." Economic underdevelopment, by Sharp's account, had left the region and its inhabitants in a kind of pristine state, the descriptions of which echoed and presaged a century's worth of sociological theorizing that ran from William Goodell Frost through Roscoe Giffin and beyond. "Immune from that continuous, grinding, mental pressure, due to an attempt to 'make a living,' from which all of us in the modern world suffer," Sharp observed, southern mountaineers lived in something close to an "ideal state of things," which, along with the region's putatively uniform "racial heritage," sustained folk traditions inherited directly from the "original settlers . . . who left the shores of Britain some time in the eighteenth century." As a result, Sharp and Campbell concluded in their pioneering 1917 study, *English Folk Songs from the Southern Appalachians*, the musical culture of the southern mountains was "far less affected by modern musical influences than the most remote and secluded English village." Indeed, so cut off from the wider world was the typical southern "hillsman," Sharp claimed, that "the only music, or, at any rate, the only secular music that he hears and has, therefore, an opportunity of learning is that which his British forefathers brought with them from their native country and has since survived by oral tradition."[15]

As it did in other contexts, the nearsightedness that imbued itself in such putatively sympathetic academic assessments of the region's unchanging traditionalism found much common ground with the more explicitly hostile popular reception that greeted the earliest country music recordings. Then, and for the next quarter-century or more, southern rural music was known in the trade press as "hillbilly music"—a marketing innovation that likely owed its origins in equal measure to the influential New York–based music promoter Ralph S. Peer, who arranged the first country recordings for Okeh Records in 1923 and later claimed to have "originated the terms 'Hillbilly' and 'Race' as applied to the record business"; and the North Carolina–born country musician Al Hopkins, who separately from Peer and along with his three brothers began recording as a band called The Hill Billies in 1925.[16] Whatever the direct impetus may have been, the use of the generic epithet to categorize the musical recordings then emerging from the white rural South also reflected the potency of the popular race-thinking of the day. "Theirs is a community all unto themselves," Abel Green, music editor for *Variety* magazine, wrote about the "mountaineer type of illiterate white," in a 1926 review of the newly available "Hill Billy" recordings. "Illiterate and ignorant, with the intelligence of morons, the sing-song, nasal-twanging vocalizing of a Vernon Dalhart or a Carson Robison . . . intrigues their interest"—and, presumably, no one else's (or at least no one whose cultural standards were sophisticated enough to prefer the popular music of the day). In either case, the southern hillbilly was represented as a relic of a premodern lifestyle, and his musical tastes likewise understood as a cultural holdover of the seclusion and provincialism of the mountain and the farm. Sympathetic listeners, like Sharp, might elevate the musical culture of rural southern whites by ethnologizing its origins in the ballad tradition of Appalachia's English and Scotch Irish ancestors; while the less so, like Abel Green, might degrade the same music by pathologizing it as the picking and twanging of a primitive people. But this was condescension whichever way you put it, and the implication behind either articulation of the genre's traditionalism was that hillbilly music, like the region from which it hailed, was backward.[17]

The reality, of course, was far more complicated. On the one hand, not only did many of the earliest country musicians and promoters wholeheartedly reject the hillbilly epithet, but their actual musical backgrounds often belied the notion that they were nothing more than untrained rustics and folk primitives.[18] Bradley Kincaid, who long after becoming the first major country radio star still liked to tell interviewers he was raised "back at the edge of the Cumberlands, where the boulevard dwindles down to a squirrel's path and loses itself at the foot of the giant trees," nonetheless recalled the stylistic adjustment he had to make when he began playing on the *National Barn Dance* program on Chicago's WLS in 1925. "I was interested in semi-classical music [i.e., light opera]. I had been studying, taking voice and studying music" at Berea College, where he met and eventually married a woman who had graduated from the Oberlin Conservatory of Music. By the time *Barn Dance* talent scouts, eager to capitalize on the growing interest in southern rural music, recruited Kincaid to perform on the show, "I had gotten so far away from the folksongs that I didn't even have a guitar. But when [they] asked me to come down and do a program, I was hungry you know?" Likewise, Doc Hopkins (no relation to Al), who learned to play the banjo and the guitar growing up in Harlan County and later became a founding member of the Cumberland Ridge

Runners, one of the more successful country acts of the 1930s, recalled similarly ambivalent feelings about the "traditional" music that Cecil Sharp and others associated with the region of his birth. "I knew these old folk-songs and ballads, plenty of them, but I was a little ashamed to play them. I wanted to play and sing, learn the new popular songs."[19]

Even those early country musicians who hailed from the more geographically remote portions of the upper South, in other words, were not so totally unfamiliar with the outside world and what Sharp dismissed as "modern street-songs."[20] Furthermore, the portrayal of the rural South as a static and stagnant regional backwater, which both Sharp and someone like Abel Green took largely for granted, was itself increasingly out of date, as optimistic local boosters touting a New South had been insisting for going on half a century. In fact, there was no separating the birth of commercial country music in the 1920s from the by-then already decades-old processes of industrialization and urbanization that had churned up older ways of life across the rural South. For someone like Hank Williams—a southern hill-billy who spent much of his adult life as a wage-laboring spot-welder and struggling barroom musician, before becoming a wildly self-destructive mass-entertainment celebrity—the bit about smelling a lot of manure was as much metaphoric as it was literal. Horseshit and hard work were no less the hillbilly's lot off the farm as they had been on it.

Indeed, fundamentally modern concerns and fundamentally working-class experiences had so thoroughly suffused themselves into the lives of rural white southerners that they were ubiquitous throughout the earliest country recordings produced and sold under the rubric of hillbilly music. Southern cotton, king among cash crops, ruled the world's market through the Civil War, and the forms of debt peonage—sharecropping, tenant farm-ing, crop liens, the "mortgage system"—which replaced the slave planta-tion as the engines of capitalist agriculture after the war were among rural farmers' first introductions to the harsh discipline of the marketplace. As a result, an early blues like "The Ballad of the Boll Weevil," which likely origi-nated with Black sharecroppers in South Texas and evoked the underlying precariousness of a world in which "the merchant got half the cotton, / the boll weevil got the rest," was familiar enough to the white Dacula, Georgia-born chicken farmer and renowned fiddler Gid Tanner that he made it one of his first recordings for Columbia in March 1924.[21] Timbering not only employed thousands up and down the Appalachian range, despite Cecil Sharp's impressions to the contrary, but had also brought market-driven globalization to even that supposedly remote corner of the American hin-terland, where by 1901 the *Lexington Morning Herald* was reporting that a shipment of close to one million dollars' worth of Kentucky white oak was on its way to Austria, to be used to make barrel staves. "Lay down late, but you get up soon, / ain't seen nothin' but the stars and the moon," went one song that described the around-the-clock work schedules dictated by the far-flung forces of supply and demand to the turpentine and lumber camps of north Florida. For one of his final recordings, Hank Williams would memorialize the "sweatin' and swearin'" working days his father, Lon Williams, had put in for the W.T. Smith Lumber Company of Chapman, Alabama, in a song called "The Log Train." Hardly "immune" from the need to make a living, as Sharp had put it, Lon Williams's life was, in fact, one of "grinding pressure" and a strict regimentation that would have been increasingly familiar to other rural southerners who had come to rely on wage work to supplement or replace traditional livelihoods. "Every mornin' at the break of day, / he'd grab his bucket and be on his way. / Winter or summer, sunshine or rain, / every mornin' he'd run that ole log train."[22]

"The whistle of the ole log train" beckoned a young Hank and many other southern children to supper, and in doing so it gave the lie to any notion that the broader region endured in a state of permanent isolation. By the turn of the twentieth century, in fact, nine out of ten southerners lived in a county with access to the railroad, which by then had even penetrated the barely accessible hollows of the West Virginia mountains. Among the many lasting changes begotten by the coming of the railroads would be generations' worth of country songs about trains—from Vernon Dalhart's "The Wreck of the Old '97," one of the first country hits, to Johnny Cash's "Folsom Prison Blues."[23] The expansion of mine and mill employment throughout the South, meanwhile, not only provided new subjective experiences for rural songwriters to narrate, but, as country music historian Bill C. Malone has noted, also impacted in fundamental ways the kinds of formal arrangements that early country musicians employed. "Appalachian coal camps and Piedmont textile villages encouraged a degree of social cohesion and community consciousness that was not always possible in the scattered rural or forested districts of the South," Malone points out—an especially propitious development since "many mill workers brought fiddles, banjoes, and other string instruments when they relocated from their rural homes." As a result, some of the most successful early string bands, like Charlie Poole's North Carolina Ramblers, traced their origins to these more densely populated areas that were then being produced by the engine of industrialization.[24] Much to his chagrin, Sharp observed the effects of these kinds of developments

as well: during his comparatively less productive travels collecting traditional ballads in the eastern Kentucky coalfields, Sharp noted that "when
there is coal and good wages to be earned, the families soon drop their
old-fashioned ways and begin to ape town manners."[25]

From the outset, then, hillbilly music was the music not of a premodern folk culture, nor a society of backward primitives, but of a people confronting the powerful economic forces then transforming the social and
cultural landscape all around them. Highways, too, were a symbol of this
southern world in flux, and as the total mileage of paved roads interpen-
etrating the region grew threefold in the period between 1914 and 1930,
the road and its open-ended possibilities left no less indelible an imprint
on early country music as the emergence of wage work or the proliferation of company-controlled mining camps.[26] Like those other markers of
economic progress, the meaning invested in the symbol of the highway
was often ambiguous. To be sure, for many southerners it signified nothing less than the "newfound mobility" of a region freed from the historic
shackles of geographic isolation and economic stagnation—an alternative
to claustrophobic lives dominated by rural poverty, the seclusion of the
family farm and the mountain hollow, and the close surveillance of the
small town and the insular religious community. But it was not for nothing
that the primary supplier of road-construction manpower across the South
in the first decades of the twentieth century was convict labor—an inescapable reminder that here, as elsewhere, the visions of progress embraced by
proponents of the New South often came at a cost, and one borne most
frequently and heavily by the region's poor and working classes. "Oh, I'm
going down this road feeling bad," sings the chain-gang-sentenced protago-
nist of Henry Whitter's 1924 single "Lonesome Road Blues," one of the very
earliest country recordings and a mainstay for country, blues, and bluegrass
musicians in the decades since. "Oh, I'm going if I never come back."[27]

Country artists from Whitter to Uncle Dave Macon to Clarence Ash-
ley to Fiddlin' Jim McCarroll, and many lesser lights besides all recorded
highway songs during the 1920s and 1930s. But it was the first significant
highway hit produced by the genre that most effectively captured the sense
of unease that the highway's arrival often beckoned forth in country's earliest practitioners. Dorsey Dixon's 1937 composition "I Didn't Hear Nobody
Pray"—which would become one of Roy Acuff's most successful singles
when he recorded an amended version and released it as "Wreck on the
Highway" in 1942—is, at first glance at least, a dour piece of pious moral-
izing.[28] The narrator tells the real-life story of a horrific car crash in Rockingham, North Carolina, in which two people were killed; the highway is

the scene of their bloody end and alcohol the contributing factor, but it is really the whole desacralized social order that Dixon is inveighing against. Grisly descriptions of the aftermath of the accident couch the main message of the song: "Whiskey and glass all together, / was mixed up with blood where they lay. / Death played her hand in destruction, / but I didn't hear nobody pray." That final line is repeated throughout as a kind of sermonic refrain, and Dixon leaves it intentionally unresolved whether it is the dead couple or his audience who he is accusing of being insufficiently penitent. More than booze and fast cars, it is pervasive irreligiousness that Dixon sees as the scourge of contemporary society. Or rather, they are all of a piece—the whiskey, windshield glass, and blood all "run together," an impure mixture of a distinctly modern and secular vintage. And not incidentally, they flow into one another on the pavement of the highway.[29]

Still, it is impossible to read "I Didn't Hear Nobody Pray" as simply the teetotaling sermonizing of a devout anti-modernist. More so than any other highway song of the period, "I Didn't Hear Nobody Pray" captured the ambiguities at the heart of the convergence between the commercial and the traditional out of which sprung early hillbilly music, and which were so immediately caught up in the image of the road. Dixon himself had grown up poor in South Carolina and worked for more than three decades in the textile mills of the Carolina Piedmont while writing and recording songs with his brother, Howard—who played the steel guitar and worked in the mills, too, straight up until he died of a heart attack while on the job in 1961. Like other rural southerners of both races during the early decades of the twentieth century, Dixon rejected the more mainstream Protestant churches, which many saw as having made too easy an accommodation with "the vanity, materialism, and spiritual complacency" that seemed to prevail in New South middle-class and urban society. Instead, in the early 1930s Dixon became a Free Will Baptist, a schismatic denomination that combined biblical orthodoxy with a working-class character that made it especially popular within the Carolina mill villages and throughout the region's mining communities.[30] Dixon thought of his musical career first and foremost as a means of spreading the Gospel—but it was not beside the point that he would often complement his more didactic compositions about local tragedies, like "I Didn't Hear Nobody Pray," with a roster of songs about industrial labor and poverty.[31] In fact, when the wave of labor unrest that swept the southern Piedmont in the late 1920s and early 1930s reached the Aleo mill in East Rockingham, where the Dixon brothers worked, it was noted that the striking workers liked to pass their time on the picket line singing the protest songs that Dorsey had written.[32]

Viewed within this context, Dixon's version of fundamentalist Christianity did not deny modern life so much as deplore the hegemonic moral logic of its dominant system of production. In the eastern Kentucky coal towns that would become the backbone of the United Mine Workers, or the cotton fields of southeastern Missouri and Arkansas from which emerged the Southern Tenant Farmers Union in the 1930s, Holiness and Pentecostal churches like the Free Will Baptists often provided the vocabulary and ethical cosmology for some of the most valiant labor struggles that rural southerners would ever engage in.[33] Dixon's were the kind of religious people who might have voted for William Jennings Bryan or even Eugene Debs, both of whom drew support for their respective visions of the cooperative commonwealth from religiously conservative southern white common folk.[34] Evangelizing the Gospel and recounting the hardships of mill labor, in other words, were not such incommensurable identities for hillbilly songwriters in the early decades of the twentieth century, and Dorsey Dixon was not the only Carolina millhand who might see in the flowering roadways of the New South the creeping of the marketplace and its corrosive amorality. A wreck on the highway, indeed.

Dixon's take on the highway in "I Didn't Hear Nobody Pray" was an unusually pessimistic one. By contrast, the most popular country musician of Dixon's generation, Jimmie Rodgers, made a career out of singing songs about hopping trains and living the rambling lifestyle. In Rodgers's music, the new roadways and train lines of the period more often represented a way out, rather than another link in the chain; and songs like "Waiting for a Train" "My Rough and Rowdy Ways," "Away Out on the Mountain" or "Peach Pickin' Time in Georgia," made the all-too-familiar experiences of rural displacement sound like a hobohemian frolic. To be sure, Rodgers's rambling bonhomie was in some good measure a pretense. As his biographer Nolan Porterfield has written, "If the life of Jimmie Rodgers can be characterized by a single element, it would be impermanence," an existential throughline uniting a "nomadic adolescence" and an "erratic" career as an "itinerant railroader" that would have been all too familiar to many working-class southerners (Rodgers himself was born in Meridian, Mississippi, which boomed with the railroads after the Civil War). It was while working on the railroads, in fact, that Rodgers contracted an ultimately fatal case of tuberculosis, which killed him at just thirty-five; like Dixon, in other words, Rodgers was familiar with the darker side of industrial life. But the "Singing Brakeman," as they called Rodgers, kept yearning after the sound of the train whistle, and his famous yodel was like a howl at the moon, with all the barely sublimated lupine sexuality it evoked.[35]

It is worth noting that Rodgers was one of the extremely few country musicians, then or since, whose repertoire included virtually no religious songs. And yet there are clearly ways in which two hillbilly singers like Dixon and Rodgers had far more in common than not. Both demonstrated how so-called hillbilly music emerged from and gave voice to a rural proletariat confronting an uneasy transition and increasingly displaced by economic forces beyond its control. Dixon's may have been a more traditional and in many ways more trenchant form of criticism. But there was also something in Rodgers's music that presaged the restlessness and refusal of conformity that would come to define later, more fully formed countercultural expressions like the postwar Beat movement—one reason, perhaps, why Jimmie Rodgers has had a more enduring influence on postwar country, rock, and blues than has Dixon.[36] In either case, the highways and railroads they fixated on embodied as clearly as anything else the forces of economic progress that were transforming life and labor across the rural South during the first decades of the twentieth century. It was no surprise, in other words, that a significant subgenre of early country music was about hitting the road, moving on, leaving behind life's impoverishments, be they economic, familial, cultural, or spiritual. Dixon wanted to escape the venality of mill society; Rodgers just wanted to "grab a train and ride"—but for both these hillbillies, the open road led not backward but forward.[37]

## Tragedy and Nostalgia in the Postwar Highway Song

Not since Jimmie Rodgers had a country musician so intentionally and effectively assumed the posture of the rambler as did Hank Williams during his abbreviated but transformative stint as the "King of the Hillbillies." Williams had been particularly taken with cowboy culture from an early age, even briefly running away from home to join a Texas rodeo when he was a teen; and he would embrace the rugged frontier lifestyle, or at least the appearance thereof, throughout his career. He always dressed as a cowboy while performing (once he became successful, in gaudy $300 suits special-ordered from the same Hollywood tailor that would later outfit Elvis Presley), and he named his longtime backing group "The Drifting Cowboys." Drinking and fighting were inevitable occupational hazards in the honky-tonks where he got his start performing, and as Williams's not infrequent brushes with the law began to attract the attention of gossip-hungry local media outlets—"Famous Song Composer Is Arrested Here," announced one headline in the *Shreveport Times*—they burnished his own reputation for "rough and rowdy ways." Under the nom de plume "Luke the Drifter," he recorded a series of spoken-word narrations and talking-blues, delivered in the sermonizing style of an itinerant preacher. Songs about traveling filled his body of work—from "Pan American," a salute to the Louisville & Nashville train that had whistled through the Alabama countryside during his youth, to "I'm a Long Gone Daddy," a rollicking break-up song that gleefully promises "I'm leaving now / I'm a long gone daddy, I don't need you anyhow." It was no exaggeration to say, as Williams himself boasted on one of his more popular singles from 1951, that "when the Lord made me, he made a ramblin' man."[38]

But as critical to his commercial success as was the rambling mantle Williams had picked up from Rodgers, even more significant to the future of country music was the tragic persona that became Williams's defining attribute, and uniquely so in the aftermath of his sudden and unexpected demise. "The lonesome Alabama country boy who rose to fame and riches with an $8 guitar and a melancholy voice" had been having premonitions of his own death, reported the *Nashville Tennessean* the day after the news of Williams's death broke. Allen Rankin, a Montgomery newspaper columnist and one of Williams's earliest supporters, spoke directly to the dead singer when he bemoaned "the obsession to catch down on paper and wax all the thousands of lyrics and melodies that reeled through your brain, that helped kill you young. It is often so with turbulent souls." Williams was, in the words of the influential country music promoter Charlie Lamb, a "star-crossed troubadour," a "wandering minstrel" and "sad-faced cowboy," "the baleful balladeer from Montgomery"—in sum, "the image of country music."[39] In some ways, this was always only an imperfect or incomplete encapsulation of Williams's music, as a closer listen to the mordant humor of "I'll Never Get Out of This World Alive," the frolicking playfulness of "Jambalaya," or the novelty slapstick of "Kaw-Liga" made clear.[40] Yet in life and especially in the aftermath of his death, Williams's comically irreverent side would be increasingly overshadowed by his more doleful and portentous output. Few songs communicated that mood in Williams's music more powerfully than "Lost Highway," a maudlin number about hard living and its consequences that would go on to become one of his most frequently covered recordings. It would also be Williams's most significant contribution to the catalog of country highways songs.

Williams released "Lost Highway" as a B-side in 1949, after it had first been recorded a year earlier by a Texas songwriter named Leon Payne. "In the early days of Leon's career, he hitchhiked from one place to another, finding jobs wherever he could," Payne's widow, Myrtie, would later recall about the song's origins. "Once he was in California hitchhiking to Alba, Texas, to visit his sick mother. He was unable to get a ride and finally got help from the Salvation Army. It was while he was waiting for help that he wrote that song."[41] In Williams's hands, though, the song takes on a different meaning altogether. Instead of a song about the dusty and disreputable life of a tramp far from home and family, Williams's version plays like a very personal kind of morality play. Thanks to his very public struggles with alcohol and women, the references to a life brought low by gambling, drinking, and "a woman's lies" take on a seedy verisimilitude that Payne's original could never possess. "I was just a lad, nearly twenty-two. / Neither good nor bad, just a kid like you," when temptation and weakness leads him astray. Lost, in the spiritual sense, it is "too late to pray" on the highway that Williams is traveling. "Now boys don't start to ramblin' round. / On this road of sin are you sorrow bound. / Take my advice or you'll curse the day, / you started rollin' down that lost highway." When Williams turned up dead on a West Virginia highway a few years later, the ominous implications of a line like "for a life of sin I have paid the cost" was not lost on anybody.[42]

Lachrymose, self-pitying, condemned—this, presumably, was what Charlie Lamb had in mind when he described Williams as "the image of country music." And indeed, for a musical genre that traditionally had been dismissed by mainstream audiences as the dissonant yodeling of so many illiterate hillbillies, the weightiness of pathos may have been Williams's most enduring contribution to the genre: a little Puccini to balance the opera buffa of the *Grand Ole Opry*. "Hank Williams was not a great musician by the yardstick of symphony and opera," one newspaper editorialized after his death, "but he won the hearts of a multitude as Stephen Foster did." That the two were even mentioned in the same breath counted as something close to historic in the movement of country music into a kind of middle-class respectability denied the genre by the condescension of its earliest critics. Nobody ran the risk, in other words, of confusing Williams with a "singing brakeman," and it was not only because he had never worked on the railroads.[43]

There was another kind of tragedy here, too, however. Hank Williams did not singlehandedly change the direction of country music, but as one of its most influential practitioners at a critical juncture in its history, he would have a considerable impact on what was to come. And in this way, "Lost Highway" was doubly significant: not only did it contribute to the turbulent-soul identity for which Williams would be immortalized and which later singers would seek to imitate, but it also signaled a change in the meaning of the highway itself. In the decades after Payne and Williams recorded their versions of "Lost Highway"—a period that, not incidentally, overlapped with the passage of the Interstate Highway Act and the heyday of chrome plating and tailfins—dozens of country music songs would be released in which the action, whether literal or metaphoric, took place on the pavement of the highway. On tracks like bluegrass luminary Bill Monroe's "Highway of Sorrow"; or Dottie West's ode to the bright lights and big city, "Route 65 to Nashville"; or Jim Reeves's forlorn "Highway to Nowhere"; or Porter Wagoner's Country Music Association Award–winning "Carroll County Accident"; or country iconoclast Townes Van Zandt's searching "Highway Kind," the highway could mean many different things. But as country music began to shed its hillbilly roots and appeal to an ever-widening audience of northern, urban, and middle-class listeners at the other end of the interstate, no longer did it stand so naturally for the southern rural working class's critical engagement with a contested capitalist modernity. Instead, as Hank Williams helped send country music "over the top," in historian Diane Pecknold's phrasing, the highway would come to operate as an increasingly backward-looking symbol, in a musical genre that was beginning to resonate with the growing conservative tendencies in postwar American culture.[44]

As a symbol loaded with potential meaning, the refashioning of the highway in postwar country music was, first and foremost, a function of the consolidation of the economic apparatus of country music recording and distribution as a "culture industry" per se, along the lines of Max Horkheimer and Theodor Adorno's definition of the concept. Even the earliest country music, of course, had always been in some basic way commercial—in fact, as Cecil Sharp's lament about "town manners" had made clear, commerce was changing musical folkways even before the invention of electrical recording devices. Hillbilly may have been a pejorative label in its origins, but it also had been an effective marketing category for the early recording and broadcast outfits, which repackaged classically trained singers like Bradley Kincaid as folk primitives, dressed even relatively urbane country artists like Jimmie Rodgers in hayseed garb, and broadcast them all on barn dance radio shows that decorated the most cutting-edge of recording studios and soundstages with hay bales and other artifacts of farm-life "authenticity." By the time the *Grand Ole Opry* and the R.J. Reynolds Tobacco Company teamed up to launch the Camel Caravan to entertain American soldiers abroad—a traveling revue that played nearly two hundred concerts at sixty-eight army camps, hospitals, airfields, and operating bases by the end of 1942 alone—it was clear that there was big money to be made in the field of country music.[45]

But it was only really beginning in the 1950s that country music became, in Horkheimer and Adorno's phrasing, "a system which is uniform as a whole and in every part"—and, even more significantly, one that could reach beyond the limitations of class and region that inevitably circumscribed the market appeal of the hillbilly label. By the era of the Camel Caravan, there was no mistaking the fact that country music was still very much, and very narrowly, hillbilly music: a contemporaneous study conducted by the Army of the radio-listening habits of more than thirty-two hundred enlisted men found the popularity of "hill-billy and western music" to be overwhelmingly concentrated among the rural lower and working classes, fully 67 percent of whom reported a fondness for the genre. By contrast, the study found, "only 19 percent of the high school or college men from the larger cities cared for it." But as the accelerating traffic along the hillbilly highway carried country music's traditional audience in growing numbers to non-southern cities, an ever-widening market was beginning to present itself. According to Horkheimer and Adorno, the logic of the culture industry was perfectly tailored to the prerogatives of an economic order based on true mass production and mass consumption, a system in which imitation was "absolute" and the factory-like operations of cultural production generated commodities that were "cyclically recurrent and rigidly invariable types." The studio system in American moviemaking was an ideal example; in the realm of country music, this productive logic generated what came to be called the "Nashville Sound."[46]

The Nashville Sound emerged in the mid to late 1950s from the recording studios of influential local producers like Owen Bradley and Chet Atkins, and very quickly began to redefine the sound and style of country music.[47] By design, the Nashville Sound was intended to make country music sound and feel more like mainstream pop music, which not only continued to sell more records but also was still considered a more respectable and sophisticated—a more middle-class—alternative to country. Famously, when asked once to define the Nashville Sound, Atkins glibly replied that it was "the sound of money." In effect, the Nashville Sound took the hillbilly out of country music: it emphasized smoother vocals and sophisticated editing, more string arrangements and background harmonies, fewer fiddles, and less twang. As D. K. Wilgus writes, "The music was not all a bland, homogenized style—though this trend was ever present—but it moved away from country, whether to rock or to pop. The cool, relaxed 'Nashville' sound predominated." And in so doing, the Nashville Sound succeeded in stripping country music of the lingering resonances of its origins among the southern rural working class, and helped turn it into cultural commodity suited for true mass consumption.[48]

This presented both opportunities and challenges for the industry. The opportunities were obvious: to transcend country's traditionally region-bound identity, to expand the geography of touring and record sales revenues, to market the country sound to the nation's rapidly growing (and consuming) middle classes. The challenge was in capitalizing on those opportunities without turning off country music's base—the same rural folk who may have moved to Chicago or Detroit and left the farm for the factory for good, but who still at this time composed the largest portion of the country music market.

The answer, for the country music industry, would lie in what Horkheimer and Adorno identified as "the predominance of the effect," an innovation of the culture industry that amounted to the elevation of style over content. Where once style—"the technical detail"—had encouraged "rebellious" aesthetic experimentations with form "as a vehicle of protest against the organization," amid the high modernism of the mid-twentieth century the stylistic effect now only worked to "subserve the formula"; to discourage formal deviations and to reinforce the broader imperative of cultural mass-consumption. The country music industry would also turn to a very particular kind of effect during these years—although in this case it might be just as appropriate to call it an affect. Complementing the "cyclically recurrent and rigidly invariable" production values of the Nashville Sound recordings was an increasing reliance on the emotive language of nostalgia, especially as it was bound up with a set of images and feelings associated with a fanciful recreation of a bygone rural southern past. Both were designed to smooth the rougher edges of country's less polished roots as the music of poor white country people—in the first case, by making that music *sound* more like the pop music that middle-class listeners preferred; and in the second by disassociating the *feelings* the music was meant to invoke from any grounding in the real experiences of region and class that had defined the country genre for its earliest practitioners. Where artistic style might once have moved freely as an independent variable, Horkheimer and Adorno wrote, even potentially as a vehicle of protest, it now was subsumed entirely by the apparatus of mass production; the style of the culture industry was "the negation of style." In a similar vein, nostalgia would prove to be the negation of country music's working-class style.[49]

The critical theorist Susan Stewart has defined nostalgia as something more ideological in nature than the word's etymology—from the Greek *nostos*, meaning "homecoming," and *algos*, meaning "pain" or "ache"—or a strictly literalist translation of the word as the feeling of homesickness would immediately suggest. Homesickness is the particular ache that is felt for a specific time and place called home; it is no coincidence that the word's roots trace to the *Odyssey*, to Odysseus's longing for a return to Ithaca and Penelope. On the other hand, as Stewart writes, "Nostalgia is a sadness without an object, a sadness which creates a longing that of necessity is inauthentic because it does not take part in lived experience." This past "has never existed except as narrative"—home, one might say, not as it is or used to be but as we always wished it was—and its invocation is both backward-looking and in some fundamental way ahistorical. "Hostile to history and its invisible origins, and yet longing for an impossibly pure context of lived experience at a place of origin," Stewart continues, "nostalgia wears a distinctly utopian face, a face that turns toward a future-past, a past which has only ideological reality."[50]

This nostalgic affect was written all over the postwar country highway song. Indeed, if there was a unifying narrative throughline to the voluminous catalog of highway songs produced during these years, it was home—going home, missing home, leaving home and regretting it, begging the departed to come back home, returning home to die. Many songs made this theme explicit. The Bailes Brothers were "Traveling the Highway Home" in 1952; Curly Dan and Wilma Ann were driving "South on 23" in 1963; Kenny Price was "Southern Bound" in 1968; and Porter Wagoner was on the "Highway Headin' South" in 1974—all of them imploring, like John Denver in 1971, "Take Me Home, Country Roads." Southern Missouri–born Wynn Stewart's long-lost girlfriend finally returns to his small town after a crash on the highway in "Long Black Limousine" (1958), while Loretta Lynn rues the day she lost her man to the big city in "Blue Kentucky Girl" (1965). Even Glen Campbell, the smooth boy-wonder of 1960s country music, as perfect a product of the Nashville Sound as there ever was, who looked much more comfortable on television or in sun-soaked Hollywood where he preferred to record than down on the Arkansas farm on which he was raised, eschewed the "highways come between us" for the "backroads by the rivers of my memories," and took home two Grammys in 1967 for "Gentle on My Mind."[51]

At times, these highway songs could capture the special poignancy associated with the experiences of dispossession and dislocation that often came with the hillbilly's postwar urban migration—much like Steve Earle's "Hillbilly Highway" would, in 1986. You could hear it in a song like "The Ballad of Barbara," Johnny Cash's 1973 reinterpretation of "Barbara Allen," the traditional Scotch-English ballad about unrequited love. After abandoning "my land and my people" in the southern town in which he was born, the singer ends up in an unnamed northern city, "in a world that's all concrete and steel." He meets a woman there, falls in love and marries her, and they move into a "fancy downtown flat," where the singer slowly begins to pine after the quiet life he left behind. He asks Barbara to leave with him but she scorns him, literally transforming herself into the cold and heartless place he has come to despise: "She turned into concrete and steel, / and she said, 'I'll take the city.'" From the unnaturalness of the building materials to the conspicuous displays of wealth and his ultimate emasculation at the hands of his wife—besotted in her own way with town manners—Cash's song is a hillbilly parable of urban alienation and class defeat. As in the original, "The Ballad of Barbara" ends with the singer chastened and alone, but in this case better off for it. "Now the cars go by on the interstate, / and my pack is on my shoulder. / But I'm goin' home, where I belong, / much wiser now and older."[52]

But more often than not, the feeling expressed in these songs amounted to a kind of wallowing self-pity, at once abject and artificial-sounding, and the resolutions they offered were clearly little more than a Nashville-produced special effect. Nobody quite captured the spirit of nostalgia in postwar country music like Bobby Bare, who had a series of hits in the 1960s—"Detroit City," "500 Miles Away from Home," "The Streets of Baltimore"—which all took as their subject the homesick country boy in the big city. In "Detroit City," which made it all the way to number six on the *Billboard* country charts and won a Grammy in 1963, the singer goes north to find work in the auto industry, but all he does is dream "about those cotton fields and home." He writes boastful letters to his family about how well he is doing, but really it is just a long procession of empty workdays and lonely nights. "From the letters I write they think I'm doing fine. / But by day I make the cars, and by night I make the bars, / if only they could read between the lines." By the end, he decides to swallow "my foolish pride, / and put it on a southbound freight and ride," back to the filial embrace of those familiar cotton fields. The song closes with Bare, a tremble in his voice, warbling, "I wanna go home. / I wanna go home. / Oh, how I wanna go home."[53]

Bobby Bare grew up on the Ohio side of the Ohio River, right where it makes a triangle with Kentucky and West Virginia along the Allegheny Plateau: a southerly part of the state in many ways, but not exactly cotton country. That little agronomic exaggeration was telling because it was such a transparent piece of artifice.[54] Short of magnolia blossoms, one would be hard-pressed to think of a more obvious symbol for a left-behind South—unless, of course, you followed the model of more than a few contemporary country musicians and southern rockers and went all in for flag-waving Confederate nationalism.[55] But given the record's success, Bare apparently knew his audience would appreciate where he was coming from—even if he did not quite come from there.

Less visible, then, in the postwar highway song was the "lived experience" of industrial modernity, with its liberating possibilities and stifling realities, which had once made country a kind of music of everyday life of the southern white working class. In its place was an only ideological reality: a rural past that was no more "real" than the Elizabethan arcadias Cecil Sharp and the other ballad collectors had hoped to find when they journeyed into the southern mountains a half century earlier. When Glen Campbell sang of country back roads, or Bare yearned for those lost cotton fields, the emotional response these songs evoked was exactly what Stewart meant by "inauthentic"—a longing for an imagined and imaginary "simple life" that did not recall an actual time or place or former way of life but was always only a fantasy. All this was a marked shift from how the highway had operated in song during Dorsey Dixon and Jimmie Rodgers's day. Where once the highway had symbolized country's desire to transcend the limitations of a social order in transition, the southbound highway in postwar country music increasingly came to operate as a conservative myth or fable—and one that would have lasting implications for the genre's class associations and political orientation.

## "The City's Goin' Country"

Nostalgia had always played a role in country music's appeal. "The type of program most popular in my home is singing of old songs and the cowboy, western, and southern songs," wrote one fan of the *National Barn Dance* in a 1935 letter to the radio station. "We do not care for popular dance music which is one reason we are glad for WLS who does not seem to have much of that." "I think they ought to cut out all the jazz music on Saturday nights and have old-time music," commented Frank Keans of Louisa, Virginia, echoing a common sentiment expressed by the program's listeners, who tended to pit jazz (or "city," "popular," or "modern" music) against the kind of music they associated with bygone eras or places in their own lives. "WLS's biggest feature . . . is music as our fathers, mothers, uncles and aunts used to sing and dance to," exclaimed Gene Jones. "Songs that were written from life and could be sung by people who didn't have time or money to take lessons and study notes." "I came to Chicago to live two years ago," Ida Haines explained. "I miss the friendliness we have in a small town, but I have WLS still to listen to." "I am a steady listener to your barn dance programs, and enjoy them very much," wrote one "Ex-Cowboy" who had since moved to the city. "I have ridden many years on the plains and am still a cowboy at heart and, consequently, know a real natural born rider when I see one."[56]

Furthermore, as the expanding geography of the genre's fan base came to resemble something like a country music diaspora, it was not uncommon for listeners who, like Ida Haines and the Ex-Cowboy, hailed from small towns and rural areas where country had naturally thrived, to see and feel in the music something like a direct linkage with home. "Colonel" Jim Wilson grew up in western Kentucky and moved to Detroit with his family right after World War II. There, while working at a record store in the southwestern part of the city near Ford's massive River Rouge complex, he witnessed firsthand the way country music helped mediate the attachments of other displaced southerners. "You had an awful lot of people who had migrated in to the Detroit area to work in the auto factories and so forth," Wilson recalled. "The music that was available there, or records, was kind of a bridge to close that gap of homesickness and so forth, that they could come in and buy some records, country or hillbilly records, that gave them a tie or closeness to the music that they'd left behind." Although it would still be some years until Detroit got its first radio station dedicated to country music, many of Wilson's customers listened religiously to WCKY out of Cincinnati. "The music they played was that which a majority of the migrant workers who'd come up from Kentucky, Tennessee, West Virginia" had grown up listening to.[57]

Twenty years later, listeners to John Morris's weekly country radio show, on WNRS out of Ann Arbor, Michigan, still felt much the same way. "I am an old Kentuckian, Murray, Kentucky, Calloway County," one wrote in a letter to Morris. "I've been in Michigan since 1937. But as a boy at home I used to buy all of the Carter Family and Jimmie Rodgers records, and I love to hear them again after so long." "My wife and I are hilly bills too," commented another. "We both love to hear the gospel records you play." For some, the nostalgic associations evoked by the music were all that made a life of regional and cultural displacement bearable. "It really brings back good memories," explained one of Morris's regular listeners. "If it wasn't for your program, I would probably be living in the South."[58] For others, like a group of southern-born activists in Chicago's Uptown neighborhood, who tried unsuccessfully in the late 1960s to mobilize public support behind a mixed-use, low- and moderate-income housing development they proposed calling "Hank Williams Village," country music was a way to bring home closer to them.[59]

A housing project named for the King of the Hillbillies, in the middle of Chicago's much-maligned hillbilly ghetto, would have been an irony befitting country music's journey from the margins to the mainstream of American popular culture in the decades after World War II. By then, it was not only ex-cowboys and old Kentuckians who were patronizing the music. Country records were outselling many other popular music genres, and the number of radio stations programming exclusively country music had exploded nationally, from just 97 in 1963 to 298 by 1966. Significantly, much of that growth had come in places far removed from the region of country music's birth. When Chicago's WJJD radio station decided to switch to an all-country format, in 1965, country records accounted for as much as 35 percent of total sales in the city for some of the major labels, and the station was soon attracting close to one in four of the city's daily radio listeners. A survey of dozens of radio markets as far-flung as Seattle, Long Island, and Ypsilanti found that "without exception, [stations] reported an improvement in ratings, billings or both" after increasing their country programming. In the process, the genre's booming success helped wipe away much of what remained of the original taint of the hillbilly label. "Contrary to the belief of some," *Broadcasting* magazine observed, with an eye especially to the growing advertising market on country radio stations, "the listeners are not overalled hayseeds driving up in Model A Ford trucks."[60] More than half of WJJD's audience, the station was proud to report, had median family incomes at or above the national average, and one in eight had incomes roughly twice as high. "The typical County music listener" no longer represented what *Variety* had once written off as a community unto itself, another trade publication concluded, but rather had become the very quintessence of middle-class conventionality. "He lives in San Francisco or New Haven or Cleveland; he's 45 and most likely owns a brand-new Chevrolet; he also owns his home and has a wife and two children to make some noise in it; he spends his days operating a machine that requires an experienced hand at the controls; his annual salary is about $6,000 a year, most of which he spends on consumer goods for his family and the rest of which he saves."[61]

It was a further irony, then, that just as country's audience was becoming less hillbilly and more urban, a rising wave of nostalgic anti-urbanism came to suffuse itself throughout the music. Ranging from the bathetic

Featured here in a 1965 advertisement in *Broadcasting* magazine, the so-called
Western Gentlemen—Don Chapman, Roy Stingley, Stan Scott, Chris Lane,
and John Trotter—were the five key producers and on-air personalities who
shepherded WJJD through its transition to being Chicago's first all-country
radio station. In Chicago and other midwestern cities during these years, the
rising popularity of country music was one of the most notable outgrowths of
the Transappalachian migration, and marked a radical shift from the earlier
disdain that urban audiences had shown for "hillbilly music."
*Broadcasting* Magazine/Future Publishing, Ltd.

in the case of Bobby Bare, to the dyspeptic in the case of someone like Hank Williams Jr.—son and namesake of the king himself, whose roaring "A Country Boy Can Survive" blared about shooting a New York City mugger with "my old .45"—country music in these years stood out even within the long tradition of anti-urbanism in American arts and letters for the hostility it expressed toward the big city.[62] Landing somewhere in the middle, Buck Owens—who, before lampooning his own hillbilly roots as the host of the corn-pone television variety show *Hee Haw* from its premiere in 1969 until 1986 had largely pioneered what came to be known as the "Bakersfield Sound" of West Coast country music, which emerged from the cradle of the Okie migration to Southern California— spoke for many with the title of his 1970 hit "I Wouldn't Live in New York City (If They Gave Me the Whole Damn Town)." "Talk about a bummer, it's the biggest one around," Owens sang over Doyle Holly's recognizable, lonesome-prairie bass guitar; "Sodom and Gomorrah was tame to what I found."[63]

Opinions such as these had always had their place in country music; what was notable now, the oral historian Marc Landy remarked at the time, was that its ruralist ethos no longer seemed to "appeal solely to Southerners and transplanted Southerners." Rather than region, Landy contended, it was a shared cultural experience that seemed to unite country's traditional fans with its more recent converts. "These Canadians, Bostonians and Jerseyites," who were tuning in in growing numbers to the new "countrypolitan" radio stations, "are also poor, white, adult and relative newcomers to the city," an urban fan base that found itself increasingly alienated from a "hostile urban environment." Landy's description of country's growing audience was acutely sensitive to the changing cultural politics of the moment. "At the same time that the South is losing its distinctiveness as a region, its music has become dominant nationally." In the process, "the blend of conservatism and the rebelliousness which has long characterized southern value systems has now taken hold among the 'forgotten Americans.'"[64] "The city's goin' country" was how the singing Wilburn Brothers put it, who had their own popular syndicated television show that was then beaming the familiar notes of ruralist nostalgia into living rooms in dozens of urban markets across the nation: "That dusty, winding, country road that Daddy used to drive / It's a four-lane highway now, speed limit sixty-five."[65]

Teddy and Doyle Wilburn shared with Bobby Bare and Hank Williams Jr. more than just a savvy appreciation for the widening marketability of songs about "the mundane terrors of the urban ooze."[66] The four were also outspoken supporters of the great restorationist hero of the little man and the defeated South, George Wallace, joining a flotilla of country singers who lined up behind the Alabama governor during his unsuccessful yet deeply polarizing bids for the presidency. Buck Owens was likewise drawn to southern conservatives—like Texas governor Preston Smith, at whose 1969 inaugural ball he would perform—although he had sat out the previous year's presidential race. Harry Dent, Richard Nixon's key southern strategist, did manage to recruit for the Republican a few country mainstays, most notably Roy Acuff and Tex Ritter. But aside from a scattering of aging stars singing along to the hastily composed Nixon campaign jingle "Bring Our Country Back" ("How far down the road has our country gone, / in this time of trouble and strife?"), country music proved overwhelmingly to be Wallace country. "During the 1968 Presidential campaign, [Nashville's] Music Row was practically a battlefield command post for George Wallace," observed the journalist Paul Hemphill; and in the aftermath of his defeat, more than one stalwart of the industry likely mourned the lost opportunity to have "the biggest country-music fan we ever had as President."[67]

And what a country music fan he was. When Hollywood's first biopic devoted to the life and death of Hank Williams, *Your Cheatin' Heart*—a schlocky affair with the extraordinarily unlikely George Hamilton cast in the lead role—had its premiere in November 1964, Governor Wallace celebrated by declaring it "Hank Williams Week" in Alabama.[68] Throughout the 1968 campaign, Wallace liked to bring a country band on stage with him during his barnstorming tours through northern cities—prompting one wag at a Boston College student paper to describe his rallies as "Doc Wallace's Musical Revue and Medicine Show"—and often, it would be "an ole Hank Williams favorite" that got things started.[69] After Hank Williams Jr. became one of Wallace's more famous endorsers, appearing with the candidate throughout the campaign, the Wallace family would later return the favor, with the governor's country music–playing son, George Wallace Jr., touring with Hank Jr.'s band for a number of years. And as George Sr. was gearing up for his final campaign for public office, in 1982, at least one astute listener noted the appropriate timing behind the recent release of Hank Williams Jr.'s "A Country Boy Can Survive," an "unauthorized campaign anthem" that nonetheless evoked "the same fierce anger which, in part, propels the Wallace candidacy."[70]

This probably was not what the music critic Tom Piazza had in mind when, in a long review-essay published in conjunction with the 1998 release of Mercury Records' *The Complete Hank Williams* boxed set, he proposed that "if there has been a gravitational center to country music since World War II, Hank Williams occupies it."[71] In fact, very few country music critics and scholars draw any kind of connection between Williams and the political culture of George Wallace and other denizens of the New Right.[72] And yet it is undeniable that in the decades since Hank Williams helped send country music "over the top"—cementing its mainstream acceptability and earning its national audience once and for all—country had become the major field of American popular culture most visibly associated with political conservatism.

One explanation for why postwar country music found itself so at home in the Wallace campaign was the pungent notes of ruralist ressentiment that echoed through both. Wallace's race-baiting, law-and-order campaign rhetoric made much of non-urban America's fear and loathing of the inner city—the portrayal of New York as the mugging capital of America appeared in Wallace's speeches long before Hank Jr. set it to song in "A Country Boy Can Survive"—and his tactical juxtaposing of out-of-touch cosmopolitan elites with the aggrieved common folk could have been lifted directly from a country songbook. When the *National Review* issued its oft-quoted criticism of Wallace's "country and western Marxism," it was this political style—as much as the substantive issues they disagreed on, like Wallace's support for social security, collective bargaining, and other forms of "egregious welfare-statism"—that the magazine was objecting to. From that citadel of elite conservatism, Wallace was still just a little too hillbilly—too comfortable marching, as the *Review* put it, "to the Nashville station."[73]

Nor was it a coincidence that the litany of potential supporters that Wallace liked to trot out on the campaign trail—"the bus driver, the truck driver, the beautician, the fireman, the policeman, and the steelworker"—echoed almost precisely the types of blue-collar and lower-middle-class trades that made up country music's new audience: the "bricklayers and plumbers, carpenters, truck drivers and stevedores . . . electricians, machinists, electronic specialists, technicians, and craftsmen," as Tex Ritter had once described them.[74] The undercurrent of anti-urbanism that wound its way through postwar country may have been a tonic to all those displaced southerners who struggled in the factories and ghettos of industrial America, but it also appealed in growing numbers to the urban ethnics, white flighters, and suburban warriors who were then remaking the landscape of American politics and cultural life. Many of these "forgotten Americans" had come to fear or resent competition over status and resources with Black Americans, and to regard the city as an increasingly alien cultural and social landscape—to them, postwar country music's nostalgic attachment to an idealized rural past represented a no less appealing kind of escapism. *Billboard* was right: country music was fast becoming a "native art," but not of the historic white yeomanry so much as the new suburban and ex-urban white middling classes, who shared their hostility to the postwar city but felt none of early country's unease about the culture of the market. Those highways led only to strip malls and subdivisions.[75]

Country and western Marxism was not nearly so new a phenomenon as the *National Review* may have thought it was when coining the phrase. Fiddlin' John Carson had laid down an ode to the Georgia Populist Tom Watson (an accomplished fiddler himself) in 1923, "Tom Watson Special," a year after Watson's death and a decade and a half after Watson's populism had taken on a vicious, anti-Catholic and white supremacist cast. Apparently unperturbed by these developments, Carson sings proudly, "Got a Watson dog and a Watson cat. / I'm a Tom Watson man from my shoes to my hat." Tom T. Hall, one of the more prolific and successful country songwriters in the postwar period, once said about country music that it "has always reflected the mood of working people, so it went the way they went." Hall left out the racial qualifier and was too quick to treat "the music" as an organic and depersonalized medium rather than as a realm of strategic cultural production—but otherwise he was more or less right. The experience of dispossession and the politics of resentment, as Tom Watson well knew, had always kept close company in the lives of white working people; and if country music could lay some genuine claim to being the music for (if not necessarily always of) this class, it was because to some considerable degree it had, from its inception, been able to evoke the special poignancy of that experience.[76]

Perhaps no country musician of the postwar period was more adept at expressing those kinds of feelings and experiences than Hank Williams. This was another way of thinking about what D. K. Wilgus had in mind, when he wrote that Williams most thoroughly "presented—in fact he was—the dichotomy, the polarization of the urban hillbilly"; a "polarization of city and country" that was at the heart of country music's evolution throughout the course of the twentieth century.[77] And while his songs largely avoided the more explicitly political or politicized themes that came to preoccupy later generations of postwar country singers, it was his signature style that helped make country music the soundtrack of the right-wing populism that had become an increasingly potent force in American life by the end of the 1960s. For it was Hank Williams—the Hank Williams of "Lost Highway," rather than the Hank Williams of "I'll

Never Get Out of This World Alive"—who gave country music its defining tragic cast, and the name of that tragedy was nostalgia. There is a
straight path from Williams mourning the day he "started rollin' down
that lost highway," to Bobby Bare moaning "I wanna go home," and it is
not altogether different from the one that leads to Wallace's most famous
restorationist mantra, "Segregation now, segregation tomorrow, segregation forever." The line between the benign fantasies of the simple rural life
of the Old South, and the economic apartheid and *herrenvolk* democracy
upon which all that rested, was a blurry one. More to the point, those
fantasies signaled the end of early country's critical modernism, the economic enclosure of hillbilly music by the productive logics of midcentury
consumerism, the final acquiescence of country and its listeners to the
cultural status quo of the newly dominant middle classes.

## Lost Highway

The tragedy of "Lost Highway" is that it mistakes symptoms for causes.
An itinerant lifestyle and reckless substance abuse did not cause Williams's
depression but was a symptom of it; the highway did not bring about the
demise of rural life but was another symptom of the galloping progress
of capitalist modernity. There is good in that version of modernity, as
Jimmie Rodgers recognized, and there is bad, as Dorsey Dixon did—but
either way, as no less a critic of capitalist modernity than Marx himself
understood, it defines the parameters of the world we live in and can be
a rich source of material for critique, experience, and political engagement. Beginning with "Lost Highway," postwar country music puts its
head in the metaphoric sand. From then on, the highways only go in one
direction.

Few country music songs (and, indeed, few country musicians) of the
postwar period revel so unabashedly in that kind of head-burying than
Hank Williams Jr.'s "A Country Boy Can Survive." Released in the early
1980s, against the backdrop of rising unemployment and inflation and the
renewed fears of nuclear conflict that marked the beginning of the Reagan presidency, the song opens on an appropriately apocalyptic note ("The
preacher man says it's the end of time") before settling into its main message, a muscular rendition of backwoods survivalism that could double as
the recruitment pitch for a secessionist militia. The singer touts his many
country-bred talents—"I can plow a field all day long, / I can catch cat-
fish from dusk 'til dawn. . . . / Ain't too many things these old boys can't
do"—while sneering at his comparably inept friend, who grew up in the city,

learned only how "to be a businessman," and ends up dead at the hands of a man with a switchblade. Even though "the interest is up and the stock market's down, / and you only get mugged if you go downtown," a similarly sordid fate, the singer makes clear, does not await him and his kind: "'Cause you can't starve us out and you can't make us run / 'Cause we're them old boys raised on shotguns. / And we say grace and we say 'Ma'am,' / and if you ain't into that we don't give a damn." The vision offered, ultimately, is one not of rural isolation but rural *isolationism*, a hillbilly *revanche* that turns Cecil Sharp on his head and retreats into the wilderness as an escape from the urban decay of modern life: "I live back in the woods, you see, / my woman and the kids, and the dogs, and me. / I got a shotgun, a rifle, and a 4-wheel drive. / And a country boy can survive."[78]

It is unfair, perhaps, to visit the sins of the son upon the father, but there is a way of reading Susan Stewart's definition of the concept by which it is not Odysseus but rather Oedipus who in some way invents the tragedy of nostalgia. It is his overriding if only subconscious desire for an object he can never attain—his father's crown, his mother's bed—that leads Oedipus to take the wrong turn at the crossroads where he encounters his father Laius; had he taken a different road than the one that leads him back to a past he cannot possess without destroying himself, who knows what would have happened to him? Highways lead forward and backward—and, for that matter, outward and inward, side to side, and back and forth. Hank Williams and his successors got lost because they took the highway toward an unobtainable past of rural simplicity which was code for all kinds of backward provincialisms. The postwar turn in country music was a tragic one because it was nostalgic, and because it was nostalgic it was conservative, bound to the very premodern forms—orthodox religiosity, the patriarchal family, ethnic provincialism, feudalistic norms of deference at the workplace—that the highway promised to obliterate when it first came on the scene. It did not have to be that way; and to be sure, it would be to mistake symptoms and causes to say that because country music moved right during these years, so did the country. But those highways do run in the same direction.

By the beginning of the 1970s, James Gregory has argued, the widespread popularity of country music, and the genre's clear association with a nationally ascendant right-wing political movement, was one of the clearest indicators of the "diaspora effect" that a half century's worth of southern white out-migration had had on the broader arenas of American culture and politics. "Guided by a southern-origin institution of popular culture," Gregory writes, "white working-class conservatism had moved

Willie Nelson, Gov. George Wallace, Hank Williams, Jr. & Shelton Hank Williams, III

HANK WILLIAMS, JR. FAN CLUB
P. O. Box 1061, Cullman, Ala. 35055
Teressa Smith, Pres.    PHOTO BY THE PELICAN C.B. JOURNAL, BATON ROUGE, LA.

Hank Williams Jr. poses for a photograph with his son, Shelton Hank Williams III, Willie Nelson, and Alabama governor George Wallace, sometime in the mid-1970s. Hank Williams Jr. was one of many outspoken supporters of Wallace's presidential campaigns in 1968 and 1972 in the country music business; he also toured extensively during the early 1970s with Wallace's country musician son, George Wallace Jr.

into another phase," one that couched the explicitly racist backlash-politics of the George Wallace campaigns in country music's more muted—though no less racially coded—nostalgic traditionalism. In so doing, country music had become a kind of unifying lingua franca for the forces seeking to roll back the political accomplishments of New Deal liberalism, most notably in the fields of civil rights and social welfare policy. The city had gone country, as the Wilburn Brothers had put it; and as the famous meetings between President Nixon and Johnny Cash in 1970 and again in 1972—the first for a three-song performance before invited guests, the second to discuss the issue of prison reform—seemed to suggest, the hill-billies had taken the White House.[79]

The problem with this way of narrating the place of country music in the rise of the New Right—which, it must be said, has been the default narrative since more or less the moment that Merle Haggard released the hippie-bashing anthem, "Okie from Muskogee," in 1969—is that it is too inclined to treat country music the same way Cecil Sharp or Abel Green once did: as the unchanging cultural expression of a backward-leaning rural folk, hell-bent on preserving an increasingly outmoded way of life.[80] If it is true that the city went country in the decades after World War II, it is only because in key ways country music was "citified" during these years as well. The stylistic changes implemented by the Nashville Sound producers, the new exposure afforded by an expanding universe of urban radio stations, the convergence between urban and rural listening habits and musical tastes—all of these factors combined to resolve the midcentury polarization between city and country through a kind of negotiated truce. What resulted from that truce was the expunging of the most disruptive elements of country music as an explicitly working-class music, even as its more nostalgic evocations were salvaged in the name of mass market respectability, increased record sales, and the comforts of a shared whiteness.

The more sweeping condemnations of country music as an inherently reactionary cultural form overlook that more critical spirit animating early hillbilly music—and indeed hillbilly culture generally. And in doing so, they echo the similar denunciations of the cultural habits and political behavior of rural white southerners that were such constants throughout the decades of southern migration to the Midwest. Whether it was the fears of wage competition and strikebreaking, which neglected the very real patterns of shop-floor radicalism that the earliest southern migrants brought with them to northern workplaces; or the projections of an imported southern racial "psychology," which obscured the indigenous roots of midwestern racial violence; or the invention of distinctive cultural origins for rural southern poverty, which ultimately isolated displaced southern whites from other poor and working-class communities in mid-twentieth-century America—time and time again, the misuses of hillbilly culture have distorted its more radical, modern, or inclusive character into one that is exclusively conservative, traditionalist, and racist. Indeed, it is one more final, tragic irony that one of the most enduring historical contributions of the hillbilly highway—the Americanization of country music—has come at the cost of hearing the hillbilly on his own terms.

# Conclusion

RACIAL TENSION BOILED over at Muncie's Southside High School in the fall of 1967. Built as the city's second high school only five years earlier to accommodate the rapidly growing neighborhoods south of the White River, Southside was, in this and other ways, a direct creation of the postwar surge in the Transappalachian migration. Constructed along Macedonia Avenue just down the street from the old Ball Brothers plant—which, in a piece of ominous symbolism that presaged the difficult years ahead for Muncie, had closed the same year the new school opened—Southside sat close to what for decades had been the heart of the city's expansive community of working-class white southerners. And in what was likely intended as much in recognition of that regional background as it was a nod to the school's local coordinates, Southside became Muncie's first semi-officially sanctioned marker of the city's recently augmented southern cultural identity. When the school opened its doors in 1962, its athletic teams became known as the Rebels, and a Confederate flag was hung from the flagpole out front. For years to come, rebel yells and renditions of "Dixie" would issue forth from local radio stations on game days. Inside Southside's hallways and classrooms, however, school spirit gave rise to racial discord that before too long would spill into the streets of Muncie.[1]

The catalyst for the trouble that took place at Southside, which would eventually lead to a joint investigation by the Indiana Civil Rights Commission and the United States Commission on Civil Rights, was what a group of Black parents identified as the "forms of subtle and overt discrimination" to which Black students at the school were repeatedly subjected. In addition to suffering the indignity of the school's Confederate insignia, Black students, who made up roughly 11 percent of the student body at the time, objected to being effectively denied the opportunity to participate in the school's honor club, choral group (known as "The Southern Aires"), cheer-leading squad, and other extracurricular activities; of no Black student ever being named homecoming queen (who went by the title of "Southern Belle") or chosen to participate in the school-wide pageant; and of the systematic indifference or outright hostility Black students encountered when raising these and other issues with Southside's all-white teachers and administrators. When Black students and parents approached Hurley Goodall, the education secretary of the Muncie Human Rights Commission, about these problems, and he secured an audience with a group that included the Southside principal and some teachers, the meeting quickly "became very heated and deteriorated." After Goodall tried to raise the issue of the school flying the Confederate flag, which he noted was "working on the Negro youth psychologically," the Southside principal, Claude Williams, responded that it was the first he had heard of the matter and dismissed Goodall's concern as excessive. "These are just students and everything will be all right," Williams told Goodall as the meeting drew to a frustrating close.[2]

As it turned out, Goodall's concern was well placed. In the late morning on October 19, chaos broke out in the halls of Southside, as Black and white students engaged in what amounted to a mini-race riot. The fighting went on for close to an hour, with the combatants only being subdued with the arrival of the police and the use of tear gas. An emergency meeting of the Muncie Human Rights Commission and the Muncie school board was convened the following week, at which a variety of recommendations for action were discussed—among them a commitment to increasing Black participation in extracurricular organizations and activities, the creation of an interracial "student relations committee" that would include both student and parent representatives, and the initiation of an "orderly procedure" to select new school nicknames that were not fraught with "so much emotionalism" and "that everyone can be proud of for many years to come." By the beginning of the following year, however, the situation had only continued to deteriorate. Not only had Principal Williams taken no action on the various recommendations of the Human Rights Commission, but bus service to and from the main Black community that fed into Southside had also been inexplicably discontinued. When a popular Black basketball player was expelled after a fight with a white student, who himself went unpunished, simmering tensions exploded once again. A second school-wide melee broke out on January 30, and again police were needed to quell the disturbance.[3]

In the midst of four years of intensifying urban unrest around the country, Muncie seemed to be teetering on the brink of its own local race war. Street altercations between Black and white youths, especially on Muncie's southside, were becoming increasingly common and increasingly bloody. One Black teenager explained that people were angered by "the situation at Southside High School" and were "taking it out" on whites. Sharon Brown, who was in junior high school on the east side of Muncie around the same time, remembered starting to see police deputies stationed on the street corners along her walk home. One day, Sharon recalled, "A Black girl that was my friend whispered in my ear and said, 'Don't any of you white girls go in the bathroom alone—they're carrying razor blades in their bra, to cut you up when you go in there.'"[4] For their part, a group of Black teens told a committee that had been appointed by the mayor to study the uptick in violence, that it was "boys from Shedtown [who] caused many of the problems." Meanwhile, outside agitators had gotten wind of what was going on, and threatened to destabilize the situation further. Two weeks after the second school riot, the Grand Dragon of the Indiana Ku Klux Klan announced plans for a "street walk" through downtown Muncie, during which upward of seventy-five robed and hooded Klansmen would distribute literature "to acquaint the people of Muncie and Delaware County with our program and our purposes." The Klan claimed the rally had nothing to do with the recent disturbances at Southside High School—but the coincidence of the timing was not lost on any of the concerned parties.[5]

Despite the Klan's attempts at provocation, a further escalation of racial tensions in the city would be avoided. The altercations at Southside were the most dramatic instances of racial conflict to occur in Muncie during these years. In the end, the fact that the unrest did not spread much farther than Southside was likely a function of the size of Muncie's Black population, which never exceeded 10 percent of the city overall and remained overwhelmingly concentrated in just two neighborhoods. The kinds of large-scale upheavals that had recently taken place in cities like Detroit, Los Angeles, or Newark were unlikely to recur in a setting where Black residents were so totally outnumbered and effectively surrounded.

Nevertheless, for the community of white southerners in Muncie, which had grown so dramatically since the early days of the hillbilly highway, the conflict at Southside was fraught with meaning. Jim Delk's parents moved to Muncie from Fentress County, Tennessee, in the 1940s, found work in a series of local factories, and ended up raising Jim, his four older brothers, and his younger sister in a small house in the southeastern part of the city. All the Delk kids went to Southside, as did the cousins and the other neighborhood kids who also hailed from the South. Even though the school was one of the places where the imprint of the Transappalachian migration was most strongly felt during these years, it was not only southern students who went to Southside. Jim also remembers the better-off children "saying hillbilly-this, and hillbilly-that" when he and his siblings showed up for school, and being made acutely aware of the differences—in everything from the food they ate, to the clothes they wore, to the number of hot showers they could afford to take weekly—between life in their home and those of their classmates. For children like the Delks, then, the school's "rebel pride" represented a kind of validation that was still otherwise hard to come by outside of the family home and the neighborhood. Jim started high school in 1970, just after the worst of the race violence at Southside, but one of his older brothers was "very much in the middle of all of it." "One kid that lived up the street, I distinctly remember, he had an old '46, '47 Chevy pickup truck. Drove it down in front of the high school with two rebel flags hanging off the back of it." At times like that, Jim noted years later, "the other classes went away," and whatever complexity may have otherwise existed in the relationship between transplanted southerners and their northern white peers disappeared. "It was just black and white."[6]

Jim's remarks were telling. It had not always been so black and white when it came to where families like his fit into the racial and class hierarchies of places like Muncie. But over time, the hillbilly highway had finally led toward a qualified form of belonging for the rural white southerners who had been traveling its circuits since the early part of the twentieth century. Thanks to the generalized elevation of working-class living standards during these years, the mainstreaming of southern cultural forms like the evangelical church and country music, and, above all, to their shared and transcendent whiteness, the walls separating the hillbilly ghetto from the rest of midwestern society had become more porous than ever by the end of the 1960s. The power of that shared whiteness was in evidence in the repurposed Confederate iconography that adorned Southside High School—and especially so during moments when the privileges tied up with that unifying racial identity came under threat and, as Jim put it, "the other classes went away." And it was in evidence, too, in other key Muncie institutions, like UAW Local 287. The cornerstone of the local labor movement since it had played its pioneering role in the formative struggles of the 1930s, Local 287 used its considerable bargaining power to ensure that wages at Warner Gear were the best in the city throughout the middle decades of the century—and, also, to preserve language in its contract that gave "preference in hiring to the son of any employee with seniority" until as late as 1971. For the children and grandchildren of those southern-born workers lucky enough to get a job on the line at Warner Gear, that control over hiring amounted to an inside-track on the kinds of well-paying industrial jobs that were becoming increasingly difficult to come by in Muncie—even at Warner Gear itself, where the workforce declined from as much as fifty-three hundred in 1963, to under two thousand by the beginning of the 1970s. For Black Munsonians, it meant that another southern relic—the grandfather clause—effectively barred them from employment as anything other than janitors at Warner Gear until well after the passage of the 1964 Civil Rights Act.[7]

But as the hillbilly taunts that Jim also recalled made clear, the divides of class and culture that had always set poor and working-class white southerners apart in Muncie endured in meaningful ways as well. Indeed, there was good reason why, if racial tension was to surface anywhere during this period, it had surfaced at Southside. Southside's catchment zone included the neighborhood that had for some time been Muncie's most visible hillbilly ghetto, Shedtown; as well as what had become, in more recent years, the main settlement area for an influx of poor Black migrants from the South, a distressed neighborhood just south of downtown known as Industry. The racial and class composition of those two neighborhoods revealed in stark terms the larger patterns of racial segregation and integrated poverty that by that point set life in Muncie's southside apart from elsewhere in the city. By the latter half of the 1960s, Shedtown had become one of the most densely populated areas in the city, with a poverty rate of 20 percent and a Black population of just 0.04 percent. Industry, meanwhile, had a Black population of close to 80 percent, as well as the highest poverty rate of any census tract in Muncie, with roughly one in three families living below the poverty threshold. Overall, in the census tracts south of the White River, where poor and working-class southerners of either race were increasingly coming to cluster in adjacent yet racially distinct neighborhoods, the poverty rate was on average more than two-thirds higher than in the census tracts north of the river. If Whitely, the other historically Black neighborhood in Muncie, which lay just to the north of the river on the city's eastern edge, was excluded from the count, the incidence of poverty in the southern half of the city was more than twice as high as it was in the northern half.[8]

By some measure, then, the Confederate symbolism and the fighting—even the effort that went into keeping Black students off the honor roll and the Southern Aires—was about a battle for control not only of Southside High School but of the southside itself. As such, it echoed similar defensive battles that working-class white ethnics of various backgrounds, from the Irish of South Boston to the Italians of Brooklyn, were then carrying out against Black urban residents and their allies in liberal city governments.[9] For Transappalachian whites in Muncie—likewise relegated to the least desirable neighborhoods in an era when those with the means to leave the city were doing so in droves; and confined overwhelmingly to blue-collar occupations at a time when the local industrial economy was already beginning to flatline—the outcome of this struggle would prove to be, at best, a pyrrhic victory. Yet it was one that they would fight to whatever extent they could over the limited sites of institutional power to which they had access: over the schools that primarily served their communities; over the boundaries of their southside neighborhoods, none of which, in 1970, had Black populations of larger than 2 percent; over the better-paid factory jobs that had made it possible for some southern migrants to leave behind lives of working-class insecurity for good.

In some cases, like the Local 287 hiring clause, the fortifications of racial privilege that working-class southerners were able to erect around their relatively tenuous position in midwestern urban society would eventually be dismantled. In other cases, like Southside's rebel nomenclature, which remained unchanged until the school closed in 2014—a casualty of the city's plummeting population, especially on the southside, after deindustrialization picked up in earnest in the 1980s—they would not.[10] Either way, there was no denying that by the end of the period of the hillbilly highway, the twin-engines of racial change and a slowing economy were combining to make Muncie's white working class, which had never been a particularly radical group, increasingly conservative in its orientation. In a county and state that traditionally leaned Republican, Muncie's working class, and especially its organized working class, had been the bedrock of local Democratic support throughout the New Deal era; it was thanks almost entirely to this labor vote, for instance, that Adlai Stevenson scored six points higher against Dwight Eisenhower in Delaware County in 1956 than he did statewide, and four points higher than he did nationally. Similar margins were evident for Democratic candidates in Delaware County throughout the immediate postwar period. But by the end of the 1960s, even that labor vote was beginning to abandon Democratic liberalism. In 1968 George Wallace won 13 percent of the Delaware County vote—two points better than he did elsewhere in Indiana and four points higher than his national returns. Hubert Humphrey, meanwhile, received the lowest portion of the vote by a Democratic presidential candidate—38 percent—since before World War II. And the tide only continued to turn toward the right. Just two weeks before the failed assassination attempt that ended his 1972 election bid, Wallace won 37 percent of the vote in Delaware County in the Democratic primary. On his way to a national landslide later that fall, Richard Nixon took Delaware County with an overwhelming 64 percent of the vote, leaving George McGovern with even less of a turnout than Humphrey had received four years earlier. Remarking on Muncie's recent political tendencies in the aftermath of the 1972 election, the Democratic mayor, Paul Cooley—a member of the founding cadre of Local 287—hardly exaggerated when he quipped: "If Jacob Javits were in Muncie, he'd be considered a Communist. Even James Buckley would be considered extremely liberal."[11]

As has been ably demonstrated elsewhere, the rightward turn of Muncie's white working class during these years was part of a broader, regionwide phenomenon, and not one that was limited to those southern-born whites who had migrated north over the last half century. In fact, there is ample enough evidence to suggest that the most immediate forms taken by this conservative renaissance among white midwesterners—such as support for Wallace's avowedly racist presidential campaigns—were more commonly seen in other groups entirely. One analysis of Wallace's results in the Milwaukee area during the 1964 election, for instance, identified "middle- and upper-class, conservative, native-stock Republicans" as his main supporters; another, which focused on primary returns in Wisconsin and Indiana, identified Wallace's working-class voters as "predominantly Catholic." In the Uptown neighborhood of Chicago, ward-level voting returns in 1968 indicate that Wallace's support (6 percent) was well under the citywide average (12 percent), and much lower than it was in the south Chicago wards where second- and third-generation European immigrants had fought residential desegregation with the greatest fervor through the postwar period, and now gave Wallace vote shares of as high as 17 percent. Wallace's surprising returns in many midwestern cities may have been a sign of southern politics "coming North," but it was not primarily because transplanted southerners themselves had brought it there.[12]

If anything, the forces that undermined the Transappalachian working class's identification with Democratic liberalism reached farther back than the backlash politics of the 1960s and 1970s—although not so far back as was often implied in the familiar accusations about the ineluctable traditionalism of this particular group of working people. The taint of a degraded region and a discarded way of life had never been fully expunged from migrants along the hillbilly highway. In part, of course, this was because of the great lengths to which those migrants went, throughout their long trial of dispossession and displacement, to maintain attachments to the region they had come from and the rural lifestyles they had known there. But the positions of marginality they had always occupied as a result, in the factory and union hierarchies they came to move within as well as in the civic and political institutional life of their new homes, also revealed something about the shifting terrain of class politics within the heart of the twentieth-century New Deal Order. By the decades after World War II, a growing divide would emerge between a liberal political establishment composed increasingly of the rising middle classes, whose ideological worldview saw no necessary tension between the structural relations of a capitalist economy and the egalitarian ideals of a pluralist democracy; and those segments of the broader industrial working class for whom the promise of embourgeoisement was already turning out to be a false coin. Residents of the hillbilly ghettos of the Midwest were by no means the only working-class Americans who confounded this vision of a future of universalized abundance. But their whiteness, rather ironically, set them apart yet again, distancing them further than ever before from the main directions of postwar liberalism.

In this way, however, the Transappalachian working class would prove to be less a relic of the past than a harbinger of the future. By the beginning of the 1970s, the hillbilly ghetto may not have been as visible a phenomenon as it once had been. But as the midwestern industrial economy began hemorrhaging jobs en masse over subsequent decades, it was not so much that the borders of the ghetto disappeared as that they began moving ominously outward. Muncie's manufacturing workforce collapsed from eighteen thousand in 1970 to just ten thousand by the first half of the 1980s; after stabilizing for a bit during the 1990s, it would plummet to less than five thousand by the early years of the new century. Similar rates of contraction would be seen throughout the Midwest during these decades, with the region losing roughly two million manufacturing jobs between 1977 and 2000. Black midwesterners, of course—many of whom shared roots in the rural South with some of their white neighbors— would experience the worst effects of regional deindustrialization. But a new sense of precariousness began to creep into the homes of even the longer-established and better-positioned blue-collar communities in the white Midwest. After Ronald Reagan's reelection landslide in 1984, the Democratic pollster Stanley Greenberg traveled to suburban Macomb County, Michigan, to explain the party's sudden reversal of fortune in a working-class community in which almost 40 percent of households included a union member and had gone for the national Democratic ticket by a margin of three to one as recently as 1964. The so-called Reagan Democrats that Greenberg met were composed overwhelmingly of Catholic immigrants and their offspring, the Ukrainians, Poles, Hungarians, and Romanians who had long formed the backbone of Detroit's automotive workforce and filled the ranks of the United Auto Workers—and whose middle-class aspirations had largely come to fruition in a county where nearly four in five families owned their home and the median household income stood $7,000 above the national average. The Reagan Democrat was about as far a cry from the southern hillbilly as you could get. "But the slide, then collapse, of auto jobs and the erosion of union contracts called into question the bigger contract that New Deal Democrats had signed with middle-class America," Greenberg concluded—fanning the flames of a wider electoral realignment that would permanently transform the class composition of modern American politics. Over the remainder of the twentieth century (and well into the twenty-first), the Democratic Party would never be without a white working-class problem again.[13]

Around the same time Greenberg went to Macomb County, the UAW negotiated a clause into its master contract with General Motors, which allowed autoworkers to request a transfer to another factory anywhere in the country if the plant they were working at was slated for closure. Itself a response to the ongoing collapse of the domestic auto industry, the relocation clause was also a testament to the enduring strength of the UAW, and the extraordinary economic security it had been able to create for a significant portion of the industrial workforce over the previous half century. Because autoworkers held on to whatever seniority they had accrued in their previous positions when relocating between plants, the relocation clause meant that midcareer workers would not lose out on what had long been one of the crown jewels of the UAW contract: the full pension and health benefits that autoworkers qualified for after thirty years with the company, which would protect them and their families through retirement and old age. After decades of absorbing working-class migrants from the southern hinterland, now midwestern auto plants expelled them to factories far outside of the staggering Rust Belt—in California, in Texas, even in the rural southeast, where states like Kentucky, Tennessee, and Alabama became newly attractive locations for automakers seeking to take advantage of lower wages and lighter regulations. Tony Ball had been laid off at a GM plant in Wyandotte, Michigan, picking up odd jobs on the side and trying to make ends meet, when an opportunity to relocate to a newly opened plant in Tennessee presented itself, and he jumped at it without hesitation. "I was a fitter-welder, working in a fabrication shop making twelve dollars an hour with a wife and two kids, and I'm thinking, 'Man, I can go back to General Motors, in a brand-new plant—I'm good for the next twenty years. I'm gonna take my happy little butt down there, move my family to Tennessee, get 'em out of Michigan, and retire a happy man.'"

Rarely, though, did things turn out so easily for the thousands of auto-workers who made similar moves during these decades. Thirty years was a long time, and with layoffs following layoffs, first relocations were usually not last relocations. "I've been shuffled here and there," a fifty-four-year-old GM worker named John Roberts complained, after moving to his fourth GM plant. "I'm tired." The flip side of retiring a happy man, after all, was never retiring at all, and a dull sense of compulsion kept families like the Macombers shuttling back and forth between Indiana and California despite the perennial disruptions it caused their teenage children. "I don't feel like I owe my whole life to the company, yet I put my whole life into it." Frank Macomber remarked, with equal parts regret and resentment. "We shouldn't be moving around all over."

As they crossed paths on the new migratory circuits of the country's postindustrial present, workers like Frank Macomber, John Roberts, and Tony Ball would devise a nickname for themselves: "GM gypsies." As Steve Earle might have put it, the hillbilly highway goes on and on.[14]

# ACKNOWLEDGMENTS

ALTHOUGH WRITING A BOOK is mostly an individual endeavor, many people lent helping hands toward the completion of this one. My first and most earnest thanks go to the dozens of individuals who agreed to sit for interviews with me about their experiences along the hillbilly highway. They gave me, a stranger, hours of their time—and even more preciously, their stories and the stories of their family members, friends, and neighbors. I could not have written this book the way I wanted to without their extraordinary generosity. Many of their names appear throughout the chapters of this book; those that do not can be found in the complete list of oral history interviewees that appears alongside my other sources. Additional gratitude goes to Willie Beaty of Jamestown, Tennessee, and Janelle Taylor of Pelham, Tennessee, along with the volunteers and staff at the Grundy County (Tennessee) Historical Society, the Fentress County (Tennessee) Historical Society, the Fentress County Senior Citizens Center in Jamestown, Tennessee, and the Forest Park Senior Center in Muncie, Indiana, for helping connect me to people who were willing to share their experiences; and in a number of cases for providing me with workspace in which to conduct interviews and other research. More thanks to Willie for leading me on that hike at Big South Fork, a much-needed break from work that I still remember fondly; and to Kay Wood Conatser of Pall Mall, Tennessee, for sharing her time and expertise with me on multiple occasions, and for granting me permission to use personal and family documents in this book. Extra special thanks to Joliange Wright, whose friendship came before everything and set me out on this particular highway in the first place.

I owe a similar debt of gratitude to the many archivists and librarians who helped me navigate the document-based research that made up the bulk of this project, as well as to those individuals and institutions whose support, both financial and otherwise, was particularly important along the way. Staff at the Alexander M. Bracken Library and the Center for Middletown Studies at Ball State University; the Center for Documentary Research and Practice at Indiana University; the Francis S. Hutchins Library at Berea College; the Frist Library and Archive at the Country Music Hall of Fame and Museum; the University Libraries at the University of Akron; and the Walter P. Reuther Library of Labor and Urban

Affairs at Wayne State University, were especially generous with their time. On two separate trips to Muncie—the first of which, in 2011, set me on the trajectory that would eventually lead to this book, although I did not yet know that then—James Connolly of the Center for Middletown Studies went out of his way to connect me with historical resources and local contacts, and even arranged a convenient and comfortable place for me to stay while I was in town conducting research. Although the book I have produced is not quite a Middletown study, Jim's help from beginning to end has meant a great deal to it—and to me. Similarly, the Collaborative for Southern Appalachian Studies, based at the University of the South in Sewanee, Tennessee, was a bedrock of support throughout years of research. In addition to several invaluable travel grants, the Collaborative provided resources, introductions, and logistical assistance on a series of trips through Indiana, Kentucky, and Tennessee, as well as numerous opportunities to present my work to a lively and engaging group of scholars, students, and community activists. To John Willis, Karen Yu, and Sabeth Jackson at Sewanee, and Linda Mayes at Yale University: thanks for always giving me such a friendly welcome whenever I am "on the mountain."

I have worked at a few different institutions in the decade it took to research and write this book. At Yale, thanks to Jean-Christophe Agnew, Beverly Gage, and Jennifer Klein, for guiding the project through its larval form; and to Michael Denning and Alexander Nemerov, whose contributions were more indirect but who each shaped my development as a scholar during these years in enduring ways. Additional thanks to all my friends and comrades in GESO/Local 33, UNITE HERE Locals 34 and 35, and New Haven Rising—especially Lisa Furchtgott, Aaron Greenberg, Stephanie Greenlea, David Huyssen, Kate Irving, Marcy Kaufman, Lukas Moe, Adam Patten, Mark Rivera, Anita Seth, Josh Stanley, Susan Valentine, and Lindsay Zafir—with whom I shared many of my most intellectually enriching and politically meaningful experiences during graduate school. For four years, I was lucky to come home to an apartment I shared with two of the best labor historians I know, Hillary Taylor and Gabe Winant. Ted Fertik and Sochie Nnaemeka: thanks for being family.

I completed the final stages of this book while on a postdoctoral fellowship at the Society of Fellows at Dartmouth College and after joining the history faculty at the University of Miami. At Dartmouth, thanks to the Society for research funds and the Department of History for office space and other resources. For their support, discussions of my work, friendship, and in some cases all three, thanks to Randall Balmer, Robert Bonner, Matthew Delmont, Mona Domosh, Udi Greenberg, Sean Griffin, Joshua

Kaiser, Laura McDaniel, Jennifer Miller, Alexander Smith, Yana Stain-ova, Derek Woods—and especially Stefan Link and Garrett Dash Nelson. My colleagues in the Department of History at the University of Miami, meanwhile, have gone above and beyond to help me wrap up the book while juggling the challenges of teaching and service work (not to mention the compounding effects of the COVID-19 pandemic), and I am grateful to have been able to call such a collegial community my home base over the last four years. Special thanks also to the College of Arts and Sciences and the Center for the Humanities at the University of Miami, for providing funds and fellowship time without which I could not have crossed the finish line.

Before the final manuscript came together, it benefited immensely from close readings by a generous group of scholars. Thanks to Nancy Isenberg and Kim Phillips-Fein for extended feedback on an early draft; to Stefan Link and Lisa McGirr for the same on a later one; and to Jackson Lears for working with me to tease out the argument in a shorter version of what would eventually become chapter 6. I am especially grateful to Gary Gerstle, who read the manuscript at multiple stages along the way and helped steer it through the publication process at Princeton University Press. At Princeton, thanks to Eric Crahan for signing the book, to Bridget Flannery-McCoy for shepherding it through peer-review, and to Alena Chekanov for providing particularly thoughtful editorial suggestions while guiding the book into production. Jaden Young, Natalie Jones, and Beth Nauman-Montana did impeccable work finishing the job, and I am grateful to all of them for the time and careful attention they gave to my writing.

Finally, I am thankful for the love and support of my family, without whom I would not have made it to the end of this process. Thanks to my in-laws, Barbara and Mike, for keeping me well-stocked with good beer and cheering me on when my spirits got low. Thanks to my sister, Emma, and to my parents, Jill and Steve, for their unwavering faith in my ability to complete this book—even, and maybe most especially, at those moments when I found it hardest to hold on to that faith myself. My mother, a veteran journalist who never met a deadline she could not meet, was then as always a source of inspiration. I am particularly grateful to my father, who has spent more time helping me become the scholar and writer that I am than anyone else. I know he takes as much pride in seeing this book finally make its way into print as I do. I wish my uncle Jonny and my mother-in-law, Nina, who both passed away before this project was completed, were around to celebrate with me now. I miss them both every day.

If I lost some family during the years spent writing this book, I was also lucky enough to gain two incredible children. Sabina and Baz were not around when this project was getting started, but I am so grateful for every day with them now—and glad, too, that I took long enough in wrapping everything up that they have gotten old enough to be able to really appreciate this milestone along with their mom and dad. The only thing they have not been able to comprehend as I have scrambled to finish the book under their watchful, waiting eyes, is why I would ever choose to take another minute away from building Legos, playing hockey, pitching baseballs, or reading books with them to work on another one. They make a good point. Elena, you are and always have been my tireless supporter, my most devoted reader, my daily companion, my best friend, and my true love. As you are my partner in life, you have been my partner in the years spent laboring on this book—and when our working days were through, it was always my sweetest reward to be alone with you. Compared to all we have this book isn't much. But I have worked hard on it and I dedicate it to you.

NOTES

## Introduction

1. Natural gas and oil were first discovered around Muncie in 1876 and encouraged local business and political interests to form drilling companies and seek out reserves they could tap at a profit. When he sunk the Eaton well in 1886, Cranell was working for a group of investors that included Eaton businessman George Washington Carter; William Worthington, the superintendent of the Fort Wayne, Cincinnati, and Louisville Railroad; and Robert C. Bell, a state senator from Fort Wayne. James A. Glass, "The Gas Boom in East Central Indiana," *Indiana Magazine of History* 96, no. 4 (December 2000): 313–35. Muncie got its enduring nickname of "Middletown" when the Lynds selected the Indiana city to be the anonymized setting of their anthropological study of a "representative" American community. See Robert S. Lynd and Helen Merrell Lynd, *Middletown: A Study in Contemporary American Culture* (New York: Harcourt Brace Jovanovich, 1929).

2. Muncie's population in 1886 was roughly 5,500; in 1890, it had grown to 11,345; and by 1900, 20,942. Glass, "The Gas Boom in East Central Indiana," 317–18; Dwight W. Hoover, *Magic Middletown* (Bloomington: Indiana University Press, 1986), 2.

3. Ibid.

4. Kenny Lewis and Jean Koons, oral history interview with author, Muncie, Indiana, March 16, 2016, audio recording and transcript in author's possession. John Bartlow Martin, "Is Muncie Still Middletown?" *Harper's Magazine*, July 1944, 105; Frederic Alexander Birmingham, *Ball Corporation: The First Century* (Indianapolis: Curtis Publishing, 1980), 139–40.

5. Wesley Reagan, oral history interview with author, Jamestown, Tennessee, March 18, 2015, audio recording and transcript in author's possession. Kenny Lewis, oral history, March 16, 2016; Martin, "Is Muncie Still Middletown?," 98; Margaret Ripley Wolfe, "Appalachians in Muncie: A Case Study of an American Exodus," *Locus* 4, no. 2 (Spring 1992): 181; Lynd and Lynd, *Middletown*, 58n13.

6. Kenny Lewis, oral history interview; Martin, "Is Muncie Still Middletown?," 98, 103.

7. Estimates of the total number of white southerners who migrated to the Midwest during these years range from a low of six million to as high as ten million. Much of the uncertainty stems from the difficulties associated with producing accurate figures from inconsistent census data and the unusually high rates of temporary and return migration that characterized the southern Appalachian migration to the Midwest. For a sense of the variance in numbers that scholars have put forward for the overall scale of the migration, see, for example, Jacqueline Jones, *The Dispossessed: America's Underclasses from the Civil War to the Present* (New York: Basic Books, 1992), 251; Phillip J. Obermiller, Thomas E. Wagner, and E. Bruce Tucker, eds., *Appalachian Odyssey: Historical Perspectives on the Great Migration* (Westport, CT: Praeger, 2000), xii; Chad Berry, "Southern White Migration to the Midwest:

An Overview," in *Appalachian Odyssey*, eds. Obermiller, Wagner, and Tucker, 4; and James N. Gregory, *The Southern Diaspora: How the Great Migrations of Black and White Southerners Transformed America* (Chapel Hill: University of North Carolina Press, 2005), 13–14. For more extended discussions of the challenges of using census data to generate precise measurements of the migration, see James N. Gregory, "The Southern Diaspora and the Urban Dispossessed: Demonstrating the Census Public Use Microdata Samples," *Journal of American History* 82, no. 1 (June 1995): 111–34; and J. Trent Alexander, "'They're Never Here More Than a Year': Return Migration in the Southern Exodus, 1940–1970," *Journal of Social History* 38, no. 3 (Spring 2005): 653–71.

8. Arthur Kornhauser, *Attitudes of Detroit People Toward Detroit: Summary of a Detailed Report* (Detroit: Wayne State University Press, 1952), 13. Wesley Reagan, oral history interview.

9. "Muncie, Ind. Is the Great U.S. 'Middletown,'" *Life*, May 10, 1937, 16–25.

10. Gregory has done the most extensive quantitative work to compare social outcomes for different groups of southern migrants and nonmigrant communities during the twentieth century; see Gregory, "The Southern Diaspora and the Urban Dispossessed," 111–34, and Gregory, *The Southern Diaspora*, tables A.1–A.24. Local real estate developer Charles H. Huber, founder of Huber Homes Inc., began construction on what would come to be known as Huber Heights, Ohio, in 1956. Wesley Reagan, oral history interview.

11. The frequency of return migration, as well as the variety of forms it took, is covered more extensively in chapter 2; for numerical assessments of the scale of this phenomenon, and comparisons with other groups of southern migrants, see Gregory, *The Southern Diaspora*, 16–17; and Alexander, "'They're Never Here More Than a Year,'" 656. Wesley Reagan, oral history interview.

12. Wesley Reagan, oral history interview. As should be obvious—and as is discussed at greater length in chapter 2—the *agency* that southern white migrants were able to exert by returning to the South for any number of reasons was also an example of a *privilege* afforded them by their white skin. Black southerners during the era of Jim Crow were not nearly so free to return to the South after leaving the region, and as a result they did so far less frequently.

13. An only partial summary of more recent scholarly and popular writing about the Great Migration includes James R. Grossman, *Land of Hope: Chicago, Black Southerners, and the Great Migration* (Chicago: University of Chicago Press, 1989); Nicholas Lemann, *The Promised Land: The Great Black Migration and How It Changed America* (New York: Alfred A. Knopf, 1991); Joe William Trotter Jr., ed., *The Great Migration in Historical Perspective: New Dimensions of Race, Class, and Gender* (Bloomington: Indiana University Press, 1991); Kimberley L. Phillips, *AlabamaNorth: African-American Migrants, Community, and Working-Class Activism in Cleveland, 1915-45* (Urbana: University of Illinois Press, 1999); Davarian Baldwin, *Chicago's New Negroes: Modernity, the Great Migration, and Black Urban Life* (Chapel Hill: University of North Carolina Press, 2009); Donna Jean Murch, *Living for the City: Migration, Education, and the Rise of the Black Panther Party in Oakland, California* (Chapel Hill: University of North Carolina Press, 2011); Isabel Wilkerson, *The Warmth of Other Suns: The Epic Story of America's Great Migration* (New York: Vintage Books, 2011);

Marcia Chatelain, *South Side Girls: Growing Up in the Great Migration* (Durham, NC: Duke University Press, 2015); and Brian McCammack, *Landscapes of Hope: Nature and the Great Migration in Chicago* (Cambridge, MA: Harvard University Press, 2017). The Great Migration has also been the subject of a nationwide traveling exhibit first mounted at the National Museum of American History in Washington, DC, in 1987, as well as two seminal exhibitions at New York's Museum of Modern Art, in 1995 and 2015, organized around Jacob Lawrence's "Migration Series" paintings. It also figures prominently in the Smithsonian's newly created National Museum of African American History and Culture, which opened in 2016.

14. Recent works on the Okie migration to California and its far-reaching cultural and political implications include James N. Gregory, *American Exodus: The Dust Bowl Migration and Okie Culture in California* (New York: Oxford University Press, 1991); Marilynn S. Johnson, *The Second Gold Rush: Oakland and the East Bay in World War II* (Berkeley: University of California Press, 1996); Gregory, *The Southern Diaspora*; Peter La Chapelle, *Proud to Be an Okie: Cultural Politics, Country Music, and Migration to Southern California* (Berkeley: University of California Press, 2007); Darren Dochuk, *From Bible Belt to Sunbelt: Plain-Folk Religion, Grassroots Politics, and the Rise of Evangelical Conservatism* (New York: W. W. Norton, 2011); and Erin Royston Battat, *Ain't Got No Home: America's Great Migrations and the Making of an Interracial Left* (Chapel Hill: University of North Carolina Press, 2014). Other important books that highlight connections between white southerners and California's New Right include Lisa McGirr, *Suburban Warriors: The Origins of the New American Right* (Princeton, NJ: Princeton University Press, 2001); Becky M. Nicolaides, *My Blue Heaven: Life and Politics in the Working-Class Suburbs of Los Angeles, 1920–1965* (Chicago: University of Chicago Press, 2002); and Kathryn S. Olmstead, *Right Out of California: The 1930s and the Big Business Roots of Modern Conservatism* (New York: The New Press, 2015).

15. One of these country songs, Steve Earle's 1986 single "Hillbilly Highway" is discussed later in the introduction; many others appear in chapter 6. The literary masterpiece is Harriette Arnow's *The Dollmaker*, originally published in 1954 and discussed here in chapter 4. For more extended assessments of and responses to Vance's controversial memoir, see the various essays included in Anthony Harkins and Meredith McCarroll, eds., *Appalachian Reckoning: A Region Responds to Hillbilly Elegy* (Morgantown: West Virginia University Press, 2019). For its part, the film version of *Hillbilly Elegy* was feted with three nominations—for worst director, screenplay, and supporting actress—at the 41st Golden Raspberry Awards.

16. Chad Berry, *Southern Migrants, Northern Exiles* (Urbana: University of Illinois Press, 2000), 5–6. Appearing the same year was Obermiller, Wagner, and Tucker, eds., *Appalachian Odyssey*, an edited volume that collected a dozen historically grounded essays on the southern Appalachian migration—although five of the twelve essays had been published previously.

17. In the years since Berry's book was published, several sterling historical dissertations have been produced on white southerners in the Midwest. But at this writing none have been turned into books. See especially J. Trent Alexander, "Great Migrations: Race and Community in the Southern Exodus, 1917–1970" (PhD diss., Carnegie Mellon University, 2001); Susan Allyn Johnson, "Industrial Voyagers: A Case Study

of Appalachian Migration to Akron, Ohio, 1900–1940" (PhD diss., The Ohio State University, 2006); and Jesse Ambrose Montgomery, "Storming Hillbilly Heaven: The Young Patriots Organization, Radical Culture, and the Long Battle for Uptown, Chicago" (PhD diss., Vanderbilt University, 2020).

18. Scholars working in other disciplines, especially sociology and ethnicity and migration studies, have produced a somewhat larger body of work on southern Appalachian migrants in the Midwest over the last few decades. But their interests have remained largely parochial, focused primarily on narrower case studies and more preoccupied with assessing the extent to which rural southern whites assimilated urban cultural habits or preserved regionally specific ethnic traditions in their new homes. Exemplary works in this tradition include Harry K. Schwarzweller, James S. Brown, and J. J. Mangalam, *Mountain Families in Transition: A Case Study of Appalachian Migration* (University Park: Pennsylvania State University Press, 1971); William Philliber, *Appalachian Migrants in Urban America: Cultural Conflict or Ethnic Group Formation?* (New York: Praeger, 1981); William W. Philliber and Clyde B. McCoy, eds., *The Invisible Minority: Urban Appalachians* (Lexington: University of Kentucky Press, 1981); Kathryn M. Borman and Phillip J. Obermiller, eds., *From Mountain to Metropolis: Appalachian Migrants in American Cities* (Westport, CT: Bergin & Garvey, 1994); and Roger Guy, *From Diversity to Unity: Southern and Appalachian Migrants in Uptown Chicago, 1950–1970* (Lanham, MD: Lexington Books, 2007).

19. See, for instance, Peter Friedlander, *The Emergence of a UAW Local, 1936–1939: A Study in Class and Culture* (Pittsburgh: University of Pittsburgh Press, 1975); Lizabeth Cohen, *Making a New Deal: Industrial Workers in Chicago, 1919–1939* (New York: Cambridge University Press, 1990); and Nelson Lichtenstein, *The Most Dangerous Man in Detroit: Walter Reuther and the Fate of American Labor* (New York: Basic Books, 1995). Immigrant ethnic identities and traditions are foundational in other canonical accounts of the CIO's founding generations outside of the Midwest; see Steve Fraser, *Labor Will Rule: Sidney Hillman and the Rise of American Labor* (New York: Free Press, 1991); and Annelise Orleck, *Common Sense and a Little Fire: Women and Working-Class Politics in the United States, 1900–1965* (Chapel Hill: University of North Carolina Press, 1995).

20. The descriptions quoted above appear, respectively, in Friedlander, *The Emergence of a UAW Local*, 127; Thomas J. Sugrue, *The Origins of the Urban Crisis: Race and Inequality in Postwar Detroit* (Princeton, NJ: Princeton University Press, 1996), 20; and Jones, *The Dispossessed*, 260–61.

21. For standard accounts of the War on Poverty's origins, for good and ill, in the growing preoccupation with Black poverty in declining inner cities, see, among many others, Michael B. Katz, *The Undeserving Poor: From the War on Poverty to the War on Welfare* (New York: Pantheon Books, 1989); Jill Quadagno, *The Color of Welfare: How Racism Undermined the War on Poverty* (New York: Oxford University Press, 1994); James T. Patterson, *America's Struggle against Poverty in the Twentieth Century* (Cambridge, MA: Harvard University Press, 2000); and Julian Zelizer, *The Fierce Urgency of Now: Lyndon Johnson, Congress, and the Great Society* (New York: Penguin, 2015).

22. Lauren St. John, *Hardcore Troubadour: The Life and Near Death of Steve Earle* (New York: Fourth Estate, 2003), 4–19. For Earle's account of life in Schertz, see

"Schertz, Texas (Monologue)," Steve Earle, *Just an American Boy*, Artemis Records 51256, 2003.

23. "Hillbilly Highway," Steve Earle, *Guitar Town*, MCA Records 5713, 1986.

24. Jefferson Cowie, *Capital Moves: RCA's Seventy-Year Quest for Cheap Labor* (Ithaca, NY: Cornell University Press, 1999) is the standout historical account of the stages of twentieth-century capital flight that preceded global off-shoring. As the economists Teresa Fort, Justin Pierce, and Peter Schott note, "between 1977 and 2000, combined manufacturing employment in the New England, Mid-Atlantic, and East North Central [i.e., Midwest] regions [fell] by 2.3 million, while the increase for all other regions as a whole [was] 0.8 million." See Teresa C. Fort, Justin R. Pierce, and Peter K. Schott, "New Perspectives on the Decline of US Manufacturing Employment," *Journal of Economic Perspectives* 32, no. 2 (Spring 2018): 64.

25. "Snake Oil," Steve Earle, *Copperhead Road*, UNI Records, UNID-7, 1988. As Earle mused to a reporter after the release of *Copperhead Road*, "To me the most interesting phenomenon of this Reagan Administration is that he really has succeeded in convincing people that he is for the working man. They really believe it, man. They bought it. And you can't turn it around. It was the most frustrating thing in the world for me. That's where 'Snake Oil' came from." "Steve Earle Plays to a New Generation," *Los Angeles Times*, December 4, 1988.

26. The literature here is extensive, but a representative sampling includes Seymour Martin Lipset, *Political Man: The Social Bases of Politics* (New York: Doubleday, 1960); Jonathan Rieder, *Canarsie: The Jews and Italians of Brooklyn against Liberalism* (Cambridge, MA: Harvard University, 1985); Thomas Byrne Edsall and Mary D. Edsall, *Chain Reaction: The Impact of Race, Rights, and Taxes on American Politics* (New York: W. W. Norton, 1990); Dan T. Carter, *The Politics of Rage: George Wallace, the Origins of the New Conservatism, and the Transformation of American Politics* (Baton Rouge: Louisiana State University Press, 1995); Thomas Frank, *What's the Matter with Kansas? How Conservatives Won the Heart of America* (New York: Metropolitan Books, 2004); Jefferson Cowie, *Stayin' Alive: The 1970s and the Last Days of the Working Class* (New York: The New Press, 2010); Arlie Russell Hochschild, *Strangers in Their Own Land: Anger and Mourning on the American Right* (New York: The New Press, 2016); Joan C. Williams, *White Working Class: Overcoming Class Cluelessness in America* (Cambridge, MA: Harvard Business Review Press, 2017); and Daniel Martinez HoSang and Joseph E. Lowndes, *Producers, Parasites, Patriots: Race and the New Right-Wing Politics of Precarity* (Minneapolis: University of Minnesota Press, 2019).

27. On the longer history of the white poor generally—and the rural white poor in particular—as an exceptional and problematic group in American culture and political discourse, see especially Anthony Harkins, *Hillbilly: A Cultural History of an American Icon* (New York: Oxford University Press, 2004) and Nancy Isenberg, *White Trash: The 400-Year Untold History of Class in America* (New York: Viking, 2016).

28. Frank Rich, "No Sympathy for the Hillbilly," *New York*, March 20, 2017.

29. Robert S. Lynd and Helen Merrell Lynd, *Middletown in Transition: A Study in Cultural Conflicts* (New York: Harcourt, Brace, 1937), 104n4.

30. Rich, "No Sympathy for the Hillbilly"; Karl Marx and Friedrich Engels, *The Communist Manifesto* (New York: Oxford University Press, 1998 [1848]), 14.

## 1. Changes on the Land: Agrarianism, Industrialization, and Displacement in the Appalachian South

1. *Economic and Social Problems and Conditions of the Southern Appalachians*, United States Department of Agriculture, Miscellaneous Publication No. 205 (Washington, DC, 1935), 2.

2. Roy Castle, oral history interview with Kathy Shearer, Dante, Virginia, October 1, 1998. Dante History Project Records, Box 1, Folder 9, Archives of Appalachia, Charles C. Sherrod Library, East Tennessee State University, Johnson City, TN. On farming conditions in Scott County and southwestern Virginia at the turn of the twentieth century, see *Economic and Social Problems and Conditions of the Southern Appalachians*, 16-20, 52-56.

3. In every state in southern Appalachia, farm debt-to-equity ratios were higher in 1945 than they had been in 1900; see U.S. Bureau of the Census, *United States Census of Agriculture, 1950. Vol. 5, Part 8, Farm-Mortgage Debt* (Washington, DC, 1952), 14 (table 14). For foreclosure rates, see Lee J. Alston, "Farm Foreclosure Rates in the United States during the Interwar Period," *Journal of Economic History* 43, no. 4 (December 1983): 885-903. Jack Temple Kirby discusses the "age of tenancy" and its successor, the "age of hired labor," in Jack Temple Kirby, *Rural Worlds Lost: The American South, 1920-1960* (Baton Rouge: Louisiana State University Press, 1987), esp. 67-68. Total farms and acreage statistics are drawn from U.S. Bureau of the Census, *United States Census of Agriculture: 1959, Volume 2, Part 1, Farms and Land in Farms* (Washington, DC, 1962), 53ff (table 21).

4. In 1954, 75 percent of all farms in the most rural portions of southern Appalachia had farm sales of less than $1,200 annually; by contrast, the national farm average in 1954 was $5,153 per annum. These and other quality-of-life measurements are discussed at length in Thomas R. Ford, ed., *The Southern Appalachian Region: A Survey* (Lexington: University of Kentucky Press, 1962), 93-94 and passim.

5. *Economic and Social Problems and Conditions of the Southern Appalachians*, 32, 38; John C. Belcher, "Population Growth and Characteristics," in Ford, ed., *The Southern Appalachian Region*, 42-43.

6. Steven Stoll's *Ramp Hollow: The Ordeal of Appalachia* (New York: Hill and Wang, 2017) offers a longer history of the social experience of "ejectment and enclosure" in Appalachia, spanning the period between the 1790s and the 1930s (xiv). The narrower chronology offered in this chapter—from the end of the nineteenth century to the years immediately following World War II—is determined, on the one hand, by the intensified rate of displacement that occurred during this period; and, on the other, by the overlapping increase in regional out-migration, which picked up in earnest during and after World War I. For the anecdotes included above, see Crandall A. Shifflett, *Coal Towns: Life, Work, and Culture in Company Towns of Southern Appalachia, 1880-1960* (Knoxville: University of Tennessee Press, 1991), 22 (Minor); Katharine C. Shearer, ed., *Memories from Dante: The Life of a Coal Town* (Abingdon, VA: People's Incorporated, 2001), 43 (Phillips); Michael J. McDonald and John Muldowny, *TVA and the Dispossessed: The Resettlement of Population in the Norris Dam Area* (Knoxville: University of Tennessee Press, 1982), 141 (Union County farmers); and George F.

Poteet, oral history interview with Karen Gatz, Anderson, Indiana, June 19, 1982, #82-55-1,2. Center for the Study of History and Memory, Indiana University, Bloomington, IN.

7. Margie [Hayes] Lawson, oral history interview with Kathy Shearer, March 12, 1998. Dante History Project, Box 2, Folder 4, Archives of Appalachia; Ralph W. Stone, "Coal Mining at Dante, VA.," in *Contributions to Economic Geology, 1906, Part II: Coal, lignite, and peat—Coal fields of Pennsylvania, Kentucky, Virginia, and Alabama*, United States Geological Survey Bulletin 316-A (Washington, DC, 1907), 69–75; Chester K. Wentworth, "The Geological and Coal Resources of Russell County, Virginia," Virginia Geological Survey Bulletin No. 22 (Charlottesville: University of Virginia, 1922); Shearer, ed., *Memories from Dante*, 51–77.

8. Margie [Hayes] Lawson, oral history interview. Dante History Project, Box 2, Folder 4, Archives of Appalachia.

9. Land acquisitions for what would become the Norris Dam and Reservoir, a massive storage reservoir and hydroelectric power facility constructed at the intersection of the Clinch and Powell Rivers, began in the summer of 1933, just weeks after Franklin Roosevelt had signed the Tennessee Valley Authority Act into law. Construction of the dam would be completed in 1937. The best account of the Norris Dam project is McDonald and Muldowny, *TVA and the Dispossessed*.

10. Myers Hill quoted in McDonald and Muldowny, *TVA and the Dispossessed*, 34–35, 38.

11. James L. Hensley, oral history interview with Greer Warren, Anderson, Indiana, June 19, 1982, #82-58-1,2. Center for the Study of History and Memory. In one measure of the effect that mechanization was having on cotton production during these years, the average labor input per hundredweight of cotton fell from 33.82 hours in 1940 to just 24.57 by 1946. By 1952 it had fallen all the way to 4.82 hours. Kirby, *Rural Worlds Lost*, 69.

12. Steven Stoll argues something similar about the relationship between land and the "makeshift" arrangements that sustained traditional agrarian communities in southern Appalachia in *Ramp Hollow*.

13. Margie [Hayes] Lawson, oral history interview. Dante History Project, Box 2, Folder 4, Archives of Appalachia; McDonald and Muldowny, *TVA and the Dispossessed*, 4, 35.

14. Schwarzweller, Brown, and Mangalam, *Mountain Families in Transition*, 18.

15. Schwarzweller, Brown, and Mangalam, *Mountain Families in Transition*, 18–19; Margie [Hayes] Lawson, oral history interview. Dante History Project, Box 2, Folder 4, Archives of Appalachia.

16. *Economic and Social Problems and Conditions of the Southern Appalachians*, 131–34, 161–62.

17. McDonald and Muldowny, *TVA and the Dispossessed*, 102 (table 20); Messer quoted in Shifflett, *Coal Towns*, 24. See also George E. Vincent, "A Retarded Frontier," *American Journal of Sociology* 4, no. 1 (July 1898): 1–20; Jack E. Weller, *Yesterday's People: Life in Contemporary Appalachia* (Lexington: University of Kentucky Press, 1965).

18. Margie [Hayes] Lawson, oral history interview. Dante History Project, Box 2, Folder 4, Archives of Appalachia.

19. Clarence Phillips, oral history interview with Kathy Shearer, October 29, 1997, Dante History Project, Box 2, Folder 9; and Margie [Hayes] Lawson, oral history interview, Box 2, Folder 4, Archives of Appalachia. On production in the southwest Virginia coalfield, see United States Department of the Interior, Geological Survey, *Coal Resources of Virginia, Geological Survey Circular 171* (Washington, DC, 1952), esp. 8, 42–43. Coal industry employment data for southwest Virginia comes from United States Department of Commerce, Bureau of Mines, *Mineral Resources of the United States, 1931, Part II-Nonmetals* (Washington, DC, 1933), 484. On Dante, see Shearer, ed., *Memories from Dante*, 175–215; Leland B. Tate, *An Economic and Social Survey of Russell County* (Charlottesville: University of Virginia Press, 1931).

20. U.S. Bureau of the Census, *Fifteenth Census of the United States, 1930: Agriculture, Volume 4, Chapter 2, Size of Farms* (Washington, DC, 1932), 91ff (table 9). See also *Economic and Social Problems and Conditions of the Southern Appalachians*, 16; Ronald D. Eller, *Miners, Millhands, and Mountaineers: Industrialization in the Appalachian South, 1880–1930* (Knoxville: University of Tennessee Press, 1982), 137; Ronald D. Eller, "Industrialization and Social Change," in *Colonialism and Modern America: The Appalachian Case*, eds. Helen Matthews Lewis, Linda Johnson, and Donald Askins (Boone, NC: Appalachian Consortium Press, 1978), 40; Paul Salstrom, *Appalachia's Path to Dependency: Rethinking a Region's Economic History, 1730–1940* (Lexington: University Press of Kentucky, 1984), 26.

21. Department of the Interior, United States Geological Survey, *Mineral Resources of the United States, Calendar Year 1911, Part II-Nonmetals* (Washington, DC, 1912), 138–43; U.S. Department of Commerce, Bureau of Mines, *Mineral Resources of the United States, 1927, Part II-Nonmetals* (Washington, DC, 1930), 464–65; U.S. Department of Commerce, Bureau of Mines, *Mineral Resources of the United States, 1930, Part II-Nonmetals* (Washington, DC, 1932); U.S. Bureau of the Census, *U.S. Census of Mineral Industries: 1954, Volume 2, Area Statistics* (Washington, DC, 1958), 116–5, 147–3. See also *Economic and Social Problems and Conditions of the Southern Appalachians*, 35–39; Harold A. Gibbard, "Extractive Industries and Forestry," in Ford, ed., *The Southern Appalachian Region*, 104–10, 117–18.

22. Calculations drawn from U.S. Bureau of Census, *Fifteenth Census of the United States, Manufactures: 1929, Volume 3, Reports By States* (Washington, DC, 1932); *Economic and Social Problems and Conditions of the Southern Appalachians*, 85–89. Average wages for the specific industry groupings named here are computed by comparing total wages paid to total wage earners in each category, and for the manufacturing sector overall, as reported in the 1929 Census of Manufactures. See also Eller, *Miners, Millhands, and Mountaineers*, 154–57.

23. See U.S. Bureau of the Census, *Manufactures: 1929* (table 10). See also Calvin B. Hoover and B. U. Ratchford, *Economic Resources and Policies of the South* (New York: The Macmillan Company, 1951), 20, 34, 55 156; Paul E. Mertz, *New Deal Policy and Southern Rural Poverty* (Baton Rouge: Louisiana State University Press, 1978), 3; Eller, "Industrialization and Social Change," 39; Gavin Wright, *Old South, New South: Revolutions in the Southern Economy Since the Civil War* (New York: Basic Books, 1986), 160 (table 6.2); Jacquelyn Dowd Hall et al., *Like a Family: The Making of a Southern Cotton Mill World* (Chapel Hill: University of North Carolina Press, 1987), map 1.

24. Calculations from U.S. Bureau of the Census, *Fifteenth Census, Agriculture, Volume 2, Part 2, The Southern States* (Washington, DC, 1932); and *Sixteenth Census of the United States: 1940, Agriculture, Volume 3, Part 1, Farms and Farm Property* (Washington, DC, 1943). See also Roy E. Proctor and T. Kelley White, "Agriculture: A Reassessment," in Ford, ed., *The Southern Appalachian Region*, 92, 97; and Alfred J. Gray, "Local, State, and Regional Planning," in Ford, ed., *The Southern Appalachian Region*, 170; Hickum quoted in Hall et al., *Like a Family*, 38–39.

25. *Historical Statistics of the United States, 1789–1945* (Washington, DC, 1949), 97–100; *Economic and Social Problems and Conditions of the Southern Appalachians*, 5–6; Hoover and Ratchford, *Economic Resources and Policies of the South*, 395 (table XC); Mertz, *New Deal Policy and Southern Rural Poverty*, 5. For the earliest articulations of the concept of "internal colonialism," commonly associated with the work of the sociologist Robert Blauner, as it applied to southern Appalachia, see the essays included in Helen Matthews Lewis, Linda Johnson, and Donald Askins, eds., *Colonialism in Modern America: The Appalachian Case* (Boone, NC: The Appalachian Consortium Press, 1978). Other notable installments in this literature include John Gaventa, *Power and Powerlessness: Quiescence and Rebellion in an Appalachian Valley* (Urbana: University of Illinois Press, 1982), and Eller, *Miners, Millhands, and Mountaineers*.

26. Resettlement Administration, *What the Resettlement Administration Has Done* (Washington, DC, 1936), 13–14; Proctor and White, "Agriculture," 100; John Alexander Williams, *Appalachia: A History* (Chapel Hill: University of North Carolina Press, 2002), 314–17; Gavin Wright, "The New Deal and the Modernization of the South," *Federal History* 2 (2010), 59. For more extended discussions of rural land use and economic development during the New Deal, see especially Jason Scott Smith, *Building New Deal Liberalism: The Political Economy of Public Works, 1933–1956* (New York: Cambridge University Press, 2006), and Sarah T. Phillips, *This Land, This Nation: Conservation, Rural America, and the New Deal* (New York: Cambridge University Press, 2007).

27. Helen M. Lewis and Edward E. Knipe, "The Colonialism Model: The Appalachian Case," in *Colonialism in Modern America*, eds. Lewis, Johnson, and Askins, 20; and James Branscome, "The Federal Government in Appalachia: TVA," in *Colonialism in Modern America*, eds. Lewis, Johnson, and Askins, 283–93; David E. Whisnant, *Modernizing the Mountaineer: People, Power, and Planning in Appalachia* (Boone, NC: Appalachian Consortium Press, 1980), 50–54; McDonald and Muldowny, *TVA and the Dispossessed*, 4, 35.

28. *Economic and Social Problems and Conditions of the Southern Appalachians*, 5.

29. Margie [Hayes] Lawson, oral history interview. Dante History Project, Box 2, Folder 4, Archives of Appalachia; Hickum quoted on Hall et al., *Like a Family*, 39; McDonald and Muldowny, *TVA and the Dispossessed*, 239, 247.

30. Compared to 61 percent of these white farm operators, only 48 percent of Black operators of noncommercial farms in the South reported a hundred days or more of work off the farm in 1954—although the disparity should be understood as a reflection of the persistence of racial discrimination in nonagricultural forms of employment throughout the region, rather than a sign of relatively higher standards of living among Black farmers.

31. Calculations drawn from U.S. Bureau of the Census, *Thirteenth Census of the United States Taken in the Year 1910, Agriculture, Volumes 6 and 7, Reports by States* (Washington, DC, 1914) and U.S. Bureau of the Census, *United States Census of Agriculture: 1954, Volume 2, General Report, Statistics By Subject* (Washington, DC, 1956). See also *Economic and Social Problems and Conditions of the Southern Appalachians*, 120, 136; Hoover and Ratchford, *Economic Resources and Policies of the South*, 60; Williams, *Appalachia*, 12–13, 312.

32. For mining workforce ratios and migration figures by county, see "Percent of Gainful Workers Over 10 in Mining, 1930," produced by W.P.A. Project 9678-0 (n.d.), James S. Brown Collection, Box 228, Folder 17; and "Migration Data" (n.d.), Brown Collection, Box 64, Folder 16, Special Collections Research Center, Margaret I. King Library, University of Kentucky, Lexington, KY. For population figures, see U.S. Department of Commerce, Bureau of the Census, *Fifteenth Census of the United States: 1930, Population Bulletin, Kentucky: Number and Distribution of Inhabitants* (Washington, DC, 1931), 431–35. See also *Mineral Resources of the United States, 1927*, 464–65; *Economic and Social Problems and Conditions of the Southern Appalachians*, 120, 136; James S. Brown and George A. Hillery Jr., "The Great Migration, 1940–1960," in Ford, ed., *The Southern Appalachian Region*, 59, 74.

33. Mary Breckinridge, "The Corn-Bread Line," *Survey*, August 15, 1930. The mining company officials are quoted in Shifflett, *Coal Towns*, 22–23. *Economic and Social Problems and Conditions of the Southern Appalachians*, 135. See also "Migration Data," Brown Collection, Box 64, Folder 16, King Library.

34. Raiford Blackstone, oral history interview with Kathy Shearer, St. Paul, Virginia, October 3, 1997, Box 1 Folder 2; Gladys Carter, oral history interview with Kathy Shearer, Dante, Virginia, October 10, 1997, Box 1, Folder 7, Dante History Project Records, Archives of Appalachia. The "keenest observer" is James S. Brown, "The Southern Appalachians and the Nation: A Tightening Web of Relationships" [final corrected manuscript] reproduced by the University of Kentucky Agricultural Experiment Station (May 1963). Brown Collection, Box 44, Folder 8, King Library. See also Hall et al., *Like a Family*, 252–58.

35. Roy Castle, oral history interview. Dante History Project Records, Box 1, Folder 9, Archives of Appalachia. The United States Coal Commission investigation is quoted in Williams, *Appalachia*, 260. For detailed descriptions of life in southern company towns, see, among many others, Hall et al., *Like a Family*; Eller, *Miners, Millhands, and Mountaineers*; and Shifflett, *Coal Towns*.

36. As with other sectors of the industrial economy, the years immediately following the passage of the National Labor Relations Act of 1935 were a watershed for organizing in the Appalachian coal industry. In that time, United Mine Workers of America locals in Kentucky, Tennessee, and Alabama were able to sign up 85 percent of the area workforce as members, while total union membership in West Virginia increased from a few thousand in 1931 to roughly three hundred thousand by the beginning of the 1940s. For the Harlan County workforce data, see U.S. Geological Survey, *Mineral Resources of the United States, 1922, Part II-Nonmetals* (Washington, DC, 1925), 598–99. See also Shifflett, *Coal Towns*, 109–12; Jones, *The Dispossessed*, 162–65; Williams, *Appalachia*, 278–81.

37. Emory Cook, oral history interview with Kathy Shearer, Dante, Virginia, February 25, 1998. Dante History Project Records, Box 1, Folder 12; Clarence Phillips,

oral history interview, Box 2, Folder 9; and Roy Castle, Box 1, Folder 9, Archives of Appalachia. See also John W. Hevener, *Which Side Are You On? The Harlan County Coal Miners, 1931–1939* (Urbana: University of Illinois Press, 2002), 5, 34–35.

38. Bureau of the Census, *Thirteenth Census: 1930, Volume 3, Population by States* (Washington, DC, 1932). Also, Elizabeth Gyetvay, Betty Sabo, Rose White, Lucille Whitaker, and Ponnie Sabo, interview with Kathy Shearer, Castlewood, Virginia, June 4, 1998. Dante History Project Records, Box 1, Folder 18, Archives of Appalachia. Jones, *The Dispossessed*, 144. See also Shearer, ed., *Memories from Dante*, 217–55.

39. See, for instance, Karl Polanyi, *The Great Transformation* (New York: Farrar & Reinhart, 1944); Maurice Dobb, *Studies in the Development of Capitalism* (London: Routledge, 1946); T. H. Aston and C.H.E. Philpin, eds., *The Brenner Debate: Agrarian Class Structure and Economic Development in Pre-Industrial Europe* (New York: Cambridge University Press, 1985 [1983]).

40. Thomas Ford, "The Passing of Provincialism," in Ford, ed., *The Southern Appalachian Region*, 29.

41. Gibbard, "Extractive Industries and Forestry," 103–10.

42. "Appalachian Migrants to Specified Metropolitan Areas from Specified Southern Appalachian State Economic Areas, Percentage Comparison for Three Time Periods, 1950, 1960, 1970," special tabulations provided by the U.S. Bureau of the Census and U.S. Department of Agriculture (no date), Brown Collection, Box 176, Folder 17; and "Net Migration by Decades, S. Apps., 1930–1977," handwritten chart (no date), Brown Collection, Box 228, Folder 9, King Library. See also Williams, *Appalachia*; President's Appalachian Regional Commission (Washington, DC, 1964), esp. Appendix C; Brown and Hillery Jr., "The Great Migration," table 17; and Gibbard, "Extractive Industries and Forestry," table 27.

43. Margie [Hayes] Lawson, oral history interview. Dante History Project, Box 2, Folder 4, Archives of Appalachia.

## 2. On the Road: Migration and the Making of a Transregional Working Class

1. Brooks quoted in Joe Creason, "Nonstop Bus Line, Paducah to Detroit," *The Courier-Journal Magazine*, August 15, 1954.

2. Charlie Wood, diary entry for August 5, 1943, copy in author's possession (courtesy of Kay Wood Conatser).

3. Charlie Wood, diary entry for April 22, 1944, copy in author's possession; Kay Wood Conatser quoted in email communication with author, March 8, 2019.

4. Helen Sells, oral history interview with author, Jamestown, Tennessee, March 17, 2015. Audio recording and transcript in author's possession. The column—penned by Mrs. Clifton Mace—first began appearing in the mid-1930s and ran until 1963; after the *Fentress County News* ceased publication in the mid-1940s, Mace's column appeared in the *Upper Cumberland Times* for the duration of its run. See Wolfe, "Appalachians in Muncie," 181.

5. Farm data for Fentress County drawn from Bureau of the Census, *Thirteenth Census of the United States: 1910, Volume 7: Reports by States* (Washington, DC, 1913); *United States Census of Agriculture: 1925, Volume 1, Reports By States* (Washington, DC, 1927); and *United States Census of Agriculture: 1945, Volume 1, Reports By States*

(Washington, DC, 1946). See also Helen Sells, oral history interview with author; Belcher, "Population Growth and Characteristics," 169–76.

6. Leonard and Libby Anderson, oral history interview with author, Jamestown, Tennessee, March 18, 2015. Audio recording and transcript in author's possession. The "perpetual transience" line can be found in Jones, *The Dispossessed*, 166.

7. In the case of the major twentieth-century migrations out of the American South, see, for example, Robert Coles, *The South Goes North* (New York: Little, Brown, 1978); Nicholas Lemann, *The Promised Land: The Great Black Migration and How It Changed America* (New York: Alfred A. Knopf, 1991); Dochuk, *From Bible Belt to Sunbelt*; J. D. Vance, *Hillbilly Elegy: A Memoir of a Family and a Culture in Crisis* (New York: Harper, 2016).

8. Joyce Crouch, oral history interview with author, Jamestown, Tennessee, March 16, 2015. Audio recording and transcript in author's possession.

9. John C. Campbell, *The Southern Highlander and His Homeland* (New York: Russell Sage Foundation, 1921), 242; *Economic and Social Problems and Conditions of the Southern Appalachians*, United States Department of Agriculture, Miscellaneous Publication No. 205 (Washington, DC, 1935), 76–79, fig. 92.

10. Over the next seven years, the Public Works Administration alone would loan or grant $1.3 billion to support federal and nonfederal street, road, and highway construction projects throughout the country. Smith, *Building New Deal Liberalism*, 95.

11. Carter Goodrich et al., *Migration and Economic Opportunity: The Report of the Study of Population Redistribution* (Philadelphia: University of Pennsylvania Press, 1936), 119–20, 683.

12. On the development of this transportation infrastructure in the South, and its social and cultural effects on the region, see, among others, Claudette Stager and Martha Carver, eds., *Looking Beyond the Highway: Dixie Roads and Culture* (Knoxville: University of Tennessee Press, 2006); Tammy Ingram, *Dixie Highway: Road Building and the Making of the Modern South, 1900–1930* (Chapel Hill: University of North Carolina Press, 2014).

13. Goodrich et al., *Migration and Economic Opportunity*, 118–19.

14. "Percentage of Total Southern Appalachian Migrants to Specified Metropolitan Areas from Specified Southern Appalachian State Economic and Metropolitan Areas, 1955–1960," special tabulations from the U.S. Bureau of the Census (n.d.). James S. Brown Collection, Box 137, Folder 4, Special Collections Research Center, Margaret I. King Library, University of Kentucky, Lexington, KY.

15. Alvin Cullum York—one of the most decorated American soldiers during World War I and the subject of a rousingly patriotic biographical film starring Gary Cooper and directed by Howard Hawks, *Sergeant York*, which was the highest-grossing movie of 1941—remains Fentress County's most famous native son. Farmland and a gristmill York operated nine miles north of Jamestown was designated a National Historic Landmark in 1977, and today is the site of a state historic park; he also founded the Alvin C. York Industrial Institute in Jamestown in 1929, which now operates as the York Institute and is Jamestown's state-administered public high school. State Route 42 through northern Fentress County, meanwhile, became State Route 111 in the late 1980s. See also, "Readin', Rightin', Rt. 23," Dwight Yoakam, *Hillbilly Deluxe*, Reprise 9 25567-2, 1987.

16. Chris Meiman, "Halfway House," in *The Encyclopedia of Northern Kentucky*, eds. Paul A. Tenkotte and James C. Claypool (Lexington: University Press of Kentucky, 2009), 429.

17. Doug Voiles, oral history interview with author, Pine Haven, Tennessee, April 3, 2015; Leonard and Libby Anderson, oral history interview; audio recordings and print transcripts in author's possession. According to Margaret Ripley Wolfe, Willard Voiles held the record for most taxi trips between Muncie and Jamestown over the duration of the Transappalachian migration; see Wolfe, "Appalachians in Muncie," 181.

18. "The Polk Brooks Story," *Paducah Sun-Democrat*, January 31, 1975; Loring M. Lawrence, "Fifty Years of the Paducah Express," *Bus Industry* 6, no. 5 (October 1979): 12–21. By Brooks's later recollections, there were as many as nine other taxi drivers regularly carrying passengers between the Jackson Purchase area and Michigan during the period he started driving. See Ora Brooks, *Brooks Bus Line: No "Common Carrier"* (self-pub., 1985), 4n2. The "one long Detroit caravan" line is found in Dorothy and Kerby Jennings, *The Story of Calloway County, 1822–1976* (self-pub., 1978), 234.

19. Mimeographed copy of company brochure (c. 1953). Brooks Bus Line Records, Box 1, Folder 3; and Memo from Jack Brooks to Ora Brooks [plus attachments] (c. 1984). Brooks Bus Line Records, Box 1, Folder 2, Special Collection and Archives, Forrest C. Pogue Library, Murray State University, Murray, KY. Additional details of the Brooks Bus Line story are gleaned from Creason, "Nonstop Bus Line"; Jon Lowell, "The Paducah Express," *Newsweek*, January 20, 1975; "The Polk Brooks Story," *Paducah Sun-Democrat*; Lawrence, "Fifty Years of the Paducah Express"; "Golden Anniversary Year for Brooks Bus Line," *Bus Ride*, October 1979; Brooks, *Brooks Bus Line*.

20. According to the Motor Carrier Act of 1935, which put interstate commercial transportation and trucking under federal regulation, bus companies and other "common carriers" had to prove that there was a "public convenience and necessity" served by a proposed route before the ICC would certify it. Doing so required companies to demonstrate not only that there was sufficient public demand to justify the creation of a proposed route, but also, among other things, that the route's approval would not saturate the local market and exert a downward pressure on prices and service. As Brooks Bus Line expanded, the company periodically applied to the ICC to add new stops along its Paducah-to-Detroit route, some of which were approved and some of which were declined (but all of which were opposed by regional competitors as well as national rivals like Greyhound). Brooks, *Brooks Bus Line*, esp. 1–27. The quoted passage above is from Interstate Commerce Commission, Division 5, *Applicant's Brief in Support of Application for Certificate of Public Convenience and Necessity* (Form BMC-9) (Hearing held November 10, 1938, at Paducah, Kentucky) [brief and excerpts from transcript]. Brooks Bus Line Records, Box 1, Folder 3, Pogue Library. For more on Brooks's repeat customers, see, for instance, Lowell, "The Paducah Express."

21. Memo from Jack Brooks to Ora Brooks [plus attachments] (c. 1984). Brooks Bus Line Records, Box 1, Folder 2, Pogue Library. "The Polk Brooks Story," *Paducah Sun-Democrat*; F. M. Hall, "Brooks Feels Technology Killed Chiefs," *Paducah Sun-Democrat*, July 20, 1977. See also Jennings and Jennings, *The Story of Calloway County*, 234–36.

22. Creason, "Nonstop Bus Line."

23. *Applicant's Brief*, November 10, 1938. Brooks Bus Line Records, Box 1, Folder 3, Pogue Library. See also Creason, "Nonstop Bus Line"; Brooks, *Brooks Bus Line*, 1–5.

24. Calculated from handwritten data sets, produced for a study initiated by the Agricultural Extension Service at the University of Kentucky (c. 1959). Brown Collection, Box 130, Folder 5, King Library. Brooks quoted in Creason, "Nonstop Bus Line." On the importance of family connections in organizing the hillbilly highway's characteristic chain-migrations, see especially Schwarzweller, Brown, and Mangalam, *Mountain Families in Transition*; and Berry, *Southern Migrants, Northern Exiles*.

25. Wood diary, entries from April 14 through June 5, 1944; copy in author's possession.

26. Chicago Commission on Human Relations, *A Summary of Work of the Migration Services Department, Mayor's Committee on New Residents, January 1957–1959* (March 1959) [unpublished report]. Council of the Southern Mountain Records, Box 270, Folder 2. Special Collections and Archives, Francis S. Hutchins Library, Berea College, Berea, KY. The Indianapolis teacher is Anne J. Mallot. See oral history interview with Richard Phelps, March 24, 1976, #76-30-1,2. Indiana University Center for the Study of History and Memory, Bloomington, IN. The factory manager is quoted in Eldon Dee Smith, "Migration and Adjustment Experiences of Rural Migrant Workers in Indianapolis" (PhD diss., University of Wisconsin, 1953), 205. The description of Brooks's passengers can be found in "Golden Anniversary Year for Brooks Bus Line." Berry also describes the importance of these kinds of migratory habits in *Southern Migrants, Northern Exiles*.

27. A snapshot of Charlie's remittance schedule can be gleaned from diary entries from April 29, May 6, May 13, and May 19, 1944. Wood diary; copy in author's possession. Howard W. Beers, "Changes in Return Migrants: Habits and Attitudes of Selected Rural Men and Women before and after Their Absence as Migrants . . . ," unpublished manuscript (c. 1947). Brown Collection, Box 122, Folder 10, King Library. The unnamed Kentucky migrant is quoted here as well.

28. Leonard and Libby Anderson, oral history interview; Frances Hurd, oral history interview with author, Jamestown, Tennessee, March 20, 2015; audio recording and print transcript in author's possession.

29. As the study's author, Roger Guy, points out, non-southern landlords also preferred to have southern women perform the role of building manager because it allowed them "to remain aloof from the often dirty business of collecting rent and dealing with tenant complaints"—the latter being a particularly common problem due to the substandard quality of many of the buildings in the neighborhoods where southern Appalachian migrants tended to live. Guy, *From Diversity to Unity*, 58–59.

30. An unparalleled depiction of the "domestic" worlds of southern Appalachian women in the urban Midwest is Harriette Arnow's exceptional 1954 novel *The Dollmaker*—which draws, very loosely, on Arnow's own experiences leaving eastern Kentucky for Detroit during World War II. A more quantitatively informed analysis of migrant women's labor force participation is Katherine J. Curtis White, "Women in the Great Migration: Economic Activity of Black and White Southern-Born Female Migrants in 1920, 1940, and 1970," *Social Science History* 29, no. 3 (Fall 2005): 413–55. For the Magoffin County data cited here, see "Table 11: War Location of Resident Population, 15 and Over, by Family Status, Age, and Sex" (1948–1949) [handwritten

statistical table], Brown Collection, Box 122, Folder 9; as well as data sets for Agricultural Extension Service study, Brown Collection, Box 130, Folder 5, King Library.

31. Brooks Bus Line (J. Polk Brooks d/b/a), *Local Express Tariff No. 1, naming Express and Newspaper Rates and Charges*, November 1, 1949. Brooks Bus Line Records, Box 1, Folder 5, Pogue Library. Kay Wood Conatser quoted in email communication with author, March 8, 2019. On the prevalence of traditional home-remedies of southern origin in Appalachian migrant communities in the Midwest, see, for instance, Virginia McCoy-Watkins, "Urban Appalachian Health Behavior," in *Perspectives on Urban Appalachians: An Introduction to Mountain Life, Migration, and Urban Adaptation, and a Guide to the Improvement of Social Services*, eds. Steven Weiland and Phillip Obermiller (Cincinnati: Ohio Urban Appalachian Awareness Project, 1978).

32. Timothy J. Smith II and Tom Des Jean, "The Geography of Illegal Distillery Sites in the Big South Fork National River and Recreation Area," conference paper presented at the 20th Annual Meeting of the Current Research in Tennessee Archaeology Conference, Nashville, Tennessee (2007); paper in author's possession. See also Doug Voiles, oral history interview; Jennings and Jennings, *The Story of Calloway County*, 239. On the ubiquity of moonshining in the economic life of the rural South, and the interstate distribution networks that thrived throughout the middle decades of the twentieth century, see Daniel S. Pierce, *Tar Heel Lightnin': How Secret Stills and Fast Cars Made North Carolina the Moonshine Capital of the World* (Chapel Hill: University of North Carolina Press, 2019), esp. 187–209.

33. "Record of Funeral [Otis Burroughs]," Yearly No. 47 (August 30, 1958), and "Record of Funeral," Yearly No. 46 (September 12, 1959), *Roth Funeral Records, 1958–1962*, 4, 75; "Record of Funeral [Robert Hampton]," Yearly No. 51 (November 3, 1967), *Roth Funeral Records, 1967–1973*, 43; "Record of Funeral [Virginia Rust]," Yearly No. 49 (March 29, 1976), *Roth Funeral Records, 1975–1977*, 86; "Record of Funeral [Mildred Smith]," Yearly No. 97 (May 28, 1977), *Roth Funeral Records, 1977–1978*, 44 [Bound ledger books]. Local and Family History Room, McCracken County Public Library, Paducah, KY.

34. Author's calculations, based on the bound record books of Jennings Funeral Home (known as Jamestown Funeral Home until 1977), which were transcribed by R. J. Ellis and C. S. Posey in 2000–2001. Of the roughly nine hundred eighty funerals conducted between 1968 and 1982 for which records exist, at least eighty-three involved decedents from the Midwest. See *Funeral Home Records from Jennings Funeral Home, Jamestown, Fentress Co., TN, formerly Jamestown Funeral Home, Books I and II*. Cemetery and Funeral Home Records, Tennessee State Library and Archives, Nashville, TN. These figures closely track the findings of Phillip Obermiller and Ray Rappold, whose 1994 study of "postdeath migration" is the only other attempt that has been made to quantify the frequency with which southern Appalachian migrants elected to be buried in this way. Obermiller and Rappold estimate that 10 percent of permanently relocated southerners, mostly drawn from the first generations of migrants, made this choice; see Phillip J. Obermiller and Ray Rappold, "The Sense of Place and Cultural Identity among Urban Appalachians: A Study in Postdeath Migration," in *From Mountain to Metropolis*, eds. Borman and Obermiller, 27–29.

35. Deborah Vansau McCauley, *Appalachian Mountain Religion: A History* (Urbana: University of Illinois Press, 1995), 432. Alan Jabbour and Karen Singer

Jabbour, *Decoration Day in the Mountains: Traditions of Cemetery Decoration in the Southern Appalachians* (Chapel Hill: University of North Carolina Press, 2010), is the most detailed treatment of Decoration Day traditions in southern Appalachia. The burial cost numbers appear in Obermiller and Rappold, "The Sense of Place and Cultural Identity among Urban Appalachians," 29.

36. As Jabbour and Jabbour note, Decoration Days—alternately known in some parts of southern Appalachia as "homecoming"—have "long provided an occasion for community members from afar to return to their homeplace." *Decoration Day in the Mountains*, vii. Nor was this particular aspect of the tradition taken lightly; as the editor of the Jasper, Alabama, *Daily Mountain Eagle* has recalled from his own childhood experiences, "kinfolk who do not show up for Decoration were always talked about in a negative light." James Phillips, "Decoration: A Tradition in Appalachia," *Daily Mountain Eagle*, May 20, 2018.

37. Brooks quoted in Creason, "Nonstop Bus Line." See also holiday bus schedules and ridership [handwritten chart] (n.d.). Brooks Bus Line Records, Box 1, Folder 6, Pogue Library.

38. Joyce Crouch, oral history interview with author; Ray Owens, oral history interview with author, Jamestown, Tennessee, March 17, 2015. Audio recording and transcript in author's possession. Shelby quoted in Berry, *Southern Migrants, Northern Exiles*, 119.

39. *Upper Cumberland Times* (Jamestown, TN), July 7, 1955; *Morgan County News* (Wartburg, TN), January 4, 1974; Mary Cantrell, "Jellico Social Scene," *Campbell County Times* (LaFollette, TN), March 14, 1975; *Pickett County Press* (Byrdstown, TN), May 25, 1975.

40. Over the years, ridership on the Paducah-to-Detroit run tended to fluctuate closely with the business cycle, peaking during boom periods for the midwestern industrial economy (such as World War II, when the number of passengers on Brooks buses regularly exceeded twenty thousand per year); and slowing markedly during slack ones (like the recessions of 1953 and 1958, when ridership fell off by close to 20 percent from previous years). See Memo from Jack Brooks to Ora Brooks [plus attachments], (c. 1984). Brooks Bus Line Records, Box 1, Folder 2, Pogue Library. The quoted Akron industrialist is Paul W. Litchfield, president of the Goodyear Tire and Rubber Company. See Litchfield, "The Future of the Rubber Industry," speech to the East Akron Board of Trade, April 20, 1922. Goodyear Collection, Series VII: Labor, Subseries: Personnel, Box 12, Folder: April 20, 1922, University Libraries, University of Akron, Akron, OH. See also Erdmann Doane Beynon, "The Southern White Laborer Migrates to Michigan," *American Sociological Review* 3, no. 3 (June 1938): esp. 337–38; Philip Harsham, "Recession Reverses East Kentuckians' Migration," *Louisville Courier-Journal*, July 17, 1958; Lowell, "The Paducah Express."

41. Franklin Hargis, oral history interview with author, March 9, 2015, Jamestown, Tennessee; and Forrest David "Hamp" Nunley, oral history interview with author, March 26, 2015, Pelham, Tennessee. Audio recordings and transcripts in author's possession. See also Joyce Crouch, oral history interview with author; Charlie Wood, diary entries for July 21 and August 5, 1943.

42. As James Gregory explains, "Since 1940, census takers have asked respondents where they lived at some previous date, usually five years earlier. This interval leads

to severe undercounts of mobility, since any two-way moves that have taken place within the five-year interval remain unrecorded and some people forget exactly where they lived five years back." Gregory, *The Southern Diaspora*, 16. See also Alexander, "'They're Never Here More Than a Year,'" 653–71; Christine Leibbrand, Catherine Massey, J. Trent Alexander, and Stewart Tolnay, "Great Migration's Great Return? An Examination of Second-Generation Return Migration to the South," *Social Science Research* 81 (July 2019): 117–31.

43. Gregory, *The Southern Diaspora*, 16. Likewise, as J. Trent Alexander has noted, "The Great Migration contained a strong and significant counterstream long before the heralded turnaround of the 1970s, particularly for southern whites." Alexander, "'They're Never Here More Than a Year,'" 665.

44. See, for instance, Elizabeth Rauh Bethel, *Promiseland: A Century of Life in a Negro Community* (Columbia: University of South Carolina Press, 1997 [1981]), 190–92; Earl Lewis, "Afro-American Adaptive Strategies: The Visiting Habits of Kith and Kin among Black Norfolkians during the First Great Migration," *Journal of Family History* 12, no. 4 (1987): 407–20; Grossman, *Land of Hope*, 91–93. Significantly, visiting tended to be more frequent among middle-class migrants; as Kimberley L. Phillips observes in her study of Black southerners in Cleveland, many working-class migrants, whether because of limited budgets or restrictive work schedules, "simply never returned 'down South' to visit loved ones." Phillips, *AlabamaNorth*, 140. The daughter of a migrant quoted above is Wilkerson, *The Warmth of Other Suns*, 366.

45. Throughout the first half of the twentieth century, the ownership rate among Black farm operators in the South never exceeded 35 percent, and typically hovered closer to 20 percent. By comparison, white farm ownership in the South during these years never dropped below 50 percent, and usually approached 60 percent or above. In 1930, when owner-operators accounted for only 21 percent of Black farmers in the South, about 59 percent of farms in southern Appalachia were owner-operated. See Arthur M. Ford, *Political Economics of Rural Poverty in the South* (Cambridge, MA: Ballinger Publishing Company, 1973), 20–21.

46. Compared to the 35 percent decline in the southern white population, Flint's population of southern-born African Americans dropped by 19 percent between 1930 and 1934. Turnover—the total rate of migration into and out of Flint, as a proportion of the overall population—was also considerably higher among white southerners (70 percent) than among Black southerners (41 percent) in Flint during these years. Beynon, "The Southern White Laborer Migrates to Michigan," 337.

47. According to one suggestive study, white southerners accounted for as much as 85 or 90 percent of migrants who left and returned to the southeast in an eight-year time window in the 1960s. For a sense of scale, whites composed somewhat less than 70 percent of all migrants who left the South over the course of the same decade. See B. F. Kiker and Earle C. Traynham Jr., *Return Migration and Nonreturn Migration for the Southeast: 1960–1970* (Columbia: University of South Carolina, 1974), 42; Gregory, *The Southern Diaspora*, 15.

48. Stewart E. Tolnay, "Migration Experience and Family Patterns in the 'Promised Land,'" *Journal of Family History* 23, no. 1 (1998): 85, 88n3. The best estimates arrived at by Alexander and Gregory put the overall rate of return migration for Black southerners somewhere between one-third and one-fourth of the rate for

white southerners in the decades between 1910 and 1970. But since these estimates rely on datasets that most commonly underreport the types of short-term and cyclical migrations that were far more frequently made by southern Appalachian migrants, it seems quite likely that the actual gap in return rates was significantly higher. Alexander, "'They're Never Here More Than a Year,'" 656; Gregory, *The Southern Diaspora*, 16–17. On the "Great Return Migration," see, among others, Carol Stack, *Call to Home: African Americans Reclaim the Rural South* (New York: Basic Books, 1996).

49. President's National Advisory Commission on Rural Poverty, *Rural Poverty in the United States* (Washington, DC, 1968), 289–90. See also Neil Fligstein, *Going North: Migration of Blacks and Whites from the South, 1900–1950* (New York: Academic Press, 1981); Wright, *Old South, New South*, quoted on 197.

50. There is limited but compelling statistical evidence that the spatial distribution of white mob violence in the South correlated directly with increased rates of Black migration, at least during the period of the "first" Great Migration during and after World War I. See Stewart E. Tolnay and E. M. Beck, "Racial Violence and Black Migration in the American South, 1910 to 1930," *American Sociological Review* 57, no. 1 (February 1992): 113. Hill is quoted in William M. Tuttle Jr., *Race Riot: Chicago in the Red Summer of 1919* (Urbana: University of Illinois Press, 1996 [1970]), 86. Stokes quoted in Phillips, *AlabamaNorth*, 255.

51. Arna Bontemps and Jack Conroy, *Anyplace But Here* (New York: Hill and Wang, 1966 [1945]), 171. The description of Till is Wilkerson's. See *The Warmth of Other Suns*, 369.

52. Berry, *Southern Migrants, Northern Exiles*, 7 and passim. Brown quoted in James S. Brown, "The Appalachian Family: A Somewhat Detailed Description of a Nonexistent Phenomenon," talk delivered at the Annual Meeting of the Commission on Religion in Appalachia, Charleston, West Virginia, October 3, 1967 [final corrected manuscript, reprinted by the Kentucky Agricultural Experiment Station]. Brown Collection, Box 44, Folder 15, King Library.

## 3. Green Peas and Hotheads: The Paradox of the Hillbilly Highway

1. Quoted in Lynd and Lynd, *Middletown*, 58n13.

2. *Akron Beacon Journal*, June 1, 1938.

3. Deac Martin, "The Paradox of Akron," *Nation's Business* (June 1937): 27–29, 148–50. On Martin's other occupation, as an "amateur singer" and court-historian of the SPEBSQSA, see Lynn Abbott, "'Play That Barber Shop Chord': A Case for the African-American Origin of Barbershop Harmony," *American Music* 10, no. 3 (Autumn 1992): 289–325.

4. Of course, saying so is not to suggest that northern employers did not also develop strategies to recruit rural Black southerners during these years—as they most certainly did. See, among others, Grossman, *Land of Hope*; and Phillips, *AlabamaNorth*.

5. Louis Adamic, "The Hill-Billies Come to Detroit," *The Nation*, February 13, 1935. The employers from Muncie and Flint are quoted in Lynd and Lynd, *Middletown in Transition*, 450; and Beynon, "The Southern White Laborer Migrates to Michigan," 339.

6. "Destroy the Black Legion," *Class Struggle* 6, nos. 3/4 (August 1936). *Class Struggle* was the semi-regular newsletter of the Communist League of Struggle, the Trotskyist sect led by veteran textile industry organizers Albert Weisbord and Vera Buch during the 1930s. On the meaning of the term *lumpenproletariat*, see Marx and Engels: "The lumpenproletariat, that passively rotting mass thrown off by the lowest layers of old society, may, here and there, be swept into the movement by a proletarian revolution; its conditions of life, however, prepare it far more for the part of a bribed tool of reactionary intrigue." Marx and Engels, *The Communist Manifesto*, 14.

7. *Akron Beacon Journal*, May 23, 1936.

8. On the 1919 strike wave, see, among many others, Jeremy Brecher, *Strike! Revised and Updated Edition* (Cambridge, MA: South End Press, 1997), 115–59. For wartime wage, hour, and price data, see Bureau of Labor Statistics, Bulletin No. 852, "War and Postwar Wages, Prices, and Hours, 1914–23 and 1939–44" (Washington, DC, 1945), esp. tables 1, 4, 6; on wartime labor policy, see Joseph A. McCartin, *Labor's Great War: The Struggle for Industrial Democracy and the Origins of Modern American Labor Relations, 1912–1921* (Chapel Hill: University of North Carolina Press, 1997).

9. The 1924 law also established an outright ban on immigration from all Asian countries—extending the ban that had already been in place on Chinese nationals since the enactment of the Chinese Exclusion Act in 1882—but given the relative lack of Asian immigrants across the landscape of Transappalachia, it seems fair to say that the national quotas imposed on European immigrants were "most significant" for midwestern employers. On the political context that produced the Johnson-Reed Act, see especially Mae Ngai, *Impossible Subjects: Illegal Aliens and the Making of Modern America* (Princeton, NJ: Princeton University Press, 2004). The immigration numbers quoted here are from Bureau of the Census, *Historical Statistics of the United States, 1789–1945* (Washington, DC, 1949), 99.

10. Kenneth C. Beede, "Housing Market Analysis for Akron, Ohio," prepared for the Federal Housing Administration (Washington, DC: Federal Housing Administration, 1938), 218–25 (table no. 21); Ruth McKenney, *Industrial Valley* (New York: Harcourt, Brace and Company, 1939), xiii; Alfred Winslow Jones, *Life, Liberty, and Property: A Story of Conflict and a Measurement of Conflicting Rights* (Philadelphia: J.P. Lippincott, 1941), 35–42, 56–57, 60–61.

11. John House, "Birth of a Union" (n.d.) [unpublished memoir], 10–11. Manuscript copy, Daniel Nelson Collection, Box 4, Special Collections, University Libraries, University of Akron, Akron, OH. For a firsthand report on the rapid and unregulated growth that accompanied Akron's reputation as a city of opportunity during these years, see Edward Mott Wooley, "Akron: Standing Room Only!" *McClure's Magazine* 49 (July 1917): 13–15.

12. Charles E. Gibbons, "The Onion Workers," *The American Child* 1, no. 4 (February 1920): 414; Paul S. Taylor, "Migratory Farm Labor in the United States," *Monthly Labor Review* 44, no. 3 (March 1937): 541–44; Carey McWilliams, *Ill Fares the Land: Migrants and Migratory Labor in the United States* (Boston: Little, Brown, 1942), 130–67.

13. The story about the sign in the Armco plant in Middletown is recounted in John Leslie Thompson, "Industrialization in the Miami Valley: A Case Study of

Interregional Migration" (PhD diss., University of Wisconsin–Madison, 1955), 134–
37. The Muncie executive is quoted in Lynd and Lynd, *Middletown*, 58n13. See also
Adamic, "The Hill-Billies Come to Detroit"; Kirby, *Rural Worlds Lost*, 327–28; Wolfe,
"Appalachians in Muncie," 185; Berry, *Southern Migrants, Northern Exiles*, 18–23.

14. See Merrill Cregar, oral history interview with Kenneth B. West, February 27,
1980; Cloyse Crane, oral history interview with Neil Leighton, February 27, 1980;
Orvell Simmons, oral history interview with Kenneth B. West, February 28, 1980;
Andrew Havrilla, oral history interview with Kenneth B. West, April 4, 1980; Norman
Bully, oral history interview with Kenneth B. West, June 26, 1980; Peggy and Melvin
Echard, oral history with Kenneth West, June 27, 1980. Labor History Project Collection, Genesee Historical Collections Center, Frances Willson Thompson Library, University of Michigan-Flint, Flint, Michigan. The anecdote about company-chartered
buses is related in Adamic, "The Hill-Billies Come to Detroit."

15. Yoak is quoted in Roberta Lieberman, "Appalachian Migrants to Akron, Ohio,
1920–1950" (April 1973) [unpublished paper], 27. Nelson Collection, Box 6, University
Libraries; details about Yoak's career are recounted in the January 5, 1944, issue of the
*Wingfoot Clan*, the Goodyear company newspaper. The quoted advertisement ran in
*Wheeling Register* editions between March 17 and 30, and April 12 and 23, 1918. See also
"Sales since 1907," (n.d.). Goodyear Tire & Rubber Company Records, Series I: Admin-
istration, Box 2, Folder: Business Rubber Charts, Financial Figures, Special Collections,
University Libraries; Harold S. Roberts, *The Rubber Workers: Labor Organization and
Collective Bargaining in the Rubber Industry* (New York: Harper & Brothers, 1944), 19.

16. "Goodyear—Average Yearly Wage Hourly Employees," and "Av. Hourly Earnings
Comparison," statistics compiled by Commercial Research Dept. (September 14, 1936).
Goodyear Records, Series VIII: Labor, Subseries: Labor Relations, Box 1, University
Libraries; Daniel Nelson, *American Rubber Workers and Organized Labor, 1900–1941*
(Princeton, NJ: Princeton University Press, 1988), 11, 90–91. The best accounts of the
1913 strike and the early organizing efforts in Akron's rubber plants are Roberts, *The
Rubber Workers*, chs. 2 and 3; and Nelson, *American Rubber Workers*, chs. 1 and 2.

17. *Akron Beacon Journal*, May 1, 1922, and November 24, 1927. House, "Birth of
a Union," 10. Nelson Collection, Box 4, University Libraries; Nelson, *American Rubber Workers*, 91.

18. Weak unions, the intensive mechanization of production, and a viciously
anti-labor judiciary all contributed to the creation of what Bernstein aptly
described as an "unbalanced society" for American workers during the 1920s. See
Irving Bernstein, *The Lean Years: A History of the American Worker, 1920–1933*
(Boston: Houghton Mifflin, 1960), esp. 47ff.; David Montgomery, *The Fall of the
House of Labor: The Workplace, the State, and American Labor Activism, 1865–1925*
(New York: Cambridge University Press, 1989); William Forbath, *Law and the
Shaping of the American Labor Movement* (Cambridge, MA: Harvard University
Press, 1991).

19. "Goodyear—Average Yearly Wage Hourly Employees," September 14, 1936.
Goodyear Records, Series VIII: Labor, Subseries: Labor Relations, Box 1, University
Libraries. See also Adamic, "The Hill-Billies Come to Detroit"; Daniel Boyd Crowder,
"Profile in Progress: A History of Local 287, UAW-CIO" (PhD diss., Ball State Uni-
versity, 1969).

20. Lynd and Lynd, *Middletown in Transition*, 25–26, 453.

21. Layoffs were a perennial frustration for Akron rubber workers during these years, as the tiremakers constantly expanded and contracted their workforces to keep up with fluctuations in orders coming in from Detroit. In one rather extreme example from 1923, the year after House got to Akron, local rubber employment peaked at 45,084 in April, fell to 27,442 in July, and rebounded to 35,831 by December. Beede, "Housing Market Analysis for Akron, Ohio."

22. House, "Birth of a Union," 10–16; See also "Floaters," *Wingfoot Clan*, October 1, 1912; Boris Stern, "Labor Productivity in the Automobile Tire Industry," *Bulletin of the United States Bureau of Labor Statistics*, No. 585 (July 1933), esp. 31–37; Nelson, *American Rubber Workers*, 90–93, 114–15.

23. Lucian and Jane Gupton, oral history interview with Timothy Borden and Jane Armstrong, Kokomo, Indiana, June 27, 1996. Indiana University Center for the Study of History and Memory, Indiana University, Bloomington, Indiana, #96-67-1. Lloyd Jones, oral history interview with Jack W. Skeels, March 10, 1960. UAW Oral Histories, #WPR 0479. Walter P. Reuther Library of Labor and Urban Affairs, Wayne State University, Detroit, MI. The best account of working conditions at Ford during these pre-UAW years is Stephen Meyer III, *The Five Dollar Day: Labor Management and Social Conflict in the Ford Motor Company, 1908–1921* (Albany, NY: SUNY Press, 1981).

24. The Goodyear ad from 1920 is quoted in Jones, *Life, Liberty, and Property*, 62. See also Lynd and Lynd, *Middletown*, 58n13; Lieberman, "Appalachian Migrants to Akron," Nelson Collection, Box 6, University Libraries.

25. House, "Birth of a Union," 14, Nelson Collection, Box 4, University Libraries. On Hannah's interview style, see Nelson, *American Rubber Workers*, 90–91.

26. Merrill Cregar, oral history interview, February 27, 1980. Labor History Project Collection, Thompson Library; Adamic, "The Hill-Billies Come to Detroit"; Lynd and Lynd, *Middletown in Transition*, 36, 450; Jones, *Life, Liberty, and Property*, 64. On the longer history of the cultural discourse surrounding the biological deficiencies of the rural poor, see especially Isenberg, *White Trash*.

27. Shannon Johnson, Phyllis Johnson, and Dawn Peters, oral history interview with author, Cowan, Indiana, March 17, 2016; audio recording and transcript in author's possession. The Akronites are quoted in *Akron Beacon Journal*, May 3, 1922; and Gerald Udell, "The Speech of Akron, Ohio: The Segmental Phonology—A Study of the Effects of Rapid Industrialization on the Speech of a Community" (PhD diss., University of Chicago, 1966), 78. See also Adamic, "The Hill-Billies Come to Detroit"; Beynon, "The Southern White Laborer Migrates to Michigan," 334; Johnson, "Industrial Voyagers," esp. 115–39.

28. James Cannon, "The Coming American Revolution" (1946), reprinted in James P. Cannon, *Speeches for Socialism* (New York: Pathfinder Press, 2008 [1969], 413; "The Struggle of the Unemployed" [unsigned pamphlet], Communist League of Struggle (May 1935). The Albert & Vera Weisbord Foundation, Chicago; http://www.weisbord.org/Unemployed.htm, accessed January 27, 2020.

29. Widick reflects on his earlier uncertainties about Akron's southern rubber workers in B. J. Widick, *Detroit: City of Race and Class Violence* (Chicago: Quadrangle Books, 1972), 66–67. For a broader framing of Widick's career, see his profile

in Nelson Lichtenstein, *A Contest of Ideas: Capital, Politics, and Labor* (Urbana: University of Illinois Press, 2013).

30. Walter White, Thurgood Marshall, and the National Association for the Advancement of Colored People, "What Caused the Detroit Riot?: An Analysis" (New York: National Association for the Advancement of Colored People, 1943), 9. Macdonald is quoted in "Fascism and the American Scene"; see his introduction to the American edition of Daniel Guerin, *Fascism and Big Business* (New York: Pioneer Publishers, 1939), 26–27. For more contemporary examples of this line of thinking within left-wing and liberal circles, see, for instance, Forrest Davis, "Labor Spies and the Black Legion," *The New Republic*, June 17, 1936; and Bontemps and Conroy, *Anyplace But Here*, 292.

31. For the discussion of rural migrants at the first UAW meeting, see *Official Proceedings, First Session, National Council of the United Automobile Workers Federal Labor Unions* (July 9–14, 1934). UAW President's Office: Homer Martin Records, Box 2, Folder 2, Reuther Library. The Muncie quotes come from Lynd and Lynd, *Middletown in Transition*, 27, 36. See also *Historical Statistics of the United States*, 95.

32. Lloyd Jones, oral history interview. UAW Oral Histories, Reuther Library; House, "Birth of a Union," 19. Nelson Collection, Box 4, University Libraries. See also Widick, *Detroit*, 67.

33. Joseph Wilson, oral history interview with Greer T. Warren, Anderson, Indiana, March 19, 1982. Center for the Study of History and Memory, Indiana University, #82-015. Joseph Arthur Pound, *The Turning Wheel: The Story of General Motors through Twenty-Five Years, 1909–1933* (New York: Doubleday, Doran, 1934), 466–67; Victor Reuther, *The Brothers Reuther and the Story of the UAW* (Boston: Houghton Mifflin, 1976), 172; Robert H. Zieger, *The CIO: 1935–1955* (Chapel Hill: University of North Carolina Press, 1995), 45; Glass, "The Gas Boom in East Central Indiana," 318–19, 330. The Toledo Auto-Lite Strike was a month-and-half-long battle in the spring of 1934, which involved some ten thousand workers at the Toledo, Ohio–based Electric Auto-Lite sparkplug factory and marked the first major organizing victory in the midwestern automobile industry.

34. Joseph Wilson also spoke to the toughness of the former miners he worked alongside at Guide Lamp: "They'd kill you! Harlan, Kentucky, hey—I wouldn't walk in that place without . . . I had a sign that said, 'I'm a union man.' Tennessee, a lot of that down there . . ." Joseph Wilson, oral history interview, Center for the Study of History and Memory. See also Ted Davis, oral history interview with Greer Warren, Anderson, Indiana, March 5, 1982. Indiana University Center for the Study of History and Memory, #82-12-1. Reuther quoted in Reuther, *The Brothers Reuther*, 179, 182. Other details about the Guide Lamp strike are drawn from "Pickets Hurt in Clash with Police," *Associated Press*, January 26, 1937; and Claude E. Hoffman, *Sit-Down in Anderson: UAW Local 663, Anderson, Indiana* (Detroit: Wayne State University Press, 1968).

35. "The History of UAW-Local 287, 1937–1981" (unsigned, n.d.). UAW-CIO, Local 287 Records and Photographs, Box 1, Folder: History, Archives and Special Collections, Alexander M. Bracken Library, Ball State University, Muncie, IN. "Borg Warner Historical Review" (c. 1978) [company-produced pamphlet]. Warner Gear Division Collection, Box 3, Folder 4, Bracken Library. *The Labor Beacon* (Local 287), May 1956; Crowder, "Profile in Progress," esp. 62–92.

36. In the original worksheets of the 1940 census, three hundred five Muncie residents are identifiable as current employees of Warner Gear. Of them, fifty-nine were born in southern states—and more than half of them (thirty-two) in Tennessee. It is worth noting that the representation of southern-born workers would likely have been higher around this time at other Muncie manufacturers, since Warner Gear, even before it was unionized, was among the very best-paid and most desirable local places of employment. The newest arrivals to the city's industrial workforce were more commonly concentrated in less well-paying jobs, at the likes of Ball Brothers, Frank Foundry, Maerhofer's (a local meat-packer), or Durham Manufacturing, which made furniture. Digitized reproductions of the worksheets are available at https://1940census.archives.gov.

37. In 1953, more than three decades after he began his career at Warner Gear and just seven years before his death, Babbitt was serving as a delegate to the Delaware County CIO, as well as the District Auto Council for UAW locals in the region. See "Special Meeting for the Nomination of Officers and Delegates" (May 23, 1953). Local 287 Records, Box 2, Folder: UAW-CIO Local 287 Minutes, 1953/4/3—1953/10/12. Bracken Library; *Muncie Evening Press*, January 26, 1960.

38. See "Copy of the Record of Committee-Men and Stewards of Local 287 U.A.W.A functioning in the Warner Gear & on the first Union Contract, 1937–1938" (n.d.). Local 287 Records, Box 8, Folder: Negotiating Notes 1938, Bracken Library. The names appearing there were cross-referenced against the original worksheets for the 1940 census; since it is not possible to identify state-of-birth information for all ninety-nine individuals, it is possible—even likely—that more than thirteen of them hailed originally from southern states. In 1940, meanwhile, 6 percent of native-born white men in Indiana were born in the South. Bureau of the Census, *Sixteenth Census of the United States: 1940, Population, State of Birth of the Native Population* (Washington, DC, 1944).

39. Of course, this begs the question of whether Norman had perhaps been a "labor spy" all along—although no positive indication that he played such a role has been identified. On labor spying and other forms of anti-union sabotage, see, for instance, Robert Michael Smith, *From Blackjacks to Briefcases: A History of Commercialized Strikebreaking and Unionbusting in the United States* (Athens: The Ohio University Press, 2003).

40. *Muncie Star Press*, June 9, 1941; *Labor Beacon*, May 1956; "The History of UAW-Local 287," Local 287 Records, Box 1, Folder: History, Bracken Library; Crowder, "Profile in Progress," 78–80.

41. For an overview of how the wave of sit-down strikes between 1936 and 1939 shaped twentieth-century industrial relations, see Jim Pope, "Worker Lawmaking, Sit-Down Strikes, and the Shaping of American Industrial Relations, 1935–1958," *Law and History Review* 24, no. 1 (Spring 2006): 45–113.

42. For accounts of the 1936 Goodyear strike and its aftermath that highlight the important role played by southern migrants, see McKenney, *Industrial Valley*; Rose Pesotta, *Bread upon the Waters* (New York: Dodd, Mead, 1944), esp. chs. 19–21; and Nelson, *American Rubber Workers*. The quoted "observer" is Edward Levinson, then the labor editor at the *New York Post*, in *Labor on the March* (New York: Harper and Brothers, 1938), 185.

43. "For Information: Resume of sitdowns, intimidations, and violence at the Akron plant of The Goodyear Tire & Rubber Company from the date of strike settlement, March 21, 1936, through December 31, 1936" (January 4, 1937); and *In the Matter of The Goodyear Tire & Rubber Company and United Rubber Workers of America*, "Respondent's Offer of Proof Under Section 25 of its Answer, Before the National Labor Relations Board," Case No. VII-2378 (June 5, 1939). Goodyear Collection, Series VIII: Labor, Subseries: Labor Relations, Box 1, University Libraries. The specifics of the Goodyear strike settlement are reprinted in "Terms of Settlement," *Wingfoot Clan*, March 26, 1936. See also *Akron Beacon Journal*, May 21, 1936, and June 1, 1938.

44. Jones, *Life, Liberty, and Property*, 67.

45. Descriptions of the sit-downs in Department 251, as well as the "molasses" comment, appear in *In the Matter*, "Respondent's Offer of Proof"; details about the fourth-shift's greater rate of strike participation appear there, as well as in J. V. DuRoss, written affidavit, re: "May 6, 1936" (April 17, 1939); and C. H. Nichols, written affidavit, re: "Goodyear Assembly" (May 2, 1939). The line about "fourth-shift radicals" is quoted from Goebel Butler, written affidavit, re: "November 3, 1937" (April 18, 1939). Goodyear Collection, Series VIII: Labor, Subseries: Labor Relations, Box 1, University Libraries. House uses the term "hotheads" in his oral history interview with Daniel Nelson, quoted in Nelson, *American Rubber Workers*; he describes his own efforts to "stop the sit-downs" at length in House, "Birth of a Union," 30ff. Nelson Collection, Box 4, University Libraries.

46. Nelson identifies Jones as a Georgian, drawing on the later recollections of one of his coworkers at Goodyear. However, 1940 census records suggest that Jones was likely born in West Virginia. See Nelson, *American Rubber Workers*, 183–84, n57.

47. Harry Brownfield, written affidavit, re: [no subject] (April 24, 1939); *In the Matter*, "Respondent's Offer of Proof." Goodyear Collection, Series VIII: Labor, Subseries: Labor Relations, Box 1, University Libraries. For more on Jones and Lesley, see also Daniel Nelson, "Origins of the Sit-Down Era: Worker Militancy and Innovation in the Rubber Industry, 1934–1938," *Labor History* 23, no. 2 (1982): 210–16.

48. In the statement he gave the Akron police after being arrested, Jones claimed that the plant supervisors and nonunion workers were held in the bullpen "merely for their own safe keeping," but did not otherwise attempt to disguise what he and the other workers had done: "No, I mean this, that we are in there to get a square deal. . . . If you got to step out of line a little bit to get that square deal, you get it." "Statement of James Jones" (May 24, 1936). Goodyear Collection, Series VIII: Labor, Subseries: Labor Relations, Box 1, University Libraries.

49. A. F. Bonifay, written affidavit, re: "General Statement" (April 14, 1939); Joe McGrath, written affidavit, re: [no subject], (April 10, 1939); R. E. Cook, written affidavit, re: "July 29, 1936" (April 18, 1939); *In the Matter*, "Respondent's Offer of Proof." Goodyear Collection, Series VIII: Labor, Subseries: Labor Relations, Box 1. For a transcript of the labor-management committee meeting in which Giles and Twyman were disciplined, and Twyman offered his halfhearted apology, see "Meeting between

Goodyear Committee and Local #2 Committee" (March 11, 1937). Nelson Collection, Box 6, University Libraries.

50. The equivalent organization at Goodrich during these years was called the 10 Year Club, which rather succinctly conveys the correlation between long service and anti-URW attitudes among the Akron rubber industry workforce. See "Minutes of 141st Meeting of Local #5" (June 4, 1939). United Rubber Workers BF Goodrich Local 5 Collection, Box F-1 [bound ledger], University Libraries.

51. The latter is the conclusion drawn in the most detailed study of the Akron Klan, John Lee Maples, "The Akron, Ohio Ku Klux Klan, 1921–1928" (MA thesis, University of Akron, 1974), 111. Nelson and Susan Allyn Johnson come to similar conclusions in their respective studies of Akron's rubber workers and its southern Appalachian migrant population. See Nelson, *American Rubber Workers*, 99–101; Johnson, "Industrial Voyagers," 191–93. For more on the Stahl-Mate Club and groups like it, see Benjamin Stolberg, "Vigilantism, 1937," *The Nation*, August 14, 1937.

52. *In the Matter*, "Official Report of the Proceedings Before the National Labor Relations Board," 6231–6820. Goodyear Collection, Series VIII: Labor, Subseries: Labor Relations, Box 3, University Libraries.

53. This period was also marked by persistent unrest at the two other Akron tire-makers, as well as at a number of the smaller rubber producers in the city; for the best accounts of the wider scope of the conflict, see Roberts, *The Rubber Workers*, esp. chs. 6 and 7; and Nelson, *American Rubber Workers*, esp. chs. 8–10.

54. House, "Birth of a Union," 40. Nelson Collection, Box 4, University Libraries. See also Martin, "The Paradox of Akron"; Roberts, *The Rubber Workers*, 251.

55. Wm. E. Denny, written affidavit "Limitation of Production" (April 12, 1939); Goodyear Collection, Series VIII: Labor, Subseries: Labor Relations, Box 1. Slusser's remarks are quoted from "Talk by C.C. Slusser—October 11 to Supervision" (October 11, 1937) [typewritten speech]. Goodyear Collection, Series: VIII: Labor, Subseries: Personnel, Box 3, Folder 18—Personnel 'S', University Libraries. For the company's estimates of production losses during the sit-downs, see *In the Matter*, "Official Report of the Proceedings," Case Nos. VIII-R-184 and VIII-C-378, 3280ff. Goodyear Collection, Series VIII: Labor, Subseries: Labor Relations, Box 3, University Libraries.

56. House, "Birth of a Union," 42. Nelson Collection, Box 4, University Libraries.

57. The early warning from Local 2 leaders is quoted in George Roberts to William Green, July 1936 [letter]. George B. Roberts Collection, Series I: Miscellaneous, Box 1, Folder 9, Reuther Library. For the account of the labor-management committee's intervention, see "Meeting Between Goodyear and Local #2" (March 3, 1937) [meeting minutes]. Nelson Collection, Box 6. See also House, "Birth of a Union," 30–40. Nelson Collection, Box 4, University Libraries.

58. On the final, successful push to win a contract at Goodyear—which was not ratified until October 28, 1941—see Nelson, *American Rubber Workers*, 314–20.

59. For a representative sample of what is a very long list, see Friedlander, *The Emergence of a UAW Local*; Cohen, *Making a New Deal*; Fraser, *Labor Will Rule*; Lichtenstein, *The Most Dangerous Man in Detroit*; Zieger, *The CIO*; Michael Denning, *The Cultural Front: The Laboring of American Culture in the Twentieth Century* (New York: Verso, 1998).

60. This was true not only of John House but also men like Sherman Dalrymple, a West Virginia farmer-turned-tire builder who rose from the presidency of Goodrich Local 5 to become the URW's first international president. See Daniel Nelson, "The Leadership of the United Rubber Workers, 1933–42," *Detroit in Perspective* 5, no. 3 (Spring 1981): esp. 23–24.

61. House, "Birth of a Union," 23. Nelson Collection, Box 4, University Libraries; Nelson, *American Rubber Workers*, 7. In *Industrial Valley*, her book about the rubber workers' struggle, Ruth McKenney gives a larger role to the Communists and especially local party secretary James Keller. But McKenney was a member of the Communist Party herself, and so her account should be taken with a grain of salt.

62. See, for instance, Irving Howe and B. J. Widick, *The UAW and Walter Reuther* (New York: Random House, 1973 [1949]), 51; Friedlander, *The Emergence of a UAW Local*, 127–31. Despite being one of the most sensitive studies of ethnicity in the workplace during the early years of auto unionism, Friedlander relies almost entirely on limited anecdotal accounts to draw a uniquely reductive portrait of the "conservative tendencies" of southern white autoworkers; see 146n66. Matthew Pehl offers a much more nuanced account of southern white conservativism during this period—but still one that tends to overdetermine the allegiance that Detroit's southern-born white working class showed to "reactionary and antimodernist" figures like Norris. Matthew Pehl, "'Apostles of Fascism,' 'Communist Clergy,' and the UAW: Political Ideology and Working-Class Religion in Detroit, 1919–1945," *Journal of American History* 99, no. 2 (September 2012): 440–65.

63. Lichtenstein has argued that the "recrudescence of right-wing agitation and red-baiting," which took the form of Black Legion activity in midwestern cities where the CIO was on the rise, was more a rearguard attempt by an established "plebian elite"—"the Protestant lower middle class and the old labor aristocracy of northern European descent"—to hold onto its place in the disintegrating social hierarchy, rather than an expression of vitriolic nativism or anti-Black racism on the part of southern white newcomers. Lichtenstein, *The Most Dangerous Man in Detroit*, 113. This echoes firsthand anecdotal accounts from the period, such as Henry Kraus, *The Many and the Few: A Chronicle of the Dynamic Auto Workers* (Urbana: University of Illinois Press, 1984 [1947]; as well as later assessments of the right-wing popular movements of the 1930s, such as Alan Brinkley, *Voices of Protest: Huey Long, Father Coughlin and the Great Depression* (New York: Vintage Books, 1983).

64. On the quick rise and fall in Martin's support in the eastern Indiana cities, see "Labor Developments of Interest" [typewritten memo] (August 24, 1938), Michael Manning Collection, Box 1, Folder 9, Reuther Library. See also Friedlander, *The Emergence of a UAW Local*, 128–29; and Lichtenstein, *The Most Dangerous Man in Detroit*, 112, 138.

65. Lloyd Jones, oral history, March 10, 1960. UAW Oral Histories, #WPR 0479, Reuther Library.

66. Such is the charge leveled against southern white workers in the Midwest in Jones, *The Dispossessed*, 260–61. Notably, among the scholarly sources that Jones relies on most extensively in this part of her discussion is Friedlander, *The Emergence of a UAW Local*; see 357n42, and 359n50.

67. *In the Matter*, "Official Report of the Proceedings Before the National Labor Relations Board." Goodyear Collection, Series VIII: Labor, Subseries: Labor Relations, Box 3, University Libraries.

68. By the middle of the 1930s, Kelsey-Hayes, along with the other major automotive plants concentrated on Detroit's west side, had been folded into a single amalgamated UAW local—Local 174, or the West Side Local—a massive, hundred-thousand-worker-strong body that would become the springboard to national power for Local 174 president Walter Reuther. In early December 1936 Kelsey-Hayes was the site of an extended sit-down strike that helped solidify Local 174's place in the Detroit auto industry; Mullin was one of the key rank-and-file leaders during the strike. On Kelsey-Hayes and the West Side Local more generally, see Frank Boles, "Walter Reuther and the Kelsey-Hayes Strike of 1936," *Detroit in Perspective* 4 (Winter 1980): 74–90; and Lichtenstein, *The Most Dangerous Man in Detroit*, esp. ch. 5.

69. After 1936, when Kelsey-Hayes recognized Local 174 as the nonexclusive bargaining agent for the company's employees, the company and the union began "operating under a contract in which only the grievance procedure is in writing." Regular meetings between the union committee and plant management used an "unsigned, proposed draft of contract" as the basis for implementing additional provisions that were put in effect verbally. See *In the Matter of: Kelsey-Hayes Wheel Company, Detroit, Michigan, and Local 174, UAW-CIO*, "Memorandum for the Company," Before the National War Labor Board, Region XI, Detroit, Michigan, Case no. 111-15152-3. Local 174 Collection, Series III, Box 6, Folder: Kelsey-Hayes, Reuther Library.

70. For the "scorekeeper" episode, see "Arbitration Proceedings," Kelsey-Hayes Wheel Co. and Local Union No. 174 UAW-CIO (May 13, 1944). UAW Local 78 Collection, Series II, Box 1, Folder 2, Reuther Library. For the "undisciplined mob" episode, see *In the Matter*, "Memorandum of the Company." Local 174 Collection, Series III, Box 6, Folder: Kelsey-Hayes, Reuther Library.

71. "Hillbilly anarchist" is Reuther's retrospective description of Mullin from an interview with Nelson Lichtenstein, quoted in Lichtenstein, *The Most Dangerous Man in Detroit*, 71 and 458n74. But Reuther had far more damning things to say at the time, as found in the reports of a labor spy within Local 174 that capture Reuther calling Mullin a "playboy" and an "opportunist" using "underhanded tactics" against those "who do not agree with him or see eye-to-eye with him on union tactics," and threatening Mullin that he "had better watch how he conducts himself, as already the Kelsey-Hayes Division of the local is on the verge of being suspended." See "Labor Developments of Interest" [typewritten memo] (April 1940). Manning Collection, Box 1, Folder 9, Reuther Library.

72. Chester Mullin to The Executive Board and the Members of the Joint Council, July 23, 1941 [letter]. UAW Local 78 Collection, Series II, Box 1, Folder 14, Reuther Library. Lloyd T. Jones, "To Kelsey-Hayes Workers" [letter to the editor] *Kelsey-Hayes Picket*, October 1941. UAW President's Office: Walter P. Reuther Collection, Box 9, Folder 23, Reuther Library.

73. Gilbert Gilbert to Walter P. Reuther, December 24, 1946 [letter]. The George F. Addes—UAW Secretary-Treasurer Collection, Series V: Appeal Cases, Box 76, Folder 12, Reuther Library. On the 1945 wildcat strike and the administratorship of the Kelsey-Hayes unit, see "Kelsey Hayes Strike" (September 10–18, 1945) [typed

executive board meeting minutes], and "Kelsey Hayes Administratorship Re: Exten-
sion of Time" (November 7-12, 1945) [typed minutes of executive board meeting].
Addes—UAW Secretary-Treasurer Collection, Series V: Appeal Cases, Box 76, Folder 12,
Reuther Library; and Lichtenstein, *The Most Dangerous Man in Detroit*, 217-19.

74. "Way Down Yonder in the Paw Paw Patch" is a traditional folk song with roots
in southern Appalachia. It refers to the pawpaw, an indigenous fruit tree that grows
in the eastern United States and Canada, especially in hardwood forests and in hilly
habitats. Wild harvesting of pawpaws, eaten raw or baked, was common throughout
the region—but it would have been the popular song, rather than the local foodways
it stemmed from, that Mullin's antagonists had in mind when they used it to tarnish
his reputation during Local 174's internal battles. See "Where Oh Where Is the West
Side Local??" (n.d.), [typewritten flier]. Walter P. Reuther Collection, Box 1, Folder 2,
Reuther Library.

75. Pope, "Worker Lawmaking," 46-47.

76. Lest the brief portrait of Chester Mullin presented here come off as too one-
dimensional, it is worth noting the role he played in a wartime walkout by white
Kelsey-Hayes workers who opposed the integration of Black workers into factory
positions outside of the lowest-paid and most menial jobs in the McGraw Avenue
foundry room. "Our committee men Mullin, Hindle, and John Hodge, took the position that they were representing their departments," a group of rightfully aggrieved
Black foundry workers wrote to the UAW executive board, "and their position was
against these workers being absorbed into other departments, contrary to CIO princi-
ples." Such racist, anti-integrationist positions were not unusual among white workers of all backgrounds, of course, and especially so during World War II, when federal
support for nondiscriminatory hiring prompted violent hate strikes by white workers
in cities across the country. In fact, according to the same Black foundry workers,
the very "Jim Crow seniority" provisions that Mullin and the other white committee men were accused of defending had first been "permitted" in 1937 by the entire
Local 174 executive leadership—including "Walter Reuther, Chairman of the West
Side Local." See Kelsey Hayes Foundry Workers Division #174 to General Executive
Board and George F. Addes (February 5, 1941) [letter]. Walter P. Reuther Collection,
Box 9, Folder 23, Reuther Library.

77. The "ate at the vitals" line is quoted from the discussion of the emergence of
the midcentury "workplace rule of law" in David Brody, *Workers in Industrial America* (New York: Oxford University Press, 1980), esp. 199-207.

78. Chester Mullin to Emil Mazey, October 26, 1948 [letter]. Addes—UAW
Secretary-Treasurer Collection, Series V: Appeals, Box 76, Folder 12, Reuther Library.

## 4. An Other America: Hillbilly Ghettos after World War II

1. Devereux quoted in Norma Lee Browning, "Girl Reporter Visits Jungles of Hillbillies," *Chicago Tribune*, March 3, 1957.

2. Michael Harrington, *The Other America: Poverty in the United States* (New
York: Penguin, 1966 [1962]), 100.

3. Oral History Interview with Harriette Arnow, April 1976. Interview G-0006.
Southern Oral History Program Collection (#4007), Southern Historical Collection,

The Wilson Library, University of North Carolina at Chapel Hill. Harriette Arnow, *The Dollmaker* (New York: Avon, 1972 [1954]), 169.

4. "Population of the City of Detroit By Census Tracts, 1950 Compared with 1940," compiled by Research Department, *Detroit Free Press*, Detroit Commission on Community Relations Records/Human Rights Department (DCCR) Records, Part 3, Box 12, Folder 54. Walter P. Reuther Library, Archives of Labor and Urban Affairs, Wayne State University, Detroit, MI. Gregory, *The Southern Diaspora*, 15. See also Johnson, *The Second Gold Rush*, for an exemplary account of the wartime migration's effect on housing and neighborhoods.

5. No less significant than the number of casualties was the way Detroit city government responded to the Sojourner Truth riot. Buckling to white resistance, the Detroit Housing Commission adopted a resolution after the riot that committed the city to maintaining residential segregation in all wartime housing projects, along with a policy that public housing construction would "not change the racial pattern of a neighborhood," which remained in effect throughout the remainder of the war and afterward. See Joe T. Darden et al., *Detroit: Race and Uneven Development* (Philadelphia: Temple University Press, 1987), esp. ch. 4; and Thomas Sugrue, *The Origins of the Urban Crisis*, 41–43 and ch. 3.

6. Arnow, *The Dollmaker*, 313. See also Oral History Interview with Harriette Arnow, April 1976; John Hartigan Jr., *Racial Situations: Class Predicaments of Whiteness in Detroit* (Princeton, NJ: Princeton University Press, 1999), 299n14.

7. The migration ban was first proposed by United States attorney general Francis Biddle, and then picked up by local officials like Detroit's police commissioner, John Witherspoon. Other local officials opposed the idea from the outset, however, and it was soon dropped. "Biddle Plan Unworkable, Says Leaders," *Detroit News*, August 13, 1943. Jefferies is quoted in Dominic J. Capeci Jr. and Martha Wilkerson, *Layered Violence: The Detroit Rioters of 1943* (Jackson: University Press of Mississippi, 2009), 31; see, as well, the discussion of the riot and the misrepresentations of southern white responsibility, in Hartigan Jr., *Racial Situations*, esp. ch. 1. Other quoted remarks above appear in Walter White, Thurgood Marshall, and the National Association for the Advancement of Colored People, "What Caused the Detroit Riot?: An Analysis" (New York: National Association for the Advancement of Colored People, 1943), 5; and Alfred McClung Lee and Norman Daymond Humphrey, *Race Riot* (New York: Dryden Press, 1943), 91.

8. Kornhauser, *Attitudes of Detroit People Toward Detroit*, 13. Browning, "Girl Reporter Visits Jungles of Hillbillies."

9. On the residential patterning of southern Appalachian migrants over the medium and long term, see most notably Gregory, "The Southern Diaspora and the Urban Dispossessed," 111–34; Berry, *Southern Migrants, Northern Exiles*.

10. James A. Maxwell, "Down from the Hills and into the Slums," *The Reporter*, December 13, 1956.

11. Gene Myers, oral history interview with author, Hillsboro, Tennessee, March 23, 2015; audio recording and transcript in author's possession; James L. Nicholson and Robert Ewing Corlew, *Grundy County* (Memphis: Memphis State University Press, 1982), 97–98, 114–17.

12. "Percentage of Total Southern Appalachian Migrants to Specific Metropolitan Areas from Specified Southern Appalachian State Economic and Metropolitan Areas,

1955 to 1960," special tabulations from the U.S. Bureau of the Census, Brown Collection, Box 137, Folder 4, University of Kentucky Special Collections. See also, Janelle Taylor, oral history interview with author, Pelham, Tennessee, March 26, 2015, audio recording and transcript in author's possession; Gene Myers, oral history interview. The most extended studies of southern whites in Cleveland are John D. Photiadis, *Social and Sociopsychological Characteristics of West Virginians in Their Own State and in Cleveland, Ohio* (Morgantown: West Virginia University Press, 1975); and Gene B. Peterson, Laure M. Sharp, and Thomas F. Drury, *Southern Newcomers to Northern Cities: Work and Social Adjustment in Cleveland* (New York: Praeger, 1977).

13. Forrest David "Hamp" Nunley, oral history interview with author, Pelham, Tennessee, March 26, 2015, audio recording and transcript in author's possession. Julian Krawcheck, "Southerners' Influx Poses Social Problems," *Cleveland Press*, January 29, 1958; Krawcheck, "Southern Pupils Do OK in Schools," *Cleveland Press*, February 3, 1958. As Krawcheck noted at the time, only accounting for the southern-born "does not include hundreds of other pupils [in the Cleveland school system]—perhaps as many as 2000—who were born in Cleveland of southern parents."

14. An unusual exception to the seasonal cycles that characterized this migrant stream came in 1934, when a strike broke out in the Hardin County onion marshes, led largely by "stranded" migrant workers from Kentucky who attempted to organize a union. See McWilliams, *Ill Fares the Land*, 132–36; and Berry, *Southern Migrants, Northern Exiles*, 53–55. On residential patterning in Akron, see Johnson, "Industrial Voyagers," 220 (table 8). On Flint, see Beynon, "The Southern White Laborer Migrates to Michigan," 334–35.

15. Noting the roughly twenty-five million American soldiers and civilians who relocated to a new county or state between 1940 and 1947, the Census Bureau concluded that "probably never before in the history of the United States has there been an internal population movement of such magnitude." Quoted in Johnson, *The Second Gold Rush*, 2.

16. James Stephen Brown, "Current and Anticipated Rural Migration, Humphreys County, Tennessee," prepared for the United States Department of Agriculture (June 1945). James S. Brown Collection, Box 44, Folder 8, Special Collections Research Center, Margaret I. King Library, University of Kentucky, Lexington, KY. U.S. Bureau of the Census, *U.S. Census of the Population: 1960. Subject Reports. State of Birth. State of Residence in 1960 and State of Birth of Native Population by Age, Color, and Sex* (Washington, DC, 1962), 9. Belcher, "Population Growth and Characteristics," 38 (table 4), and Brown and Hillery Jr., "The Great Migration, 1940–1960," 58–59 (tables 8 and 9).

17. By comparison, the rural nonfarm population accounted for just over 40 percent of net migration losses from southern Appalachia during the 1940s. See Brown and Hillery Jr., "The Great Migration," 72 (table 16).

18. "Net Migration, by Decades, S Apps, 1930–1979," [handwritten chart] (n.d.). Brown Collection, Box 228, Folder 9, King Library. See also Belcher, "Population Growth and Characteristics," 39–41; Brown and Hillery Jr., "The Great Migration," 61–76; Gibbard, "Extractive Industries and Foresty," 110 (table 28); Jerome Pickard, "Appalachian Population Growing, Income Catching Up," *Appalachia: Journal of the Appalachian Regional Commission* 12, no. 5: 44 (table 2).

19. Notably, the racial composition of the city's southern-born population became demonstrably whiter over the same period. Black southerners composed nearly half (48 percent) of southern-born residents of Indianapolis in 1940, but just one-third (33 percent) of the city's southern-born residents in 1960. In a significant way, then, the wartime and postwar influx of southern migrants to Indianapolis was driven largely by traffic along the hillbilly highway. See U.S. Bureau of the Census, *Sixteenth Census of the United States: 1940*, 69; and *U.S. Census of the Population: 1960. Subject Reports. State of Birth . . .* , 174. See also Alexander, "Great Migrations"; and Alexander, "'They're Never Here More Than a Year,'" 658.

20. The Stringtown residents are quoted in Barbara Tapp, Michael J. Tapp, oral history interview with Richard Phelps, March 21, 1976, #76-22-1,2; and Charles H. Dix, oral history interview with Richard Phelps, March 20, 1976, #76-19-1. Center for the Study of History and Memory, Indiana University, Bloomington, IN. South Lebanon's Kentucky-born migrants were the subject of one of the very earliest studies of postwar migration to the industrial Midwest, in James Brown's doctoral thesis, "Social Organization of an Isolated Kentucky Mountain Neighborhood" (PhD diss., Harvard University, 1950). The quote above is from Brown's coauthored follow-up study: Schwarzweller, Brown, and Mangalam, *Mountain Families in Transition*, 124. See also Guy, *From Diversity to Unity*, 32–40.

21. In general, male migrants who had been employed in manual occupations prior to leaving the South outnumbered those in professional trades by roughly a factor of five during the postwar period. See Brown and Hillery Jr., "The Great Migration," 69–71 (table 15).

22. John D. Photiadis, "Occupational Adjustment of Appalachians in Cleveland," in *The Invisible Minority*, eds. Philliber and McCoy, 142–46.

23. Even though 80 percent of new migrants fell into this below-average category when it came to income, roughly 40 percent of them lived in suburban communities rather than inner-city Cincinnati. Philliber, *Appalachian Migrants in Urban America*, 20–21.

24. Darden et al., *Detroit*, 100–3. Another study of postwar suburbanization in Detroit found that in the inner-ring suburbs that received significant numbers of southern white migrants, average family incomes were as much as one-third lower than they were in the more middle-class suburbs that developed within the belt that stretched eighteen to twenty-two miles from the city center. See Reynolds Farley, "Components of Suburban Population Growth," in *The Changing Face of the Suburbs*, ed. Barry Schwartz (Chicago: University of Chicago Press, 1976), 31–34. On "Hazeltucky," see, for instance, "Appalachia's Hillbillies Trek North for Jobs," *New York Times*, March 29, 1973.

25. Hamp Nunley, oral history interview. The quote regarding low property values in Five Points comes from the worksheets accompanying the Home Owners' Loan Corporation's color-coded "mortgage security" map of Cleveland, produced in 1939. Like other low-income, heavily industrial neighborhoods, Five Points was "redlined" on the map—even though, notably, the compiler of the map recorded the presence of only two African American families then living in the neighborhood. Robert K. Nelson, LaDale Winling, Richard Marciano, Nathan Connolly, et al., "Mapping Inequality: Redlining in New Deal America, 1935–1940," *American Panorama: An*

*Atlas of United States History*, eds. Robert K. Nelson and Edward L. Ayers, accessed August 26, 2021, https://dsl.richmond.edu/panorama/redlining/#loc=10/41.49/-81 .985&city=cleveland-oh&area=D25. On the class as well as race-based origins of residential redlining, see Garrett Dash Nelson, "Redlining, Race, and the Color of Money," *Dissent*, July 8, 2021.

26. Richard W. Bricker, *Muncie, Indiana: Hard Times and Good Times from 1925 through 1950* (Shoeacres, TX: self-pub., 2010), 26. Already by the end of the 1930s, the Lynds had noted that the city's growing population of "'poor whites' from the Kentucky, Tennessee, and West Virginia mountains" were clustering in "the ramshackle, unpainted cottages on the outlying paved streets." Lynd and Lynd, *Middletown in Transition*. See also Carmel L. Jones, "Migration, Religion, and Occupational Mobility of Southern Appalachians in Muncie, Indiana" (EdD diss., Ball State University, 1978), 177–79; on Chicago, see Lewis Killian, "The Adjustment of Southern White Migrants to Northern Urban Norms," *Social Forces* 32 (October 1953): 66.

27. Richard Greene, "Seen and Heard in Our Neighborhood," *Muncie Star*, January 5, 1946, and February 6, 1946. The description of Shedtown comes from the worksheets that accompanied the HOLC maps of the city produced in 1937; see Nelson et al., "Mapping Inequality," *American Panorama*, accessed on September 11, 2021, https://dsl.richmond.edu/panorama/redlining/#loc=15/40.169/-85.362&city =muncie-in&area=D6. On population change and housing conditions in wartime Muncie, see also Martin, "Is Muncie Still Middletown?," 97–109.

28. Address given by Richard F. Huegli, Managing Director, United Community Services of Metropolitan Detroit, May 24, 1961 [typed manuscript]. DCCR Records, Part 3, Box 11, Folder 12. See also Detroit Housing Commission, "Some Facts About the Housing Situation in Detroit" (April 1949), DCCR Records, Part 3, Box 25, Folder 127; and *Detroit Area Study* data (1952), [handwritten note], DCCR Records, Part 3, Box 11, Folder 10, Reuther Library. On Indianapolis, see Shane Davies and Gary L. Fowler, "The Disadvantaged Urban Migrant in Indianapolis," *Economic Geography* 48, no. 2 (April 1972): 160; on Cincinnati, see Grace G. Leybourne, "Urban Adjustments of Migrants from the Southern Appalachian Plateaus," *Social Forces* 16, no. 2 (December 1937): 244–45; on Chicago, see Guy, *From Diversity to Unity*, 32–40.

29. Uptown's decline and transformation is most ably captured by Roger Guy in a series of articles and books, including "The Media, the Police, and Southern White Migrant Identity in Chicago, 1955–1970," *Journal of Urban History* 26, no. 3 (March 2000): 329–49; Guy, *From Diversity to Unity*; and Guy, *When Architecture Meets Activism: The Transformative Experience of Hank Williams Village in the Windy City* (Lanham, MD: Lexington Books, 2018); and in Jesse Ambrose Montgomery's dissertation, "Storming Hillbilly Heaven." See also Leybourne, "Urban Adjustments of Migrants from the Southern Plateaus," 244–45; Lynd and Lynd, *Middletown in Transition*, 166n39.

30. The Stringtown residents are quoted in Tapp and Tapp, oral history interview, #76-22-1,2, and Nannie Lewis, Mary Willoughby, oral history interview with Richard Phelps, March 24, 1976. Indiana University Center for the Study of History and Memory, #76-25-1. "Study Made by Group of Teachers at Jefferson Int. School" (1938) [typewritten copy], Lewis B. Larkin Papers, Box 10, Folder 10, Reuther Library. See also Killian, "The Adjustment of Southern White Migrants," 68; William Collins,

"Mountaineers Come and Go," *Cincinnati Enquirer*, July 15, 1957; Ben R. Huelsman, "Urban Anthropology and the Southern Mountaineer," *Proceedings of the Indiana Academy of Science* 78 (1968): 101.

31. Lake View Newcomer Committee, "James and Donna Fair" (February 1961) [unpublished case study], Council of the Southern Mountains Records, 1912–1970, Box 270, Folder 2, Special Collections & Archives, Hutchins Library, Berea College, Berea, KY. As noted in the report, the names James and Donna Fair were fictionalized to preserve the anonymity of the family.

32. J. Trent Alexander has found that southerners employed in professional and technical occupations during the 1960s made up less than one in five of southern migrants who remained in the North, but more than one in four of the southern migrants who returned to the South. Likewise, rates of return migration during the second half of that decade were nearly three times higher among migrants to Indianapolis than to Cincinnati, which Alexander attributes to the comparatively prosperous conditions in those parts of southern Appalachia from which most Indianapolis-bound migrants hailed during these years (western Kentucky and Tennessee), relative to those in the eastern Kentucky coalfields that produced the majority of migrants to Cincinnati. See Alexander, "'They're Never Here More Than a Year,'" esp. 657–61.

33. Hal Bruno, "Chicago's Hillbilly Ghetto," *The Reporter*, June 4, 1964; Tapp and Tapp, oral history interview with Richard Phelps, Center for the Study of History and Memory.

34. See "ACTION Inc. City Target Areas" [map] (November 1966). Black Muncie History Project, Box 2, Folder 23, Archives and Special Collections, Alexander M. Bracken Library, Ball State University, Muncie, IN; and Jones, "Migration, Religion, and Occupational Mobility of Southern Appalachians in Muncie, Indiana," 177 (table 32).

35. Dan McKee and Phillip J. Obermiller, "The Invisible Neighborhood: Appalachians in Ohio Cities," in *Perspectives on Urban Appalachians*, eds. Weiland and Obermiller, 214.

36. M. W. Newman, "Chicago's Uptown Battles Blight, Flight," *Chicago Daily News*, April 22, 1959; Report by Lynnae King, included in *Chicago Student Health Project—Summer 1968*, sponsored by Student Health Organization of Chicago and Presbyterian-St. Luke's Hospital (Bethesda, MD: Health Services and Mental Health Administration, 1970), 14–15. See also Todd Gitlin and Nanci Hollander, *Uptown: Poor Whites in Chicago* (New York: Harper & Row, 1970), xix, 77–81; Guy, *From Diversity to Unity*, 38–39. The quote from the *Daily News* appears in Jesse Montgomery, "Sing Me Back Home: Country Music and Radical Community Organizing in Uptown Chicago," *Journal of Popular Music Studies* 32, no. 2 (June 2020): 95.

37. Cincinnati Planning Commission investigation, cited in "The Basin Area: An Appraisal of its Leisure-Time Services," report of the Community Health and Welfare Council of the Cincinnati Area (May 1959). CSM Records, Box 270, Folder 3. The quoted director of health education is E. Russell Porter, "When Cultures Meet— Mountain and Urban," *Nursing Outlook* 11, no. 6 (June 1963). See also Zane L. Miller and Bruce Tucker, *Changing Plans for America's Inner Cities: Cincinnati's Over-the-Rhine and Twentieth-Century Urbanism* (Columbus: The Ohio State University Press, 1998).

38. Gregory, "The Southern Diaspora and the Urban Dispossessed," 123 (table 8) and passim.

39. On the social and cultural significance of the working-class saloon, see, among others, Jon M. Kingsdale, "The 'Poor Man's Club': Social Functions of the Working-Class Saloon," *American Quarterly* 25, no. 4 (October 1973): 472–89; E. E. LeMasters, *Blue-Collar Aristocrats: Life-Styles at a Working-Class Tavern* (Madison: University of Wisconsin Press, 1975); David Halle, *America's Working Man: Work, Home, and Politics among Blue-Collar Property Owners* (Chicago: University of Chicago Press, 1984); Julie Lindquist, *A Place to Stand: Politics and Persuasion in a Working-Class Bar* (New York: Oxford University Press, 2002); Aaron Fox, *Real Country: Music and Language in Working-Class Culture* (Durham, NC: Duke University Press, 2004).

40. The precise origins of Uptown's "Hillbilly Heaven" nickname is unclear, but it probably dates to the release of Hal Southern's "I Dreamed of a Hillbilly Heaven," a popular country novelty song first released in 1951 (right around the beginning of postwar migrant surge) and later recorded by the likes of Eddie Dean, Tex Ritter, and Loretta Lynn, Dolly Parton, and Tammy Wynette. The Uptown resident quoted is Doug Youngblood, interviewed in Guy Carawan and Candie Carawan, *Voices from the Mountains* (New York: Alfred A. Knopf, 1975), 71; the line about "drunks of both sexes" comes from an editorial in an Uptown community newspaper, the *Edgewater Uptown News*, quoted in Guy, "The Media, The Police, and Southern White Migrant Identity in Chicago," 337. See also Albert Votaw, "The Hillbillies Invade Chicago," *Harper's*, February 1958. On southern "low culture," see, for example, Pete Daniel, *Lost Revolutions: The South in the 1950s* (Chapel Hill: University of North Carolina Press, 2000), 91ff.

41. Browning, "Girl Reporter Visits Jungles of Hillbillies"; "Martin-McCoy Migrants Boom Hillbilly Talent in Detroit," *Billboard*, December 4, 1943.

42. Omer and Amanda Hicks, oral history interview with author, March 19, 2015, Jamestown, Tennessee; audio recording and transcript in author's possession.

43. Wesley Reagan, oral history interview with author, March 18, 2015, Jamestown, Tennessee; audio recording and transcript in author's possession.

44. "Martin-McCoy Migrants." A little over half a year later, *Billboard* was hailing the Jefferson Inn as "Motor City's now famed hill-billy night spot." "Coinmen You Know," *Billboard*, July 15, 1944. See also Craig Maki with Keith Cady, *Detroit Country Music: Mountaineers, Cowboys, and Rockabillies* (Ann Arbor: University of Michigan Press, 2013), 2–7.

45. Topper quoted in Bernard Asbel, "National Barn Dance," *Chicago* (October 1954). See also Montgomery, "Storming Hillbilly Heaven," 121; Devin Hunter, "Growing Diversity: Urban Renewal, Community Activism, and the Politics of Cultural Diversity in Uptown, Chicago, 1940–1970" (PhD diss., Loyola University Chicago, 2015).

46. Hamp Nunley, oral history interview.

47. Bob Barnet, "After the Ball," *Muncie Star Press*, May 26, 1945; Browning, "Girl Reporter Visits Jungles of Hillbillies." Hamp Nunley, oral history interview; Janelle Taylor, oral history interview. Breeding quoted in Maki with Cady, *Detroit Country Music*, 59.

48. "Champ Bad Man Sliced Up a Bit," *Muncie Star Press*, September 5, 1937. Gregory, *American Exodus*, 143ff.

49. Harry Woodward Jr., for the Lake View Newcomer Committee, "Analysis of Arrest Records Town Hall Police Station," report for Lake View Newcomer Committee (June 1961) [unpublished report]. CSM Records, Box 270, Folder 2, Hutchins Library. The Nineteenth District commander is John Fahey, quoted in Council of the Southern Mountains, Inc., "Report on a meeting held in connection with the Chicago Office of the Council of the Southern Mountains" (November 18, 1963) [typewritten meeting minutes and report]. CSM Records, Box 270, Folder 13, Hutchins Library. The chief investigator of the Chicago Crime Commission is quoted in Browning, "Girl Reporter Visits Jungles of Hillbillies."

50. William Collins, "Code of Hills Fails in City," *Cincinnati Enquirer*, July 13, 1957. In his study of southern Appalachian migrants in Cincinnati, William Philliber likewise found that migrants were roughly twice as likely as white natives of Cincinnati to have arrest records, and nearly three times as likely as white migrants to the city from places other than the South. Only Black Cincinnatians were more likely to have arrest records. Philliber, *Appalachian Migrants in Urban America*, 103–4.

51. The quoted Cincinnati police representative is Lieutenant Robert Roncker; see Roncker, "The Southern Appalachian Migrant: A social study of his attitudes, customs, and environment" (August 1959) [unpublished report]. CSM Records, Box 267, Folder 4, Hutchins Library. The Chicago lieutenant is quoted in Browning, "Girl Reporter Visits Jungles of Hillbillies."

52. Guy, "The Media, the Police, and Southern White Migrant Identity in Chicago," 338.

53. Wolfe, "Appalachians in Muncie," 165.

54. Gitlin and Hollander, *Uptown*, 375–76. See also, "Analysis of Arrest Records Town Hall Police Station," CSM Records, Box 270, Folder 2, Hutchins Library.

55. Guy, "The Media, the Police, and Southern White Migrant Identity in Chicago," 335–36. By the late 1960s, systematic police bias and brutality against southern migrants in Uptown became a primary impetus for the political organizing done by local community groups like Jobs or Income Now (JOIN) and later the Young Patriots' Organization, whose membership was largely composed of southern Appalachian migrants. See especially Gitlin and Hollander, *Uptown*; Amy Sonnie and James Tracy, *Hillbilly Nationalists, Urban Race Rebels, and Black Power: Community Organizing in Radical Times* (New York: Melville House, 2011); Jakobi Williams, *From the Bullet to the Ballot: The Illinois Chapter of the Black Panther Party and Racial Coalition Politics in Chicago* (Chapel Hill, NC: University of North Carolina Press, 2015); and Montgomery, "Storming Hillbilly Heaven."

56. Maloney quoted in Ohio Advisory Committee to the United States Commission on Civil Rights, *Policing in Cincinnati, Ohio: Official Policy and Vs. Civilian Reality* (Cincinnati, OH: 1981), 2–4, 69. On the occurrence of police profiling and brutality in Cincinnati's migrant communities, and the response of community organizations like the Urban Appalachian Council, see Phillip J. Obermiller and Michael E. Maloney, "Living City, Feeling Country: The Current Status and Future Prospects of Urban Appalachians," in *From Mountain to Metropolis*, eds. Borman and Obermiller, 3–13; and Thomas E. Wagner and Phillip J. Obermiller, *Valuing Our Past, Creating Our Future: The Founding of the Urban Appalachian Council* (Berea, KY: Berea College Press, 1999).

57. Lewis Killian, *White Southerners* (New York: Random House, 1970), 109–10; Maxwell, "Down from the Hills and into the Slums."

58. Sharon Brown, oral history interview with author, March 18, 2015, James-town, Tennessee; audio recording and transcript in author's possession. See also Edwin White, "Religious Ideals in the Highlands," *Mountain Life & Work* 27, no. 2 (1952); Jones, "Migration, Religion, and Occupational Mobility of Southern Appala-chians in Muncie, Indiana," 232.

59. "The Southern White Migrant to Lake View" (July 1960). CSM Records, Box 270, Folder 2, Hutchins Library.

60. Boyd, "Detroit's Southern Whites and the Store-Front Churches," DCCR Rec-ords, Part 3, Box 11, Folder 10, Reuther Library.

61. "Biggest Baptist Church," *Life*, July 25, 1949, 59–62; Mark Price, "Preacher Was on a Mission in 1920s," *Akron Beacon Journal*, October 14, 2018. See also Dallas Billington, *God Is Real: A Testament in the Form of an Autobiography* (New York: McKay, 1962); Elmer L. Towns, *The Ten Largest Sunday Schools and What Makes Them Grow* (Grand Rapids: Baker Book House, 1969), 14–22. Johnson, "Industrial Voyagers," 199–210.

62. Leon McBeth, "Expansion of the Southern Baptist Convention to 1951," *Bap-tist History and Heritage* 17, no. 3 (July 1982): 32. Gregory, *The Southern Diaspora*, 204; Berry, *Southern Migrants, Northern Exiles*, 149–53.

63. James Gregory has summarized the southern migration as a "migration of Bap-tists, millions of Baptists," and notes that "in most southern states, well over half of white churchgoers were Baptists, as were about three-quarters of African-American worshipers." Gregory, *The Southern Diaspora*, 204. In addition to Lewis Killian's account, quoted above, Holiness or Pentecostal churches are cited explicitly in Votaw, "The Hillbillies Invade Chicago"; "Hill Folk Stick to 'Old-Time' Religion," *The Catholic Telegraph-Register*, April 29, 1960; Donald Janson, "30,000 Hill People Now Cluster in Chicago," *New York Times*, August 31, 1963; and many other accounts from the period.

64. The complaint about "assimilation" is found in Boyd, "Detroit's Southern Whites and the Store-Front Churches," DCCR Records, Part 3, Box 11, Folder 10, Reuther Library; the minister's wife offers her opinion in "Ministry to the South-ern Mountaineer," *A Report of the Research Work Done by an Episcopal Church in the Inner-City of Cincinnati, Ohio* (1959), CSM Records, Box 35, Folder 5, Hutchins Library. On Pentecostalism, the Holiness tradition and other charismatic churches in the Upper South, see, among others, McCauley, *Appalachian Mountain Religion*; David L. Kimbrough, *Taking Up Serpents: Snake Handlers of Eastern Kentucky* (Cha-pel Hill: University of North Carolina Press, 1995); Bill J. Leonard, *Christianity in Appalachia: Profiles in Regional Pluralism* (Knoxville: University of Tennessee Press, 1999); and Richard J. Callahan Jr., *Work and Faith in the Kentucky Coal Fields: Sub-ject to Dust* (Bloomington: Indiana University Press, 2009).

65. Lynd and Lynd, *Middletown in Transition*, 297–301; see also Jones, "Migra-tion, Religion, and Occupational Mobility of Southern Appalachians in Muncie, Indi-ana." The Cincinnati numbers appear in Philliber, *Appalachian Migrants in Urban America*, 91–92.

66. Christian Ministries of Delaware County, "Churches of Delaware County" (1976) [published report]. Churches of Delaware County Directory, 1976 (SC-576), Stoeckel Archives of Local History, Archives and Special Collections, Alexander M.

Bracken Library, Ball State University, Muncie, Indiana. Lynd and Lynd, *Middletown in Transition*, 297–301.

67. "A Faith That Can't Be Rattled," *Indianapolis Star*, July 23, 1995; Kimbrough, *Taking Up Serpents*, 174–81. On South Lebanon, see Schwarzweller, Brown, and Mangalam, *Mountain Families in Transition*, 135–38.

68. Donovan quoted in Council of the Southern Mountains, Inc., *Report on a meeting held in connection with the opening of the Chicago Office of the Council of the Southern Mountains* [in-house report, n.d. (c. November 1963)], CSM Records, Box 270, Folder 13, Hutchins Library. The "git happy" line appears in "Ministry to the Southern Mountaineer" (1959), CSM Records, Box 35, Folder 5, Hutchins Library. The Detroit pastor is quoted in Boyd, "Detroit's Southern Whites and the Store-Front Churches" (1958), DCCR Records, Part 3, Box 11, Folder 10, Reuther Library. The "lower class" description appears in William E. Powles, "The Southern Appalachian Migrant: Country Boy Turned Blue-Collarite," in *Blue-Collar Word: Studies of the American Worker*, eds. Arthur B. Shostak and William Gomberg (Englewood Cliffs, NJ: Prentice-Hall, 1964), 276.

69. Boyd, "Detroit's Southern Whites and the Store-Front Churches," DCCR Records, Part 3, Box 11, Folder 10, Reuther Library. *Report on a Workshop Sponsored by the Mayor's Friendly Relations Committee and the Social Service Association of Greater Cincinnati* (April 1954). CSM Records, Box 268, Folder 5, Hutchins Library. On the transformation of the congregation at Akron Baptist Temple, see Towns, *The Ten Largest Sunday Schools*, 21.

70. Hartigan Jr., *Racial Situations*, 88–102, 316n22; "'Disgrace to the Race,'" 152–54. Elam quoted in Guy, *When Architecture Meets Activism*, 74.

71. Boyd, "Detroit's Southern Whites and the Store-Front Churches," DCCR Records, Part 3, Box 11, Folder 10, Reuther Library; the Cincinnati social workers are quoted in *Report on a Workshop* (April 1954). CSM Records, Box 268, Folder 5, Hutchins Library.

72. Mabel Guffey, oral history interview with author, March 16, 2015, Jamestown, Tennessee; audio recording and transcript in author's possession.

73. The minister is quoted in Lynd and Lynd, *Middletown in Transition*, 298. Kirby Garrett, oral history interview with author, March 18, 2016, Muncie, Indiana; audio recording and transcript in author's possession; Sharon Brown, oral history interview. The "havens" line appears in McBeth, "Expansion of the Southern Baptist Convention to 1951," 40.

74. A group of social service providers and city officials from Detroit identified this relative dispersion as a particular challenge in their efforts to address the social welfare issues confronting southern whites in the city: "One of the major problems is defining the size, characteristics, location, and nature of the problems of our in-migrant group." "Workshop on Urban Adjustment of Southern Appalachian Migrants," report of representatives from Detroit (July 23, 1960) [unpublished memorandum]. CSM Records, Box 267, Folder 8, Hutchins Library. Hartigan Jr. likewise identifies this pattern and its effects on southern white racial formation in Detroit, in *Racial Situations*, esp. ch. 1.

75. Gitlin and Hollander, *Uptown*, xix; Gregory, *The Southern Diaspora*, 164; on the suburbanization of second- and third-generation Appalachian migrants to the Midwest, see Fowler, "The Residential Distribution of Urban Appalachians."

76. Jacqueline Jones, "Southern Diaspora: Origins of the Northern 'Underclass,'" in *The "Underclass" Debate: Views from History*, ed. Michael B. Katz (Princeton, NJ: Princeton University Press, 1993), 52. Gregory, *The Southern Diaspora*, and Berry, *Southern Migrants, Northern Exiles*, make a version of this argument as well—emphasizing so strongly the underappreciated generational mobility of southern white migrants that they downplay the significant role that migrant poverty played in broader policy conversations during the 1950s and 1960s.

77. Bruno, "Chicago's Hillbilly Ghetto." On Chicago, see especially Arnold Hirsch, *Making the Second Ghetto: Race and Housing in Chicago, 1940–1960* (New York: Cambridge University Press, 1983). For a comparable narrative of resistance and flight in Detroit, see Darden et al., *Detroit*; and Sugrue, *The Origins of the Urban Crisis*.

78. Population data by decade, Black Muncie History Project Records, Box 2, Folder 15, Archives and Special Collections, Bracken Library. Hirsch, *Making the Second Ghetto*, 24; Jon C. Teaford, *The Rough Road to Renaissance: Urban Revitalization in America, 1940–1985* (Baltimore: Johns Hopkins University Press, 1990), 126; Farley, "Components of Suburban Population Growth," 6–7, 10–11 (tables 1–2).

79. Daniel Seligman, "The Enduring Slums," in *The Exploding Metropolis: A Study of the Assault on Urbanism and How Our Cities Can Resist It*, eds. William H. Whyte et al. (New York: Doubleday Books, 1958), 96. Votaw, "The Hillbillies Invade Chicago." On Votaw's role in the Uptown Chicago Commission, see Guy, *From Diversity to Unity*, 36–40.

80. It is perhaps not beside the point that one of the many charges leveled against Gertie Nevels by her resentful Irish American neighbor is that she is a "nigger-loven . . . hillbilly." Arnow, *The Dollmaker*, 349.

81. Daniel Bell, *The End of Ideology: On the Exhaustion of Political Ideas in the Fifties* (New York: Free Press, 1960); Steve Fraser and Gary Gerstle, eds., *The Rise and Fall of the New Deal Order, 1930–1980* (Princeton, NJ: Princeton University Press, 1989); Lizabeth Cohen, *A Consumer's Republic: The Politics of Mass Consumption in Postwar America* (New York: Knopf, 2003); Robert O. Self, *All in the Family: The Realignment of American Democracy Since the 1960s* (New York: Hill and Wang, 2013).

82. Gregory, "The Southern Diaspora and the Urban Dispossessed," 123–29.

83. Harrington, *The Other America*, 96–100, 140–41.

84. See, for instance, Katz, *The Undeserving Poor*; and Alice O'Connor, *Poverty Knowledge: Social Science, Social Policy, and the Poor in Twentieth-Century U.S. History* (Princeton, NJ: Princeton University Press, 2001).

85. Maxwell, "Down from the Hills and into the Slums." The remark about "time and the clock" appears in Lloyd Baldwin, "The Cumberlands: A Lost Land? A Radio Documentary," radio teleplay for WCKY-Cincinnati, September 16–20, 1963 [typewritten transcript]. Urban Appalachian Council Records, 1930–1964, Box 4, Folder 10, Hutchins Library. The Cleveland minister is Reverend Donald L. Benedict, "The Integration of Southern Appalachian Migrants into Northern Urban Centers" (July 1959) [unpublished report], CSM Records, Box 267, Folder 4, Hutchins Library. Whyte is quoted in William H. Whyte, "Are Cities Un-American?" in *The Exploding Metropolis*, 28.

86. Harrington, *The Other America*, 99; Roscoe Giffin, "The Southern Mountaineer in Cincinnati," reprinted in *Report on a Workshop* (April 1954). CSM Records, Box 268, Folder 5, Hutchins Library. On time and the transition to industrial life, see

especially Tamara K. Harevan, *Family Time and Industrial Time: The Relationship Between the Family and Work in a New England Industrial Community* (New York: Cambridge University Press, 1982).

87. The nature and extent of Southern Appalachia's Scotch Irish "identity" has long been an object of fascination and debate among academics, political commentators, and lay observers alike. Some of the more well-known arguments for the Scotch Irish influence on the region, and especially the political and cultural behavior of the region's white common folk, are David Hackett Fisher, *Albion's Seed: Four British Folkways in America* (New York: Oxford University Press, 1989); James Webb, *Born Fighting: How the Scots-Irish Shaped America* (New York: Broadway Books, 2004); and, most recently, the self-proclaimed "Scots-Irish hillbilly" J. D. Vance's *Hillbilly Elegy*. But much recent scholarship in the field of Appalachian Studies has made clear that the claims of a singular or even predominant Scotch Irish cultural tradition within the region significantly overstates the portion of the region's population who could ever claim such a heritage. In fact, as one such scholar notes, "In reality, the most prominent European groups to settle the region were German, English, and Scots-Irish from Ulster (not the Scottish highlands)." Emily Satterwhite, *Dear Appalachia: Readers, Identity, and Popular Fiction Since 1878* (Lexington: University of Kentucky Press, 2011), 142; see also Richard A. Straw and H. Tyler Blethen, eds., *High Mountains Rising: Appalachia in Time and Place* (Urbana: University of Illinois Press, 2004).

## 5. *"An Exaggerated Version of the Same Thing":* *Southern Appalachian Migrants, Cultures* *of Poverty, and Postwar Liberalism*

1. Paul Ylvisaker, "The University in a Changing Urban Environment," November 3, 1958, speech before 44th Annual Meeting of the Association of Urban Universities, Omaha, Nebraska, Paul N. Ylvisaker Papers, HUGFP 142, Box 19, Folder: Speeches 1958–1960, Harvard University Archives, Cambridge, MA.

2. Lyndon Baines Johnson, "Commencement Address at Howard University: 'To Fulfill These Rights,' June 4, 1965," *Public Papers of the Presidents of the United States: Lyndon B. Johnson, 1965* (Vol. II) (Washington, DC, 1966), 638.

3. On the MFRC's stance on racial integration and justice issues, as well as its relationship to Cincinnati's local civil rights movement, see Robert A. Burnham, "The Mayor's Friendly Relations Committee: Cultural Pluralism and the Struggle for Black Advancement," in *Race and the City: Work, Community, and Protest in Cincinnati, 1820–1970*, ed. Henry Louis Taylor Jr. (Urbana: University of Illinois Press, 1993), 258–79; and Michael Washington, "The Stirrings of the Modern Civil Rights Movement in Cincinnati, Ohio, 1943–1953," in *Groundwork: Local Black Freedom Movements in America*, eds. Jeanne Theoharis and Komozi Woodard (New York: New York University Press, 2005).

4. By one estimate, roughly two out of every five new migrants to Cincinnati from southern Appalachia first settled in the city's poorest neighborhoods during these years. Philliber, *Appalachian Migrants in Urban America*, 20–21; see also "Study Completed on Mountaineers," *New York Times*, October 10, 1954. Marshall Bragdon,

"Introduction to Fourth Printing," *Report of a Workshop on the Southern Mountaineer in Cincinnati* (March 1960 [April 29, 1954]), sponsored by the Mayor's Friendly Relations Committee and the Social Service Association of Greater Cincinnati. Council of the Southern Mountains (CSM) Records,1912–1970, Box 268, Folder 5, Francis S. Hutchins Library, Berea College, Berea, KY. The "second minority" quote appears in Phillip J. Obermiller and Thomas E. Wagner, "Cincinnati's 'Second Minority': The Emergence of Appalachian Advocacy, 1953–1973," in *Appalachian Odyssey*, eds. Obermiller, Wagner, and Tucker, 194–95, which also provides further background on Bragdon and the MFRC's activities.

5. Bragdon, "Introduction to Fourth Printing," and Roscoe Giffin, "The Southern Mountaineer in Cincinnati," edited transcript of remarks, both included in *Report of a Workshop* (March 1960 [April 29, 1954]). CSM Records, Box 268, Folder 5, Hutchins Library. A useful intellectual biography of Giffin, as well as a framing for his thinking about the issue of "urban adjustment," is Bruce Tucker, "Transforming Mountain Folk: Roscoe Giffin and the Invention of Urban Appalachia," in *Appalachian Odyssey*, eds. Obermiller, Wagner, and Tucker, 69–98.

6. "Part II—Discussion Sections," edited reports, included in *Report of a Workshop* (March 1960 [April 29, 1954]).

7. "Part II—Discussion Sections," and Giffin, "A Commentary on the Discussion Sections," both included in *Report of a Workshop* (March 1960 [April 29, 1954]).

8. Bragdon, "Introduction to Fourth Printing," and "Part IV—'The Workshop Has Helped Me Thus . . . ,'" both included in *Report of a Workshop* (March 1960 [April 29, 1954]). CSM Records, Box 268, Folder 5, Hutchins Library; "Study Completed on Mountaineers," *New York Times*, October 10, 1954. The wider reception of the Cincinnati workshop is detailed in Obermiller and Wagner, "Cincinnati's 'Second Minority,'" esp. 195–98.

9. "Minutes of the Meeting, Committee on Urban Adjustment" (November 30, 1959) [typewritten minutes]. Detroit Commission on Community Relations (DCCR)/ Human Rights Department Records, Part 3, Box 11, Folder 10, Walter P. Reuther Library, Wayne State University, Detroit, MI. The quoted chairman is Mel Ravitz, "The New Resident and His Education," *New City*, December 15, 1962. On the origins of Chicago's Committee on New Residents, see Margaret S. Madden et al., "Mayor's Committee on New Residents, Migration Services Department" (February 3, 1961) [typewritten memorandum]. CSM Records, Box 270, Folder 2, Hutchins Library. Obermiller and Wagner, "Cincinnati's 'Second Minority,'" 196.

10. Interview with Paul Ylvisaker, Ford Foundation Oral History Project, Sept/ Oct 1973. Ylvisaker Papers, HUGFP 142, Box 5, Folder: Ford Foundation Oral History Project, Harvard University Archives.

11. Nor was Giffin the first in his discipline to deploy the language of "urban adjustment" when discussing the migration of southern whites to northern cites. As early as 1937 the sociologist Grace Leybourne was writing in *Social Forces* about "Urban Adjustments of Migrants from the Southern Appalachian Plateaus"; although as Leybourne's use of the plural suggests, she more had in mind the effects that urban migration had on the employment patterns and residential habits of rural southerners—how migration had "adjusted" them—than the cultural obstacles to integration that would be Giffin's later focus. Leybourne, "Urban Adjustments of

Migrants from the Southern Appalachian Plateaus," 238–46. By the time *Social Forces* revisited the topic in 1953—just six months before the Cincinnati workshop—in Lewis Killian's "The Adjustment of Southern White Migrants to Northern Urban Norms," the emphasis had shifted squarely on to the more cultural and behavioral implications of the term. Killian, "The Adjustment of Southern White Migrants to Northern Urban Norms," 66–69. What distinguished Killian's work from Giffin's was the programmatic intent that guided so much of the latter's work, especially with civic organizations like the MFRC: Giffin's own faith that social scientists and policy professionals could yet further "adjust" southern migrants and in so doing "transform Appalachians in cities from tradition-bound relics of another age into exemplars of modern American urban citizenship." Tucker, "Transforming Mountain Folk," 71.

12. Lake View Newcomer Committee, "Summary of Visits to Southern White Families" (February 1961) [typewritten report]. CSM Records, Box 270, Folder 2, Hutchins Library; "Study Made by Group of Teachers at Jefferson Int. School," mimeographed copy (1938). Lewis B. Larkin Papers, Box 10, Folder 10, Reuther Library.

13. George Henderson, "Poor Southern Whites: A Neglected Urban Problem," *Journal of Secondary Education* 41, no. 3 (March 1966): 113; emphasis in original.

14. Maxwell, "Down from the Hills and into the Slums"; Collins, "Code of Hills Fails in City." Reverend Donald L. Benedict, "The Integration of Southern Appalachian Migrants into Northern Urban Centers" (July 1959) [typewritten report]. CSM Records, Box 267, Folder 4, Hutchins Library. For more on the feuding-hillbilly stereotype, see, among others, Harkins, *Hillbilly*, esp. ch. 5; and Clyde B. McCoy and Virginia McCoy Watkins, "Stereotypes of Appalachian Migrants," in *The Invisible Minority*, eds. Philliber and McCoy, 20–34.

15. Ellen J. Stekert, "Focus for Conflict: Southern Mountain Medical Beliefs in Detroit," *The Journal of American Folklore* 83, no. 328 (April 1970): 119. The Dayton representative is Nell Agenbroad, quoted in "Suggestions for Integrating the Southern Appalachian Migrants," typewritten report from The Dayton Group (1959). CSM Records, Box 267, Folder 4, Hutchins Library. The Chicago director of Migration Services is Margaret Madden, quoted in "Minutes of Meeting of Committee on Urban Adjustment of Southern Appalachian Migrants" (September 26, 1959) [typewritten meeting minutes]. CSM Records, Box 266, Folder 1, Hutchins Library. The Cincinnati doctor is quoted in Maxwell, "Down from the Hills and into the Slums." For a more sympathetic assessment of the persistence of home remedies and other traditional forms of health care in migrant communities, see McCoy-Watkins, "Urban Appalachian Health Behavior," in *Perspectives on Urban Appalachians*, eds. Weiland and Obermiller.

16. Giffin, "The Southern Mountaineer in Cincinnati," and "Part IV—'The Workshop Has Helped Me Thus ... ,'" in *Report of a Workshop* (March 1960 [April 29, 1954]).

17. Seligman, "The Enduring Slums," 95.

18. Giffin's understanding of group identity in migrant communities shared much with Oscar Handlin's, whose classic immigration history *The Uprooted* had been published to wide acclaim just two years earlier. Giffin included *The Uprooted* in a short list of references published along with his remarks in the MFRC's report on the 1954 workshop, which were "suggestive of the rich literature concerned with the adjustment of migrant groups in the U.S." Noting that most of these works, like *The Uprooted*, were concerned primarily with the experiences of migrants from

non-"Anglo-Saxon" countries and cultures, Giffin observed that "the case of the Southern Mountaineer is unique in that we have here as nearly pure an Anglo-Saxon population as is to be found who are encountering the same sort of difficulties that practically all other migrants faced." Giffin, "The Southern Mountaineer in Cincinnati," in *Report of a Workshop* (March 1960 [April 29, 1954]).

19. For a contemporary statement of this new way of thinking, see, among others, C. Wright Mills, *The Sociological Imagination* (New York: Oxford University Press, 1959).

20. Giffin, "The Southern Mountaineer in Cincinnati," in *Report of a Workshop* (March 1960 [April 29, 1954]). As Alice O'Connor has noted, two "fundamental convictions" underlay the behavioral science movement during these years: "one that all problems . . . could be traced to individual behavior and human relationships; the other that methodologically rigorous research could uncover the 'laws' of human behavior so that enlightened, democratic leaders might set society on a more rational course." O'Connor, *Poverty Knowledge*, 102–7.

21. Giffin, "The Southern Mountaineer in Cincinnati," in *Report of a Workshop* (March 1960 [April 29, 1954]).

22. William Goodell Frost, "Our Contemporary Ancestors in the Southern Mountains," *Atlantic Monthly* 83 (March 1899): 311–19.

23. Howard W. Odum, "The Way of the South," *Social Forces* 23, no. 3 (March 1945): 261–62. On the influence of the southern regionalists on New Deal and postwar development initiatives, see Bruce J. Schulman, *From Cotton Belt to Sunbelt: Federal Policy, Economic Development, and the Transformation of the South* (New York: Oxford University Press, 1991), esp. 50–62; on their influence on contemporary thinking about the relationship between place, culture, and poverty, see O'Connor, *Poverty Knowledge*, esp. 67–73.

24. Harry Caudill, *Night Comes to the Cumberlands: A Biography of a Depressed Area* (Boston: Little, Brown, 1963); Weller, *Yesterday's People*. On the influence of these particular texts, as well as the longer tradition from which they emerged, on the War on Poverty, see Thomas Kiffmeyer, "Looking Back to the City in the Hills: The Council of the Southern Mountains and a Longer View on the War on Poverty in the Appalachian South, 1913–1970," in *The War on Poverty: A New Grassroots History, 1964–1980*, eds. Annelise Orleck and Lisa Gayle Hazirjian (Athens: University of Georgia Press, 2011), 359–86, and Whisnant, *Modernizing the Mountaineer*.

25. See, for instance, Roscoe Giffin, "Newcomers from the Southern Mountains," reprinted in *Selected Papers* (Chicago: Institute on Cultural Patterns of Newcomers, 1960 [1958]). Urban Appalachian Council (UAC) Records, Box 5, Folder 3, Hutchins Library; as well as the reference in Chicago Commission on Human Relations, "Southern Appalachian Tour Workshop, July 13–18, 1959," detailed minutes and report (July 1959). CSM Records, Box 267, Folder 1, Hutchins Library.

26. Giffin, "The Southern Mountaineer in Cincinnati," in *Report of a Workshop* (March 1960 [April 29, 1954]); Giffin, "Newcomers from the Southern Mountains," reprinted in *Selected Papers*. UAC Records, Box 5, Folder 3, Hutchins Library. Porter, "When Cultures Meet," 418; emphasis in the original.

27. James S. Brown, "Migratory Streams from the Southern Appalachians to Specified Metropolitan Areas in the Midwest, 1949–1950," table 1, mimeographed copy (April 1966). James S. Brown Papers, 1917–2005, Box 135, Folder 14, Special

Collections Research Center, Margaret I. King Library, University of Kentucky, Lexington, KY. The quoted "observer" is William Meyers, an executive at the Uptown-based Combined Insurance Company of America, and one of the primary driving forces behind the creation of the Chicago Southern Center, which provided aid and resources to local migrants. Quoted in Letter from Bill Meyers to Miss Canterbury (October 7, 1963). CSM Records, Box 73, Folder 16, Hutchins Library. For more on the activities of the Southern Center, see Phillip J. Obermiller and Thomas E. Wagner, "'Hands-Across-the-Ohio': The Urban Initiatives of the Council of the Southern Mountains, 1954–1971," in *Appalachian Odyssey*, eds. Obermiller, Wagner, and Tucker, 121–40; and Guy, *From Diversity to Unity*, esp. ch. 5.

28. Lake View Newcomer Committee, "Summary of Visits to Southern White Families," unpublished report (February 1961). CSM Records, Box 270, Folder 2, Hutchins Library; Harry Woodward Jr., "Analysis of Arrest Records Town Hall Police Station," report for Lake View Newcomer Committee (June 1961). CSM Records, Box 270, Folder 2, Hutchins Library.

29. John Fahey, quoted in Council of the Southern Mountains, Inc., "Report on a meeting . . ." (November 18, 1963). CSM Records, Box 270, Folder 13, Hutchins Library.

30. As Jacqueline Jones has written, "Social workers and scholars alike have spent much time and effort trying to define a distinctive Appalachian culture without realizing that many of the traits ascribed to this group were common to rural folk in general"; that they reflected "less a 'Kentucky way' than a rural way of life." Jones, "Southern Diaspora," 47.

31. Porter, "When Cultures Meet," 418.

32. Wagner and Obermiller, *Valuing Our Past, Creating Our Future*, 9; additional charitable efforts in Over-the-Rhine and other migrant communities are detailed in William Collins, "Many Aiding Migrants," *Cincinnati Enquirer*, July 17, 1957.

33. William Collins, "Many Migrants Win Out," *Cincinnati Enquirer*, July 16, 1957. As the newspaper's executive editor noted in a brief introduction to the articles, which were reprinted in pamphlet-form under the title "From the Freedom of the Mountains to the Hurly-Burly City" in response to widespread reader interest, "I am sure that any fair-minded person who reads these articles will find it clear that the *Enquirer*'s purpose was to explore an important population movement as it affects our city and that the eventual result of it will be to the good of both the city and its mountain people." *Cincinnati Enquirer*, "From the Freedom of the Mountains to the Hurly-Burly City" (July 1957), mimeographed copy, UAC Records, Box 5, Folder 2, Hutchins Library.

34. Bragdon quoted in Obermiller and Wagner, "Cincinnati's 'Second Minority,'" 196. The community activist is Louise Spiegel, who spent years on the boards of the Cincinnati Human Relations Commission (the successor to the MFRC) and Urban Appalachian Council, among other Cincinnati civic organizations; quoted in Wagner and Obermiller, *Valuing Our Past, Creating Our Future*, 14. Spiegel's impression—that the MFRC's investment in the urban Appalachian initiative was largely determined by the amount of time and energy that Bragdon was able to devote to it—would be corroborated by Bragdon himself, who would later write, "At MFRC with its $30,000 annual budget, I would crudely guess that approximately $1,000 worth of staff is given to this function." Letter from Marshall Bragdon to P. F. Ayer (November 13, 1961). CSM Records, Box 35, Folder 5, Hutchins Library.

35. As the writer of one such series, Evelyn Stewart of the *Detroit Free Press*, put it in a letter to a colleague of Bragdon's, "my city editor is very much interested in giving whatever space it needs to good constructive stories about the southern migrants"—especially in the wake of "the trouble we had before," when the *Free Press* had published less favorable reports on Detroit's southern whites and had received a considerable backlash from its southern readership. In addition to the *Free Press* and the *Enquirer*, similarly "constructive" series appeared during these years in the *Chicago Tribune* and the *Cleveland Press*, as well as in smaller local papers throughout the region. Letter from Evelyn Stewart to Perley Ayer (May 29 [1961?]). CSM Records, Box 266, Folder 8, Hutchins Library.

36. Votaw, "The Hillbillies Invade Chicago." For the "direct pipe-line quote," see report of "Miss [Margaret] Madden," in Council of the Southern Mountains, "Minutes of Meeting of Committee on Urban Adjustment of Southern Appalachian Migrants" (September 26, 1959). CSM Records, Box 266, Folder 1, Hutchins Library.

37. Roscoe Giffin, "From Cinder Hollow to Cincinnati," *Mountain Life and Work* (Fall 1956); Ayer quoted in Obermiller and Wagner, "'Hands-Across-the-Ohio,'" 122; see also Obermiller and Wagner, "Cincinnati's 'Second Minority,'" 196–97. On the history of the Council of the Southern Mountains and its relationship to Berea College, see Whisnant, *Modernizing the Mountaineer*, esp. ch. 1.

38. Alice O'Connor, "The Ford Foundation and Philanthropic Activism in the 1960s," in *Philanthropic Foundations: New Scholarship, New Possibilities*, ed. Ellen Condliffe Lagemann (Bloomington: Indiana University Press, 1999), 172. Ford had been the first of its peers, in 1951, to launch an in-house research and programming initiative devoted to the behavioral sciences, and established the hugely influential Center for Advanced Studies in the Behavioral Sciences in Palo Alto in 1954. See also O'Connor, *Poverty Knowledge*, 102–4.

39. Ylvisaker, "The University in a Changing Urban Environment" (November 3, 1958). Ylvisaker Papers, HUGFP 142, Box 19, Folder: Speeches 1958–1960, Harvard University Archives; Interview with Paul Ylvisaker, Ylvisaker Papers, HUGFP 142, Box 5, Folder: Ford Foundation Oral History Project, Harvard University Archives.

40. Interview with Paul Ylvisaker, Ylvisaker Papers, HUGFP 142 Box 5, Folder: Ford Foundation Oral History Project, Harvard University Archives. On the Ford study's treatment of southern Appalachia as a "problem area," see especially Rupert B. Vance, "The Region: A New Survey," in *The Southern Appalachian Region: A Survey*, ed. Thomas R. Ford (Lexington: University Press of Kentucky, 1962), 3–8. See also Obermiller and Wagner, "Cincinnati's 'Second Minority,'" 198.

41. Interview with Paul Ylvisaker, Ylvisaker Papers, HUGFP 142, Box 5, Folder: Ford Foundation Oral History Project, Harvard University Archives. On the Ford Foundation's timidity about addressing racial matters head-on during the 1950s, see Alice O'Connor, "Community Action, Urban Reform, and the Fight against Poverty: The Ford Foundation's Gray Areas Program," *Journal of Urban History* 22, no. 5 (July 1996): esp. 592–95.

42. Gissen's description of the initial discussions that went into the planning of the 1959 Berea workshop, along with the "native habitat" quote, appears in Ira Gissen, "The Mountain Migrant: The Problem-Centered Workshop at Berea," *Journal of Human Relations* 9 (Autumn 1960): 69. Ylvisaker's account of being approached by

Weatherford appears in Interview with Paul Ylvisaker, Ylvisaker Papers, HUGFP 142, Box 5, Folder: Ford Foundation Oral History Project, Harvard University Archives. Louis Smith, the long-acting Dean of Berea College, directed the formal request to Perley Ayer to "head up the enterprise" in January 1959; see Letter from Louis Smith to Perley Ayer (January 7, 1959). CSM Records, Box 266, Folder 8, Hutchins Library—which also includes another useful summary of the origins of the workshop and especially of the roles played therein by Roscoe Giffin and W. D. Weatherford. Bragdon's description of the MFRC's role in devising the idea for the workshop, and its work alongside Ayer to enlist participation from other midwestern urban representatives, appears in Letter from Marshall Bragdon to Paul Ylvisaker (February 22, 1959). CSM Records, Box 266, Folder 3, Hutchins Library. Weatherford's plans for the bus tour—which included stops in Beverly, Pineville, and Middleboro in southeastern Kentucky, followed by Gatlinburg and Crossville in Tennessee—are detailed in Letter from W. D. Weatherford to Marshall Bragdon (May 13, 1959). CSM Records, Box 266, Folder 3, Hutchins Library. Ultimately, the steering committee responsible for planning and administering the 1959 workshop, which was financed entirely by the Ford Foundation and sponsored by Berea College, would be composed of Bragdon, Giffin, Ayer, Weatherford, Gissen, Wendell Pierce of the Cincinnati school system, Thomas Ford of the University of Kentucky, and Helen Caskey, a professor of education at the Teachers' College at the University of Cincinnati; see Berea College, *A Workshop on Urban Adjustment of Southern Appalachian Migrants*, official brochure (1959). CSM Records, Box 267, Folder 1, Hutchins Library. See also Bruce Tucker, "Imagining Appalachians: The Berea Workshop on the Urban Adjustment of Southern Appalachian Migrants," in *Appalachian Odyssey*, eds. Obermiller, Wagner, and Tucker, 97–120.

43. "Minutes of Meeting of Committee on Urban Adjustment" (September 26, 1959). CSM Records, Box 266, Folder 1, Hutchins Library. The quotes from Cullen and the Chicago delegation appear in "Southern Appalachian Tour Workshop" (c. July 1959). CSM Records, Box 267, Folder 1, Hutchins Library; the Cincinnati attendee is quoted in Ethel Slade, "Evaluation of S.A.M. Workshop," unpublished report (August 8, 1959). CSM Records, Box 266, Folder 8, Hutchins Library. Details about the workshop participants are drawn from *A Workshop on Urban Adjustment*, official brochure (1959), and "Registered Delegates to the Workshop on Urban Adjustment of Southern Appalachian Migrants" (1959) [typewritten roster]. CSM Records, Box 267, Folder 1, Hutchins Library.

44. A roster of workshop alumni through 1966 has 233 names on it, including the director of the Bernard van Leer Foundation, a philanthropic foundation based in the Netherlands that specializes in early childhood development. "Participants—Workshop on Urban Adjustment of Southern Appalachian Migrants, 1959–1966" (c. 1966) [typewritten roster]. CSM Records, Box 267, Folder 1, Hutchins Library. An additional twenty-four names appear on a list of participants for the 1967 workshop, and eighteen participants are listed for the tenth and final workshop in 1968. See "Participants—Ninth Workshop on Urban Adjustment of Southern Appalachian Migrants, July 7–19, 1967" (July 1967) [typewritten roster]. CSM Records, Box 269, Folder 3, Hutchins Library; and "Participants—Tenth Workshop on Urban Adjustment of Southern Appalachian Migrants, July 12–24, 1968" (July 1968) [typewritten roster]. CSM Records, Box 269, Folder 7, Hutchins Library.

45. Obermiller and Wagner, "'Hands-Across-the-Ohio,'" 123–26.

46. Interview with Paul Ylvisaker, Ylvisaker Papers, HUGFP 142, Box 5, Folder: Ford Foundation Oral History Project, Harvard University Archives. Cullen quoted in "Southern Appalachian Tour Workshop . . ." (c. July 1959). CSM Records, Box 267, Folder 1, Hutchins Library.

47. O'Connor notes that Ylvisaker borrowed the idea of urban "gray areas" from one economist in particular: "Raymond Vernon, who, as director of the Regional Plan Association's New York Metropolitan Regional Study in the late 1950s had written about the 'growing obsolescence' of central cities in the face of suburbanization and economic change." Ylvisaker took Vernon's notion of a "'gray belt' of potential slums," and shifted the original emphasis from infrastructural decline to "its sociological dimensions." O'Connor, "Community Action, Urban Reform, and the Fight against Poverty," 605–6.

48. Interview with Paul Ylvisaker, Ylvisaker Papers, HUGFP 142, Box 5, Folder: Ford Foundation Oral History Project, Harvard University Archives. Cullen quoted in "Southern Appalachian Tour Workshop . . ." (c. July 1959). CSM Records, Box 267, Folder 1, Hutchins Library.

49. The following year, Washington, DC, San Francisco, and Buffalo were added to the list of grantees. Peter Marris and Martin Rein, *Dilemmas of Social Reform: Poverty and Community Action in the United States*, 2nd ed. (Chicago: Aldine, 1973 [1967]), 16–17.

50. Ford Foundation officers seemed to use these various terms relatively interchangeably as well. Ylvisaker, for instance, preferred "culturally disadvantaged"; while Peter Marris, who in 1964 the Ford Foundation brought in as an independent observer of its gray area projects, wrote about the target populations of the foundation's Great Cities programming as the "culturally handicapped." See Interview with Paul Ylvisaker, Ylvisaker Papers, HUGFP 142, Box 5, Folder: Ford Foundation Oral History Project, Harvard University Archives; Marris and Rein, *Dilemmas of Social Reform*, 16. Whatever the particular preference may have been, the overarching influence of the behavioral framework and the language of pathology that Roscoe Giffin and others had been deploying since the early 1950s is clearly evident. See also O'Connor, "Community Action, Urban Reform, and the Fight against Poverty," 608.

51. Great Cities appropriation figures are taken from Ford Foundation, "Review Paper: Public Affairs: Gray Areas Program," internal report (September 1964). Ylvisaker Papers, HUGFP 142, Box 5, Folder: Ford Foundation: Gray Areas Program Review Paper, 1964, Harvard University Archives. See also Marris and Rein, *Dilemmas of Social Reform*, 16–18; O'Connor, "Community Action, Urban Reform, and the Fight against Poverty," 609.

52. The stepping-stone quote appears in Morris and Rein, *Dilemmas of Social Reform*, 16. Ylvisaker's quoted remarks at the 1963 American Municipal Conference in Houston, Texas, appear in O'Connor, "Community Action, Urban Reform, and the Fight against Poverty," 609. The Gray Areas appropriation figures appear in "Review Paper: Public Affairs: Gray Areas Program" (September 1964). Ylvisaker Papers, HUGFP 142, Box 5, Folder: Ford Foundation: Gray Areas Program Review Paper, 1964, Harvard University Archives. For more on specific Gray Area program initiatives within the context of the postwar urban crisis and the formative period of the War

on Poverty, see, for instance, Robert Halpern, *Rebuilding the Inner City: A History of Neighborhood Initiatives to Address Poverty in the United States* (New York: Columbia University Press, 1995); Guian McKee, *The Problem of Jobs: Liberalism, Race, and Deindustrialization in Philadelphia* (Chicago: University of Chicago Press, 2010); Karen Ferguson, *Top Down: The Ford Foundation, Black Power, and the Reinvention of Racial Liberalism* (Philadelphia: University of Pennsylvania Press, 2013).

53. For an overview of the planning and development stages of the War on Poverty, see Carl M. Brauer, "Kennedy, Johnson, and the War on Poverty," *The Journal of American History* 69, no. 1 (June 1982): 98–119.

54. Accounts of Ylvisaker's role in the drafting of the Economic Opportunity Act are drawn from oral histories with William Cannon, William Capron, Frederick Hayes, Sargent Shriver, and James Sundquist, excerpted in Michael Gillette, *Launching the War on Poverty: An Oral History* (New York: Oxford University Press, 1996), 18, 52, 59, 62–63, 83. See also O'Connor, "Community Action, Urban Reform, and the Fight against Poverty," 611–13.

55. For background on Mynatt and his early experiences organizing in white southerners in Over-the-Rhine, see Wagner and Obermiller, *Valuing Our Past, Creating Our Future*; the exchange between Mynatt and Shriver is described on 27–28. For more on the work of The Hub and other community action programs in Over-the-Rhine during this period, see also Miller and Tucker, *Changing Plans in America's Inner Cities*, esp. chs. 5 and 6.

56. The new organization, founded in November 1968, would be called United Appalachian Cincinnati, and set as its agenda, "to promote the self-awareness and self-activity of the Appalachian people in Cincinnati, to encourage our urban institutions to respond to the needs and interests of Appalachians, and to show our community at large the power and the beauty of our culture." Wagner and Obermiller, *Valuing Our Past, Creating Our Future*, 28–37; Faber quoted on 28. See also Miller and Tucker, *Changing Plans for America's Inner Cities*, 72–83; Bruce Tucker, "Toward a New Ethnicity: Urban Appalachian Ethnic Consciousness in Cincinnati, 1950–1987," in *Appalachian Odyssey*, eds. Obermiler, Wagner, and Tucker, 159–80.

57. For a contemporary account of this struggle, from one such Washington liberal who was then beginning his ideological journey to the neoconservative right, see Daniel Patrick Moynihan, *Maximum Feasible Misunderstanding: Community Action in the War on Poverty* (New York: Free Press, 1969). A very different perspective, also from the time, is offered in Maurice R. Berube and Marilyn Gittel, eds., *Confrontation at Ocean-Hill Brownsville* (New York: Praeger, 1969). For a good historical analysis of the effects that the political controversy surrounding the meaning and application of the "maximum feasible participation" principle in the antipoverty programs of the period, see Quadagno, *The Color of Welfare*.

58. On the efforts of the War on Poverty in southern Appalachia, see, among others, Whisnant, *Modernizing the Mountaineer*; Thomas Kiffmeyer, *Reformers to Radicals: The Appalachian Volunteers and the War on Poverty* (Lexington: University Press of Kentucky, 2008), and Ronald D. Eller, *Uneven Ground: Appalachia since 1945* (Lexington: University Press of Kentucky, 2008), esp. chs. 2 and 3.

59. Maloney quoted in Bruce Tucker, "Michael Maloney: Interviewed by Bruce Tucker," *Appalachian Journal* 17, no. 1 (Fall 1989): 43–44.

60. U.S. Congress, Senate, Committee on Labor and Public Welfare, *Hearings Before the Subcommittee on Employment, Manpower, and Poverty: Examining the War on Poverty, Part 13*, 90 Cong., 1 sess., May 18, 1967, pp. 4194–99. Hunter, "Growing Diversity," 281, 315–16.

61. Monroe Karmin, "Model City Muddle," *Wall Street Journal*, February 20, 1968.

62. The application process and selection criteria are detailed in Ford Foundation, "Review Paper: Public Affairs: Gray Areas Program," internal report (September 1964). Ylvisaker Papers, HUGFP 142, Box 5, Folder: Ford Foundation: Gray Areas Program Review Paper, 1964, Harvard University Archives. See also O'Connor, "Community Action, Urban Reform, and the Fight against Poverty," 610–11.

63. Richard Goodwin was a special assistant to Lyndon Johnson. Baker quoted in Gillette, *Launching the War on Poverty*, 71–72, 123.

64. Jones, "Southern Diaspora," 52; Tucker, "Michael Maloney," 47–48. See also Miller and Tucker, *Changing Plans for America's Inner-Cities*, xv–xxi.

65. Oscar Lewis, *La Vida: A Puerto Rican Family in the Culture of Poverty—San Juan and New York* (New York: Random House, 1965), xlii, xlvii–xlviii; see also, Lewis, *Five Families: Mexican Case Studies in the Culture of Poverty* (New York: Basic Books, 1959).

66. Lewis, *La Vida*, xlv. On the misappropriation of Lewis's original theory, see Katz, *The Undeserving Poor*, 16–29.

67. Daniel Patrick Moynihan, "The Negro Family: The Case for National Action," reprinted in Lee Rainwater and William Yancey, *The Moynihan Report and the Politics of Controversy* (Cambridge, MA: MIT Press, 1967 [1965]), 39–125. The initial use of the "cycle of poverty" concept—which did not appear in Lewis's original work on the culture of poverty—in the 1963 prospectus of the North Carolina Fund is discussed in Marris and Rein, *Dilemmas of Social Reform*, 38–39.

68. On the various controversies over the intentions and implications of the report, see Yancey and Rainwater, *The Moynihan Report and the Politics of Controversy*; and Moynihan, *Maximum Feasible Misunderstanding*.

69. Johnson, "Commencement Address at Howard University," *Public Papers of the Presidents*, 638.

70. O'Connor, "Community Action, Urban Reform, and the Fight against Poverty," 617.

71. Mark J. Stern, "Poverty and Family Composition since 1940," in Katz, ed., *The "Underclass" Debate*, 225.

72. Teaford, *The Rough Road to Renaissance*, 125.

73. Marris and Rein, *Dilemmas of Social Reform*, 11.

74. On just some of the implications of this conservative triumph, see, for instance, the collected essays in Katz, ed., *The "Underclass" Debate*.

## 6. Lost Highways: Country Music and the Rise and Fall of Hillbilly Culture

1. "Lost Highway," Hank Williams, *The Complete Hank Williams*, Mercury 314 536 007-2, 1998[1949].

2. "A Country Boy Can Survive," Hank Williams Jr., *The Pressure Is On*, Elektra SE-535, 1981.

3. "'King of the Hillbillies' Dies in Sleep in Auto," *Associated Press*, January 2, 1953; Roger M. Williams, *Sing a Sad Song: The Life and Times of Hank Williams*, 2nd ed. (Urbana: University of Illinois Press, 1981), 212–14. An earlier version of this chapter was first published as Max Fraser, "Lost Highways," *Raritan Quarterly Review* 35, no. 3 (Winter 2016): 117–44.

4. Charles Carr quoted in Peter Cooper, "Retracing a Ghostly Night Ride," *Nashville Tennessean*, January 1, 2003. Excerpts of Audrey Mae Williams's divorce complaint appear in Patrick Huber, Steve Goodson, and David M. Anderson, eds., *The Hank Williams Reader* (New York: Oxford University Press, 2014), 38–47. The Harry Stone and Oscar Davis quotes appear in Roger Williams's hagiographic biography, *Sing a Sad Song*, 171–208.

5. "Top Country & Western Records," *Billboard*, January 3, 1953; Williams, *Sing a Sad Song*, 198–200.

6. "Mystery Shrouds the Death of Singer Hank Williams," *Knoxville Journal*, January 2, 1953; Doug Morris, "Hank Williams' Death Still Issue," *Knoxville Journal*, December 15, 1982; Williams, *Sing a Sad Song*, 213–18. The *Montgomery Advertiser* is quoted in Huber, Goodson, and Anderson, eds., *The Hank Williams Reader*, 4.

7. According to the editors of an academic press anthology devoted to the singer—the existence of which is itself a testament to the remarkable scope of what one could be excused for calling the field of "Hank Williams Studies"—Williams "has been the subject of at least fifteen biographies, more than seventeen hundred articles in newspapers, magazines, and scholarly journals, and scores of essays, encyclopedia entries, album reviews, liner notes, poems, plays, novels, and short stories." Published in 2014, the editors missed *I Saw the Light* (2015), the second major motion picture made about Hank Williams's life, starring Tom Hiddleston in the lead role, by just a year. Huber, Goodson, and Anderson, eds., *The Hank Williams Reader*, 8.

8. Mark J. Price, "Influential Akron Disc Jockey Proud to Be a Hillbilly," *Akron Beacon Journal*, August 25, 2013; Clyde B. McCoy and James S. Brown, "Appalachian Migration to Midwestern Cities," in *The Invisible Minority*, eds. Philliber and McCoy, 46; Williams, *Sing a Sad Song*, 2.

9. Timothy A. Patterson, "Hillbilly Music among the Flatlanders: Early Midwestern Barn Dances," *Journal of Country Music* 6, no. 1 (Spring 1975): 15. Lynd and Lynd, *Middletown in Transition*, 264. On the Blue Ridge Ramblers tours, see Charles Wolfe, "Up North with the Blue Ridge Ramblers: Jennie Bowman's 1931 Tour Diary," *Journal of Country Music* 6, no. 3 (Fall 1975): 136–44.

10. Interview with Henry Glover by John W. Rumble, March 1, 1983, OHC128, and Interview with Steve Cisler by John W. Rumble, February 20, 1984, OH59, in the Country Music Foundation Oral History Project, Country Music Hall of Fame and Museum, Nashville, Tennessee.

11. Barbara Myers, oral history interview with author, March 27, 2015, Tracy City, Tennessee; audio recording and transcript in author's possession. D. K. Wilgus, "Country-Western Music and the Urban Hillbilly," *Journal of American Folklore* 83 no. 238 (April–June 1970): 172; Mark Ribowsky, *Hank: The Short Life and Long Country Road of Hank Williams* (New York: Liveright, 2016), 240–41, 253.

12. Wilgus, "Country-Western Music and the Urban Hillbilly," 172. As Diane Pecknold has noted, the extraordinary attention generated by Williams's death at the

beginning of 1953 was "the first of a series of events that combined to propel the country music industry into the biggest promotional windfall it had experienced in its short history." Diane Pecknold, *The Selling Sound: The Rise of the Country Music Industry* (Durham, NC: Duke University Press, 2007), 72.

13. "Country & Western Business is Big Business," *Billboard*, December 5, 1953, 41. The "radio dial" quote appears in Jones, "Southern Diaspora," 49. For discussions of the assimilation experiences of these and other earlier groups of white (im)migrants, see, for instance, Gary Gerstle, *Working-Class Americanism: The Politics of Labor in a Textile City, 1914–1960* (New York: Cambridge University Press, 1989); David R. Roediger, *The Wages of Whiteness: Race and the Remaking of the American Working Class* (New York: Verso, 1991); and Matthew Frye Jacobson, *Whiteness of a Different Color: European Immigrants and the Alchemy of Race* (Cambridge, MA: Harvard University Press, 1998).

14. Williams quoted in Rufus Jarman, "Country Music Goes to Town," *Nation's Business*, February 1953. On Williams's time in the Mobile shipyards and its impact on his musical career, see also George Lipsitz, *Rainbow at Midnight: Labor and Culture in the 1940s* (Urbana: University of Illinois Press, 1994), 23–29; and Williams, *Sing a Sad Song*, 52–55.

15. Olive Dame Campbell and Cecil Sharp, *English Folk Songs from the Southern Appalachians: Comprising 122 Songs and Ballads and 323 Tunes* (New York: G.P. Putnam's Sons, 1917), iv–ix.

16. As the folklorist Archie Green notes, the hillbilly label proved to be an extraordinarily capacious one, at one point or another encompassing a truly "kaleidoscopic variety" of musical subgenres, including: "old time, familiar tunes, Dixie, mountain, sacred, gospel, country, cowboy, western, country-western, hill and range, western swing, Nashville, rockabilly, bluegrass." By 1929 Sears, Roebuck, had decided to list all recordings of white rural musics that it sold through its mail-order catalog under the generic "hillbilly" label, and Montgomery Ward followed suit the next year—and as those retail heavyweights went, so went the country (so to speak). Archie Green, "Hillbilly Music: Source and Symbol," *Journal of American Folklore* 78, no. 309 (July 1965), reprinted in Green, *Torching the Fink Books and Other Essays on Vernacular Culture* (Chapel Hill: University of North Carolina Press, 2001), 10–13, 34. Peer quoted on 13.

17. Abel Green, "'Hill Billy' Music," *Variety*, December 29, 1926. For more on this point about the ethnological condescension practiced by the likes of Campbell and Sharp, see David E. Whisnant, *All That Is Native and Fine: The Politics of Culture in an American Region* (Chapel Hill: University of North Carolina Press, 1983), 51–58; Bill C. Malone, *Don't Get above Your Raisin': Country Music and the Southern Working Class* (Urbana: University of Illinois Press, 2002), 327n51.

18. John Lair, the "impresario" behind first WLS's *National Barn Dance* and later the *Renfro Valley Barn Dance*, broadcast out of Cincinnati and then Mt. Vernon, Kentucky, had this to say: "Hill billies in radio? They ain't no such thing. Mountaineers and folk from the hill country, maybe, but no hill billies." George Hay, for many years the announcer for the *Grand Ole Opry* in the character of "The Solemn Old Judge," echoed Lair's sentiment: "We never use the word [hillbilly] because it was coined in derision. Furthermore, there is no such animal." Both quoted in Green, "Hillbilly Music," 35.

19. Interview with Bradley Kincaid by Dorothy Gable, November 2, 1967, OH332; Interview with Kincaid by Douglas B. Green, July 10, 1974, OH83; Interview with Doc Hopkins by Douglas B. Green, June 11, 1974, OH74, Country Music Foundation. Kincaid's "squirrel path" anecdote is repeated in both of these oral histories, and was commonly incorporated into his performing persona throughout his career. In reality, though, Kincaid grew up in Garrard County, Kentucky, a largely rural but long-settled area in the Bluegrass region of the state about thirty miles south of Lexington.

20. Campbell and Sharp, *English Folk Songs from the Southern Appalachians*, ix.

21. "Boll Weevil Blues," Gid Tanner and His Skillet Lickers, Columbia 15016D-81604, 1924, shellac; see also Bill C. Malone, *Country Music U.S.A.*, rev. ed. (Austin: University of Texas Press, 1985), 50–52; Malone, *Don't Get above Your Raisin'*, 31, 270n8. Tanner was the first country musician to sign with Columbia, which soon became the preeminent hillbilly record label. As Green notes, when Columbia launched its "Familiar Tunes—Old and New" series in January 1925, it became "the first company to see the possibilities in an exclusive white folk series." Green, "Hillbilly Music," 26.

22. "The Log Train," Hank Williams, *The Complete Hank Williams*, Mercury 314 536 007-2, 1998 [1952]; see also Malone, *Country Music U.S.A.*, 239; The song quoted is "You Better Lie Down," by the blues singer Emmett Murray, discussed in Alton C. Morris, *Folksongs of Florida* (Gainesville: University Press of Florida, 1950), 10–11. The *Lexington Morning Herald* is quoted in Whisnant, *All That Is Native and Fine*, 72–74.

23. "The Wreck of the Old '97," Vernon Dalhart, Victor 19427, 1924; "Folsom Prison Blues," Johnny Cash, *With His Hot and Blue Guitar*, Sun LP 1220, 1957. On the origins of Dalhart's early hit, see Green, "Hillbilly Music," 27–29. The railroad county statistic comes from Edward L. Ayers, *The Promise of the New South: Life After Reconstruction* (New York: Oxford University Press, 1992), 9–13.

24. On the musical culture of the Piedmont mill villages, see especially Patrick Huber, *Linthead Stomp: The Creation of Country Music in the Piedmont South* (Chapel Hill: University of North Carolina Press, 2008).

25. Malone, *Don't Get above Your Raisin'*, 33–34; Sharp quoted in Whisnant, *All That Is Native and Fine*, 121. A not dissimilar development followed on the heels of the 1894 discovery by the Water Development Authority in Corsicana, Texas, of the first commercially viable oilfield in the state. The oil boom that followed and swept through Louisiana, Arkansas, and Oklahoma brought one more wave of industrialization to another primarily rural part of the South. As local farmers followed the model of their coal-country brethren and flocked to oilfields in search of good wages, another modern tradition was born in the roadside bars that began to line the outskirts of East Texas boomtowns. Called "honky-tonks," they provided alcohol, female company, and musical entertainment to the single men working the fields. Town manners were spreading fast. See Malone, *Don't Get above Your Raisin'*, 35, 161–62.

26. To give a sense of just how revolutionary the "coming of the roads" was for the rural South during this period, as recently as 1904 there were fewer miles of surfaced roads across the entire region stretching from the Mississippi River to the Appalachian Mountains south of the Ohio River than there were in the state of Ohio itself. See Andrew P. Anderson, "Rural Highway Mileage, Income, and Expenditures: 1921

and 1922," United States Department of Agriculture, Bulletin No. 1279 (Washington, DC, 1925), table 7.

27. Henry Whitter, "Lonesome Road Blues," OKeh 40015-A, 1924. In Georgia, for instance, the deployment of convicts allowed the state to more than double the mileage of its surfaced roads in a matter of just five years. Howard Lawrence Preston, *Dirt Roads to Dixie: Accessibility and Modernization in the South, 1885-1935* (Knoxville: University of Tennessee Press, 1991), 5, 22, 9–69. The "newfound mobility" quote appears in Dorothy Horstman, *Sing Your Heart Out, Country Boy*, rev. ed. (Nashville: Country Music Foundation Press, 1986), 352.

28. "Wreck on the Highway," Roy Acuff, OKeh 6585, 1942. About "Wreck on the Highway," one of Acuff's biographers has gone so far as to say it is "the most perfect hillbilly song"—and again, "the epitome of hillbillyness"—as much for its "sincerity" and "emotional depth" as for the song's "whiskey, blood, glass, and double negatives [that] were utterly distasteful to sophisticates." Elizabeth Schlappi, *Roy Acuff: The Smoky Mountain Boy*, 2nd ed. (Gretna: Pelican Publishing, 1993), 123–24. Expressing similar sentiments at the time, a *Saturday Evening Post* article on the wartime "hillbilly boom" pointed to Acuff's recently recorded single as "having all the qualities in perfection" that country music's promoters were looking for. Maurice Zolotow, "Hillbilly Boom," *Saturday Evening Post*, February 12, 1944.

29. The Dixon Brothers, "I Didn't Hear Nobody Pray," *Dixon Brothers Volume 3: 1937-1938* (Document 8048, 2000 [1937]). The best account of the life and music of Dorsey and his brother, Howard, can be found in Huber, *Linthead Stomp*, 216–74.

30. As Deborah McCauley notes, the Free Will Baptists were so closely associated with the more industrialized portions of southern Appalachia that it earned a reputation as "the miner's church" by the mid-twentieth century. McCauley, *Appalachian Mountain Religion*, 23.

31. Patrick Huber, "'A Blessing to People': Dorsey Dixon and His Sacred Mission of Song," *Southern Cultures* 12, no. 4 (Winter 2006): 118–20.

32. It was primarily this side of Dixon's recording career that earned him the title of "the poet laureate of the cotton mill industry," as Archie Green would later dub him. In the mid-twentieth century, Pete Seeger and other postwar folk revivalists would rediscover and make popular a number of Dixon's more secularly minded compositions, most notably "Weave Room Blues," which begins "Working in a weave room, fighting for my life. / Trying to make a living for my kiddies and my wife." Pete Seeger, "Weave Room Blues," *Folk Songs for Young People*, Folkways Records 7532, 1959. The folk revival's renewed interest in the Dixon Brothers' labor songs led to a new album of their work being released in the early 1960s, for which Dorsey wrote the title track, "Babies in the Mill." Nancy, Dorsey, and Howard Dixon, *Babies in the Mill: Carolina Traditional, Industrial, Sacred Songs*, Testament Records 3301, 1962. Archie Green's "poet laureate" remark is quoted in Huber, *Linthead Stomp*, 218.

33. On these particular examples of the relationship between southern Pentecostalism and working-class protest, see Callahan Jr., *Work and Faith in the Kentucky Coal Fields*; and Jarod Roll, *Spirit of Rebellion: Labor and Religion in the New Cotton South* (Urbana: University of Illinois Press, 2010).

34. Although these kinds of southerners were more obviously Bryan's base, Debs's homegrown socialism also gained traction, especially in parts of the rural South and southwest where conservative Protestantism and a tradition of agrarian radicalism

or militant unionism coexisted. As Elizabeth Sanders and James Green have noted, Debs's strongest support in the region "came from the poorest farm and piney woods districts in southern Oklahoma, north-central and northeastern Texas, and western Louisiana and from the farm and coal-mining counties of southwestern Kansas and western Arkansas." Although his support was lower in the southern Appalachian states, where such traditions were much weaker, at the high-water mark of the 1912 election, Debs still managed to win 3 percent of the popular vote in states like Alabama and Kentucky. Elizabeth Sanders, *Roots of Reform: Farmers, Workers, and the American State, 1877–1917* (Chicago: University of Chicago Press, 1999), 61; James Green, *Grass Roots Socialism* (Baton Rouge: Louisiana State University Press, 1978), 12–52.

35. "Waiting for a Train" [1929]; "My Rough and Rowdy Ways" [1930]; "Away Out on the Mountain" [1928]; "Peach Pickin' Time in Georgia" [1932], Jimmie Rodgers, *Recordings: 1927–1933*, JSP Records, JSP 7704, 2002; Nolan Porterfield, *Jimmie Rodgers: The Life and Times of America's Blue Yodeler*, 2nd ed. (Urbana: University of Illinois Press, 1992), 6–7.

36. For a sense of this influence, see the essays in Mary Davis and Warren Zanes, eds., *Waiting for a Train: Jimmie Rodgers' America* (Burlington, MA: Rounder Books, 2009).

37. "Train Whistle Blues," Jimmie Rodgers, *Recordings: 1927–1933*, 2002 [1929].

38. "Pan American" [1947]; "I'm a Long Gone Daddy" [1947]; "Ramblin' Man" [1952], Hank Williams, *The Complete Hank Williams*, 1998. "Famous Song Composer Is Arrested Here," *Shreveport Times*, December 12, 1952. See also Williams, *Sing a Sad Song*, 38–42, 143.

39. H. B. Teeter, "Hank Williams Had Premonition of Death," *Nashville Tennessean*, January 2, 1953; Allen Rankin, "Rankin File: So Long, Hank. Hear You Later." *Montgomery Advertiser*, January 4, 1953; Charlie Lamb, liner notes to *Hank Williams Greatest Hits* (MGM Records E3918, 1961). Williams's singular reputation as a tragic figure—and a singer of tragic songs—would only grow over the course of his latter-day canonization as a "serious" musician. In awarding him a posthumous citation in 2010, for instance, the Pulitzer Prize Board would emphasize the special "poignancy" of Williams's music; and even the editor-academics of a recent anthology devoted to the singer's life and legacy seem most drawn to this version of the "melancholy life and tumultuous career" of the "hauntingly enigmatic" country star. *The 2010 Pulitzer Prize Winners: Special Awards and Citations*, Pulitzer Prize Board, available at http://www .pulitzer.org/citation/2010-Special-Awards-and-Citations, accessed January 14, 2015; Huber, Goodson, and Anderson, eds., *The Hank Williams Reader*, 6, 15.

40. All three songs were written or released within weeks of Williams' death, with "Jambalaya" topping the country charts as news of the tragedy broke and "Kaw-Liga" spending fourteen weeks at number one after it was released later in January 1953. For more on the humor of "I'll Never Get Out of This World Alive," see Fraser, "Lost Highways."

41. Myrtie Payne quoted in Horstman, *Sing Your Heart Out, Country Boy*, 367.

42. "Lost Highway," Williams.

43. "A Great Singer Passes," *Spokane Daily Chronicle*, January 8, 1953, quoted in Huber, Goodson, and Anderson, eds., *The Hank Williams Reader*, 68.

44. Pecknold, *The Selling Sound*, 70. "Highway of Sorrow," Bill Monroe, Decca 9 46369, 1951; "Highway to Nowhere," Jim Reeves, *Singing Down the Lane*, RCA Victor

1256, 1956: "Carroll County Accident," Porter Wagoner, RCA Victor, LSP-4116, 1969; "Highway Kind," Townes Van Zandt, *High, Low and In Between*, Poppy PYS 5700, 1972; "Route 65 to Nashville," Dottie West, *Carolina Cousins*, RCA Victor APL1-1041, 1975.

45. Malone, *Country Music, U.S.A.*, 183. For the commercial usages of hillbilly culture and the marketing of "authenticity" in early country music, see especially Richard A. Peterson, *Creating Country Music: Fabricating Authenticity* (Chicago: University of Chicago Press, 1997).

46. The U.S. Army survey results are reproduced in "Enlisted Men Prefer Music, News, Comedy," *Broadcasting*, October 5, 1942. It should be noted that all the soldiers polled in this survey were white. See also Max Horkheimer and Theodor W. Adorno, *Dialectic of Enlightenment* (New York: Seabury Press, 1972 [1944]), 120–25.

47. Pecknold's *The Selling Sound* is the best scholarly treatment of the emergence of the Nashville Sound that I have come across; equally detailed and rigorous, and benefiting from the perspective of an industry insider, is the extended discussion of the Nashville Sound producers and musicians in the second season of Tyler Mahan Coe's exemplary country music history podcast *Cocaine and Rhinestones*, released in 2022. See also Paul Hemphill, *The Nashville Sound: Bright Lights and Country Music* (New York: Simon & Schuster, 1970), Malone, *Country Music, U.S.A.*, 245–69; Jeffrey Lange, *Smile When You Call Me a Hillbilly: Country Music's Struggle for Respectability, 1939–1954* (Athens: University of Georgia Press, 2004), 198–221.

48. Wilgus, "Country-Western Music and the Urban Hillbilly," 173–74. The Atkins anecdote was repeated many times, and again in Atkins's obituary in the *New York Times*. Ben Ratliff, "Chet Atkins, 77, Is Dead; Guitarist and Producer Was Architect of the 'Nashville Sound,'" *New York Times*, July 2, 2001.

49. Horkheimer and Adorno, *Dialectic of Enlightenment*, 125–30.

50. Susan Stewart, *On Longing: Narratives of the Miniature, the Gigantic, the Souvenir, the Collection* (Durham, NC: Duke University Press, 1993), 23.

51. "Traveling the Highway Home," Kyle and Walter Bailes, *I've Got My One Way Ticket*, Old Homestead Records 70009, 1976 [1952]; "South on No. 23," Curly Dan & Wilma Ann, Happy Hearts 134-A, 1963; "Southern Bound," Kenny Price, *Southern Bound*, Boone BLPS-1214, 1968; "Highway Headin' South," Porter Wagoner, *Highway Headin' South*, RCA APL1-0713, 1974; "Take Me Home, Country Roads," John Denver, *Poems, Prayers, & Promises*, RCA Victor LSP 4499, 1971; "Long Black Limousine," Wynn Stewart, *The Challenge Years: 1958–1962*, Bear Family BFD 15261, 1988 [1958]; "Blue Kentucky Girl," Loretta Lynn, *Blue Kentucky Girl*, Decca DL 4665, 1965; "Gentle on My Mind," Glen Campbell, *Gentle on My Mind*, Capitol Records ST 2809, 1967.

52. "The Ballad of Barbara," Johnny Cash, Columbia 4-45890, 1973.

53. "Detroit City" [1963], "500 Miles Away from Home" [1963]; "The Streets of Baltimore" [1966], Bobby Bare, *The Best of Bobby Bare*, Razor & Tie, RE 2043, 1994.

54. In fairness to Bare, "Detroit City" was written by Danny Dill and Mel Tillis, two songwriters from states with actual experience in cotton production—Tennessee and Florida, respectively. For short biographical sketches of all three, see Paul Kingsbury, Michael McCall, and John W. Rumble, eds., *The Encyclopedia of Country Music: The Ultimate Guide to the Music*, 2nd ed. (New York: Oxford University Press, 2012).

55. On the imagery of the Confederacy in American country music, see, among others Melton A. McLaurin, "Songs of the South: The Changing Image of the South in Country Music," in *You Wrote My Life: Lyrical Themes in Country Music*, eds.

Melton A. McLaurin and Richard A. Peterson (Philadelphia: Gordon and Breach, 1992), 15–35; Malone, *Don't Get above Your Raisin'*, 210–53.

56. Letter from Fred M. Peterson, reprinted in "Listeners' Mike", *Stand By!*, February 16, 1935; Letter from Frank Keans, reprinted in "Listeners' Mike," *Stand By!*, March 16, 1935; Letter from Gene Jones, reprinted in "Listeners' Mike," *Stand By!*, December 14, 1935; Letter from Ida Haines, reprinted in "Listeners' Mike," *Stand By!*, November 30, 1935; Letter from an Ex-Cowboy, reprinted in "Listeners' Mike," *Stand By!*, November 27, 1937.

57. Interviews with "Colonel" Jim Wilson by John W. Rumble, February 17 and February 23, 1983, OHC329 and OHC330, Country Music Foundation. Wilson would leave his job at the Harmony music store in 1949 to become a salesman for King Records, where he covered an area that encompassed major markets in Detroit and Toledo, Ohio. Wilson worked on and off for King and later Starday Records through the mid-1970s.

58. Letters reprinted in Atelia Clarkson and W. Lynwood Montell, "Letters to a Bluegrass DJ: Social Documents of Southern White Migration in Southeastern Michigan, 1964–1974," *Southern Folklore Quarterly* 39, no. 3 (September 1975): 219, 223–25.

59. Alice Geber, "Hank Williams Lives in Uptown: The Southern Whites Have a Dream Called Hank Williams Village," *Uptown News*, September 11, 1968. See also Guy, *When Architecture Meets Activism*.

60. "The New Appeal of Country Music," *Broadcasting*, August 1, 1966; "Want a Sound of Your Own? Try C&W," *Broadcasting*, August 1, 1966.

61. "Country Is Spelled with '$', Not Cents," *Sponsor*, August 8, 1966; Pecknold, *The Selling Sound*, 143–61.

62. Williams Jr., "A Country Boy Can Survive." On the anti-urban tradition, see, for instance, Morton White and Lucia White, *The Intellectual versus the City: From Thomas Jefferson to Frank Lloyd Wright* (Cambridge, MA: Harvard University Press, 1962); and Steven Conn, *Americans against the City: Anti-Urbanism in the Twentieth Century* (New York: Oxford University Press, 2014). For contemporary assessments of this trend within country music, see Marc Landy, "Country Music: The Melody of Dislocation," *New South* 26 (Winter 1971): 67–69; and Ivan M. Tribe, "The Hillbilly versus the City: Urban Images in Country Music," *John Edwards Memorial Foundation Quarterly* 10, no. 34 (Summer 1974): 41–51.

63. "I Wouldn't Live in New York City (If They Gave Me the Whole Dang Town)," Buck Owens and His Buckaroos, *I Wouldn't Live in New York City*, Capitol Records ST628, 1970. On the Bakersfield scene, and particularly its relationship to the southern migration, see especially Gregory, *American Exodus*, 222–48; and La Chapelle, *Proud to Be an Okie*.

64. Landy, "Country Music: The Melody of Dislocation," 67–69.

65. The Wilburn Brothers, "The City's Goin' Country," Decca 33027, 1972. By 1965 *The Wilburn Brothers Show* was one of fourteen country music TV shows then available "in major cities coast-to-coast," according to *Billboard*. Claude Hall, "Country Television Programs Enjoying Coast-to-Coast Hayride," *Billboard*, November 13, 1965. *The Wilburn Brothers Show* show was also widely credited with launching the singing career of country superstar Loretta Lynn, who appeared on the program regularly between 1963 and 1971. See Loretta Lynn with George Vecsey, *Loretta Lynn: Coal Miner's Daughter* (New York: Warner Books, 1976), 129ff.

66. Landy, "Country Music: The Melody of Dislocation," 68.

67. Hemphill, *The Nashville Sound*, 110; Carter, *The Politics of Rage*, 363. The complete lyrics to "Bring Our Country Back"—written by Fred LaRue, a Texas-born aide to Nixon who would later serve time in prison for his role in the Watergate cover-up—appear in Joe McGinniss, *The Selling of the President*, 2nd ed. (New York: Penguin Books 1988 [1969]), 113.

68. Willams, *Sing a Sad Song*, 242.

69. Marty Funke, "Doc Wallace's Revue," *The Heights*, October 15, 1968; see also, for example, James T. Wooten, "16,000 in Madison Square Garden Cheer Wallace's Third-Party Candidacy," *New York Times*, October 25, 1968.

70. Allen Tullos, "Figures of Speech—Can a Country Boy Survive?" *Southern Changes* 4, no. 3 (1982): 2.

71. Tom Piazza, "Still Standing Tall Over Country," *New York Times*, November 8, 1998.

72. A notable exception might be Greil Marcus's essay on Elvis Presley in *Mystery Train: Images of America in Rock 'n' Roll Music*, 2nd ed. (New York: E.P. Dutton, 1982 [1975]), esp. 150–53. Marcus also describes Williams as a "tragic" artist, "a poet of limits, fear, and failure" whose unrivalled influence over subsequent generations of country musicians helped ensure the music's continued "withdrawing into itself"; while Presley and the other rockabilly innovators reached across the racial and rural-urban divide to give rise to a "music for the whole community." Although Marcus does not discuss politics directly in the essay, the divergent paths taken by Williams's country and Presley's rock 'n' roll are obvious musical stand-ins for the divisive regional and cultural politics of the period. For a survey of the more conventional critical and scholarly assessments of Hank Williams's cultural and political influence, see the essays and remembrances excerpted in Parts VI and VII of Huber, Goodson, and Anderson, eds., *The Hank Williams Reader*.

73. Chilton Williamson Jr., "Country & Western Marxism: To the Nashville Station," *National Review*, June 9, 1978, 711–16.

74. Wallace quoted in Edsall and Edsall, *Chain Reaction*, 77; Ritter quoted in Pecknold, *The Selling Sound*, 157.

75. For an astute treatment of the relationship between country music and a burgeoning conservative political culture in Southern California, see Gregory, *American Exodus*, ch. 8.

76. Watson quoted in Malone, *Don't Get above Your Raisin'*, 215; Hall quoted on 147.

77. Wilgus, "Country-Western Music and the Urban Hillbilly," 157, 173.

78. Williams Jr., "A Country Boy Can Survive," Elektra SE-535, 1981; on the "enduring influence" of Hank Williams Jr., see, among others, David Cantwell, "The Awkward, Enduring Influence of Hank Williams, Jr.," *New Yorker*, March 24, 2016.

79. "Johnny Cash Loath to Sing 'Cadilac' at the White House," *New York Times*, March 31, 1970; Daniel Geary, "'The Way I Would Feel about San Quentin': Johnny Cash and the Politics of Country Music," *Daedalus* 142, no. 4 (Fall 2013): 64–72; Gregory, *The Southern Diaspora*, 5, 315–16.

80. A catalogue of contemporary examples of this tendency must include—in some measure, begin with—Robert Altman's brilliant if deeply cynical takedown of county music, *Nashville*, released in 1975, which in many ways solidified the popular

association between country's crassly manipulative displays of patriotic excess during the Vietnam War era and the political gullibility of its hick audience. See a good discussion of the movie and its representation of the country music–consuming masses in Pecknold, *The Selling Sound*, ch. 6; as well as Max Fraser, "Country Music Capital," *Dissent* (Winter 2016): 15–19. Other popular as well as scholarly examples from the period include Jens Lund, "Fundamentalism, Racism and Political Reaction in Country Music," and Paul Di Maggio, Richard A. Peterson, and Jack Esco Jr., "Country Music: Ballad of the Silent Majority," both in R. Serge Denisoff and Richard A. Peterson, *The Sounds of Social Change: Studies in Popular Culture* (Chicago: Rand McNally, 1972); Florence King, "Red Necks, White Socks, and Blue Ribbon Fear," *Harper's*, July 1974, 30–34; Hemphill, *The Nashville Sound*. On Merle Haggard and the political response to "Okie from Muskogee," see Paul Hemphill, "Merle Haggard," *Atlantic Monthly*, September 1971, 98–103.

# Conclusion

1. Hurley Goodall and Elizabeth Campbell, "A City Apart," in *The Other Side of Muncie: Exploring Muncie's African-American Community*, eds. Luke Eric Lassiter, Hurley Goodall, Elizabeth Campbell, and Michelle Natasya Johnson (Walnut Creek: AltaMira Press, 2004), 68–69; see also "Muncie Pastors Look for Racial Solutions," *Muncie Evening Press*, May 27, 1968.

2. Hurley Goodall for the Muncie Human Rights Commission, "Chronological History of the Southside High School Racial Situation," unpublished manuscript with editorial markings (March 6, 1968). Black Muncie History Project Records, Box 2, Folder 21, Archives and Special Collections, Alexander M. Bracken Library, Ball State University, Muncie, IN; Indiana State Advisory Committee to the United States Commission on Civil Rights and Subcommittee of the Indiana Civil Rights Commission, "Report on Racial Antagonism at Southside High School in Muncie, Indiana" (April 24, 1968). Southside High School Racial Situation Reports, 1968 (SC 163), Folder 1, Stoeckel Archives of Local History, Bracken Library.

3. "Plaintiffs' Post-Trial Brief," in *David Banks, a minor by his mother and next friend Mrs. Rosemary Banks, et. al., vs. Muncie Community Schools, et. al.*, No. IP 69-C-79, filed in U.S. District Court, Indianapolis Division (July 18, 1969). Proposed Northwest High School, 1969 (SC 422), Folder 1, Bracken Library.

4. Sharon Brown, oral history interview with author, March 18, 2015, Jamestown, Tennessee; audio recording and transcript in author's possession.

5. "Ku Klux Klan Plans 'Street Walk' in Muncie," *Terre Haute Tribune*, February 18, 1968. The two quotes from the Black teenagers are found in Dr. Lester Hewitt et al., "Report on the Willard—Hackley Neighborhood," unpublished report (October 8, 1970). Harry L. Gudger civil rights in Indiana reports, 1968–1989 (SC 17), Folder 1, Bracken Library.

6. Jim Delk, oral history interview with author, March 24, 2016, Muncie, Indiana; audio recording and transcript in author's possession.

7. The hiring preference clause was first written into Local 287's 1945 contract and appears in all subsequent contracts until the 1971 agreement, in which it was replaced with an "Equal Employment Rights" clause. See various contracts, Local

287 Records, Box 1, Folder: Agreements—1945, and Folder: Agreements 1964–1971, Bracken Library. Local 287 maintained its restrictive hiring practices throughout these years over the objections of the national leadership of the UAW, Muncie's local civil rights movement, and the federal government; a description of the various efforts to remove the hiring clause is included in Hurley Goodall, "Biographical Sketch: Rev. Anthony J. Oliver, Sr." (May 1978). Black Muncie History Project, Box 2, Folder 8, Bracken Library. For the Warner-Gear workforce numbers, see Larry Shores, "Warner Gear Gets Pact," *Muncie Star*, March 22, 1972.

8. See maps and data-sets produced by ACTION, Inc., "City Target Areas, Social Action Programs 1971–1972," Box 2, Folder 23; and handwritten charts (n.d.), Black Muncie History Project Records, Box 2, Folder 15, Bracken Library.

9. See, for instance, Jonathan Rieder, *Canarsie: The Jews and Italians of Brooklyn Against Liberalism* (Cambridge, MA: Harvard University Press, 1985), and Ronald P. Formisano, *Boston Against Busing: Race, Class, and Ethnicity in the 1960s and 1970s* (Chapel Hill: University of North Carolina Press, 1991).

10. On the effects of deindustrialization on Muncie and especially the southside, see, among others, Max Fraser, "Down and Out in the New Middletowns," *Dissent* 59, no. 1 (Winter 2012): 27–34.

11. Cooley quoted in Douglas E. Kneeland, "Watergate Is Remote to Muncie," *New York Times*, April 25, 1973. State- and county-level election returns for elections cited above are from Secretary of the State of Indiana, *General Election Report of the Secretary of State of the State of Indiana, [Various Years]: General Election Statistics* and *Primary Election Statistics*. Indiana State Agency Documents, Indiana Division, Indiana State Library (Indianapolis, IN).

12. Secretary of the State of Illinois, *Official Vote Cast at the General Election, November 5, 1968, Judicial; Primary Election, General Primary, June 11, 1968*. Illinois State Library (Springfield, IL). See also M. Margaret Conway, "The White Backlash Re-examined: Wallace and the 1964 Primaries," *Social Science Quarterly* 49, no. 3 (December 1968): esp. 710–11.

13. For a discussion of the Macomb County Studies, and the important distinctions between the "Reagan Democrat" and the Transappalachian working class, see Stanley B. Greenberg, *Middle Class Dreams: The Politics and Power of the New American Majority* (New York: Times Books, 1995), 23ff; and Stanley Greenberg, "Unlearning the Lessons of *Hillbilly Elegy*," *The American Prospect* (Winter 2019): 42–49. Manufacturing job loss figures for Muncie and the wider Midwest are drawn from Aaron M. Malone, "Middletown No More? Globalization and the Declining Positionality of Muncie, Indiana" (MA thesis, Ohio University, 2010), 39; and Teresa C. Fort, Justin R. Pierce, and Peter K. Schott, "New Perspectives on the Decline of US Manufacturing Employment," *Journal of Economic Perspectives* 32, no. 2 (Spring 2018): 64.

14. The nickname was used commonly by General Motors workers and appeared frequently in media accounts at the time, despite its incorporation of an offensive term. See, for example, Don Lee, "'Gypsies' Travel to Keep GM Pension," *Los Angeles Times*, April 11, 1996, and Fred O. Williams and David Robinson, "General Motors' Gypsies: GM's Workers Stay Mobile to Keep Jobs," *The Buffalo News*, October 26, 1997. Tony Ball quoted in Fraser, "Down and Out in the New Middletowns."

# Archival Material

## ALEXANDER M. BRACKEN LIBRARY, BALL
## STATE UNIVERSITY, MUNCIE, INDIANA.

Archives and Special Collections.
  –Black Muncie History Project Papers (MSS.033).
  –Stoeckel Archives of Local History.
  –UAW-CIO Local 287 Records and Photographs (1935–2015) (MSS.165).
  –Warner Gear Division Collection (1918, 1928, 1946, 1976–1991) (MSS.178).

## CENTER FOR DOCUMENTARY RESEARCH AND
## PRACTICE, INDIANA UNIVERSITY,
## BLOOMINGTON, INDIANA.

Oral History Archive.
  –Generations of Auto Workers: Anderson, Indiana (042).
    –Davis, Ted (82-12-1).
    –Hensley, James (82-58-1,2).
    –Poteet, George (82-55-1,2).
    –Wilson, Joseph (82–015).
  –History: Stringtown, Indiana (059).
    –Dix, Charles H. (76-19-1).
    –Grubbs, Stephen C. (76-23-1).
    –Lewis, Nannie, and Mary Willoughby (76-25-1).
    –Malott, Anne (76-30-1,2).
    –Phelps, Richard (76-21-1).
    –Tapp, Barbara, and Michael J. Tapp (76-22-1,2).
  –Indiana Labor History Project (062).
    –Gupton, Lucian, and Jane Gupton (96-67-1).

## CHARLES C. SHERROD LIBRARY, EAST TENNESSEE
## STATE UNIVERSITY, JOHNSON CITY, TENNESSEE.

Archives of Appalachia.
  –Congress for Appalachian Development: Gordon Ebersole Collection (MS74).
  –Dante History Project Records (MS538).
    –Blackstone, Raiford.
    –Carter, Gladys.
    –Castle, Roy.
    –Cook, Emory.

–Gyetvay, Elizabeth, Betty Sabo, Rose White, Lucille Whitaker, and Ponnie Sabo.
–Hayes, Margie.
–Phillips, Clarence.
–Urban Appalachian Council Collection (MS11).

### FORREST C. POGUE LIBRARY, MURRAY STATE UNIVERSITY, MURRAY, KENTUCKY.

Special Collection and Archives.
–Brooks Bus Line Records (MS87).

### FRANCES WILLSON THOMPSON LIBRARY, UNIVERSITY OF MICHIGAN-FLINT, FLINT, MICHIGAN.

Genesee Historical Collections Center.
–Labor History Project Collection.
–Bully, Norman.
–Crane, Cloyse.
–Cregar, Merrill.
–Echard, Peggy and Melvin.
–Havrilla, Andrew.

### FRANCIS S. HUTCHINS LIBRARY, BEREA COLLEGE, BEREA, KENTUCKY.

Special Collections and Archives.
–Council of the Southern Mountains Records, 1912–1970 (BCA 0002 SAA 001).
–Urban Appalachian Council Records (BCA 0151 SAA 160).

### FRIST LIBRARY AND ARCHIVE, COUNTRY MUSIC HALL OF FAME AND MUSEUM, NASHVILLE, TENNESSEE.

Oral History Project Collection.
–Cisler, Stephen (OH59).
–Glover, Henry (OHC128).
–Hopkins, Doc (OH74).
–Kincaid, Bradley (OH83; OH332).
–Wilson, Jim (OH329; OH330).

### LOUIS ROUND WILSON LIBRARY, UNIVERSITY OF NORTH CAROLINA, CHAPEL HILL, NORTH CAROLINA.

Southern Historical Collection.
–Southern Oral History Program Collection. (4007).
–Arnow, Harriette (G-0006).

## MARGARET I. KING LIBRARY, UNIVERSITY OF KENTUCKY, LEXINGTON, KENTUCKY.

Special Collections Research Center.
 –Appalachian Regional Commission Records, 1958–2010. (90M1).
 –James S. Brown Papers, 1917–2005 (MS354).


## MCCRACKEN COUNTY PUBLIC LIBRARY, PADUCAH, KENTUCKY.

Local and Family History Room.
 –Brooks Bus Line vertical file.
 –Roth Funeral Home (Paducah, KY) Records.


## TENNESSEE STATE LIBRARY AND ARCHIVES, NASHVILLE, TENNESSEE.

 –Jennings Funeral Home (Jamestown, TN) Records.


## UNIVERSITY LIBRARIES, THE UNIVERSITY OF AKRON, AKRON, OHIO.

Special Collections and Regional History Collections.
 –Daniel Nelson Collection.
 –Goodyear Tire & Rubber Company Records (99/106).
 –United Rubber Workers (URW) Local 5 Records.


## WALTER P. REUTHER LIBRARY OF LABOR AND URBAN AFFAIRS, WAYNE STATE UNIVERSITY, DETROIT, MICHIGAN.

 –Detroit Commission on Community Relations/Human Rights Department Records (UR000267).
 –George B. Roberts Papers (LP000038).
 –Lewis B. Larkin Papers (WSP000112).
 –Michael J. Manning Collection (LP000018).
 –UAW Local 78 Collection (LP000645).
 –UAW Local 174 Records (LP00006).
 –UAW Oral Histories (LOH002229).
     –DiGaetano, Nick (WPR 0479).
     –Jones, Lloyd (WPR 0479).
 –UAW President's Office: Homer Martin Records (LR000063).
 –UAW President's Office: Walter P. Reuther Records (LR000261).
 –UAW Secretary Treasurer's Office: George Addes Records (LR00052).

## Oral Histories

All the following oral histories were conducted by the author. Audio recordings and transcripts remain in the author's possession.

–Anderson, Leonard, and Libby Anderson (March 18, 2015).
–Andrews, Elaine (March 23, 2015).
–Brown, Sharon (March 18, 2015).
–John Campbell (March 27, 2015).
–Campbell, Willene Nunley (March 27, 2015).
–Copeland, Joyce (March 19, 2015).
–Cowan, Richard (March 19, 2015).
–Crouch, Joyce (March 16, 2015).
–Delk, Jim (March 24, 2016).
–Guffey, Mabel (March 16, 2015).
–Garrett, Kirby (March 18, 2016).
–Hargis, Franklin (March 19, 2015).
–Harris, Jim, and Sue Crabtree (March 18, 2016).
–Hennessey, De (March 25, 2015).
–Hicks, Omer, and Amanda Hicks (March 19, 2015).
–Hill, Carla (April 1, 2015).
–Hoover, Betty (March 24, 2016).
–Hurd, Frances (March 20, 2015).
–Johnson, Shannon, Phyllis Johnson, and Dana Peters (March 17, 2016).
–Jones, Loyal (January 17, 2015).
–Jusko, Jonna (March 17, 2015).
–Kirkendall, Ernestine (March 27, 2015).
–Layne, Sherman (March 26, 2015).
–Lehman, Martha (March 15, 2016).
–Lewis, Kenny, and Jean Koons (March 16, 2016).
–Moore, Nadene Fultz (March 27, 2015).
–Myers, Barbara (March 27, 2015).
–Myers, Gene (March 23, 2015).
–Newsome, Wanda (March 24, 2015).
–Nunley, Forrest David (March 26, 2015).
–Owens, Ray (March 17, 2015).
–Reagan, Wesley (March 18, 2015).
–Rigsby, Loretta (March 24, 2016).
–Sells, Helen (March 17, 2015).
–Smith, Juanita (March 15, 2016).
–Taylor, Janelle (March 26, 2015).
–Voiles, Doug (April 3, 2015).
–Wheeley, Caren Crabtree (March 17, 2015).
–Wilson, David, and Susan Wilson (March 23, 2015).

## Periodicals

*Akron Beacon Journal*
*Alexandria Times-Tribune*
*The American Prospect*
*Appalachia*
*Associated Press*
*Atlantic Monthly*
*Billboard*
*Broadcasting*
*Bus Industry*
*Bus Ride*
*The Call Leader*
*Campbell County Times*
*The Catholic Telegraph-Register*
*Chicago*
*Chicago Daily News*
*Chicago Tribune*
*Cincinnati Enquirer*
*Class Struggle*
*Cleveland Press*
*Daily Mountain Eagle*
*Detroit Free Press*
*Detroit News*
*Dissent*
*Gear O'Gram*
*Harper's*
*The Heights*
*Indianapolis Star*
*Knoxville Journal*
*The Labor Beacon*
*Life*
*Louisville Courier-Journal*
*McClure's*
*Montgomery Advertiser*
*Monthly Labor Review*
*Morgan County News*
*Mountain Life and Work*
*Muncie Evening Press*
*Muncie Star*
*Muncie Star Press*
*Nashville Tennessean*
*The Nation*
*National Review*
*Nation's Business*
*New City*
*The New Republic*

*New York*
*New York Journal*
*New York Times*
*New Yorker*
*Newsweek*
*Paducah Sun*
*Paducah Sun-Democrat*
*Pickett County Press*
*The Reporter*
*Saturday Evening Post*
*Shreveport Times*
*Sponsor*
*Stand By!*
*The Student Outlook*
*Survey*
*Terre Haute Tribune*
*Textile Labor*
*Upper Cumberland Times*
*Variety*
*Wall Street Journal*
*Wheeling Register*
*Wingfoot Clan*

## Published Primary Sources

Beede, Kenneth C. "Housing Market Analysis for Akron, Ohio." Prepared for the Federal Housing Administration, Washington, DC, 1938.

Nelson, Robert K., LaDale Winling, Richard Marciano, Nathan Connolly, et al. "Mapping Inequality: Redlining in New Deal America, 1935–1940." In *American Panorama: An Atlas of United States History*, edited by Robert K. Nelson and Edward L. Ayers. Digital Scholarship Lab, University of Richmond, accessible at https://dsl.richmond.edu/panorama.

Ohio Advisory Committee, United States Commission on Civil Rights. *Policing in Cincinnati, Ohio: Official Policy and Vs. Civilian Reality*. Cincinnati, OH, 1981.

President's Appalachian Regional Commission. *Appalachia: A Report*. Washington, DC, 1964.

President's National Advisory Commission on Rural Poverty. *Rural Poverty in the United States*. Washington, DC, 1968.

Resettlement Administration. *What the Resettlement Administration Has Done*. Washington, DC, 1936.

Secretary of the State of Illinois. *Official Vote Cast at the General Election, November 5, 1968*. Springfield, IL, 1968.

Secretary of the State of Indiana. *General Election Report of the Secretary of State of the State of Indiana: General Election Statistics* and *Primary Election Statistics*. Indianapolis, IN, various years.

Stern, Boris. "Labor Productivity in the Automobile Tire Industry." Bulletin No. 585, Washington, DC, 1933.

Stone, Ralph W. "Coal Mining at Dante, VA." In *Contributions to Economic Geology, 1906*.

Student Health Organization of Chicago and Presbyterian-St. Luke's Hospital. *Chicago Student Health Project—Summer 1968*. Prepared for the Health Services and Mental Health Administration, Bethesda, MD, 1970.

United States Congress, Senate, Committee on Labor and Public Welfare.

*Hearings Before the Subcommittee on Employment, Manpower, and Poverty: Examining the War on Poverty*. Washington, DC, 1967.

United States Department of Agriculture.

> Anderson, Andrew P. "Rural Highway Mileage, Income, and Expenditures: 1921 and 1922." Bulletin No. 1279, Washington, DC, 1925.

> *Economic and Social Problems and Conditions of the Southern Appalachians*. Miscellaneous Publications No. 205, Washington, DC, 1935.

United States Department of Commerce, Bureau of the Census.

> *Thirteenth Census of the United States: 1910*. Washington, DC, 1914.

> *Census of Agriculture: 1925*. Washington, DC, 1927.

> *Fifteenth Census of the United States: 1930*. Washington, DC, 1932.

> *Sixteenth Census of the United States: 1940*. Washington, DC, 1944.

> *Census of Agriculture: 1945*. Washington, DC, 1946.

> *Historical Statistics of the United States, 1789-1945*. Washington, DC, 1949.

> *Census of Agriculture: 1950*. Washington, DC, 1952.

> *Census of Agriculture: 1954*. Washington, DC, 1956.

> *Census of Mineral Industries: 1954*. Washington, DC, 1958.

> *Census of Agriculture: 1959*. Washington, DC, 1962.

> *Census of the Population: 1960*. Washington, DC, 1962.

> "Historical Census Statistics on Population Totals by Race, 1790 to 1990, and by Hispanic Origin, 1970 to 1990, for the United States, Regions, Divisions, and Sates." Population Division Working Paper No. 56, Washington, DC, 2022.

United States Department of Commerce, Bureau of Mines.

> *Mineral Resources of the United States: 1927*. Washington, DC, 1929.

> *Mineral Resources of the United States: 1929*. Washington, DC, 1932.

> *Mineral Resources of the United States: 1931*. Washington, DC, 1933.

United States Department of the Interior.

> *Mineral Resources of the United States, 1911*. Washington, DC, 1912.

> *Mineral Resources of the United States, 1912*. Washington, DC, 1913.

> *Mineral Resources of the United States, 1921*. Washington, DC, 1924.

> *Mineral Resources of the United States, 1922*. Washington, DC, 1925.

> *Coal Resources of Virginia*. Geological Survey Circular 171. Washington, DC, 1952.

United States Department of Labor, Bureau of Labor Statistics.

United States Geological Survey Bulletin 316-A. Washington, DC, 1907.

> "War and Postwar Wages, Prices, and Hours, 1914–23 and 1939–44." Bulletin No. 852. Washington, DC, 1945.

White, Walter, and Thurgood Marshall. "What Caused the Detroit Riot?: An Analysis." Prepared for the National Association for the Advancement of Colored People, New York, July 1943.

Wentworth, Chester K. "The Geological and Coal Resources of Russell County, Virginia." Virginia Geological Survey Bulletin No. 22. Charlottesville, VA, 1922.

## Unpublished Dissertations, Thesis, Conference Papers

Alexander, J. Trent. "Great Migrations: Race and Community in the Southern Exodus, 1917–1970." PhD diss., Carnegie Mellon University, 2002.

Brown, James S. "Social Organization of an Isolated Kentucky Mountain Neighborhood." PhD diss., Harvard University, 1950.

———. "The Southern Appalachians and the Nation: A Tightening Web of Relationships." Paper delivered at the 51st Annual Conference of the Council of the Southern Mountains, Gatlinburg, Tennessee, February 1963.

———. "The Appalachian Family: A Somewhat Detailed Description of a Nonexistent Phenomenon." Paper delivered at the Annual Meeting of the Commission on Religion in Appalachia, Charleston, West Virginia, October 1967.

Crowder, Daniel Boyd. "Profile in Progress: A History of Local 287, UAW-CIO." PhD diss., Ball State University, 1969.

Hunter, Devin. "Growing Diversity: Urban Renewal, Community Activism, and the Politics of Cultural Diversity in Uptown, Chicago, 1940–1970." PhD diss., Loyola University Chicago, 2015.

Johnson, Susan Allyn. "Industrial Voyagers: A Case Study of Appalachian Migration to Akron, Ohio, 1900–1940." PhD diss., The Ohio State University, 2006.

Jones, Carmel L. "Migration, Religion, and Occupational Mobility of Southern Appalachians in Muncie, Indiana." EdD diss., Ball State University, 1978.

Malone, Aaron M. "Middletown No More? Globalization and the Declining Positionality of Muncie, Indiana." MA thesis, Ohio University, 2010.

Maples, John Lee. "The Akron, Ohio Ku Klux Klan, 1921–1928." MA thesis, University of Akron, 1974.

Montgomery, Jesse Ambrose. "Storming Hillbilly Heaven: The Young Patriot's Organization, Radical Chicago, and the Long Battle for Uptown, Chicago." PhD diss., Vanderbilt University, 2020.

Rosswurm, Kevin. "A Strike in the Rubber City: Akron, Rubber Workers, and the IWW, 1913." MA thesis, Kent State University, 1975.

Smith, Timothy J., II, and Tom Des Jean. "The Geography of Illegal Distillery Sites in the Big South Fork National River and Recreation Area." Paper delivered at the 20th Annual Meeting of the Current Research in Tennessee Archaeology Conference, Nashville, Tennessee, 2007.

Thompson, John Leslie. "Industrialization in the Miami Valley: A Case Study of Interregional Migration." PhD diss., University of Wisconsin–Madison, 1955.

Udell, Gerald. "The Speech of Akron, Ohio: The Segmental Phonology—A Study of the Effects of Rapid Industrialization on the Speech of a Community." PhD diss., University of Chicago, 1966.

Ylvisaker, Paul. "The University in a Changing Urban Environment." Paper delivered at the 44th Annual Meeting of the Association of Urban Universities, Omaha, Nebraska, November 1958.

## *Recordings*

Acuff, Roy. "Wreck on the Highway." OKeh 6585, 1942, shellac.

Bailes, Kyle, and Walter. "Traveling the Highway Home." *I've Got My One Way Ticket*. Old Homestead Records 70009, 1976 [1952].

Bare, Bobby. "Detroit City." *Detroit City and Other Hits*. RCA Victor LSP-2776, 1963, vinyl.

——. "500 Miles Away from Home." *500 Miles Away from Home*. RCA Victor LPM-2835, 1963, vinyl.

——. "The Streets of Baltimore." *The Streets of Baltimore*. RCA Victor LSP-3618, 1966, vinyl.

Campbell, Glen. "Gentle on My Mind." *Gentle on My Mind*. Capitol Records ST 2809, 1967, vinyl.

Cash, Johnny. "Folsom Prison Blues." *With His Hot and Blue Guitar*. Sun LP 1220, 1957, vinyl.

——. "The Ballad of Barbara." *The Last Gunfighter Ballad*. Columbia Records KC 34314, 1977, vinyl.

Dalhart, Vernon. "The Wreck of the Old '97." Victor 19427, 1924, shellac.

Dan, Curly & Wilma Ann and the Danville Mountain Boys. "South on No. 23." Happy Hearts Records HH-134, 1963, vinyl.

——. "North on 23." Fortune Records F-228, 1965, vinyl.

Denver, John. "Take Me Home, Country Roads." *Poems, Prayers, & Promises*. RCA Victor LSP 4449, 1971, vinyl.

Dixon Brothers, The. "I Didn't Hear Nobody Pray." *Dixon Brothers Volume 3: 1937–1938*. Document, 8048, 2000 [1937], compact disc.

Dixon, Nancy, Dorsey and Howard. "Babies in the Mill." *Babies in the Mill: Carolina Traditional, Industrial, Sacred Songs*. Testament Records 3301, 1962, vinyl.

Earle, Steve. "Hillbilly Highway." *Guitar Town*. MCA Records MCA-5713, 1986, vinyl.

——. "Snake Oil." *Copperhead Road*. UNI Records UNID-7, 1998, compact disc.

——. "Schertz, Texas (Monologue)." *Just an American Boy*. Artmemis Records 51256, 2003, compact disc.

Lynn, Loretta. "Blue Kentucky Girl." *Blue Kentucky Girl*. Decca DL 4665, 1965, vinyl.

Monroe, Bill. "Highway of Sorrow." Decca 9 46369, 1951, vinyl.

Owens, Buck, and His Buckaroos. "I Wouldn't Live in New York City (If They Gave Me the Whole Dang Town." *I Wouldn't Live in New York City*. Capitol Records ST628, 1970, vinyl.

Price, Kenny. "Southern Bound." *Southern Bound*. Boone BLPS-1214, 1968, vinyl.

Reeves, Jim. "Highway to Nowhere." *Singing Down the Lane*. RCA Victor 1256, 1956.

Rodgers, Jimmie. *Recordings 1927–1933*. JSP Records JSP 7704, 2002, compact disc.

——. "Away Out on the Mountain." [1928].

——. "Waiting for a Train." [1929].

——. "My Rough and Rowdy Ways." [1930].

——. "Train Whistle Blues." [1930].

——. "Peach Pickin' Time in Georgia." [1932].

Seeger, Pete. "Weave Room Blues." *Folk Songs for Young People*. Folkways Records 7532, 1959, vinyl.

Stewart, Wynn. "Long Black Limousine." *The Challenge Years: 1958–1962*. Bear Family Records BFD 15261, 1988 [1958], compact disc.

Tanner, Gid, and His Skillet Lickers. "Boll Weevil Blues." Columbia Records 15016D-81604, 1924, shellac.

Van Zandt, Townes. "Highway Kind." *High, Low and In Between*. Poppy PYS 5700, 1972, vinyl.

Wagoner, Porter. "The Carroll County Accident." *The Carroll County Accident*. RCA Victor LSP-4116, 1969, vinyl.

———. "Highway Headin' South." *Highway Headin' South*. RCA Victor APL1-0713, 1974, vinyl.

West, Dottie. "Route 65 to Nashville." *Carolina Cousins*. RCA Victor APL1-1041, 1975, vinyl.

Whitter, Henry. "Lonesome Road Blues." OKeh Records 40015-A, 1924, shellac.

Wilburn Brothers, The. "The City's Goin' Country." Decca 33027, 1972, vinyl.

Williams, Hank. *The Complete Hank Williams*. Mercury 314 536 007-2, 1998, compact disc.

———. "I'm a Long Gone Daddy." [1947].

———. "Pan American." [1947].

———. "Lost Highway." [1949].

———. "I'll Never Get Out of This World Alive." [1952].

———. "Jambalaya (On the Bayou)." [1952].

———. "Kaw-Liga." [1952].

———. "The Log Train." [1952].

———. "Ramblin' Man." [1953].

Williams, Hank, Jr. "A Country Boy Can Survive." *The Pressure Is On*. Elektra SE-535, 1981, vinyl.

Yoakam, Dwight. "Readin', Rightin', Rt. 23." *Hillbilly Deluxe*. Reprise 9 25567-2, 1987, compact disc.

## Books and Journal Articles

Abbott, Lynn. "'Play That Barber Shop Chord': A Case for the African-American Origin of Barbershop Harmony." *American Music* 10, no. 3 (Autumn 1992): 289–325.

Alexander, J. Trent. "'They're Never Here More Than a Year': Return Migration in the Southern Exodus, 1940–1970." *Journal of Social History* 38, no. 3 (Spring 2005): 653–71.

Alston, Lee J. "Farm Foreclosure Rates in the United States during the Interwar Period." *Journal of Economic History* 43, no. 4 (December 1983): 885–903.

Arnow, Harriette. *The Dollmaker*. New York: Avon, 1972 [1954].

Ayers, Edward L. *The Promise of the New South: Life After Reconstruction*. New York: Oxford University Press, 1992.

Barrell, John. *The Dark Side of the Landscape: The Rural Poor in English Painting, 1730–1840*. Cambridge: Cambridge University Press, 1980.

Bell, Daniel. *The End of Ideology: On the Exhaustion of Political Ideas in the Fifties*. New York: Free Press, 1960.

Bensel, Richard Franklin. *The Political Economy of American Industrialization, 1877–1900*. New York: Cambridge University Press, 2000.

Bernstein, Irving. *The Lean Years: A History of the American Worker, 1920–1933*. Boston: Houghton Mifflin, 1960.

Berry, Chad. *Southern Migrants, Northern Exiles*. Urbana: University of Illinois Press, 2000.

———. "Southern White Migration to the Midwest: An Overview." In *Appalachian Odyssey: Historical Perspectives on the Great Migration*, edited by Phillip J. Obermiller, Thomas E. Wagner, and E. Bruce Tucker, 3–26. Westport, CT: Praeger, 2000.

Bethel, Elizabeth Rauh. *Promiseland: A Century of Life in a Negro Community*. Columbia: University of South Carolina Press, 1997 [1981].

Beynon, Erdmann Doane. "The Southern White Laborer Migrates to Michigan." *American Sociological Review* 3, no. 3 (June 1938): 333–43.

Birmingham, Frederic Alexander. *Ball Corporation: The First Century*. Indianapolis: Curtis Publishing, 1980.

Boles, Frank. "Walter Reuther and the Kelsey-Hayes Strike of 1936." *Detroit in Perspective* 4 (Winter 1980): 74–90.

Bontemps, Arna, and Jack Conroy. *Anyplace But Here*. New York: Hill and Wang, 1966 [1945].

Branscome, James. "The Federal Government in Appalachia: TVA." In *Colonialism in Modern America: The Appalachian Case*, edited by Helen Matthews Lewis, Linda Johnson, and Donald Askins, 283–94. Boone: Appalachian Consortium Press, 1978.

Brauer, Carl M. "Kennedy, Johnson, and the War on Poverty." *The Journal of American History* 69, no. 1 (June 1982): 98–119.

Brecher, Jeremy. *Strike! Revised and Updated Edition*. Cambridge, MA: South End Press, 1997.

Bricker, Richard W. *Muncie, Indiana: Hard Times and Good Times from 1925 through 1950*. Shoeacres, TX: Self-published, 2010.

Brinkley, Alan. *Voices of Protest: Huey Long, Father Coughlin and the Great Depression*. New York: Vintage Books, 1983.

Brody, David. *Steelworkers in America: The Nonunion Era*. Cambridge, MA: Harvard University Press, 1960.

———. *Workers in Industrial America*. New York: Oxford University Press, 1980.

Brooks, Ora. *Brooks Bus Line: No "Common Carrier"*. Self-published, 1985.

Brown, James S., and George A. Hillery Jr. "The Great Migration: 1940–1960." In *The Southern Appalachian Region: A Survey*, edited by Thomas R. Ford, 54–78. Lexington: University of Kentucky Press, 1962.

Brown, James S., Harry K. Schwarzweller, and Joseph J. Mangalam. "Kentucky Mountain Migration and the Stem-family: An American Variation on a Theme by Le Play." *Rural Sociology* 28, no. 1 (March 1963): 48–69.

Burnham, Robert A. "The Mayor's Friendly Relations Committee: Cultural Pluralism and the Struggle for Black Advancement." In *Race and the City: Work, Community, and Protest in Cincinnati, 1820–1970*, edited by Henry Louis Taylor Jr., 258–79. Urbana: University of Illinois Press, 1993.

Callahan, Richard J., Jr. *Work and Faith in the Kentucky Coal Fields: Subject to Dust*. Bloomington: Indiana University Press, 2009.

Campbell, John C. *The Southern Highlander and His Homeland*. New York: Russell Sage Foundation, 1921.

Campbell, Olive Dame, and Cecil Sharp. *English Folk Songs from the Southern Appalachians: Comprising 122 Songs and Ballads and 323 Tunes*. New York: G.P. Putnam's Sons, 1917.

Cannon, James. *Speeches for Socialism*. New York: Pathfinder Press, 2008 [1969].

Capeci, Dominic J., Jr., and Martha Wilkerson. *Layered Violence: The Detroit Rioters of 1943*. Jackson: University Press of Mississippi, 2009.

Capozzola, Christopher. *Uncle Sam Wants You: World War I and the Making of the Modern American Citizen*. New York: Oxford University Press, 2008.

Carawan, Guy, and Candie Carawan. *Voices from the Mountains*. New York: Alfred A. Knopf, 1975.

Carter, Dan T. *The Politics of Rage: George Wallace, the Origins of the New Conservatism, and the Transformation of American Politics*. Baton Rouge: Louisiana State University Press, 1995.

Caudill, Harry. *My Land Is Dying*. New York: E.P. Dutton, 1971.

——. *Night Comes to the Cumberlands: A Biography of a Depressed Area*. New York: Little, Brown, 1963.

Clarkson, Atelia, and W. Lynwood Montell. "Letters to a Bluegrass DJ: Social Documents of Southern White Migration in Southeastern Michigan, 1964–1974." *Southern Folklore Quarterly* 39, no. 3 (September 1975): 219–32.

Cobb, James C. "From Rocky Top to Detroit City: Country Music and the Economic Transformation of the South." In *You Wrote My Life: Lyrical Themes in Country Music*, edited by Melton A. McLaurin and Richard A. Peterson, 63–80. Philadelphia: Gordon and Breach, 1992.

——. *The Selling of the South: The Southern Crusade for Industrial Development, 1936–1990*. 2nd ed. Urbana: University of Illinois Press, 1993.

Cohen, Liz. *A Consumer's Republic: The Politics of Mass Consumption in Postwar America*. New York: Knopf, 2003.

——. *Making a New Deal: Industrial Workers in Chicago, 1919–1939*. New York: Cambridge University Press, 1990.

Coles, Robert. *The South Goes North*. New York: Little, Brown, 1978.

Conway, M. Margaret. "The White Backlash Re-examined: Wallace and the 1964 Primaries." *Social Science Quarterly* 49, no. 3 (December 1968): 710–19.

Conn, Steven. *Americans against the City: Anti-Urbanism in the Twentieth Century*. New York: Oxford University Press, 2014.

Cowie, Jefferson. *Capital Moves: RCA's Seventy-Year Quest for Cheap Labor*. Ithaca, NY: Cornell University Press, 1999.

——. *Stayin' Alive: The 1970s and the Last Days of the Working Class*. New York: The New Press, 2010.

Darden, Joe T., et al. *Detroit: Race and Uneven Development*. Philadelphia: Temple University Press, 1987.

Daniel, Pete. *Lost Revolutions: The South in the 1950s*. Chapel Hill: University of North Carolina Press, 2000.

Davis, Mary, and Warren Zanes, eds. *Waiting for a Train: Jimmie Rodgers's America*. Burlington: Rounder Books, 2009.

DeNatale, Doug, and Glen Hinson. "The Southern Textile Song Tradition Reconsidered." In *Songs about Work: Essays in Occupational Culture*, edited by Archie Green, 77–107. Bloomington: Indiana University Press, 1993.

Denning, Michael. *The Cultural Front: The Laboring of American Culture in the Twentieth Century*. New York: Verso, 1998.

Di Maggio, Paul, Richard A. Peterson, and Jack Esco Jr. "Country Music: Ballad of the Silent Majority." In *The Sounds of Social Change: Studies in Popular Culture*. Chicago: Rand McNally, 1972.

Dochuk, Darren. *From Bible Belt to Sunbelt: Plain-Folk Religion, Grassroots Politics, and the Rise of Evangelical Conservatism*. New York: W. W. Norton, 2011.

Douglas, Paul H., and Frances Lamberson. "The Movement of Real Wages, 1890–1918." *American Economic Review* 11, no. 3 (September 1921): 409–26.

Drake, St. Clair, and Horace Cayton. *Black Metropolis: A Study of Negro Life in a Northern City*. Chicago: University of Chicago Press, 1945.

Dubofsky, Melvyn, and Warren Van Tine. *John L. Lewis: A Biography*. Urbana: University of Illinois Press, 1986.

Duneier, Mitchell. *Ghetto: The Invention of a Place, the History of an Idea*. New York: Farrar, Straus and Giroux, 2016.

Edsall, Thomas Byrne, and Mary D. Edsall. *Chain Reaction: The Impact of Race, Rights, and Taxes on American Politics*. New York: W. W. Norton, 1990.

Egerton, John. *The Americanization of Dixie: The Southernization of America*. New York: Harper's Magazine Press, 1974.

Eller, Ronald D. "Industrialization and Social Change in Appalachia, 1880–1930." In *Colonialism in Modern America: The Appalachian Case*, edited by Helen Matthews Lewis, Linda Johnson, and Donald Askins, 35–46. Boone: Appalachian Consortium Press, 1978.

———. *Miners, Millhands, and Mountaineers: Industrialization of the Appalachian South, 1880–1930*. Knoxville: University of Tennessee Press, 1982.

———. *Uneven Ground: Appalachia since 1945*. Lexington: University of Kentucky Press, 2008.

Farley, Reynolds. "Components of Suburban Population Growth." In *The Changing Face of the Suburbs*, edited by Barry Schwartz, 3–38. Chicago: University of Chicago Press, 1976.

Ferguson, Karen. *Top Down: The Ford Foundation, Black Power, and the Reinvention of Racial Liberalism*. Philadelphia: University of Pennsylvania Press, 2013.

Fligstein, Neil. *Going North: Migration of Blacks and Whites from the South, 1900–1950*. New York: Academic Press, 1981.

Forbath, William. *Law and the Shaping of the American Labor Movement*. Cambridge, MA: Harvard University Press, 1991.

Ford, Arthur M. *Political Economics of Rural Poverty in the South*. Cambridge, MA: Ballinger Publishing Company, 1973.

Ford, Thomas R. "The Passing of Provincialism." In *The Southern Appalachian Region: A Survey*, edited by Thomas R. Ford, 9–34. Lexington: University of Kentucky Press, 1962.

Formisano, Ronald P. *Boston Against Busing: Race, Class, and Ethnicity in the 1960s and 1970s*. Chapel Hill: University of North Carolina Press, 1991.

Fort, Teresa C., Justin R. Pierce, and Peter K. Schott. "New Perspectives on the Decline of US Manufacturing Employment." *Journal of Economic Perspectives* 32, no. 2 (Spring 2018): 47–72.

Fowler, Gary L. "The Residential Distribution of Urban Appalachians." In *The Invisible Minority: Urban Appalachians*, edited by William W. Philliber and Clyde B. McCoy, 79–94. Lexington: University of Kentucky Press, 1981.

Fox, Aaron. *Real Country: Music and Language in Working-Class Culture*. Durham, NC: Duke University Press, 2004.

Frank, Thomas. *What's the Matter with Kansas? How Conservatives Won the Heart of America*. New York: Metropolitan Books, 2004.

Fraser, Max. "Lost Highways." *Raritan Quarterly Review* 35, no. 3 (Winter 2016): 117–44.

Fraser, Steve. *Labor Will Rule: Sidney Hillman and the Rise of American Labor*. New York: Free Press, 1991.

Fraser, Steve, and Gary Gerstle, eds. *The Rise and Fall of the New Deal Order, 1930–1980*. Princeton, NJ: Princeton University Press, 1989.

Freeman, Joshua B. *Working-Class New York: Life and Labor Since World War II*. New York: The New Press, 2000.

Friedlander, Peter. *The Emergence of a UAW Local, 1936–1939*. Pittsburgh: University of Pittsburgh Press, 1975.

Gage, Beverly. *The Day Wall Street Exploded: A Story of America in Its First Age of Terror*. New York: Oxford University Press, 2009.

Gaventa, John. *Power and Powerlessness: Quiescence and Rebellion in an Appalachian Valley*. Urbana: University of Illinois Press, 1980.

Geary, Daniel. "'The Way I Feel About San Quentin': Johnny Cash and the Politics of Country Music." *Daedalus* 142, no. 4 (Fall 2013): 64–72.

Gibbard, Harold A. "Extractive Industries and Forestry." In *The Southern Appalachian Region: A Survey*, edited by Thomas R. Ford, 102–22. Lexington: University of Kentucky Press, 1962.

Gibbons, Charles E. "The Onion Workers." *The American Child* 1, no. 4 (February 1920): 406–18.

Giffin, Roscoe. "Appalachian Newcomers in Cincinnati." In *The Southern Appalachian Region: A Survey*, edited by Thomas R. Ford, 79–84. Lexington: University of Kentucky Press, 1962.

Gillette, Michael. *Launching the War on Poverty: An Oral History*. New York: Oxford University Press, 1996.

Gissen, Ira. "The Mountain Migrant: The Problem-Centered Workshop at Berea." *Journal of Human Relations* 9 (Autumn 1960): 67–73.

Gitlin, Todd, and Nanci Hollander. *Uptown: Poor Whites in Chicago*. New York: Harper & Row, 1970.

Glass, James A. "The Gas Boom in East Central Indiana." *Indiana Magazine of History* 96, no. 4 (December 2000): 313–35.

Goan, Melanie Beals. *Mary Breckinridge: The Frontier Nursing Service and Rural Health in Appalachia*. Chapel Hill: University of North Carolina Press, 2008.

Goodall, Hurley, and Elizabeth Campbell. "A City Apart." In *The Other Side of Muncie: Exploring Muncie's African American Community*, edited by Luke Eric Lassiter, Hurley Goodall, Elizabeth Campbell, and Michelle Natasya Johnson, 47–76. Walnut Creek: AltaMira Press, 2004.

Goodrich, Carter, et al. *Migration and Economic Opportunity*. Philadelphia: University of Pennsylvania Press, 1936.

Green, Archie. "Hillbilly Music: Source and Symbol." *Journal of American Folklore* 78, no. 309 (July 1965): 204–28.

——. *Torching the Fink Books and Other Essays on Vernacular Culture*. Chapel Hill: University of North Carolina Press, 2001.

Green, James. *Grass Roots Socialism*. Baton Rouge: Louisiana State University Press, 1978.

Greenberg, Stanley B. *Middle Class Dreams: The Politics and Power of the New American Majority*. New York: Times Books, 1995.

Gregory, James N. *American Exodus: The Dust Bowl Migration and Okie Culture in California*. New York: Oxford University Press, 1991.

——. "The Southern Diaspora and the Urban Dispossessed: Demonstrating the Census Public Use Microdata Samples." *Journal of American History* 82, no. 1 (June 1995): 111–34.

——. *The Southern Diaspora: How the Great Migrations of Black and White Southerners Transformed America*. Chapel Hill: University of North Carolina Press, 2005.

Grossman, James R. *Land of Hope: Chicago, Black Southerners, and the Great Migration*. Chicago: University of Chicago Press, 1989.

Guerin, Daniel. *Fascism and Big Business*. New York: Pioneer Publishers, 1939.

Guy, Roger. *From Diversity to Unity: Southern and Appalachian Migrants in Uptown Chicago, 1950–1970*. Lanham, MD: Lexington Books, 2007.

——. "The Media, the Police, and Southern White Migrant Identity in Chicago, 1955–1970." *Journal of Urban History* 26, no. 3 (March 2000): 329–49.

——. *When Architecture Meets Activism: The Transformative Experience of Hank Williams Village in the Windy City*. Lanham, MD: Lexington Books, 2016.

Hall, Jacquelyn Dowd, et al. *Like a Family: The Making of a Southern Cotton Mill World*. Chapel Hill: University of North Carolina Press, 1987.

Halle, David. *America's Working Man: Work, Home, and Politics among Blue-Collar Property Owners*. Chicago: University of Chicago Press, 1984.

Halpern, Robert. *Rebuilding the Inner City: A History of Neighborhood Initiatives to Address Poverty in the United States*. New York: Columbia University Press, 1995.

Handlin, Oscar. *The Uprooted: The Epic Story of the Great Migrations That Made the American People*. Boston: Little, Brown, 1952.

Harevan, Tamara K. *Family Time and Industrial Time: The Relationship Between the Family and Work in a New England Industrial Community*. New York: Cambridge University Press, 1982.

Haring, H. A. "Three Classes of Labor to Avoid: Prejudices and Habits Displayed by Men in Certain Occupations." *Industrial Management* 62, no. 6 (December 1921): 370–73.

Harkins, Anthony. *Hillbilly: A Cultural History of an American Icon*. New York: Oxford University Press, 2004.

Harrington, Michael. *The Other America: Poverty in the United States*. New York: Penguin, 1966 [1962].

Hartigan, John, Jr. "'Disgrace to the Race': Hillbillies and the Color Line in Detroit." In *Appalachian Odyssey: Historical Perspectives on the Great Migration*, edited by Phillip J. Obermiller, Thomas E. Wagner, and E. Bruce Tucker, 143–58. Westport, CT: Praeger, 2000.

———. *Racial Situations: Class Predicaments of Whiteness in Detroit.* Princeton, NJ: Princeton University Press, 1999.

Hemphill, Paul. *The Nashville Sound: Bright Lights and Country Music.* New York: Simon & Schuster, 1970.

Henderson, George. "Poor Southern Whites: A Neglected Urban Problem." *Journal of Secondary Education* 41, no. 3 (March 1966): 111–14.

Herman, Ellen. *The Romance of Psychology: Political Culture in the Age of Experts.* Berkeley: University of California Press, 1995.

Hevener, John W. *Which Side Are You On? The Harlan County Coal Miners, 1931–1939.* Urbana: University of Illinois Press, 2002.

Hirsch, Arnold. *Making the Second Ghetto: Race and Housing in Chicago, 1940–1960.* New York: Cambridge University Press, 1983.

Hoffman, Claude E. *Sit-Down in Anderson: UAW Local 663, Anderson, Indiana.* Detroit: Wayne State University Press, 1968.

Hofstadter, Richard. *The Age of Reform: From Bryan to FDR.* New York: Alfred A. Knopf, 1955.

Hoover, Calvin B., and B. U. Ratchford. *Economic Resources and Policies of the South.* New York: The Macmillan Company, 1951.

Hoover, Dwight W. *Magic Middletown.* Bloomington: Indiana University Press, 1986.

Horkheimer, Max, and Theodor W. Adorno. *Dialectic of Enlightenment.* New York: Seabury Press, 1972 [1944].

Horstman, Dorothy. *Sing Your Heart Out, Country Boy,* rev. ed. Nashville: Country Music Foundation Press, 1986.

Hounshell, David A. *From the American System to Mass Production, 1800–1932: The Development of Manufacturing Technology in the United States.* Baltimore: Johns Hopkins University Press, 1984.

Howe, Irving, and B. J. Widick. *The UAW and Walter Reuther.* New York: Random House, 1973 [1949].

Huber, Patrick. "'A Blessing to the People': Dorsey Dixon and His Sacred Mission of Song." *Southern Cultures* 12, no. 4 (Winter 2006): 111–31.

———. *Linthead Stomp: The Creation of Country Music in the Piedmont South.* Chapel Hill: University of North Carolina Press, 2008.

Huber, Patrick, Steve Goodson, and David M. Anderson, eds. *The Hank Williams Reader.* New York: Oxford University Press, 2014.

Huelsman, Ben R. "Urban Anthropology and the Southern Mountaineer." *Proceedings of the Indiana Academy of Science* 78 (1968): 97–103.

Ignatiev, Noel. *How the Irish Became White.* New York: Routledge, 1995.

Ingram, Tammy. *Dixie Highway: Road Building and the Making of the Modern South, 1900–1930.* Chapel Hill: University of North Carolina Press, 2014.

Isenberg, Nancy. *White Trash: The 400-Year Untold History of Class in America.* New York: Viking, 2016.

Jabbour, Alan, and Karen Singer Jabbour. *Decoration Day in the Mountains: Traditions of Cemetery Decoration in the Southern Appalachians.* Chapel Hill: University of North Carolina Press, 2010.

Jackson, Kenneth. *Crabgrass Frontier: The Suburbanization of the United States.* New York: Oxford University Press, 1985.

Jacobson, Matthew Frye. *Whiteness of a Different Color: European Immigrants and the Alchemy of Race.* Cambridge, MA: Harvard University Press, 1998.

Jennings, Dorothy, and Kerby Jennings. *The Story of Calloway County, 1822–1976.* Self- published, 1980.

Johnson, Marilynn S. *The Second Gold Rush: Oakland and the East Bay in World War II.* Berkeley: University of California Press, 1996.

———. "Urban Arsenals: War Housing and Social Change in Richmond and Oakland, California, 1941–1945." *Pacific Historical Review* 60, no. 3 (August 1991): 283–308.

Jones, Alfred Winslow. *Life, Liberty, and Property: A Story of Conflict and a Measurement of Conflicting Rights.* Philadelphia: J.P. Lippincott, 1941.

Jones, Jacqueline. *The Dispossessed: America's Underclasses from the Civil War to the Present.* New York: Basic Books, 1992.

———. "Southern Diaspora: Origins of the Northern 'Underclass.'" In *The "Underclass" Debate: Views from History,* edited by Michael B. Katz, 27–54. Princeton, NJ: Princeton University Press, 1993.

Katz, Michael B. *The Undeserving Poor: From the War on Poverty to the War on Welfare.* New York: Pantheon Books, 1989.

Kazin, Michael. *A Godly Hero: The Life of William Jennings Bryan.* New York: Knopf, 2006.

Kennedy, Randall. *Nigger: The Strange Career of a Troublesome Word.* New York: Pantheon, 2002.

Kiffmeyer, Thomas. "Looking Back to the City in the Hills: The Council of the Southern Mountains and a Longer View on the War on Poverty in the Appalachian South, 1913–1970." In *The War on Poverty: A New Grassroots History, 1964–1980,* edited by Annelise Orleck and Lisa Gayle Hazirjian, 359–86. Athens: University of Georgia Press, 2011.

———. *Reformers to Radicals: The Appalachian Volunteers and the War on Poverty.* Lexington: University of Kentucky Press, 2008.

Kiker, B. F., and Earle C. Traynham Jr. *Return Migration and Nonreturn Migration for the Southeast: 1960–1970.* Columbia: University of South Carolina Press, 1974.

Killian, Lewis. "The Adjustment of Southern White Migrants to Northern Urban Norms." *Social Forces* 32, no. 1 (October 1953): 66–69.

———. *White Southerners.* New York: Random House, 1970.

Kimbrough, David L. *Taking Up Serpents: Snake Handlers of Eastern Kentucky.* Chapel Hill: University of North Carolina Press, 1995.

Kingsdale, Jon M. "The 'Poor Man's Club': Social Functions of the Working-Class Saloon." *American Quarterly* 25, no. 4 (October 1973): 472–89.

Kirby, Jack Temple. *Rural Worlds Lost: The American South, 1920–1960.* Baton Rouge: Louisiana State University Press, 1987.

Kornhauser, Arthur. *Attitudes of Detroit People Toward Detroit: Summary of a Detailed Report.* Detroit: Wayne State University Press, 1952.

Kraus, Henry. *Heroes of Unwritten Story: The UAW, 1934–1939.* Urbana: University of Illinois Press, 1993.

———. *The Many and the Few: A Chronicle of the Dynamic Auto Workers.* Urbana: University of Illinois Press, 1985 [1947].

La Chapelle, Peter. *Proud to Be an Okie: Cultural Politics, Country Music, and Migration to Southern California.* Berkeley: University of California Press, 2007.

Landy, Marc. "Country Music: The Melody of Dislocation." *New South* 26 (Winter 1971): 67–69.

Lange, Jeffrey. *Smile When You Call Me a Hillbilly: Country Music's Struggle for Respectability, 1939–1954.* Athens: University of Georgia Press, 2004.

Lassiter, Matthew D. *The Silent Majority: Suburban Politics in the Sunbelt South.* Princeton, NJ: Princeton University Press, 2006.

Lee, Alfred McClung, and Norman Daymond Humphrey. *Race Riot.* New York: Dryden Press, 1943.

Leibbrand, Christine, Catherine Massey, J. Trent Alexander, and Stewart Tolnay. "Great Migration's Great Return? An Examination of Second-Generation Return Migration to the South." *Social Science Research* 8 (July 2019): 117–31.

Lemann, Nicholas. *The Promised Land: The Great Black Migration and How It Changed America.* New York: Alfred A. Knopf, 1991.

LeMasters, E. E. *Blue-Collar Aristocrats: Life-Styles at a Working-Class Tavern.* Madison: University of Wisconsin Press, 1975.

Leonard, Bill J. *Christianity in Appalachia: Profiles in Regional Pluralism.* Knoxville: University of Tennessee Press, 1999.

Levenstein, Harvey A. *Communism, Anti-Communism, and the CIO.* Westport, CT: Greenwood Press, 1981.

Levinson, Edward. *Labor on the March.* New York: Harper and Brothers, 1938.

Lewis, Earl. "Afro-American Adaptive Strategies: The Visiting Habits of Kith and Kin among Black Norfolkians during the First Great Migration." *Journal of Family History* 12, no. 4 (1987): 407–20.

Lewis, Helen M., and Edward E. Knipe. "The Colonialism Model: The Appalachian Case." In *Colonialism in Modern America: The Appalachian Case,* edited by Helen Matthews Lewis, Linda Johnson, and Donald Askins, 9–32. Boone: Appalachian Consortium Press, 1978.

Lewis, Oscar. *Five Families: Mexican Case Studies in the Culture of Poverty.* New York: Basic Books,    1959.

——. *La Vida: A Puerto Rican Family in the Culture of Poverty—San Juan and New York.* New York: Random House, 1965.

Leybourne, Grace G. "Urban Adjustments of Migrants from the Southern Appalachian Plateaus." *Social Forces* 16, no. 2 (December 1937): 238–46.

Lichtenstein, Nelson. *A Contest of Ideas: Capital, Politics, and Labor.* Urbana: University of Illinois Press, 2013.

——. *The Most Dangerous Man in Detroit: Walter Reuther and the Fate of American Labor.* New York: Basic Books, 1995.

Lichtfield, Paul W. *Industrial Voyage.* New York: Doubleday, 1954.

Lindquist, Julie. *A Place to Stand: Politics and Persuasion in a Working-Class Bar.* New York: Oxford University Press, 2002.

Lipset, Seymour Martin. *Political Man: The Social Bases of Politics.* New York: Doubleday, 1960.

Lipset, Seymour Martin, and Earl Raab. *The Politics of Unreason: Right-Wing Extremism in America.* New York: Harper & Row, 1970.

Lipsitz, George. *Rainbow at Midnight: Labor and Culture in the 1940s*. Urban: University of Illinois Press, 1994.

Lowndes, Joseph. *From the New Deal to the New Right: Race and the Suburban Origins of Modern Conservatism*. New Haven, CT: Yale University Press, 2008.

Lund, Jens. "Fundamentalism, Racism and Political Reaction in Country Music." In *The Sounds of Social Change: Studies in Popular Culture*, edited by R. Serge Denisoff and Richard A. Peterson, 79–91. Chicago: Rand McNally, 1972.

Lynd, Robert S., and Helen Merrell Lynd. *Middletown: A Study in Contemporary American Culture*. New York: Harcourt Brace Jovanovich, 1957 [1929].

———. *Middletown in Transition: A Study in Cultural Conflicts*. New York: Harcourt, Brace, 1937.

Lynn, Loretta, with George Vescey. *Loretta Lynn: Coal Miner's Daughter*. New York: Warner Books, 1976.

Maclean, Nancy. *Freedom Is Not Enough: The Opening of the American Workplace*. Cambridge, MA: Harvard University Press, 2008.

Maki, Craig, with Keith Cady. *Detroit Country Music: Mountaineers, Cowboys, and Rockabillies*. Ann Arbor: University of Michigan Press, 2013.

Malone, Bill C. *Country Music U.S.A.*, rev. ed. Austin: University of Texas Press, 1985.

———. *Don't Get above Your Raisin': Country Music and the Southern Working Class*. Urbana: University of Illinois Press, 2002.

Marcus, Greil. *Mystery Train: Images of American in Rock 'n' Roll Music*. 2nd ed. New York: E.P. Dutton, 1982 [1975].

Marcuse, Herbert. *One-Dimensional Man: Studies in the Ideology of Advanced Industrial Society*. Boston: Beacon Press, 1964.

Marris, Peter, and Martin Rein. *Dilemmas of Social Reform: Poverty and Community Action in the United States*. 2nd ed. Chicago: Aldine, 1973 [1967].

Marx, Karl. *Capital, Volume I: A Critique of Political Economy*. New York: Penguin Classics, 1992 [1887].

———. *The Eighteenth Brumaire of Louis Bonaparte*. New York: Mondial, 2005 [1852].

Marx, Karl, and Friedrich Engels. *The Communist Manifesto*. New York: Oxford University Press, 1998 [1848].

Mathewson, Stanley B. *Restriction of Output Among Unorganized Workers*. New York: Viking Press, 1931.

May, Elaine Tyler. *Homeward Bound: American Families in the Cold War Era*. New York: Basic Books, 1988.

McBeth, Leon. "Expansion of the Southern Baptist Convention to 1951." *Baptist History and Heritage* 17, no. 3 (July 1982): 32–43.

McCartin, Joseph A. *Labor's Great War: The Struggle for Industrial Democracy and the Origins of Modern American Labor Relations, 1912–1921*. Chapel Hill: University of North Carolina Press, 1997.

McCauley, Deborah Vansau. *Appalachian Mountain Religion: A History*. Urbana: University of Illinois Press, 1995.

McCoy, Clyde B., and James S. Brown. "Appalachian Migration to Midwestern Cities." In *The Invisible Minority: Urban Appalachians*, edited by William W. Philliber and Clyde B. McCoy, 35–78. Lexington: University of Kentucky Press, 1981.

McCoy, Clyde B., and Virginia McCoy Watkins. "Stereotypes of Appalachian Migrants." In *The Invisible Minority: Urban Appalachians*, edited by William W. Philliber and Clyde B. McCoy, 20–34. Lexington: University of Kentucky Press, 1981.

McDonald, Michael J., and John Muldowny. *TVA and the Dispossessed: The Resettlement of Population in the Norris Dam Area*. Knoxville: University of Tennessee Press, 1982.

McGinniss, Joe. *The Selling of the President*. 2nd ed. New York: Penguin Books, 1988 [1969].

McGirr, Lisa. *Suburban Warriors: The Origins of the New American Right*. Princeton, NJ: Princeton University Press, 2001.

McKee, Guian. *The Problem of Jobs: Liberalism, Race, and Deindustrialization in Philadelphia*. Chicago: University of Chicago Press, 2010.

McKenney, Ruth. *Industrial Valley*. New York: Harcourt, Brace. 1939.

McLaurin, Melton A. "Songs of the South: The Changing Image of the South in Country Music." In *You Wrote My Life: Lyrical Themes in Country Music*, edited by Melton A. McLaurin and Richard A. Peterson, 15–35. Philadelphia: Gordon and Breach, 1992.

McWilliams, Carey. *Ill Fares the Land: Migrants and Migratory Labor in the United States*. Boston: Little, Brown, 1942.

Mertz, Paul E. *New Deal Policy and Southern Rural Poverty*. Baton Rouge: Louisiana State University Press, 1978.

Metzgar, Jack. *Striking Steel: Solidarity Remembered*. Philadelphia: Temple University Press, 2000.

Meyer, Stephen III. *The Five Dollar Day: Labor Management and Social Control in the Ford Motor Company, 1908–1921*. Albany, NY: SUNY Press, 1981.

Miller, Zane L., and Bruce Tucker. *Changing Plans for America's Inner Cities: Cincinnati's Over-the-Rhine and Twentieth-Century Urbanism*. Columbus: The Ohio State University Press, 1998.

Mills, C. Wright. *The Sociological Imagination*. New York: Oxford University Press, 1959.

Montgomery, David. *The Fall of the House of Labor: The Workplace, the State, and American Labor Activism, 1865–1925*. New York: Cambridge University Press, 1989.

——. *Workers' Control in America: Studies in the History of Work, Technology, and Labor Struggles*. New York: Cambridge University Press, 1979.

Montgomery, Jesse. "Sing Me Back Home: Country Music and Radical Community Organizing in Uptown Chicago." *Journal of Popular Music Studies* 32, no. 2 (June 2020): 95–111.

Moore, Leonard. *Citizen Klansmen: The Ku Klux Klan in Indiana, 1921–1928*. Chapel Hill: University of North Carolina Press, 1991.

Morris, Alton C. *Folksongs of Florida*. Gainesville: University Press of Florida, 1950.

Moynihan, Daniel Patrick. *Maximum Feasible Misunderstanding: Community Action in the War on Poverty*. New York: Free Press, 1969.

Murray, Robert K. *Red Scare: A Study in National Hysteria, 1919–1920*. New York: McGraw-Hill, 1964.

Myrdal, Gunnar. *An American Dilemma: The Negro Problem and Modern Democracy*. New York: Harper & Brothers, 1944.

Nelson, Daniel. *American Rubber Workers and Organized Labor, 1900–1941*. Princeton, NJ: Princeton University Press, 1988.

———. "The Leadership of the United Rubber Workers, 1933–42." *Detroit in Perspective* 5, no. 3 (Spring 1981): 21–30.

———. "Of Mortgages and Men: A Housing Boom in Rubber City." *Timeline* 4, no. 4 (August–September 1987): 49–55.

———. "Origins of the Sit-Down Era: Worker Militancy and Innovation in the Rubber Industry, 1934–1938." *Labor History* 23, no. 2 (1982): 198–225.

Ngai, Mae N. *Impossible Subjects: Illegal Aliens and the Making of Modern America*. Princeton, NJ: Princeton University Press, 2004.

Nicholson, James L., and Robert Ewing Corlew. *Grundy County*. Memphis: Memphis State University Press, 1982.

Nickerson, Michelle, and Darren Dochuk, eds. *Sunbelt Rising: The Politics of Space, Place, and Region*. Philadelphia: University of Pennsylvania Press, 2011.

Nicolaides, Becky M. *My Blue Heaven: Life and Politics in the Working-Class Suburbs of Los Angeles, 1920–1965*. Chicago: University of Chicago Press, 2002.

O'Connor, Alice. "Community Action, Urban Reform, and the Fight against Poverty: The Ford Foundation's Gray Areas Program." *Journal of Urban History* 22, no. 5 (July 1996): 586–625.

———. "The Ford Foundation and Philanthropic Activism in the 1960s." In *Philanthropic Foundations: New Scholarship, New Possibilities*, edited by Ellen Condliffe Lagemann, 169–94. Bloomington: Indiana University Press, 1999.

———. *Poverty Knowledge: Social Science, Social Policy, and the Poor in Twentieth-Century U.S. History*. Princeton, NJ: Princeton University Press, 2001.

Obermiller, Phillip J., and Michael E. Maloney. "Living City, Feeling Country: The Current Status and Future Prospects of Urban Appalachians." In *From Mountain to Metropolis: Appalachian Migrants in American Cities*, edited by Kathryn M. Borman and Phillip J. Obermiller, 3–13. Westport: Bergin & Garvey, 1994.

Obermiller, Phillip J., and Ray Rappold. "The Sense of Place and Cultural Identity among Urban Appalachians: A Study in Postdeath Migration." In *From Mountain to Metropolis: Appalachian Migrants in American Cities*, edited by Kathryn M. Borman and Phillip J. Obermiller, 25–31. Westport, CT: Bergin & Garvey, 1994.

Obermiller, Phillip J., and Robert W. Oldendick. "Urban Appalachian Health Concerns." In *From Mountain to Metropolis: Appalachian Migrants in American Cities*, edited by Kathryn M. Borman and Phillip J. Obermiller, 51–61. Westport, CT: Bergin & Garvey, 1994.

Obermiller Phillip J., and Thomas E. Wagner. "Cincinnati's 'Second Minority': The Emergence of Appalachian Advocacy, 1953–1973." In *Appalachian Odyssey: Historical Perspectives on the Great Migration*, edited by Phillip J. Obermiller, Thomas E. Wagner, and E. Bruce Tucker, 193–214. Westport, CT: Praeger, 2000.

———. "'Hands-Across-the-Ohio': The Urban Initiatives of the Council of the Southern Mountains, 1954–1971." In *Appalachian Odyssey: Historical Perspectives on the Great Migration*, edited by Phillip J. Obermiller, Thomas E. Wagner, and E. Bruce Tucker, 121–42. Westport, CT: Praeger, 2000.

Obermiller, Phillip, et al. "Major Turning Points: Rethinking Appalachian Migration." *Appalachian Journal* 36, no. 3/4 (Spring/Summer 2009): 164–87.

Odum, Howard W. "The Way of the South." *Social Forces* 23, no. 3 (March 1945): 258–68.

Orleck, Annelise. *Common Sense and a Little Fire: Women and Working-Class Politics in the United States, 1900–1965*. Chapel Hill: University of North Carolina Press, 1995.

Ortquist, Richard T. *Depression Politics in Michigan*. New York: Garland Press, 1982.

Patterson, Timothy A. "Hillbilly Music among the Flatlanders: Early Midwestern Barn Dances." *Journal of Country Music* 6, no. 1 (Spring 1975): 12–18.

Pecknold, Diane. *The Selling Sound: The Rise of the Country Music Industry*. Durham, NC: Duke University Press, 2007.

Pehl, Matthew. "'Apostles of Fascism,' 'Communist Clergy,' and the UAW: Political Ideology and Working-Class Religion in Detroit, 1919–1945." *Journal of American History* 99, no. 2 (September 2012): 440–65.

Perelman, Michael. *The Invention of Capitalism: Classical Political Economy and the Secret History of Primitive Accumulation*. Durham, NC: Duke University Press, 2000.

Pesotta, Rose. *Bread upon the Waters*. New York: Dodd, Mead, 1944.

Peterson, Gene B., Laure M. Sharp, and Thomas F. Drury. *Southern Newcomers to Northern Cities: Work and Social Adjustment in Cleveland*. New York: Praeger, 1977.

Peterson, Joyce Shaw. *American Automobile Workers, 1900–1933*. Albany, NY: SUNY Press, 1987.

Peterson, Richard A. *Creating Country Music: Fabricating Authenticity*. Chicago: University of Chicago Press, 1997.

Philliber, William. *Appalachian Migrants in Urban America: Cultural Conflict or Ethnic Group Formation?* New York: Praeger, 1981.

Phillips, Kimberley L. *AlabamaNorth: African-American Migrants, Community, and Working-Class Activism in Cleveland, 1915–45*. Urbana: University of Illinois Press, 1999.

Phillips, Sarah T. *This Land, This Nation: Conservation, Rural America, and the New Deal*. New York: Cambridge University Press, 2007.

Photiadis, John D. "Occupational Adjustment of Appalachians in Cleveland." In *The Invisible Minority: Urban Appalachians*, edited by William W. Philliber and Clyde B. McCoy, 140–53. Lexington: University of Kentucky Press, 1981.

——. *Social and Sociopsychological Characteristics of West Virginians in Their Own State and in Cleveland, Ohio*. Morgantown: West Virginia University Press, 1975.

Pierce, Daniel S. *Tar Heel Lightnin': How Secret Stills and Fast Cars Made North Carolina the Moonshine Capital of the World*. Chapel Hill: University of North Carolina Press, 2019.

Pope, Jim. "Worker Lawmaking, Sit-Down Strikes, and the Shaping of American Industrial Relations, 1935–1938." *Law and History Review* 24, no. 1 (Spring 2006): 45–113.

Porter, E. Russell. "When Cultures Meet—Mountain and Urban." *Nursing Outlook* 11, no. 6 (June 1963): 418–20.

Porterfield, Nolan. *Jimmie Rodgers: The Life and Times of America's Blue Yodeler*. 2nd ed. Urbana: University of Illinois Press, 1992.

Post, Charles. *The American Road to Capitalism: Studies in Class Structure, Economic Development and Political Conflict, 1620–1877*. Chicago: Haymarket Books, 2012.

Pound, Arthur. *The Turning Wheel: The Story of General Motors through Twenty-Five Years, 1908–1933*. New York: Doubleday, Doran, 1934.

Powles, William E. "The Southern Appalachian Migrant: Country Boy Turned Blue-Collarite." In *Blue-Collar World: Studies of the American Worker*, edited by Arthur B. Shostak and William Gomberg, 270–81. Englewood Cliffs: Prentice-Hall, 1964.

Preston, Howard Lawrence. *Dirt Roads to Dixie: Accessibility and Modernization in the South, 1885–1935*. Knoxville: University of Tennessee Press, 1991.

Quadagno, Jill. *The Color of Welfare: How Racism Undermined the War on Poverty*. New York: Oxford University Press, 1994.

Quittmeyer, Charles L., and Lorin A. Thompson. "The Development of Manufacturing." In *The Southern Appalachian Region: A Survey*, edited by Thomas R. Ford, 123–35. Lexington: University of Kentucky Press, 1962.

Rainwater, Lee, and William Yancey. *The Moynihan Report and the Politics of Controversy*. Cambridge, MA: MIT Press, 1967.

Rieder, Jonathan. *Canarsie: The Jews and Italians of Brooklyn against Liberalism*. Cambridge, MA: Harvard University Press, 1985.

Reuther, Victor. *The Brothers Reuther and the Story of the UAW*. Boston: Houghton Mifflin, 1976.

Ribowksy, Mark. *Hank: The Short Life and Long Country Road of Hank Williams*. New York: Liveright, 2016.

Roberts, Harold S. *The Rubber Workers: Labor Organization and Collective Bargaining in the Rubber Industry*. New York: Harper & Brothers, 1944.

Roediger, David. *The Wages of Whiteness: Race and the Making of the American Working Class*. New York: Verso, 1991.

Roll, Jarod. *Spirit of Rebellion: Labor and Religion in the New Cotton South*. Urbana: University of Illinois Press, 2010.

Rosenzweig, Roy. *Eight Hours for What We Will: Workers and Leisure in an Industrial City, 1870–1920*. New York: Cambridge University Press, 1983.

Salstrom, Paul. *Appalachia's Path to Dependency: Rethinking a Region's Economic History, 1730–1940*. Lexington: University Press of Kentucky, 1984.

Sanders, Elizabeth. *Roots of Reform: Farmers, Workers, and the American State, 1877–1917*. Chicago: University of Chicago Press, 1999.

Satterwhite, Emily. *Dear Appalachia: Readers, Identity, and Popular Fiction Since 1878*. Lexington: University of Kentucky Press, 2011.

Schlappi, Elizabeth. *Roy Acuff: The Smoky Mountain Boy*. 2nd ed. Gretna: Pelican Publishing, 1993.

Schulman, Bruce J. *From Cotton Belt to Sunbelt: Federal Policy, Economic Development, and the Transformation of the South*. New York: Oxford University Press, 1991.

Schwarzweller, Harry K., James S. Brown, and J. J. Mangalam. *Mountain Families in Transition: A Case Study of Appalachian Migration*. University Park: Pennsylvania State University Press, 1971.

Self, Robert O. *All in the Family: The Realignment of American Democracy Since the 1960s*. New York: Hill and Wang, 2013.

———. *American Babylon: Race and the Struggle for Postwar Oakland*. Princeton, NJ: Princeton University Press, 2003.

Sennett, Richard, and Jonathan Cobb. *The Hidden Injuries of Class*. New York: W. W. Norton, 1972.

Shearer, Katharine C., ed. *Memories from Dante: The Life of a Coal Town*. Abingdon, VA: People's Incorporated, 2001.

Shermer, Elizabeth Tandy. *Sunbelt Capitalism: Phoenix and the Transformation of American Politics*. Philadelphia: University of Pennsylvania Press, 2013.

Shifflett, Crandall A. *Coal Towns: Life, Work, and Culture in Company Towns of Southern Appalachia, 1880–1960*. Knoxville: University of Tennessee Press, 1991.

Smith, Jason Scott. *Building New Deal Liberalism: The Political Economy of Public Works, 1933–1956*. New York: Cambridge University Press, 2006.

Smith, Robert Michael. *From Blackjacks to Briefcases: A History of Commercialized Strikebreaking and Unionbusting in the United States*. Athens: The Ohio University Press, 2003.

Sonnie, Amy, and James Tracy. *Hillbilly Nationalists, Urban Race Rebels, and Black Power: Community Organizing in Radical Times*. New York: Melville House, 2011.

St. John, Lauren. *Hardcore Troubadour: The Life and Near Death of Steve Earle*. New York: Fourth Estate, 2003.

Stack, Carol. *Call to Home: African Americans Reclaim the Rural South*. New York: Basic Books, 1996.

Stager, Claudette, and Martha Carver, eds. *Looking Beyond the Highway: Dixie Roads and Culture*. Knoxville: University of Tennessee Press, 2006.

Stein, Judith. *Pivotal Decade: How the United States Traded Factories for Finance in the Seventies*. New Haven, CT: Yale University Press, 2010.

——. *Running Steel, Running America: Race, Economic Policy, and the Decline of Liberalism*. Chapel Hill: University of North Carolina Press, 1998.

Stekert, Ellen J. "Focus for Conflict: Southern Mountain Medical Beliefs in Detroit." *The Journal of American Folklore* 82, no. 328 (April 1970): 115–47.

Stern, Mark J. "Poverty and Family Composition since 1940." In *The "Underclass" Debate: Views from History*, edited by Michael B. Katz, 220–53. Princeton, NJ: Princeton University Press, 1993.

Stewart, Susan. *On Longing: Narratives of the Miniature, the Gigantic, the Souvenir, the Collection*. Durham, NC: Duke University Press, 1993.

Stoll, Steven. *Ramp Hollow: The Ordeal of Appalachia*. New York: Hill and Wang, 2017.

Sugrue, Thomas. *The Origins of the Urban Crisis: Race and Inequality in Postwar Detroit*. Princeton, NJ: Princeton University Press, 1996.

Tate, Leland B. *An Economic and Social Survey of Russell County*. Charlottesville: University of Virginia Press, 1931.

Taylor, Frederick Winslow. "Shop Management." *Transactions of the American Society of Mechanical Engineers* 24 (1903): 1337–1480.

Taylor, Paul S. "Migratory Farm Labor in the United States." *Monthly Labor Review* 44, no. 3 (March 1937): 537–49.

Teaford, Jon C. *The Rough Road to Renaissance: Urban Revitalization in America, 1940–1985*. Baltimore: Johns Hopkins University Press, 1990.

Tenkotte, Paul A., and James C. Claypool, eds. *The Encyclopedia of Northern Kentucky*. Lexington: University Press of Kentucky, 2009.

Thompson, E. P. *Customs in Common: Studies in Traditional Popular Culture*. New York: The New Press, 1992.

——. *The Making of the English Working Class*. New York: Vintage, 1966 [1963].

Tolnay, Stewart E. "Migration Experience and Family Patterns in the 'Promised Land.'" *Journal of Family History*, 23, no. 1 (January 1998): 68–89.

Tolnay, Stewart E., and E. M. Beck. "Racial Violence and Black Migration in the American South, 1910 to 1930." *American Sociological Review* 57, no. 1 (February 1992): 103–16.

Towns, Elmer L. *The Ten Largest Sunday Schools and What Makes Them Grow*. Grand Rapids: Baker Book House, 1969.

Tribe, Ivan M. "The Hillbilly versus the City: Urban Images in Country Music." *John Edwards Memorial Foundation Quarterly* 10, no. 34 (Summer 1974): 41–51.

Trotter, Joe William, Jr. *Black Milwaukee: The Making of an Industrial Proletariat, 1915–1945*. Urbana: University of Illinois Press, 1985.

Tucker, Bruce. "Imagining Appalachians: The Berea Workshop on the Urban Adjustment of Southern Appalachian Migrants." In *Appalachian Odyssey: Historical Perspectives on the Great Migration*, edited by Phillip J. Obermiller, Thomas E. Wagner, and E. Bruce Tucker, 97–120. Westport, CT: Praeger, 2000.

——. "Michael Maloney: Interviewed by Bruce Tucker." *Appalachian Journal* 17, no. 1 (Fall 1989): 34–48.

——. "Transforming Mountain Folk: Roscoe Giffin and the Invention of Urban Appalachia." In *Appalachian Odyssey: Historical Perspectives on the Great Migration*, edited by Phillip J. Obermiller, Thomas E. Wagner, and E. Bruce Tucker, 69–96. Westport, CT: Praeger, 2000.

Tullos, Allen. "Figures of Speech—Can a Country Boy Survive?" *Southern Changes* 4, no. 3 (1982): 1–3.

Tuttle, William M., Jr. *Race Riot: Chicago in the Red Summer of 1919*. Urbana: University of Illinois Press, 1996 [1970].

Vance, J. D. *Hillbilly Elegy: A Memoir of a Family and a Culture in Crisis*. New York: Harper, 2016.

Vance, Rupert B. "The Region: A New Survey." In *The Southern Appalachian Region: A Survey*, edited by Thomas R. Ford, 1–8. Lexington: University of Kentucky Press, 1962.

Vincent, George E. "A Retarded Frontier." *American Journal of Sociology* 4, no. 1 (July 1898): 1–20.

Wagner, Thomas E., and Phillip J. Obermiller. *Valuing Our Past, Creating Our Future: The Founding of the Urban Appalachian Council*. Berea, KY: Berea College Press, 1999.

Washington, Michael. "The Stirrings of the Modern Civil Rights Movement in Cincinnati, Ohio, 1943–1953." In *Groundwork: Local Black Freedom Movements in America*, edited by Jeanne Theoharis and Komozi Woodard, 215–34. New York: New York University Press, 2005.

Watkins, Myron W. "The Labor Situation in Detroit." *Journal of Political Economy* 28, no. 10 (December 1920): 840–52.

Weiland, Steven, and Phillip Obermiller, eds. *Perspectives on Urban Appalachians: An Introduction to Mountain Life, Migration, and Urban Adaptation, and a Guide to the Improvement of Social Services*. Cincinnati: Ohio Urban Appalachian Awareness Project, 1978.

Weller, Jack E. *Yesterday's People: Life in Contemporary Appalachia*. Lexington: University of Kentucky Press, 1965.

Whisnant, David E. *All That Is Native and Fine: The Politics of Culture in an American Region*. Chapel Hill: University of North Carolina Press, 1983.

———. *Modernizing the Mountaineer: People, Power, and Planning in Appalachia*. Boone, NC: Appalachian Consortium Press, 1980.

White, Katherine J. Curtis. "Women in the Great Migration: Economic Activity of Black and White Southern-Born Female Migrants in 1920, 1940, and 1970." *Social Science History* 29, no. 3 (Fall 2005): 413–55.

White, Morton, and Lucia White. *The Intellectual versus the City: From Thomas Jefferson to Frank Lloyd Wright*. Cambridge, MA: Harvard University Press, 1962.

Whyte, William H., et al., eds. *The Exploding Metropolis: A Study of the Assault on Urbanism and How Our Cities Can Resist It*. New York: Doubleday, 1958.

Widick, B. J. *Detroit: City of Race and Class Violence*. Chicago: Quadrangle Books, 1972.

Wilgus, D. K. "Country-Western Music and the Urban Hillbilly." *Journal of American Folklore* 82, no. 238 (April–June 1970): 157–79.

Wilkerson, Isabel. *The Warmth of Other Suns: The Epic Story of America's Great Migration*. New York: Vintage Books, 2011.

Williams, Jakobi. *From the Bullet to the Ballot: The Illinois Chapter of the Black Panther Party and Racial Coalition Politics in Chicago*. Chapel Hill: University of North Carolina Press, 2015.

Williams, John Alexander. *Appalachia: A History*. Chapel Hill: University of North Carolina Press, 2002.

Williams, Roger M. *Sing a Sad Song: The Life and Times of Hank Williams*. 2nd ed. Urbana: University of Illinois Press, 1981.

Wolfe, Charles. "A Lighter Shade of Blue: White Country Blues." In *Nothing But the Blues: The Music and the Musicians*, edited by Lawrence Cohn. New York: Abbeville Press, 1993.

———. "Up North with the Blue Ridge Ramblers: Jennie Bowman's 1931 Tour Diary." *Journal of Country Music* 6, no. 3 (Fall 1975): 136–44.

Wolfe, Margaret Ripley. "Appalachians in Muncie: A Case Study of an American Exodus." *Locus* 4, no. 2 (Spring 1992): 169–89.

Woodward, C. Vann. *Origins of the New South: 1887–1913*. Baton Rouge: Louisiana State University Press, 1951.

Wright, Gavin. *Old South, New South: Revolutions in the Southern Economy Since the Civil War*. New York: Basic Books, 1986.

———. "The New Deal and the Modernization of the South," *Federal History* 2 (2010), accessed July 19, 2002, http://www.shfg.org/resources/Documents/FH%202%20 (2010)%20Wright.pdf.

———. *Tom Watson: Agrarian Rebel*. New York: Oxford University Press, 1963 [1938].

Zieger, Robert H. *The CIO: 1935–1955*. Chapel Hill: University of North Carolina Press, 1995.

# INDEX

Note: Page numbers in italic refer to photographs. Page numbers followed by an 'n' refer to notes.

## A NOTE ON THE TYPE

THIS BOOK has been composed in Miller, a Scotch Roman typeface designed by Matthew Carter and first released by Font Bureau in 1997. It resembles Monticello, the typeface developed for The Papers of Thomas Jefferson in the 1940s by C. H. Griffith and P. J. Conkwright and reinterpreted in digital form by Carter in 2003.

Pleasant Jefferson ("P. J.") Conkwright (1905–1986) was Typographer at Princeton University Press from 1939 to 1970. He was an acclaimed book designer and AIGA Medalist.